Effective Internet Search:

E-Searching Made Easy!

Skills & Strategies for Improved Search Engine Results

by Ed Baylin

(full book, printed edition, ISBN 0-921354-04-5)

More information on our book at:

www.SearchHelpCenter.com

Book Editions

Available formats: printed and e-book (electronic):

Abridged Edition: Print format, abridged edition: 252 pages; ISBN: 0-921354-06-1.

Full Edition (includes Reference Manual):

Print format:
544 (252 + Reference Manual) pages; ISBN: 0-921354-04-5, revised Aug. 23, 2005.

E-book format:
No print; 544 pages, same as full printed book; ISBN: 0-921354-03-7; ISSN: 1708-6159 Aug, 2005.

Page Size: All editions/formats are:

7.44 X 9.69 inches
189 X 246 millimeters

Book orders, updates, & reviews:
Visit our website at: www.SearchHelpCenter.com.

D1581781

Effective Internet Search: E-Searching Made Easy!
(full book, printed edition)
by Edward N. Baylin

Published by: Baylin Systems, Inc.
2809 Mozart Court, Ottawa, Ontario, Canada, K1T 2P5.
Contact us at: www.SearchHelpCenter.com

First edition, major contributor and editor: Judith Gill

Cover Design: Edward N. Baylin; Visual Creations; Bruce Maclean of Scan11 & 11th Hour Imaging

Printing history: First edition: December, 2004

ISBN: 0-921354-04-5

Dedicated to you — the searcher

This book is about helping you improve your searches — giving you the information, skills, and strategies you need to increase the effectiveness and efficiency of your Internet searches, and to conduct more targeted searches with more accurate results.

We also provide you with a unique system to explore, study and experience a variety of search engine features. Specifically:

1. **We teach you how to increase the efficiency and effectiveness of your Internet searches by explaining:**

   - Fundamental principles of how all search engines work.
   - How to select the most appropriate search engines to find what you are looking for.
   - The strengths and weaknesses of four popular search engines: AlltheWeb, AltaVista, Google, and MSN Search, plus more specialized ones like leading-edge meta search utility, Copernic.
   - General search engine features to help you find and display the most appropriate and relevant search results.
   - Specific search engine features to help you conduct more effective and complex searches.
   - Tips for handling a slew of typical search problem situations.
   - Unexpected, "quirky," and often undocumented situations you might encounter when using some search engines, and how to handle them.

2. **We equip you with an easy-to-apply generic template of search engine features to:**

   - Help you to develop Internet search skills in a more organized and systematic way by using the same pattern throughout for presenting book materials.
   - Make it easy for you to understand, remember, and quickly access specialized features of various search engines.
   - Provide you with a common pattern of search engine features applicable to any search engine.

3. **We provide you with a unique "Features Control Center" to:**

   - Permit comprehensive interlinking throughout the book.
   - Provide you with an invaluable electronic reference manual.
   - Allow you to experiment with the numerous search engine features explored in this book.

4. **We furnish you with a free** Search Tool Guide **to:**

- Help you quickly, conveniently and accurately pinpoint the information you want and need.

To see our guide, go to ToolGuide.SearchHelpCenter.com.

5. **We put top resources at your fingertips by quickly and easily linking you directly to the Internet to:**

- Complement book content with useful references, materials and tutorials from other experts.
- Connect you with the most up-to-date information and latest developments in the fast-changing evolution of search engine technology.

6. **We provide you with regular book updates to:**

- Keep you current with the latest developments in the rapidly evolving field of search engines.
- Prevent materials and resources from becoming obsolete.
- Quickly link you to the latest book changes, conveniently summarized in a central location.

Note: The book in its printed format will also be completely up-to-date because the latest electronic file is supplied to fulfill each order or set of orders on a print-on-demand basis.

Table of Contents
(Incl. Parts of Book Found in Full Editions Only)

Contents at a glance

In the e-book format, just click the appropriate Table of Contents entry to go to that page. Either use the navigation bar in the left tab in Adobe Acrobat, or click the content detail entries below.

On our websites:

1. Research on Internet Searching: ⇨ www.SearchHelpCenter.com/ support-files/effective-internet-search-research-on-searching.pdf

2. Search Engine Evolution: ⇨ www.SearchHelpCenter.com/ effective-internet-search-search-engine-evolution-1.html

3. Search Tool Guide — A free companion guide to help you quickly and efficiently locate the right search tool for every job: ⇨ ToolGuide. SearchHelpCenter.com

About this book

Chapters

1: INTRODUCTION TO SEARCHING

2: SEARCH TOOLS & STRATEGIES

3: SEARCH ENTRY BASICS

4: SAMPLE SEARCH PROJECTS

5: MORE SEARCH INTERFACES

Parts of Book Found Only in the Full Editions

Features control center

▶ Back to top

Reference manual: Search engine features

▶ Back to top

3: Primary Search Entry Interfaces

▶ Back to top

5.1: Specialized Search Entry Interfaces

▶ Back to top

5.2: Findings Display & Handling Interfaces

6.3: Findings Display & Handling Parameters

6.4: User Preference Setting Parameters

ABOUT THIS BOOK

Improve Your Searches Now!

Online searching is one of the most important and valued activities on the Internet — and search engines are the gateways to access its information.

But research tells us over fifty percent of searches fail — hence the reason for writing our book — to help you improve your search skills.

In our opinion, search fails people for one major reason — **a lack of knowledge and expertise**. Not only is it frustrating and a waste of your valuable time, but it has other significant costs attached.

We've been studying Internet searching in-depth for more than three years now, and have more than 50 years of experience between us teaching and working with computers. We'd like to share what we've learned with you to help you improve your searches.

With this in mind, we've incorporated some unique features and teaching aids in our book to assist you:

- **E-Book format:** coupled with a print version as well, permits you to take full advantage of the power of your computer and of the Internet: ⇨ www. SearchHelpCenter.com/effective-internet-search-buy-book-versions-prices-orders.html.

- **Extensive hyperlinking:** moves you back and forth both within the e-book itself, as well as in and out of the Internet: ⇨ About the Book: Book hyperlinking.

- **Search Engine Features Control Center:** allows you to easily try out and compare hundreds of search engine features from major search engines: ⇨ www.SearchHelpCenter.com/effective-internet-search-solutions-search-engine-book-features-control-center.html and FEATURES CONTROL CENTER.

- **Structured search tool selection process:** helps you choose the best search tool every time: ⇨ Chapter 2: Basic Search Strategies.
- www.SearchHelpCenter.com: our website provides you with additional free search help resources, book updates, discussion topics, research, and other valuable search information.
- ToolGuide.SearchHelpCenter.com: our companion website provides you with a free **Search Tool Guide** to help you locate your target information quickly and easily.

We have provided many more useful features to assist you in your searches. To find out more about them, keep reading, or if using our e-book version, simply click on the desired link shown here.

Table of contents	Book overview
Book hyperlinking	Search Help
Search Popularity	Improve Your Searches Now!
Why Search Fails?	Cost$ of Not Searching Well

Our featured search engines

Learn how to get the most out of your searching using Yahoo's AlltheWeb and AltaVista, Copernic Agent, Google, MSN Search, Exalead, and others.

Special audiences

Teachers

Please Contact us (www.SearchHelpCenter.com) if you are interested in:

- Creating a test bank for our book.
- Extending book usage in course management systems such as WebCT or Blackboard.
- Adding learning materials to our website for both teacher and student use.

Information specialists & librarians

- Our Discussion Topics page at www.SearchHelpCenter.com may also include additional subjects of interest.

Webmasters

- Chapter 1 discusses the inner workings of search engines.
- Chapter 5: Other user tools summarizes special interface tools available from our featured search engines.

Search engine developers

- Our Search Tool Guide (ToolGuide.SearchHelpCenter.com) acts at a meta level to those provided by individual search sites, integrating and cross-referencing materials from many search tools and search guides in one place.
- Our Features Control Center provides a template of search engine features, which compares their attributes at multiple levels of abstraction. This not only provides a generic treatment of search engine functions, but is also useful to map one search engine against another.

Advertisers & Sales Affiliates (visit www.SearchHelpCenter.com)

- Our Sales Affiliates program may be of interest.

Authors & Contributors

Authors

Edward N. Baylin, BA, MBA, has more than 32 years experience in the computer field; some 20 years teaching computers and systems theory at the college and university levels, and 12 as a systems analyst/designer and technical writer for business computer information systems. He is currently a teacher in the Computer Sciences Department at John Abbott College.

Ed is the author of three books on systems theory, including *Functional Modeling of Systems,* published by Gordon and Breach Science Publishers in 1990. His knowledge of modeling has carried over into the fields of metadata and types of thesaurus relationships, which have influenced the evolution of this book. Further, his expertise in systems led to his interest in general schema theory, originating during the dissertation phase of a PhD in systems science, ideas of which are touched upon on our website (under Discussion Topics).

Major contributor

Judith Gill, PhD, MBA, has been writing and editing for 31 years, with many successful books, magazine and newspaper articles, and syndicated columns to her credit, as well as a computer program. She also worked in radio for 15 years, and has been teaching for over 30. For the past few years, she has been specializing in creating and managing content for the Web. This is her fifth book.

For three years, Judy played a major role in writing and editing the original editions of the book, first published in fall 2004. Subsequent editions, beginning in 2005, do not contain her input. Therefore, at her strong insistence, to which we have reluctantly complied, she is no longer cited as one of its two peer co-authors. However, her contributions on the book website have been duly noted. Thanks to Judy for such extreme generosity, but, in reality, she is still the second author on this book.

Acknowledgements

Melvyn Baylin, my older brother, for the cartoons used in this book.

Darlene Canning, BA, MLIS, Computer Services Librarian, Schulich Library of Science & Engineering, McGill University, Montreal, Quebec, generously permitted us to include her article Search Engine Evolution on our website (see "Discussion Topics").

Brenda Shestowsky, BSc(N), MS, MLS, my spouse, for her support throughout this project, her editing of the text and structure, and for making this manuscript much easier to understand. Indeed, she was its original inspiration. While completing her Masters of Library Science degree, she focused my attention on the subject of search engines, prompting me to teach it to my students.

John Abbott College's Visual Creations, a student-run company from the Publication Design & Hypermedia Technology program, for producing our book cover in the Hypermedia course, taught by **Eric Girouard** in winter 2005. **Kristin Fontaine** provided the chosen cover design from among a few appealing alternatives produced by the students.

Bruce Maclean, professional graphics designer, 11th Hour/Scan11 Imaging, an old friend, for adding the final, important professional touches to the book cover.

John Beenen, BEng, for reading the very early manuscript and pointing out problems with the structure and approach.

Ed's students, including Bryant Yen, who analyzed search engines as part of course assignments during the winter 2002 semester.

Book Features

Book overview

To increase the effectiveness and efficiency of your Internet searches, key concepts will be explored in each chapter. Information is arranged sequentially, with one concept building on the next.

A. Book chapters

Each chapter contains unique content, summarized below.

Chapter 1: Introduction to Searching

Evolution of the Internet and the Web.

Introduction to search engines featured in this book.

Fundamental principles of how all search engines work.

Chapter 2: Search Tools & Strategies

Explanation of different kinds of search engines.

A simple step-by-step search strategy.

Tips to solve typical search problems.

Chapter 3: Search Entry Basics

Introduction to parameters.

Use of parameters for effective searches.

Features common to most search engine interfaces.

Basic types of search entry interfaces.

Chapter 4: Sample Search Projects

Application of search techniques to real-life problems.

Practical mini-courses on the use of numerous search engines and the meta search utility, Copernic.

Differences in search engine databases and subsequent search results produced.

Superiority of particular engines for conducting certain kinds of searches.

Quirks, technical problems and software bugs in search engines, and how to investigate and, hopefully, solve them.

Chapter 5: More Search Interfaces

User interface features to handle:

> Specialized search requirements entry.
>
> Findings display.
>
> Findings handling.
>
> Search support tools.

Chapter 6: Advanced Search Options

Advanced searching techniques, particularly the effective use of parameters and filters for various search engine interfaces including:

> Term-based filters.
>
> Metadata-based filters.
>
> Parameters to display and handle search results.
>
> Parameters to customize search engine user preferences.

B. Parts of book found only in the full editions

The following parts of the book are referenced from this abridged edition. But, they are contained only in the full editions of the book.

Features control center

A powerful electronic template of search engine features to help you:

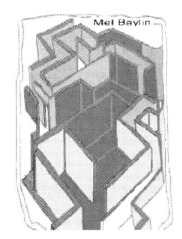

- Evaluate the relative strengths and weaknesses of various search engines.
- Experiment with summary, multi-level matrices of comparative search engine features.
- Explore cross-links between Chapters 3, 5, and 6 and their related Reference Manual sections, examining the pattern of search engine features in varying levels of detail. This linking will be explained in detail in the next section, "Book hyperlinking."

Reference manual: Search engine features

The Reference Manual serves a vital role in this book, and makes up more than half of the book content. The Reference Manual sections:

- Itemize features of search engines featured in this book including:

  - ﹙ Details of their search features/parameters.
  - ﹙ Examples using their screen interfaces.

- Hyperlink to chapter contents as seen here, allowing easy cross-reference between concepts and implementation details. The book also often links to our web-based Search Tool Guide.

Reference Manual	Chapter
3	3
5.1 - 5.3	5
6.1 - 6.4	6

For a more detailed view of the Reference Manual sections, refer to the Table of Contents, or go to www.SearchHelpCenter.com/effective-internet-search-about-book-contents.html.

Book interrelationships

To help you better visualize interrelationships between different segments of the book, look at the diagram on the next page.

Conventions used

- **Sans-serif typeface** (such as this text) is used for:
  - ﹙ The text of quotes from the Help screens of search engines. Such quotes are accompanied by a reference to the source, generally in square brackets, e.g., [Google Help].
  - ﹙ Text inside the cells of tables.
  - ﹙ Text, such as search keywords, to be typed into text boxes on forms.
  - ﹙ Depending on the edition, possibly the main text in the Reference Manual part of the book, included in the full editions. It is anticipated that many readers will use the reference materials in electronic format, while sans-serif text is preferable for reading off of the screen.
- **Quotes** are used to surround the names of various boxes on forms to be filled in to specify the search parameters — for example, "Search with this Boolean expression" could be the name of a scrolling text box in a search interface.

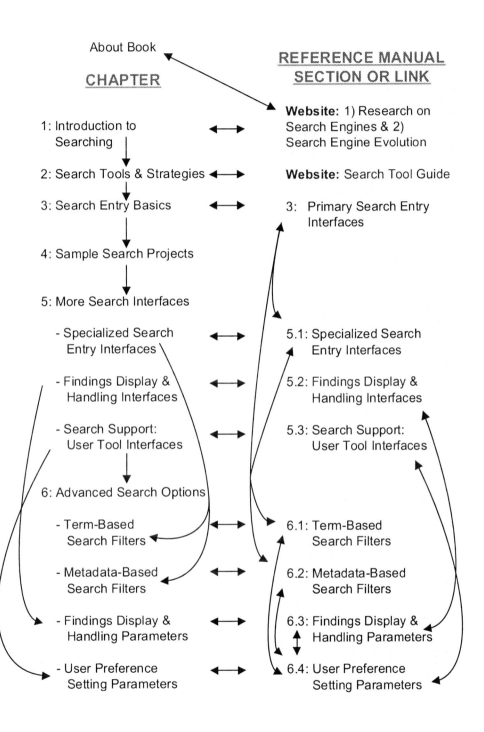

About Book

CHAPTER

**REFERENCE MANUAL
SECTION OR LINK**

1: Introduction to
   Searching

Website: 1) Research on
Search Engines & 2)
Search Engine Evolution

2: Search Tools & Strategies

Website: Search Tool Guide

3: Search Entry Basics

3:   Primary Search Entry
     Interfaces

4: Sample Search Projects

5: More Search Interfaces

- Specialized Search
  Entry Interfaces

5.1: Specialized Search
     Entry Interfaces

- Findings Display &
  Handling Interfaces

5.2: Findings Display &
     Handling Interfaces

- Search Support:
  User Tool Interfaces

5.3: Search Support:
     User Tool Interfaces

6: Advanced Search Options

- Term-Based
  Search Filters

6.1: Term-Based
     Search Filters

- Metadata-Based
  Search Filters

6.2: Metadata-Based
     Search Filters

- Findings Display &
  Handling Parameters

6.3: Findings Display &
     Handling Parameters

- User Preference
  Setting Parameters

6.4: User Preference
     Setting Parameters

- **Normal Web conventions** are used in the e-book, such as hyperlinks indicated in blue, visited links in purple, and so on.
- Icons:

  🔲 indicates an **example**.   💡 indicates a **tip**.

  🔨 indicates a **note**.   △ indicates a **warning**.

  ⇨ indicates a link to a **reference**.

- This handy **internal navigation bar** is found on Reference Manual pages, allowing you to jump back and forth comparing features for different search engines (in the e-book only):

General	AlltheWeb	AltaVista	Copernic	Google	MSN

References & Links

- **Bracketed numbers within text:** signify references and links. Used to avoid disruption of your reading, they link you to items at the end of each chapter or Reference Manual section. Example: [15].
- **References & Links:**
  - **External references & links:** links to materials *found on the Internet* are generally grouped at the end of appropriate sections.
  - **Internal book cross-link references:** links to materials *within the book* are generally grouped at the end of appropriate sub-sections.

Book hyperlinking

The flexible design of this book allows you to access it both online or in hard copy. And hyperlinks, found throughout, permit you to explore its many features.

Hyperlink tutorial

In the e-book, the unique "backbone" network of book hyperlinks allows you to:

1. **Switch back and forth between explanations of search engine features and how they work.**

   To experiment with this in the e-book:

   a. Click ⇨ here to go to a particular search engine feature. In this case, "Intelligent avoidance of formal parameter entry" (discussed in Chapter 3) appears in a discussion.

b. Once there, click on the blue text (beside this ➪ icon), signifying a hyperlink to the corresponding section of the Reference Manual. You arrive at Reference Section 3: "Intelligent avoidance of formal parameter entry," which gives details on how this feature is implemented.

c. Click on the return link beside this ➪ icon in the accompanying sidebar box to go back to your starting point. As you can see, this allows you to flip back and forth between conceptual explanations and practical applications of search engine features.

2. **Access all search engine features centrally located in the Features Control Center.**

From here you can easily try out different search engine features, experimenting with how different search engines specifically implement them. You move from master tables in the Features Control Center to either: (a) explanations in the chapters, or to (b) detailed applications in the Reference Manual.

To experiment with this in the e-book:

a. Click on the "Try it out" icon to test it on a search engine feature from one of the master tables in the Features Control Center. "Intelligent avoidance of formal parameter entry" appears in the a row of the table in a new pop-up window.

b. Click the row header "Intelligent avoidance of formal parameter entry," which takes you to an explanation of this feature in Chapter 3. After reviewing it, press the "Back" button in your browser to return to the Features Control Center.

c. Now click on one of the cells in the same row of the table to see how a particular search engine implements this feature.

For your ease of use, an internal navigator bar is repeated at several points on the page, which looks like this (you may have to scroll a little to see it):

General   AlltheWeb   AltaVista   Copernic   Google   MSN

d. Say you chose AltaVista in the previous step, but now want to look at the description for Google. Simply click "Google" on the internal navigator bar to take you there. It's as easy as that!

e. For brief notes about the specific feature you are exploring and how our selected search engines implement it, click "General" on the navigator bar, to take you directly to generalities on that feature.

> From this point forward, you could simply follow the same directions as in #1 (where you switched back and forth between explanations of search engine features and how they work). Instead you are encouraged to continue on, allowing you to further explore the many unique and powerful features of the Features Control Center.

f. Once there, notice the yellow arrow icon (⇨) you were referred to in #1 above (you end up in the same place by another route). As before, click the link to take you to the specific place in the book where your selected search engine feature is explained more fully.

g. To return to the Control Center, press the "Back" button on your browser until you reach it.

3. **Try out search engine features in the actual Internet search environment.**

For instance, when help materials for a particular search engine are quoted, a link is provided to them.

To try out this feature in the e-book:

a. Click on the picture of a finger. It will take you to a place in

Google, AltaVista, and perhaps Hotbot have particularly good image file searches.

the book having a sample results listing from MSN Search. You will notice that some of the findings in that list have hyperlinks, shown in blue. These hyperlinks are active in many cases.

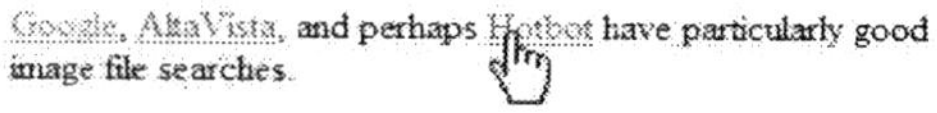

b. To find out which hyperlinks are active, float your mouse over the MSN Search findings. Where the hand icon (see above picture) appears, try out the hyperlink. If the finding is still on the Web, it should work.

c. A similar principle often applies when we show search entry forms; e.g., the "Help" link sometimes works. Even if entries in the form do not have active hyperlinks (depending on the way the form was captured for production of this book), the caption above the form will. For instance, if you scroll down the page below the MSN Search findings list you will find examples of search entry forms from AltaVista and Google, among others. Click on the text in blue in the caption above these forms to go to the Internet to try out these search entry interfaces.

d. In fact, many of the internal features of these forms themselves actually work — the radio buttons, checkboxes, and choices from drop-down menus. Click on the down arrows next to active drop-down menu boxes to see the choices they offer, as if you were active on the Internet.

Key takeaway: In the e-book, the network of hyperlinks and the Features Control Center are powerful and flexible tools to help you quickly and easily locate the information you want wherever it is located in the book and on the Internet, making it a handy reference manual now and in the future.

Effective Internet Search

E-Searching Made Easy!

Skills & Strategies for Improved Search Engine Results

Chapters

1: INTRODUCTION TO SEARCHING

In this chapter:

- Evolution of the Internet and the Web.
- Introduction to search engines featured in this book.
- Fundamental principles of how all search engines work.

Search Engine Overview

The information superhighway

> **... the Internet is ... the fastest growing new medium of all time, ... the information medium of first resort for its users.**
> - University of California, Berkeley, School of Information Management and Systems, October 2003 [1]

How big is the Internet? Estimates vary, depending on the source [26], but in 2004, some 709 to 945 million people are expected to be online [3]. In August 2005, one article [1] estimated the size as of January 2005 to be around 11.5 billion "indexable" pages (of which about 9 billion are indexed by search engines) in the visible (surface) web, and perhaps up to 500 billion pages in the invisible (deep) web (⮕ Chapter 2: Deep web search engines).

In 2003, international distribution roughly broke down as follows: Europe - 31%; Asia/Pacific (including Australia and New Zealand) - 31%; North America - 30%; Latin America - 6%; Middle East - 1%; Africa - 1% [4] (⮕ pie chart: www.sims.berkeley.edu/research/projects/how-much-info-2003/internet.htm).

The power of the Internet

> **The impact of the Internet — whether measured by the numbers of users or by the social change it is causing — cannot be overstated. A technology that practically did not exist in American homes only a few years ago is now a standard feature in nearly two-thirds of homes.**
> - USC Annenberg School Center for the Digital Future, September 2004 [5]

A recent University of California, Berkeley study claims the Internet is not only the newest, but also the fastest growing new medium of all time. In 2002, it represented the second largest source of new information after the telephone [6]. And as the accompanying table indicates, it is also the information medium of first resort for its users, with the majority ranking it ahead of television, radio, newspapers and magazines [7].

Clearly, the Internet has become an increasingly important part of our social fabric. But do you really understand what the Internet is and how it works?

What is the Internet? [8]

To help you visualize it, think of the Internet as a network of networks — or a worldwide collection of computer networks — or a vast system of computers that are linked together and cooperate with each other to exchange information. And because the Internet is a loose alliance of private organizations, universities and government agencies, it is a shared global resource that is not owned or controlled by anyone.

Sources of New Electronic Information - 2002

Medium	Terabytes
Telephone	17,300,000
Internet	532,897
Television	68,955
Radio	3,488
TOTAL	17,905,340

Source: How much information 2003 [6]

What is a terabyte (TB)? A unit for measuring computer memory or storage capacity; a unit of information equal to a trillion bytes (1,099,511,627,776) or approximately 10^{12} bytes or a thousand gigabytes. 10 TB is equivalent to the entire print collection of the U.S. Library of Congress.

The Internet began in 1969 as a United States Defense Department network called ARPAnet to ensure reliable communications in the event of nuclear war. Soon educational and research institutions were added to perform military-related work, followed later by non-military communications between academic organizations. Its rapid expansion dates back to 1989-90, when commercial entities began offering the general public access to the Internet. Coupled with the availability of reasonably-priced, yet powerful, personal computers and easy-to-use graphical operating systems, the Internet truly came into its own.

What is the Web? [8]

The Web has become a worldwide source of information and a mainstream business tool.
- IEEE/CS Computer, March 2002 [9]

Although the terms "Internet" and "Web" are used interchangeably, the Web makes up only a portion of the Internet — albeit the largest and most popular part. Short for World Wide Web, it is a group of approximately three million free, publicly-available Internet sites [10], [11] that use the same **protocol** to exchange information. Its popularity is easy to explain — because everyone can view its pages regardless of what kind of computer is used. To help visualize the relationship between the Internet and the Web, see: www.tpub.com/content/aerographer/14272/css/14272_20.htm.

Simply put, you can think of the Web as:

- A subset of the Internet.
- An Internet application — Hypertext Transfer Protocol (HTTP); others include e-mail (SMTP, POP, MAPI), File Transfer Protocol (FTP), Instant Messaging (IM), Internet Relay Chat (IRC), Network News (NNTP).
- The Internet application that accesses files using the HTTP — Hypertext Transfer Protocol (⇨ Chapter 5: Non-Web Internet applications). Many different types of files stored on web servers are accessible with this protocol, including document and multi-media formats (⇨ Chapter 6: File structure characteristics).

Searching the Internet

In the past year or so, the Internet has turned into America's go-to tool.
- John Horrigan, Senior Research Specialist, Pew Internet & American Life Project, December 2002 [12]

Search is the second most popular online activity, helping users more quickly and efficiently locate the information and webpages they want. There are many search tools available to you that can complement each other in the research process. General search engines, subject directories, meta search engines, specialized and deep web search engines can all deliver the results you want. The trick is knowing how to maximize their abilities, and use them most appropriately.

Is there a single search tool that can access every document on the Web?

The short answer is "no." The Internet is huge, and it changes and evolves too quickly for all its content to be carefully documented. Even the biggest search engines only access a small portion of the content available; estimates put it at less than 20%; some say as little as one percent.

Key takeaway: There is no "best way" or "best tool" to conduct an Internet search — and that is one of the big messages we hope you get from reading our book.

Search engines

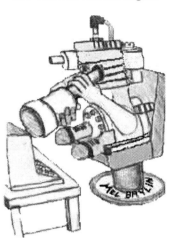

The 1-stroke search engine

> **Search engines are really the gateway to the Internet; they're the front door.**
> - iProspect CEO Frederick Marckini, April 2004 [18]

Consumer WebWatch defines the term search engine as "any major site with the ability to point or navigate hundreds of thousands of Internet users to different points of entry online, including search services, directories, portals and community sites" [13].

Studies have consistently shown that most people use search engines to locate websites and information: Pew: 84-88% [14], [17]; Georgia Tech: 87% [15]; iProspect: 77% [16]. They have become an indispensable utility for Internet users, ranking only behind e-mail in popularity and use [14], [17]. They are *one* invaluable way to find information on the Internet.

Featured search engines [19]

The four major search engines and one meta search utility (Copernic) featured in our book will provide you with the foundation to understand how most search engines work. These particular ones were selected due to their:

- Popularity and/or richness of features.
- Variety and number of specialized search interfaces.
- Connection to important sources of Internet information including the major webcrawlers owned by Google and Yahoo, and data compiled from webmasters and website authors.
- Range of search results returned including:

  › General web document (Web) listings: based on data collected by webcrawlers.
  › Subject directories: usually from listing requests by website creators.
  › Paid results: from companies paying to have their websites listed.

Featured Search Engines

Logo	Search Engine	Ownership	Main Search Source	Other Search Sources
alltheweb *** all the web, all the time	AlltheWeb www.alltheweb.com	Overture; acquired by Yahoo	Yahoo webcrawler	Paid listings, Yahoo news feeds
altavista™	AltaVista www.altavista.com	Overture; acquired by Yahoo	Yahoo webcrawler	Paid listings, Yahoo news feeds, ODP and Yahoo/ Overture subject directories
copernic⁾ See note below.	Copernic www.copernic.com	Copernic Technologies	Over 1,000 search engines grouped into 120 categories	Meta search utility; accesses other search engine sources
Google™	Google www.google.com	Google	Own webcrawler	Paid listings, ODP subject directory, trusted feeds (especially news)
see MSN Search	MSN Search www.search.msn.com	Microsoft	Own webcrawler	Trusted feeds, especially news

Note: Throughout our book, all references to Copernic are specific to only one of its many search tools, Copernic Agent Professional.

- ○ Partially human-compiled "general" data (not in subject directories): screened by humans assisted by various automated techniques.
- ○ Machine-calculated "clickthrough" data: based on the popularity of certain findings to the users searching.
- ○ Trusted feed data: automatically uploaded without human intervention such as information from journals, newspapers, and magazines.

Supplemental search engines

To better illustrate some concepts and principles, additional search engines may also be discussed, such as Exalead (www.exalead.com), Hotbot (www.hotbot.com) and Vivisimo's Clusty (www.vivisimo.com), a meta search engine.

Key takeaway: Searching the Internet is a skill. The trick is to learn to employ the most effective and efficient search techniques given your desired target information. The good news is you can improve — which is why we wrote this book.

How Search Engines Work

Catalogs and indexes

Search engines are essentially massive databases. Although the specifics of how they operate vary from one to the next, they all have three basic components:

- **a search robot(s)** (also known as **spiders** or **metacrawlers**) to gather information;
- **a database** in which to store this information;
- **a search tool** to search the database.

Basic search process: First off, it's important to understand that search engines do not search the Internet itself. What they actually do is search their own databases of information *about* the Internet, known as **catalogs**, which their host companies have gathered. Documents placed on the Internet can only be found by search engines if they have been recorded in these catalogs.

How do search engines find documents placed on the Internet? The general process goes something like this. First, document publishers can register them directly with search engines. Another method is to find them using search robots or spiders that scour the Internet looking for content. Information is gathered and then recorded (or **indexed**).

A separate indexing computer program analyzes the text, links, and other content on each new webpage found, then stores this information (called **metadata**) in the search engine's catalogs. This permits searches by keyword or other more advanced methods. Pages are located when your search matches its content.

Why do you get different results from search engines when using identical search terms? Because each search engine looks through its own catalogs to find your target content. These document collections are different, they are each indexed with varying degrees of detail, and are searched with differing levels of sophistication.

How do search engines locate information in their catalogs? By either subject or keyword. Here is a general overview of these two search methods.

Subject searches: Imagine a traditional library, where books and other materials are cataloged, indexed, and often arranged on shelves by subject. These subject-areas are established by recognized authorities such as the Library of Congress. Fairly broad general classifications are employed, which are somewhat limited in number to be manageable. As a result, they are often unable to reflect the true complexity and variety of topics covered within the materials cataloged.

Furthermore, subject searching is not always obvious or direct. For instance, to find information about the Vietnam War, you might have to follow the roundabout route of first looking under United States - then History - then Vietnam War.

Alternatively, subject searches can be very useful when you have a vague or broad idea about what you want to research, permitting you to explore a number of avenues to find your target content.

Keyword searches: Using computerized search terms, known as keywords, permits much more sophisticated and complex searches. Indexing is very comprehensive, including words from the title and content, as well as the subject (discussed in detail later on). As a result, a lot more information can be located and quite specific to your desired topic.

On the other hand, keyword searches have trouble distinguishing between words spelled the same way, but having different meanings such as the "hard" drive of your computer, a "hard" test, or a "hard" rock. This is why you often get seemingly totally irrelevant results to your search query.

"Stemming" can be a problem, too. When you enter the word "employ," you may also get back search results for "employer," "employment," and so on. Singular and plural words, and verb tenses can also be a problem (e.g., words with an "s" or an "ed").

Another consideration: most search engines only search on the specific keywords in your query, so words of similar meaning are not included in your results (e.g. "heart" versus "cardiovascular" versus "cardiac" problems).

Overall, due to the potential for locating vast quantities of information, the challenge in keyword searches is to refine them sufficiently to obtain useful and relevant documents without being overwhelmed by low-content or irrelevant documents.

Key takeaway: Both subject and keyword searches can be useful in locating your desired content. You should regard them as complementary approaches, knowledgeably selecting the correct method at the appropriate moment in your search. Later, in Chapter 2, we'll come back to discuss some of the finer points of when to use these and other kinds of searches to get the best results.

But right now, since you have a better appreciation of the general search process, let's get down to the specifics.

Importance of search engine catalogs

> **Today's search engines may be capturing as little as 1 percent of the Web, largely because of how they find and index online resources.**
> - Associated Press, March 2004 [20]

As you can see from the above quote, the importance of catalogs cannot be overstated. How a search engine gathers data, then indexes and prioritizes it into catalogs to answer user queries, is the key to understanding how a search engine works.

A search engine is simply a computer system made up of hardware, software, and **catalogs**. The software program accepts queries from and provides responses to users. Catalogs provide the data that respond to the query.

Different catalogs often require the use of separate search entry interfaces.

> Search engines may provide different interfaces for the user to request document versus sound versus video versus image files.

> The kinds of catalogs used will often affect the placement and formatting of search results on the findings display screen, as well.

Key takeaway: A knowledge and understanding of search engine catalogs will increase the likelihood that you, the user, can find the most relevant information you require quickly and efficiently, thus optimizing your Internet searches.

Catalogs, tables, and indexes

Databases are made up of tables, each row of which is usually called a **record**, and each column a **field**. You can find individual records in a table by creating sorted indexes, which are other tables used to cross-reference the basic, underlying table. In fact, you can create levels of index tables above the final, underlying data being indexed.

🔲 Take a trivial table, such as that seen here, that has just two fields, namely, first (for first name) and last (for last name). Assume that this simplistic table has just two records, with values:

Record No.	Name	
	First	Last
1	Joe	Shmo
2	Susie	Que

- Joe (first name) Shmo (last name) in the first record.
- Susie (first name) Que (last name) in the second record.

In this case, four different indexes are possible, each with two entries corresponding to the two records. The indexes, with entries sorted alphabetically, in ascending order are:

- by first, having the entries Joe and Susie;
- by first+last, having the entries JoeShmo and SusieQue;
- by last, having the entries Que and Shmo;
- by last+first, having the entries QueSusie and ShmoJoe.

In the latter index, for instance, QueSusie would point to record 2 in the table, while ShmoJoe would point to record 1.

The more a database is structured into fields, the more ways of indexing it become possible. In fact, some documents on the Internet, accessible by deep web searches (⇨ Chapter 2: Deep web search engines), are structured databases, represented as tables divided into multiple fields and records.

However, many if not most files on the Internet are like a "null table," consisting of just one record and one, big "memo" field. Such is the traditional webpage on the surface web. Nowadays, however, some webpages are coded with invisible (not shown in your browser) tags to provide some identification of fields within their single "record." The coding scheme normally used for this is known as **XML** (see the following frame).

💡 Better ways of defining fields in textual documents are now being implemented, usually using a coding scheme known as **XML** (Extended Markup Language). With this method, a document creator is able to identify the fields (meanings) of sub-strings of document text, based on discipline (domain)-specific vocabularies (ontologies). With this approach, search engines will be able to create many more different indexes for use in finding information.

🜨 **Chemistry:** as part of its particular vocabulary, uses the term "compound formula," which is a field to provide the chemical composition of a substance. The document creator indicates that the vocabulary for chemistry is to be used in the document, and places some indicators into the document to surround text that gives the compound formula field. These indicators are hidden codes that do not display to the regular computer user. The document can now be indexed by "compound formula," and located using that index.

Obviously, the more indexes a document has, the more ways there are of locating it. That's why it's easier to find information in a structured database than in a bunch of documents not structured into multiple records and fields.

However, with computers, other kinds of indexes, known as **text indexes**, become possible. More will be said about this technique below, after we deal with traditional catalogs and use of tables of **metadata** to provide higher level indexes pointing to unstructured webpages, structured databases, or webpages that have a degree of structure. **Note:** The use of metadata tables implies that multiple levels of tables and indexes are used by search engines to find the underlying data.

How catalogs work

> **Search engines are becoming the card catalog to the Web.**
> - CyberAtlas, March 13, 2003 [21]

To help visualize the cataloging (indexing) process, once again think of a traditional library. Its catalogs — which consist of both tables and their indexes — contain records made up of fields such as author, title, subject, ISBN, call number, publisher, date of publication, notes, etc. Information specialists and librarians refer to this as **metadata** — data about data; in this case, data about the documents in the library.

Similarities to a library: A library can have more than one kind of catalog — one for books, one for videotapes, another for CD's, and so on. Each catalog can and often does have its own set of metadata, that is, different fields in its records.

 A catalog of books would list an author, whereas paintings would include an artist. As a result, separate catalogs may be needed for different metadata due to the varying nature of the objects described. And by extension, different metadata imply different catalogs, or at least, different ways of viewing catalogs.

Like libraries, search engine catalogs are also created for different kinds of objects, referenced by metadata, including:

- Files for presentation media such as documents, images, sound, and video.
- Data from different Internet applications other than the Web, the most prominent being News; FTP (file transfer protocol); Public discussion boards; Chat rooms; E-mail, in some authorized cases.
- Particular kinds of information based on domain/discipline/topic such as names and addresses of people and organizations; information on patents and trademarks; and private company market research studies.

Also, as in a traditional library, search engine catalogs are also often based on the creation and maintenance of indexes based on well-defined metadata fields. To make use of this metadata, searches may enter filters to limit or expand the scope of search engine findings. As will be discussed in Chapter 3, in this book, these indexes are called **metadata-based filters** (⇨ Chapter 3: Parameter types), although search engines generally refer to them as simply **filters**.

 Author's name and file size are metadata-based filters.

Dissimilarities to a library: Although search engine catalogs are similar in many respects to those in a traditional library, there are some very important differences. This is not only due to differing data-gathering methods, to be explained shortly (⇨ Chapter 1: Catalog types and origins), but also because they use more automated methods, as follows:

1. Search engines also create **text indexes**. With these, each word particle, word, or larger character string in a document can be used to generate an index at the lowest level. The entries in this index are similar to the index at the back of a book, although more structured. Also, each index entry refers to a different webpage or part thereof, like an index that covers multiple different books. Note: Multiple levels of text indexes are in fact used.

These search engine text indexes tend to be much longer and more thorough than what you might find at the back of a book, because many more words and ordered combinations of words (called **phrases**) from the document are used to create them. Indeed, the resulting index can actually be many times larger than the document itself, due to different combinations of words of varying lengths in differing orders.

> ⇨ **Phrases** are search terms, often entered into search engines with quotation marks around them so results containing the entire phrase will be given the highest priority in listings; e.g., "digital camera ratings" as opposed to searching on each word separately.

🔢 Suppose a document consists of just two words, digital and camera. Then the text index to this document has four potential entries, namely: digital, digital camera, camera, and camera digital. If the document had just three words, 15 index entries would become possible, based on all the different combinations and permutations of words and phrases.

Text indexes allow you to search based on strings of characters found in a webpage, as opposed to metadata about that webpage. You enter these

> ⇨ For more on search filter types, see Chapter 6: Introduction.

characters, possibly along with further parameters that allow you to expand or limit the scope of text index entries used to respond to a query. In this book, the further parameters employed to do this are known as **term-based filters** (⇨ Chapter 3: Parameter types). Search engines have no well-known term for this concept, although **word filters** is sometimes used.

🔢 Wildcards (⇨ Chapter 6: Term variation filters) are term-based filters that expand the number of index entries selected in response to a query.

> ⇨ For an example of a wildcard in action, see Chapter 2: Refine your search.

🔢 If a document file contains just the two-word text shopping center, you can find the files on this topic through the value strings shopping center, or center shopping, or just the individual words center or shopping. Each of these four possibilities corresponds to a different set of textual index entries created to cross-map search queries against files. The role of term-based filters is to indicate which of these and what variations of them are to be used to find matches.

2. Search engine catalogs use metadata to assign priorities to entries in each document or file in an index, based on the **degree of relevance** to a user's query.

3. The text indexing method may be hybridized with the indexing of metadata. Thus, the value of a metadata field in a record may give rise to several textual variations for indexing purposes.

   🔲 Suppose that some metadata field gives the topic dealt with by a document being indexed. If a file's topic is shopping center, you can find the file matches through this metadata value. However, different arrangements of the words this metadata field value may also be indexed. For instance, you may not be able to use the value string center shopping or just the words shopping or center.

4. Access to the referenced data itself is made even more efficient when the catalog contains a whole or partial snapshot of the version of the referenced file last crawled. To be more technically correct, the search engine may sometimes keep a local, **cached** copy of the file *in conjunction with* its catalog. To be on the safe side, however, instead of using the cached version, the search engine can access a current version of the file on the Internet.

   Under certain circumstances, you may want to access the cached version of a page instead of accessing it on the Internet:

   - If the file owner has removed it from the Internet, the cache is the only place to go.
   - You may want to see an older version of a file.
   - The search engine may return a file that appears to have little to do with your query.
   - The cached version is for free, but you have to pay or subscribe to obtain a current version of the file.
   - The download of the file from its host server is too slow, for whatever reason, and download from a search engine server will be faster.

   In fact, with some kinds of search utilities, priorities can be further refined by using the referenced file itself. In a traditional library of books, this would be like actually going to have a quick look at the book itself to obtain more information than is available in the catalog.

   Nor does this prioritization of the findings have to stop here. Once the user reviews the search results, further guidelines can be provided to the computer to trigger another round of findings sequences to take place (⇨ Chapter 5: Post-processing of findings).

Catalog types and origins

Catalog types

To understand the full potential for creating different sorts of catalogs, think of all the possible permutations and combinations of files classified according to the following criteria:

- **File format:** document, multi-media (audio, image, video), and other file types (spreadsheet, database, program).
- **Internet application:** Web, news, discussion board, e-mail, FTP, etc.
- **Catalog topic/discipline:** general or special topic.
- **Catalog data collection method:** crawler, submission, and others.
- **Catalog listing payment method:** free or paid placement (including various ways of paying for placement such as Pay Per Click, Pay For Inclusion, and so on).

Catalog data-gathering

Search engines use various ways of collecting data for text indexes and gathering metadata into catalogs. The methodology selected influences the resulting catalog and, in turn, the data gathered for a particular kind of file or object.

Search engines collect data for their catalogs in the following ways:

1. **Data gathered by webcrawlers: crawlers**, for short; also known as **web robots** or **spiders**. They scour the Internet looking for files, including those changed since the crawler last visited the website. The data collected are organized into various webcrawler-based catalogs, often based on classifying files residing on Internet servers by file type (format).

   The different file formats include, but are not limited to:

   - **Document files**, in formats such as HTML, Adobe PDF, and Microsoft Word DOC files. Catalogs of this type are generally considered the most important because they often embed pointers to other kinds of files.
   - **Sound files**, such as MP3.
   - **Image files**, such as JPG (jpeg) and GIF.
   - **Video files**, such as MOV and QT.

   The use of the term **Web** can be very confusing. Search engines have adopted a rather idiosyncratic usage, both in relation to their catalogs and their **Web Search** interfaces. But to understand how search engines work, you must grasp their meaning.

When search engines refer to a "Web catalog," they don't mean a catalog of all files accessible by the Web Internet application. Rather, they mean a catalog that is comprised only of document files; not specific to any topic; accessed by the keyword method of search entry; based on data collected by webcrawlers; and found only on the Web. More explanation is given in the following frame.

When you do a "Web" search, the implication is your search requirements use (are "run against") these "Web" catalogs.

"Web" catalogs —versus— Catalogs of files "available on the Web"		
Catalog Criteria	Catalogs on the Web	Web Catalogs
File format	Many file formats — document, multi-media (audio, image, video), other file types (spreadsheet, database)	Document files only — but may embed pointers to other file formats within them
Topic or Discipline	General or special topic	General only
Access method	Subject & keyword search methods	Keyword search method only
Data collection method	Crawler, submission, etc.	Webcrawler only
Internet application	Web, news, discussion board, e-mail, FTP, etc.	Web only

The term **Internet application** in the last row of the above table merits further understanding. In general, a computer application may be defined as a set of computer programs that directly produce information for an end user, i.e., for use over and beyond managing or controlling the computer itself. For instance, a computerized accounting information system is such an application.

However, in telecommunications in general, and on the Internet in particular, the term usually has a rather different meaning, which we will tend to use in this book with some exceptions (identified in this note). It refers to the telecommunications protocol *immediately behind* producing information for the end user. For example, the Web application uses the HTTP (Hyper-Text Transfer Protocol). There are also protocols for news, email, and discussion boards, although news, email, and discussion boards also often occur under the aegis of the HTTP protocol (in which case they are referred to as being "web-based").

In this book, we will refer to email, news, and discussion boards as separate "Internet" applications whether or not they are web-based.

While most crawlers are controlled from central locations, some new varieties of distributed crawlers, called

> Although we speak of "crawling the Web," in truth search robots actually stay in one place when gathering metadata into catalogs.

"Grubs" (www.grub.org/), are now starting to make their appearance.

The importance of good metadata: The need for complete and well-thought-out metadata now starts to become obvious. It is collected by webcrawlers from files at websites, based on the documentation contained in the files or on the crawled website. Such documentation is created by the website authors, who can put titles and metatags into HTML document files, to provide keywords, summaries, and other descriptions of the document.

Key takeaway: Unfortunately, many webpage creators do

> **Dublin Core Metadata Initiative**
>
> Obviously, establishing universal, standardized conventions for metadata for website files is required for easy location of files or documents. Libraries and the Web are both repositories of information, organized and indexed to facilitate searching and retrieval. Unfortunately, the Web often lacks this structure. The Dublin Core Metadata Initiative was created to introduce formal metadata schemes into the Web in a consistent way.
>
> **How successful has it been?** The OCLC Online Computer Library Center, Office of Research, has tracked metadata usage on public websites from 1998 to 2002. Although there have been steady increases, they conclude, "The vast majority of metadata provided on the public Web is *ad hoc* in its creation, unstructured by any formal metadata scheme" [22].

not systematically include metadata in their documents or elsewhere on their websites. When this occurs, the webcrawler is unable to obtain standard, complete, consistent, or reliable descriptions of a website's files, thus hindering it from being easily found by search engines.

2. **Data compiled with a degree of human intervention:** for example, based on submissions about particular sites from **webmasters** (people who author or run websites), causing the webcrawler to go to a site it might not otherwise visit.

Subject directory catalogs [23] are also created from these submissions, having several pre-defined topic

⇨ See Chapter 2: Subject directories or Chapter 3: Subject directory search interfaces for more information.

categories as well as levels of sub-categories. Editors review and select sites for inclusion in their directories on the basis of previously determined selection criteria. Some search engines may also automatically cross-reference subject directories with their other types of catalogs.

Submission for inclusion in subject directories may or may not be accompanied by payment to the data collection company. Paid inclusions may be placed into a separate catalog from the non-paid ones, and receive higher priority — that is, they are usually placed on the first page of the search findings display, often in a separate section.

Subject directories are becoming less and less popular with searchers. Also, they are very expensive to build and maintain because human labor is needed. However, automated algorithms will never become good enough to replace the kind of judgments about the substance of a website that can be made by human experts. One problem is that there is a tendency for subject directory entries to become based on factors such as popularity and commercial considerations, as opposed to substance. It comes as no surprise that some of the best subject indexes on the Internet are ones maintained by professional librarians.

3. **Data automatically uploaded without human intervention from trusted feeds:** such as news, magazines, stock exchanges, and the like. A crawler may be involved in gathering information from an

⇨ For more about trusted feeds, consult the RSS standard at www.searchenginewatch.com /sereport/article.php/2175261.

assortment of trusted data feeds or it may come straight to the search engine. Like subject directory data, it is slotted into predefined categories and its metadata is ideally standard, complete, and consistent. This technology relies on systematic and standardized encoding of hidden XML tags (see above) into webpages.

4. **Data computed from patterns of access frequency:** Statistics are automatically gathered on users' reactions to search term findings.

🔢 Suppose whenever the term cat is entered, users tend to click on one particular finding more than others. The ten most popular are then collected in a catalog that makes associations between terms entered and popular websites. In a separate part of the findings display, these top 10 are listed whenever users search on the term cat.

Because catalogs based on this type of data collection method link to information in other catalogs, they are generally referred to as **clickthrough** data.

Catalog data sources

The table on the next page is intended to help you visualize the various kinds of catalogs, data-gathering methods for each, the types of files they contain, and their data sources. It soon becomes apparent that a relatively limited number of data-suppliers provide information to most of the major public search engines. Not only do they supply more than one company, but many also have their own search engines as well. The combination of data-suppliers used by each search engine also varies from company to company. SearchEngineWatch.com provides a comprehensive listing: ➪ www.searchenginewatch.com/reports/article. php/2156401.

Search engine alliances: To help picture these complex alliances, look at the interactive search engine relationship chart from Search-This Search Engine Solutions (www.search-this.com/ search_engine_decoder.asp). Because search engines evolve quickly, undoubtedly some of this information may already have changed. In particular, as webcrawler technology becomes more widely dispersed, it is possible that more and more companies will become involved in creating their own catalogs based on their own crawlers.

> Overture's acquisition of FAST and AltaVista, followed by Yahoo's purchase of Overture stand out as a particularly important series of industry consolidation events (www.searchenginewatch.com/ searchday/article.php/2234821).

Data sources: To add further complexity, although search engines share the same data sources, they may re-catalog it in unique ways. A more in-depth explanation of the search engine data-cataloging process is provided by SearchEngineWatch.com [24]. Interestingly, search engines are not very forthcoming about their data sources or collection methods: ➪ SearchEngineWatch.com for an analysis [25].

Database size: Most agree that Google, Yahoo, Microsoft, and Ask Jeeves offer the largest surface web catalogs [26]. Large crawlers collect data on many different types of files in addition to HTML (specially prepared for display on the Internet). However, the whole picture is in flux. Yahoo's crawler now replaces those of Inktomi, FAST, and AltaVista, all of whose assets are now owned by Yahoo. This includes, for example, AltaVista's huge multi-media file catalogs [26].

Catalog Types & Data Sources

Catalog Types	Data Collection Method	Catalog Descriptions & File Types	Data Sources
Crawler-based	Automatically collected: • usually by a webcrawler, the Web being the most frequent Internet application. • also by other crawler types: news, FTP, discussion board, etc.	Includes separate catalogs by file type, type of Internet application or special topic. Catalogs include most file types: document, audio, video, image, database, program, etc. Excludes catalogs of files submitted to subject directories.	Google Yahoo (includes the former FAST, AltaVista, and Inktomi) Microsoft
Subject Directories	Human-compiled; based on submissions: paid placements or free.	Includes web document files (webpages).	Open Directory Project (ODP) Yahoo
Paid listings	Human-compiled; based on submissions.	Includes web document files (webpages).	Yahoo/ Overture Google LookSmart
Clickthroughs	Automatically derived; based on search behavior.	Includes web document files (webpages).	Search engine companies

Are your search results really unbiased & the best?

Most Internet users have blind faith that search engines place the most appropriate results on the top of their search result listings. But is this really true?

Search engines are money-making enterprises. Although business models are still evolving, they earn income by selling the use of their data catalogs and search technology to other companies. Words like "enhanced" or "powered" by search engine X should clue you in to this fact. SearchEngineWatch.com provides a comprehensive listing of search providers at: www.searchenginewatch.com/reports/article.php/2156401.

Paid listings have become an increasingly important income stream for search engines since 2003. This means that many findings appearing at the top of your search results may be paid placements, and therefore, may not necessarily be the most relevant to your search query.

Paid placements are usually prominently highlighted in a different color, or referred to as "sponsored" links, results or matches; they are also known as "featured" or "partner" sites, or "additional listings." But sometimes it may be difficult to differentiate them from regular, unpaid findings.

Implications for you:

- Check the data sources of search tools you use regularly so you are aware of the companies supplying information and powering them.
- Consult disclosure links and "About Search" pages so you can identify paid listings.
- Look beyond the first page of search results.
- For more information on paid content and disclosure, consult the links given in our references for this chapter [27].
- Continue reading our book to learn more about how search engines work.

Selecting a search engine

When search engines work best [28]

Although there are many ways to search the Internet, sometimes one approach is more effective and efficient then others. Here's when using a search engine might work best to produce the results you want:

- You know exactly the information you want.
- You have a narrow or obscure topic or idea to research.
- You want to find a specific website.
- You wish to search the full text of millions of pages of documents.
- You want to retrieve a large number of documents on a subject.
- You wish to find particular types of documents, file types, languages, date last modified, and so on.
- You want to use newer retrieval technologies such as concept clustering, ranking by popularity, link ranking, and so on.

Considerations: One of the big weaknesses of search engines is you can get back literally thousands of results (matches, findings), many of dubious value.

Selecting "the best" search engine

How do you know which search engine to use?

Since all have both strengths and weaknesses, in general you should use more than one to produce the best results. An overview of the major search engines and directories is available at www.SearchEngineWatch.com, where you should be able to find articles comparing and evaluating the different search engines. For a study of just how much search engine results diverge, see ➪ searchenginewatch.com/searchday/article.php/3524411.

The table on the next page reviews some additional considerations that may affect your eventual choices.

Key takeaway: Searching the Internet is a skill. The trick is to learn to employ the most effective and efficient search techniques given your desired target information. The good news is you *can* improve.

Why Search Engines Differ

Considerations	Explanations
Some search engines may be more appropriate than others for particular searches because they:	Provide different options for selecting data such as the use of subject directories.
	Use different ways of presenting search results with respect to level of detail, relationships to other findings or subject categories, language, and formulas used to sort results pages.
	Have different specialized or advanced interfaces making the entry of certain kinds of searches more or less complicated.
	Have different features for post-processing of findings such as the ability to translate findings, to annotate results, to save and track saved searches and individual findings, and to produce concise summaries.
Search engines use different data sources or ways of organizing information, often producing diverse search results due to:	Differences in data catalogs, ways of indexing information, features, selectivity, accuracy, and retrieval technologies.
	Differences in ways of handling "stop words" — small, commonly used words, such as parts of speech: adverbs, conjunctions, prepositions, or forms of "to be": the, a, an, you, it, we, at, and, or, as, be, if, in, into, to, of, on, and with. These are often ignored even inside phrases; can be controlled in some search engines.
	Differences in prioritizing the presentation of results, using criteria particular to itself for establishing relative relevance between findings. Some search interfaces provide various options for sequencing findings on the results page.

External References & Links: Chapter 1

You will find these items, to which the above numbers in square brackets refer, at ⇨ www.searchhelpcenter.com/refchap1.htm.

2: SEARCH TOOLS & STRATEGIES

In this chapter:

- Explanation of different kinds of search engines.
- A simple step-by-step search strategy.
- Tips to solve typical search problems.

Other Ways to Search

There are many kinds of search tools on the Internet in addition to the major search engines of Google, Yahoo, MSN Search, AlltheWeb, AltaVista, and so on. These include:

- **Meta search engines**, which integrate the results of other search engines.
- **Subject directories**, often incorporated within major search engines, using different catalogs and search interfaces.
- **Specialized search engines**, again simply integrated within major search engines, using special interfaces for image searches, news, and so on.
- **Deep web search engines**, which collect data by crawling places on the Internet where major search engines don't go.

Meta search engines [1]

Unlike regular search engines, meta search engines don't create their own databases of information. Rather, they browse and integrate the results from those of other engines, attempting to extract the most relevant hits from them all.

The process generally goes like this. You enter your keyword(s) in the meta search engine's search box, which is then simultaneously transmitted to several search engines and their catalogs of webpages. Shortly after, you get results back from all the search engines queried.

When meta search engines work best

Because they access multiple databases, often simultaneously, meta search engines can be great time-savers, search results are more comprehensive, and may be integrated to remove duplicates. They are also good when:

- You want to start by getting a general feel of what is available.
- You wish to locate known works or quick facts.
- You want to retrieve a large number of documents on a subject.
- You wish to search the full text of millions of pages of documents.
- You have a narrow or obscure topic or idea to research.
- You want to search for particular types of documents, file types, source locations, date last modified, and so on.
- You wish to take advantage of newer retrieval technologies such as concept clustering, ranking by popularity, link ranking, and so on.

Considerations: Because meta search engines scour many databases to retrieve information, sometimes obtaining results may be slower. You also risk receiving incomplete search results because they may be denied access to some major databases. For instance, many of the freely-available meta search engines do not search Google, although they may access the Google catalog indirectly through other search engines. After all, source search engines want users to visit their webpages directly, most particularly to see their paid listings at the top of search results.

Meta search engines deal with this problem in different ways.

> Copernic does not select paid listings for its results. Other search engines include paid listings, but may highlight them in a different color, for example. A discussion thread on this topic is available at "Free Search Engine Forums" (www.ihelpyouservices. com/forums).

Other drawbacks: A meta search engine has to try to translate your query into language each search engine will understand [2]. Ideally, they employ the highest common denominator among the user interfaces of search engines they integrate. This may limit the sophistication level of your searches, because search syntax often varies from one search engine to the next. Further, some dumb down your search terms, or if you add another one later, you are never sure whether it has actually been transmitted.

Also, some meta search engines do not consistently query all of the search engines they claim to. Instead, to expedite the process, they search only a small portion, or they search those available at the moment you submit your keywords. This may result in shallow coverage of the Web.

Finally, meta search engine results lists may be skewed. Because they tend to retrieve the first few links from each search engine they query, many may be "sponsored" links that pay for prominent placement. Also, disclosure information, showing on the originating search engine, may be stripped away by the meta search engine's filters and ranking mechanisms [3].

Key takeaway: Ultimately, meta search engines cannot be better than the catalogs they query, which of course, affects the quality of the results you receive.

Types of meta search engines

There are several useful ways of classifying meta search engines, including the following:

1. **Metacrawlers and meta search utilities:**

   a. **Metacrawlers:** They are simple meta search engines that do not post-process results (see next).

   b. **Meta search utilities:** These are like metacrawlers, but the referenced files may actually be retrieved from the Internet, and then processed by software installed on the user's computer (or possibly on the Internet server itself). This allows looking *inside the files themselves,* as well as in the search engine's catalogs or indexes.

      Downloading the actual files facilitates or is actually required in some cases for **post-processing of findings**. This generally involves:

      - Eliminating duplicate files found at different Internet addresses (URLs).
      - Removing dead links to files referenced on the Internet.
      - Sorting results or grouping them into categories automatically or at the user's discretion.

        ☞ You might want to sort findings by certain words in the title or use the the post-processing software to dynamically create multi-level topic categories to organize the various documents.

      - Translating pages into another language.

- Performing analyses on results to produce a precise summary of essential points for each document along with a keyword summary.
- Doing search follow-up by:
    - Allowing the user to save pages found in an organized system of folders and perhaps to exchange historical search data with other users over the Internet;
    - Setting up standing orders: alerts notify you of new or updated pages conforming to your search requirements that become available in search engine catalogs.

2. **Meta search engines with search sets.**

These include meta or deep web search tools and/or all-in-one search pages that provide or allow you to create search tool **search sets**.

Search sets are lists of search engines, searchable subject directories, or internal website search tools. Each one is designed to satisfy the needs of a particular kind of search, for example, on a particular subject. Meta search engines permit you to integrate the results of several tools in a single search set.

With certain meta search engines like Copernic, you have a considerable degree of control over how to use any search set: make up your own, parallel search with any combination of the tools in a given search set, place ceilings on the number of findings per search tool in any search set, and more.

On the other hand, many meta or deep web search tools do not provide search sets, but simply give you one of the following:

- Different branches for searching different subjects, without providing search sets you can see or customize.
- Simple interfaces that do not have different branches for searching different topics.

3. **Meta search engines that cluster results into subject hierarchies.**

Such engines cluster results into meaningful subject hierarchies. These are created dynamically, based on the unique results of each search, rather than on pre-established categories.

Key takeaway: Meta search engines have not yet earned wide acceptance (www.searchengineyearbook.com/meta-search-engines.shtml). But the better ones incorporate features not yet found in regular search engines.

Both Copernic and Vivisimo's Clusty have received top rankings by SearchEngineWatch.com for their particular functionalities including sophisticated post-processing of findings — Copernic, and topical clustering of results — Vivisimo (www.searchenginewatch.com/awards/article.php/2155921). Copernic has also been recognized for its superior search utility toolbar (www.copernic.com/en/company/press/press-releases/press_53.html).

More details on specific meta search engines and their abilities:

- On our website:
  - www.searchhelpcenter.com/chap2-table-metasearch-engines.htm;
  - ToolGuide.SearchHelpCenter.com/search-tool-guide-for-effective-internet-search-tool-abilities.html.
- Elsewhere:
  - www.searchenginewatch.com/links/article.php/2156241;
  - www.searchenginewatch.com/links/article.php/2156381.

All-in-one search tools

While meta search engines access various sources in parallel, all-in-one search tools provide the ability to easily switch between tools one at a time. They may provide one or more categories, as well as sub-categories of search tools. To access them, a drop-down list of search tools might be provided. Examples of all-in-one search tools include:

- AlphaSearch (www.alphasearch.org)
- Freeality.com (www.freeality.com)
- iTools (www.itools.com)
- Langenberg.com (www.langenberg.com)
- Bruce Clay Search Hub (www.bruceclay.com/searchhub.htm)
- Others (www.searchenginewatch.com/links/article.php/2156071).

Hotbot (www.hotbot.com) may also be thought of as an all-in-one search engine for Web search, using the major search engine catalogs. It conducts advanced searches of major webcrawler-based document file catalogs, one at a time, using complex sets of filters with same look and feel regardless of catalog.

Unlike most, if not all meta and all-in-one search tools, Hotbot is able to transport filter settings from one catalog to the other using the *highest* common denominator for advanced Web search, as conducted by the major search engines. For more details on this: ⇨ Chapter 5: Links from Findings Display.

Subject directories [4]

Yahoo (www.yahoo.com) and Open Directory Project (free listings handled by volunteers: dmoz.org/about.html) are the most notable examples of general or specialized information directories that pre-organize webpages by subject. Other people-driven directories are those at about.com (bought recently by the New York Times), Zeal (owned by Looksmart), and Bluefind. Some other good ones include those at business.com, goguides.org, joeant.com, gimpsy.com, amray.com, illumirate.com, and onemission.com [⇨ www.highrankings.com/forum/index.php? &showtopic=2295].

Search directories are essentially hierarchical databases. Content is selected and classified into subject categories and sub-categories. Reviews and/or ratings are sometimes included.

Links to websites are hand-picked by real people, and classified according to the rules and guidelines set by the particular directory. Access is by keyword search or by browsing the classifications (www.searchengineshowdown.com/strat/strat2. shtml), and then doing a keyword search within one.

On the next page is an example of a human-created subject directory under development by Zenome, a Canadian Montreal-based company. What seems rather unique about this directory is the various ways in which results can be sorted, as seen in the drop-down menu.

Several flavors of subject directories exist on the Internet including general, academic, commercial, portals, and vortals:

- **Portals:** are simply gateways to information, which aggregate others people's content, centralizing all a user's Internet needs in one location; e. g., e-mail, news, online chat rooms, games, shopping, weather, and so on.
- **Vortals (vertical portals):** are subject-specific portals, catering to target audiences within in a specific industry or interest area; e.g. collectors of Barbie dolls or genealogy.

When subject directories work best

Subject directories are not as popular as they once were. However, like all search approaches, they have both advantages and disadvantages [5]. So when might a subject directory work best?

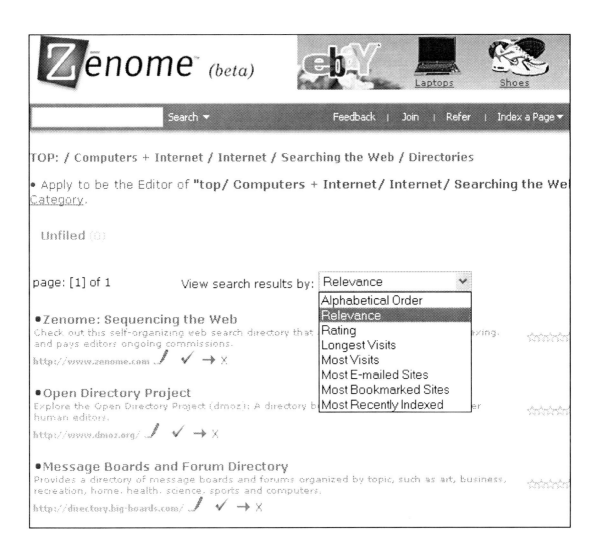

- They may give you superior results when you are looking for:

    › Top level sites for organizations;
    › General topics;
    › Commercial products;
    › Current events.

- They may also be the most direct way to find information when:

    › You have a general notion of what you are searching for;
    › You have a broad topic or idea to research;
    › You want to browse or be more vague or general with your search terms;
    › You want to control the search pattern;

⊃ You want a list of websites for your selected subject recommended and annotated by experts;

⊃ You prefer a list of websites relevant to your topic, rather than numerous individual pages within these sites;

⊃ You wish to avoid getting low-content documents;

⊃ You wish to search for the website title, annotation and assigned keywords, if available, to retrieve relevant material;

⊃ You know the specific category to search on.

EG To locate facts about a baseball player, you could search the "Sports and Leisure" subject category to find webpages on baseball.

Considerations: Subject directories place Web documents or locations into an arbitrary classification scheme or taxonomy. Because the topic categories are provided, they may be neither the most appropriate nor specific enough for your search needs. Perhaps the most important consideration is they tend to generate far fewer search results, and comb less databases to produce them.

The backbone of all subject directories is systematic and complete metadata. Unfortunately, it is often missing in files detected by Internet webcrawlers. The net result is subject directories must be at least partially compiled by hand, which is more labor intensive and thus, more costly.

Key takeaway: More importantly to you, subject directories are significantly smaller in size and less complete than search engine databases. Moreover, the quality of the data found will vary greatly, depending on such things as how widely they search for information, how current it is, and the method used to categorize findings.

Specialized search engines [6]

Search engines may also be classified as general-purpose or specialized.

General-purpose search engines

a. Can search for document files on any subject, where the files are cataloged as a result of webcrawler activity.

b. Also contain one or both of the following:

- non-specialized subject directories;
- specialized interfaccs (see below).

Specialized search engines

    a. Restrict findings based on selected criteria, such as topic, file type, target audience, country, and so on. Examples are summarized in a chart beginning on the following page.

When specialized search engines work best

- You know exactly the information you want.
- You are looking for a specific topic or website.
- You have a narrow subject or idea to research.
- You want to search for particular types of documents, file types, source locations, languages, countries, and so on.

Vertical search sites - Vearch engines [7]

Specialized search engines/tools are also known as "vertical search" or "vearch engines" (⇨ Chapter 2: Distinctions between search tools), especially when they do both surface and deep web search. They address one of the big complaints about general search engines, namely returning too many results. Vearch engines promise "to revolutionize the market by returning the smallest number of results possible in the least amount of time" (SatireWire, 2000).

What is a "vearch engine"? Essentially, it is a kind of hybrid specialized search tool, promising unprecedented speed and relevancy by cataloging only a very narrow selection of websites. For instance, think of Amazon or Cars.com. "They may not index much or any of the web external to themselves, but within their respective specialties (consumer goods and cars), users find very useful information" (Freedman Consulting, 2004). In response, the mainstream search engines have been developing more and more vearch interfaces of their own.

Vearch engines have experienced strong growth over the past few years, particularly in the sectors of shopping, classifieds, and travel. Chris Sherman of SearchEngineWatch.com says they "pose a significant threat to all of the major search engines" ... as "searchers are becoming more sophisticated, and are learning that general-purpose search engines are not always the best choice for every type of search" (June 16, 2004).

Specialized Search Engines		
Search Engine Specialty	Description	Examples
Topic-specific	Specialize in information on patents & trademarks, legal, medical, computer, shopping, travel, government, financial, science, etc.	Scirus (science): www.scirus.com/srsapp. US Patents & Trademarks Office: www.uspto.gov/main/sitesearch.htm. Lists of specialty topic search engines: • SearchEngineWatch.com: www.searchenginewatch.com/linksarticle.php/2156351. • Search Engine Yearbook: www.searchengineyearbook.com/topical-search-engines.shtml. • Binghamton University Libraries: library.lib.binghamton.edu/search/index.html#sub.
File Type	Contain multi-media files, and file types associated with blogs (see "Data source format" row below)	See our Search Tool Guide > File Format, at: toolguide.searchhelpcenter.com.
Paid Data	Include paid-only subject directory data	SearchEngineWatch.com: www.searchenginewatch.com/links/article.php/2156291.
Highly-organized catalogs	Have well-defined data fields; sometimes organized by professional librarians	• U.S. Patents Office: patft.uspto.gov/netahtml/search-adv.htm. • Library Gateways: e.g., USC Beaufort Library: www.sc.edu/beaufort/library/pages/bones/lesson4.shtml.
Target audience	Designed for particular populations	Young children, seniors, women: See our Search Tool Guide > Country, language, audience, Internet application, at: toolguide.searchhelpcenter.com.

Search Engine Specialty	Description	Examples
Non-Web Internet application	Include news, discussion boards, journals & magazines, FTP (file transfer protocol)	See our Search Tool Guide > Country, language, audience, Internet application, at: toolguide. searchhelpcenter.com.
Data source format	Collect data from personal blogs, RSS news feeds, etc.	See our Search Tool Guide > Country, language, audience, Internet application, at: toolguide. searchhelpcenter.com.
Country-specific	Contain country-specific information	See our Search Tool Guide > Country, language, audience, Internet application at: toolguide. searchhelpcenter.com.
Search Tool Abilities	e.g., Display device, ability to post-process findings, screens in your language	See our Search Tool Guide > Search tool abilities, at: toolguide. searchhelpcenter.com.

Potential advantages of using vearch engines:

- All those implied above for specialized search engines:
  - › very limited list of results;
  - › very focused;
  - › maximum relevancy;
  - › quick return of results.
- Additional resources included that general search engines might not list.

Deep web search engines [8]

> **If the most coveted commodity of the Information Age is indeed information, then the value of deep web content is immeasurable.**
> - Michael K. Bergman, University of Michigan, July 2001 [9].

A little known fact among Web users is that the Internet actually contains several layers of content, not all of which are readily visible. To help you picture these layers, see the diagram at About.com [10].

Layers commonly referred to as "the Web," also known as the **surface web** are estimated to contain 167 terabytes of information on publicly-available webpages

— the equivalent in volume to 17 times the size of the Library of Congress print collections) [11]. Although this may sound like a huge amount of information, it actually represents only a tiny portion of the entire Web.

In fact, most accessible information on the Internet — perhaps up to 90% — is not indexed by search engines. Not well known to the average Web user, this type of content comprises the **deep** or **invisible web**.

Consisting of specialized databases, dynamic websites and intranet sites, the deep web has been estimated to be 400 to 550 times larger than the surface web, including some 550 billion web-accessible documents [9]. Because of its highly structured nature, this data is usually of much better quality than that found by ordinary webcrawlers. Examples include interactive tools or documents, such as calculators and dictionaries, sometimes found on pass-protected websites, placed behind firewalls.

> The deep web is made up of thousands of specialized searchable databases. One way you can access them is to enter your search term(s) followed by the term databases or online databases; e.g., "genealogy databases" or "food nutrient online databases".

> You cannot generally find all the work phone numbers of employees in most large organizations on regular webpages. Instead, largely for protection, these are placed inside structured databases, against which you will need to generate a query using a form on a designated webpage. Although they may in theory be able to easily do it, most webcrawlers will not generate queries to find all the possible records in that database, but will simply index only the starting webpage from which the queries are generated.

One reason search engines can't locate or index much of deep web information [12] is because results are often delivered in webpages that are particular to your individual search. Therefore, it is simply easier and cheaper to dynamically generate the answer page each time for every query, rather than store all possible pages containing all possible answers to all possible queries people could make against the database.

Finding deep web content

One of the best ways to access information on the invisible web is through library gateways and subject-specific databases with direct links to them [13]. Toolbars in web browsers often provide choices for branching to deep web searches.

A meta search engine that divides search engines into categories can also provide good deep web search. Copernic, for one, divides search engines into topic categories, which you can configure and add to as you desire. You can even ask it to access new search engines for your categories.

🖰 Say you want to search Canadian news sources, for which Copernic provides a pre-built category. It will pass your query along to the internal search engines of the various Canadian news media

⚠ Some meta search engines claiming to search the deep web are simply directories of databases accessible only by deep search methods, along with a list of specialty search engines that can access them.

⇨ For a list of directories of this kind, see Search Tool Guide: Search tool abilities, at ToolGuide.SearchHelpCenter.com/search-tool-guide-for-effective-internet-search-tool-abilities.html. Try experimenting with some!

companies, such as the Globe and Mail. You may also select the Globe's individual website from the list of search engines making up the category, in case you want to search it in its native search engine. (This may be desirable when the search string passed to the search engine via Copernic doesn't do the job as well as the native search engine itself.)

Deep web search is starting to become a standard part of every main search engine, as a kind of "search with invisible tabs" [14] or using "vertical search (vsearch)" specialty interfaces. As well, deep web search abilities are often embedded in search engines as "search shortcuts": ⇨ Chapter 3: Simple search interfaces, related to intelligent avoidance of formal parameter entry using shortcuts.

When deep web search engines work best

- You want dynamically changing content; e.g., travel schedules, weather, job postings.

- You desire high-quality structured data; e.g., dictionaries, encyclopedias, calculators.
- You want information normally stored in databases; e.g., phone book listings, geographical and company data; searchable collections of laws.

Considerations: Even a deep web search engine cannot be expected to gather more than a sample, a relatively small sub-set of what is available on the deep web. The volume of information alone, coupled with dynamic ever-changing content, makes keeping up virtually impossible.

Key takeaway: Because of its enormous size, high-quality content, and phenomenal growth rate, today no serious researcher can afford to ignore the deep web.

Distinctions between search tools

For clarity and simplicity's sake, clear distinctions have been made between the search capabilities of the major search engines, subject directories, specialized, deep web and meta search engines — and which fit into each category. The reality is much more complex and ambiguous.

Most search engines, in fact, are multi-type hybrids — a blend of various search tools and utilities. Many have secondary search entry or findings display interfaces for subject directory, specialized, and/or deep web search.

For instance, although Copernic and Surfwax are both meta search engines, they can also organize other search engines into various specialized types by subject, Internet application, etc. When the source search engines are organized by subject, Copernic and Surfwax are really acting as subject directories. Each sub-category of the source search engines may also be viewed as a specialized search facility or tool. And, deep web searches may be possible, depending upon the capabilities of the source search engines.

Vertical search (vearch) engines are another example of hybrid specialized search tools. They narrow searches by only searching very targeted websites, such as those devoted to news, discussion boards, shopping, classifieds, or travel: ⇨ www.satirewire.com/news/0006/satire-vearch.shtml. Ideally, they search both the surface and the deep web within their specialty area. Also, when fielded searching of a particular topic in a subject directory is available, it could be thought of as a specialized topic search (vearch).

Key takeaway: Lines are blurring among the capabilities of various search engines and tools. If anything, they will become even more complex and confusing in the future as search engines continue to improve. But chapter information and the Reference Manual sections in this book will help you sort them out, and teach you how to make the most effective use of each.

Types of search entry interfaces

Each search engine included in this book has a number of interface screens you can use for search filter entry. You must select the ones most appropriate for your search.

	Primary		Specialized	
	Simple	**Advanced**	**Simple**	**Advanced**
Keyword Search Method	Simple Web document search	Advanced Web document search	Simple specialized search	Advanced specialized search
Subject Search Method	Simple subject directory Web document search	Advanced subject directory Web document search	Simple specialized search by narrowed subject	Advanced specialized search by narrowed subject

(Table title: Search Entry Interface Types)

Entry screens may be classified in three separate ways, as summarized in the table above.

1. **Primary vs. specialized search interfaces:**

    a. **Primary interfaces** are the basic, most frequently employed by general-purpose search engines. They search against general web document catalogs (Web catalogs), either compiled as a result of webcrawler activity or manually assembled into subject directories. For short, these are called:

      • **Web interfaces** — when the keyword search method is used.

Most Internet searches are, in effect, web searches, in the most general usage of the word "web." This is because they retrieve information about files accessible directly by the Web Internet application.

Remember, when search engines refer to a "Web catalog," they don't mean a catalog of all files accessible by the Web Internet application. Rather, they mean a catalog: comprised only of document files; not specific to any topic; accessed by the keyword method of search entry; based on data collected by webcrawlers; found on the Web only.

- **Subject directories** — when the subject search method is used. Note: These kinds of searches are generally becoming less important. For example, Google no longer has directory search in its main set of search entry interface links. On the other hand, deep web search within subject category is perhaps becoming more important.

b. **Specialized interfaces** are those generally employed by special-purpose search engines (⇨ Chapter 2: Specialized search engines). In this book, they are broken down as follows:

- **Multi-media file types:** image, video, and sound (⇨ Chapter 5: Multi-media file search interfaces).
- **Data from non-Web kinds of Internet applications,** including news, discussion board, chat, and FTP (file transfer protocol) document files (⇨ Chapter 5: Non-Web Internet application interfaces).
- **Special topics** (⇨ Chapter 5: Specialized topic search interfaces).

2. **Keyword vs. subject search interfaces:** General-purpose search engines allow you to conduct searches for web documents in two basic ways — by keyword and by subject (⇨ Chapter 1: Catalog types and origins).

a. **Keyword searches** are most popular with users. Important search terms (your keywords) are entered in a search interface to locate your desired information by looking through different Web catalogs.

🔣 Google, MSN Search, AlltheWeb, AltaVista "Web" searches.

b. **Subject searches** look for information in directories organized or classified by subject (the hierarchical subject classification method). You drill down through a series of choices until you find your desired topic sub-category, after which you may drill down some more using a keyword search within that category. This method is generally used with the following kinds of search entry interfaces:
- Subject directory: ⇨ Chapter 2: Subject directories.

- News and discussion group: ⇨ Chapter 5: Non-Web Internet application interfaces.
- Telephone numbers: when business numbers are distinguished from residential ones: ⇨ Chapter 5: Specialized topic search interfaces.
- Products for sale: ⇨ Chapter 5: Specialized topic search interfaces.

🔍 AltaVista Directory search, AltaVista News search (which breaks news topics down by area), Google Groups search (which uses the hierarchical structure of USENET discussion boards), and Google Catalog or Froogle searches (which provide categories of products for sale).

> 💡 Even if you do not search by subject category, you can still sometimes find it using the results listings, when the related subject classes in a keyword search are displayed on the results list, either for the keywords (i.e., all the findings) or for individual findings (next to each finding): ⇨ Chapter 5: Links from findings display. The reverse is also sometimes possible, when findings are grouped, sorted, or dynamically clustered by subject: ⇨ Chapter 5: Post-processing of findings.

3. **Simple vs. advanced search interfaces:**

    a. **Simple search interfaces** have less complex filter entry choices.
    b. **Advanced search interfaces** provide many more boxes and options to the searcher.

The distinction between simple and advanced search entry interfaces is more fully explored in Chapter 3.

Key takeaway: For simplicity's sake, search entry interfaces have been classified into three major types. In reality, distinctions are not quite so clear. The previous table, "Search Entry Interface Types" (see above), suggests there can be both primary and specialized subject directory or keyword search entry interfaces; also simple and advanced versions of each. But in reality, lines between them are often blurred, resulting in hybrid interfaces.

🔍 Three of the search engines featured in this book have specialized interfaces for image file search at both the simple and advanced levels, using the keyword search method.

Basic Search Strategies

	Search Tool Selection	
	Quick Steps	**Your Basic Search Strategy**
1	Go to specific website with target information.	Use on-site links. Try on-site search facilities.
2	Try a quick fix.	Replicate search strategies of people in comparable situations or looking for similar information. For example, using a general-purpose search engine such as Google: a. Use a primary search entry interface. Do a general look-up with a Web search. b. Search on your desired topic in a subject directory interface. c. Use intelligent features that allow access to deep web databases. d. Use a specialized search entry interface.
3	Select a search tool.	Choose the best one for the job in hand. Detailed selection strategies follow.
4	Use various search tools separately or in combination.	a. Scour the Internet conducting a more comprehensive search with a meta search engine, preferably one that includes deep web search. b. Use all-in-one search tools, or other tools to easily switch search requirements to other search utilities. c. Try post-processing your search results.

Your basic search strategy

- **Select your search tools.**
- **Refine your search**.
- **Post-process your findings**.

Select your search tools

A search tool is any mechanism or computer program that helps you locate information on the Web such as:

- General-purpose search engines: Google, Yahoo, MSN Search, AltaVista, AlltheWeb
- Subject directories: Yahoo, Open Directory Project, LookSmart
- Meta search engines: Copernic, Vivisimo's Clusty, HotBot
- Specialized and deep web search engines: library gateways, subject-specific databases, vearch engines

A basic search strategy for choosing the appropriate search tool is summarized on the previous page. Here's this search strategy explained in more detail.

Step 1: Go to specific website with target information

This is the most obvious place to start, if the exact website is known to you.

    a. Use the links provided on-site.
    b. Failing that, try its internal search facilities.

If Step 1 doesn't work, proceed to Step 2.

Step 2: Try a quick fix

Many search situations are similar and their results can be replicated. For example:

- Do a regular Web search with a general-purpose search engine. If this doesn't work or meet your needs, use a vertical search (vearch) interface associated with that search engine (e.g., for travel, classifieds, news, messages, phone numbers, or shopping). These specialized interfaces often search both the surface and deep web. You may also be able to access the deep web using the search shortcuts provided by your selected search engine.

- If you know the subject category for your desired search and your selected general-purpose search engine includes it, branch directly to its subject directory screen.

> Not all search engines have subject directories.

- Search discussion boards or mailing lists for discussion threads that concern a topic similar to yours, i.e., for discussions by others, perhaps including experts, discussing your topic.

Step 3: Select a search tool

If general-purpose search engines like Google and Yahoo don't meet your needs, you will need to find an appropriate search tool. Some helpful strategies to locate one are provided below.

You want to:	Suggestion
Find search engines for children.	Enter the search terms kids and search.
Find information from inside a structured database in the field of biology.	Try searching on the phrase deep web search along with the words biology databases, or try biology with the phrase online database.
Find a subject directory on a particular topic (based on Google Hacks, p. 54-56). Example: obtain a list of different evergreen trees. Find documents with titles like "Directory of Coniferous Trees," or "Directory of Evergreen Trees."	Try the search strings intitle:"directory * * trees", or intitle:"directories * * trees". In these examples, based on Google syntax: • the two asterisks are wildcards for whole words; • the quotes surround a phrase; • intitle is a field operator that restricts searching to the document title.
Find an appropriate discussion board and topic thread, such as a discussion about bee stings.	Using Google syntax, try the search strings intitle:digest "bee sting", or intitle:digest "bee sting" thread.
Find a recent obituary of someone from Canada.	Use the search string online database AND obituaries AND Canada to find an appropriate deep web search tool. Then do your search.

Another way to locate an appropriate search tool is using a **search tool guide** — a multi-level, categorized list of different types of search tools. Consider it a starting point, intended to point you toward the most important references and/or provide you with sample sites to get you going in the right direction.

Search tool guides include links to:

- Websites that specialize in discussing, categorizing, and advising on search engines or tools;
- Meta or deep web search tools;
- All-in-one search pages;
- Specialized, deep and surface web search engines and directories: library gateways, subject-specific databases, vearch engines;
- Other search tool guides.

For your convenience, we have created our own free Search Tool Guide available at: ⇨ ToolGuide.SearchHelpCenter.com.

> **🔢** Go to one of the discussion boards or mailing lists identified in our Search Tool Guide. To get there, start with the "Country, language, audience, Internet application" link. Next, choose "Discussion board applications." Then, do a search on the topic inside any discussion tool you select.

Step 4: Use various search tools separately or in combination

Here are alternatives, including ones covered in Chapter 2: Other Ways to Search:

a. **Meta search engines**: Preferably use one that has different search categories and can perform deep web searching. It also works well when a search yields few results because it scours Internet catalogs conducting a more comprehensive search.

b. **All-in-one search sites**: Use one appropriate to your needs.

c. **Search tools that easily switch between catalogs**: If you plan to enter a complex set of search requirements from a webcrawler-generated catalog, try a search tool that permits carrying them to other search utilities.

> **🔢** Hotbot allows you to easily switch between the Web catalogs of Google and Ask Jeeves, as much as possible transferring the same set of search requirements from one to another, so that you can compare results.

⇨ To learn more about how to use Hotbot to apply criteria used to obtain results from one catalog to another catalog, consult Chapter 5: Links to switch to other catalogs.

If you use the OpenSource Mozilla browser, consider NeedleSearch (needlesearch.mozdev.org), described in searchenginewatch.com/searchday/article.php/3307551.

Final note: Besides the information provided here and throughout this book, there are many other links and tools that will further expand your knowledge on effectively searching the Internet, including our own Search Tool Guide. Search professionals doing specialized research will also find help. For a comprehensive list of these tools, refer to our website (www.SearchHelpCenter.com):

- ⇨ Search Help: Online tutorials
- ⇨ Search Help: Search books & articles

Refine your search

Regardless of the search tools you select, make sure you choose appropriate search terms and define parameters to restrict or broaden the scope of your search as required (⇨ Chapter 3: Refining Search Results).

Since the most common search problem is obtaining too many results, start by using very specific search terms. Then gradually expand their scope if you don't obtain your desired results. Tara Calishain [18] refers to this as "The Principle of Onions" (⇨ vig.prenhall.com/samplechapter/0131471481.pdf).

For your convenience, we have summarized more specific search strategies in the following tables.

Check out some more tips at:
www.pandia.com/goalgetter/
recommendations.html

Quick Search Strategies

Prioritize your terms

Search Tips	Examples/Notes
1. Use terms likely used in the title of the document — given the highest priority in a search engine's logic. 2. Include expected words in a general description of the document — including its keywords. 3. Use important words contained in the body text.	1. A popular medical journal article on the Internet may have its popular terms in the title. 2. You may also see the more technical terms in the body text. 3. Some terms may not be seen on the screen at all but be in the hidden keywords inserted as metadata in the file.
Enter most important search terms first, which will tend to place the most relevant findings first.	Your subject is hormone replacement therapy for women. 1. Enter the phrase hormone replacement therapy. 2. Enter something to identify that the subject is to be applied only to women; e.g., menopause. 3. Refine your subject to include one or both of the terms hysterectomy and uterus removal. 4. Exclude the terms oophorectomy and ovary removal. Altogether your search string might look like this: "hormone replacement therapy" AND menopause AND (hysterectomy OR "uterus removal") AND NOT (oophorectomy OR "ovary removal")
Place words that should be near one another in the string. • Some search engines have special operators to do this. • This trick may also work even when special operators are unavailable.	Use Boolean operators NEAR or WITH. In the Exalead search engine, use NEXT to find words on either side of a term.

| In some search engines, place a plus sign (+) in front of search terms to give them more importance. | +menopause |

Be specific	
Search Tips	**Examples**
Sometimes, you need to ensure that certain small words or punctuation is found. Many punctuation characters and small common words (called **stop words**, e.g., articles of speech — the, a, an) are ignored in searches.	Place stop words inside a phrase or place a plus sign (+) in front of them to retain stop words. • "The World Bank" • +Your Health A to Z
Use at least three search terms.	DVD video players. There is an implicit AND between the first, second, and third terms — DVD AND video AND players.
Try combining two or more words into a phrase and use it as a term.	"DVD players" instead of DVD players. There is an implicit AND between DVD and players in the latter, while the phrase is simply taken as a single string of two words joined in a certain order.
Restrict the search to a single domain (website).	To search the tile.net mailing list for a discussion about trees, enter trees site:tile.net.
Restrict the search so that it excludes commercial sites.	To find information about canoeing, enter canoeing -site:.com.
Don't use terms that add nothing much to the query, but actually distract the search engine from producing the right results	Enter teaching style rather than documentation on teaching style.
Don't use common words unless they are part of a phrase.	• Enter canary yellow as opposed to just yellow. • To find a Shakespearian play: use some words from the language of the time, such as doth or methinks.

Use slang or discipline-specific terms geared to narrow down your search.
 	
• Slang is especially useful for searches in discussion board catalogs.
• Generally avoid slang when searching in news indexes.
• There are many dictionaries of slang and discipline-specific terminology on the Web [15].
	• Use the exact terms or phrases you are searching for. Example: If searching specifically for TCP remote_port field, use that exact phrase rather than TCP client port field.
	• For football (in the sense of soccer), as played in England, try football along with the word bloke [17, p. 17].
	• Find stock information [17, p. 48-49]; e.g., look for stock information on Intel as follows:
	
	  ○ Press releases: search for phrases such as Intel announced, Intel announces, or Intel reported.
	  ○ Financial information: search for terms such as:
	
	    ■ the word Intel along with the acronym SEC, or the word Intel accompanied by the word financials;
	    ■ the phrase Intel quarterly report;
	    ■ the word Intel along with the phrase p/e ratio.
	  ○ The company's location: search for the word Intel, along with words such as parking, or airport, or location.

Use individual discipline-specific or slang words. Don't enter more than one the first time you search.	Add one extra slang word each time you retry it until you find what you want.
Be specific, but at the same time try to minimize the number of search terms used, especially since some search engines have limits on the number of search terms that can be used. (For example, Google has a limit of 32 words, including words inside phrases.)	Search for the news item "Australians vote Jones least-liked president." • Employ a news search engine or interface, preferably one specific to Australia. • Use short search strings such as the phrases Australians vote Jones or the phrase Jones least-liked. • Set other search filters such as the date range of the news item. Search on garbage collection schedule, rather than schedule for collecting garbage.
Use search filters to narrow your search scope and be more specific. (⇨ See Chapter 6 for more in-depth discussion.)	To eliminate commercial websites when conducting a search for jobs in the non-profit sector, enter the word jobs along with a filter to remove the domain suffix .com from sites found; e.g., enter jobs NOT domain:*.com in some search engines, or jobs -site:com, depending on syntax supported.

Use nouns and objects as search terms [16]

Search Tips	Examples
Use the word stub or the singular as opposed to plural.	Use work instead of works or working. The search tool may find the other variations automatically.
To experiment, repeat nouns more than once in a search string. In some search engines, repeat product names or nouns to find shopping sites.	Use of plurals often works effectively to find shopping sites; e.g. scooters [17, p. 25].

Try synonyms or variations of terms [19]

Search Tips	Examples
Try a different spelling.	Use labour instead of labor if you want to find sites outside the U.S.
Use concept search to search on terms having meanings similar to the ones you actually use.	Use Google's tilde (~) operator in front of a word to search on the word and its synonyms.
Wildcards substitute for one or more characters when searching for text. Place them at the start, middle or end of words, which allows simultaneously searching for several words with the same root or stem. The most common wildcards are: • an asterisk (*) as a placeholder for 0 to n (or 1 to n) characters; • number sign (#) or question mark (?) for one character.	• Enter play* to find any word starting with the four letters play and with any kind of ending — playback, playboy, playbook, playdough, etc. • Enter smok* to return documents containing words such as smoke, smokers, smoking, smokes, smoked, smoking, etc. — for information on the harmful effects of smoking.
Use wildcards to act as substitutes for whole words.	Enter the search string big * clouds to find webpages containing strings of text such as big dark clouds, big gray clouds, big grey clouds, big ugly clouds, etc.

Use wildcards to help circumvent search word count limitations imposed by some search engines, as in the case of Google, which has a limit of 32 words per search string.	In Google, to save words use an asterisk *, which is not treated as a word. For instance, searching on the phrase **funny * face** will return documents having the phrases funny little face, funny silly face and funny old face.

Try other search tips & tricks

Search Tips	Examples
If the search tool has a "Find in Results" functionality that can inspect the original pages on the Internet or re-inspect the catalog findings for a given search, try to do a search that has more ambiguous criteria and then refine the search by doing a "Find in Results" procedure.	In the case of meta search engine Copernic, your original search criteria have to be somewhat simplified to find a common denominator between several search engines (⇨ Chapter 2: Meta search engines, point on "Meta search utilities"). Thus, search with simpler criteria upfront, and then refine the search using Copernic's sophisticated "Find in Results" functions.
If the search engine does not have the particular metadata field you want, try improvising your own solution by including appropriate extra search terms along with your other keywords.	Say you want to find an article published by The New York Times, but news search does not provide a field for "source" or "publisher." Try the phrase **Copyright * The New York Times Company**, where * is a wildcard acting as a placeholder for the year of publication.
Use the form "So-and-so is..." or "Such and such is..." with your search terms to learn the web's "opinion" of something, e.g., search on "hippies are" to see what you get.	Using the Googlism tool (www.googlism.com), which implements this kind of approach, simply enter your search terms, and click a radio button to select "who," "what," "where," or "when."
Experiment using a group of words both as a phrase and as a series of separate words, then compare differences in your search results.	Enter the keyword clothes once in Google, and you get many more findings than if you entered it twice [17, p. 22-24]. While the number of times a term occurs on a page may be one of the criteria used by Google in determining the relevancy ranking of the result, this example shows that word repetition in the text is only one of many criteria considered in Google's relevancy ranking algorithm.

If the search tool has two search entry interfaces that appear to have the same logic, try both. You may obtain different results in each case.	Try a complex query using operator parameters (explained in Chapter 3) as opposed to using selections from various form elements such as drop-down menu lists, radio buttons, and checkboxes: ⇨ Chapter 4 > Health-Related Search Case Example > Search strategy > AlltheWeb.
To obtain a focused list of appropriate search terms, do a preliminary search for acronyms or abbreviations by looking up terms in dictionaries and glossaries; also try monikers, aliases, nicknames, handles, or specific brand names [18, p. 86-89]. Then enter your finalized search terms in a list, separating them with OR.	You run into the telecommunications term "Orthogonal Frequency Division Multiplexing," and would like to find some synonyms and a possible acronym. Try the first initials to see if they form an acronym, by searching on phrases such as: a) OFDM stands +for (where the plus sign ensures that the word for is not dropped by the search engine); b) What is OFDM? c) OFDM is short for what? Then use the acronym and possible synonyms in your end search. To do a search on types of running shoes, first find the various brands with the phrase brands running shoes, or running shoes types, or There are * kinds of running shoes, etc. Searching on specific brands will help narrow your search.
Locate different blogs [17, p. 59-60]. Example: find information from well-known weblogs and hosting sites. Note: Blogs are weblogs that use special syntax intended to make them more easily and quickly found by webcrawlers.	Use search terms such as: • The phrases: powered by blogger, or powered by blosxom, or powered by greymatter, or powered by geeklog, or powered by pmachine; • The correct website identifiers, such as: site:blogspot.com, site:editthispage.com, or site:pitas.com, or site:ujournal.org, or site:livejournal.com, or site:radio.weblogs.com; • The phrase: a manila site.
Be creative in finding help when you get stuck.	For example, if you need help with your typing skills, search on the phrase typing tutorials.

Post-process your findings

Although we consider this an important step in your search strategy, interestingly few references include it. Perhaps this is because most general-purpose search engines can't post-process your search results with any level of sophistication. Meta search utility Copernic is one that can.

Why is it so important? In brief, post-processing allows you to:

1. Keep organized records of your search histories.

2. Manipulate the results list.

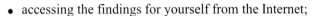

- searching within results;
- grouping;
- sorting;
- extracting findings;
- translating webpages;
- making annotations of particular findings;
- backtracking;
- accessing the findings for yourself from the Internet;
- general sifting through your findings.

Mel Baylin

3. Follow up on changes since you last did a search in your search history by tracking changes to searches or particular webpages.

To expand on the above, post-processing allows you to:

1. **Keep organized search histories**

   The first step is to organize records of completed searches into appropriate categories, say, using a system of folders hierarchically arranged. In this way, you can duplicate the same search under different conditions, modify or replace it to produce an alternative version, or delete it from the search history. Your search tool should ideally be able to record any previous annotations or record processing of findings already completed in the search histories.

2. **Manipulate the findings list**

   Each search will require different manipulations. Since Copernic provides a relatively complete set of functions, you might wish to browse some of them, referring to the Reference Manual sections below:

   >  Manipulating the findings list involves a lot of non-automated work. For instance, search engines are not capable of accurately prioritizing findings according to the authoritativeness or excellence of presentation on a website.

   - ⇨ Reference Section 5.2: Findings Display & Handling Interfaces
   - ⇨ Reference Section 6.3: Findings Display & Handling Parameters

3. Follow up on your search

> In some situations you may wish to periodically rerun your search and be notified of any new or changed findings. Or, you might want to keep track of changes to a particular finding.

Wave of the future

When conducting complex searches, you may actually spend more time processing the findings than in producing them. Therefore, this ability will become an increasingly important feature for general-purpose search engines to adopt.

At present, the few references that address post-processing of results are directed to programmers about "scraping the results list" to extract the findings into a spreadsheet for further manipulation.

> Google Hacks uses this approach
> (⇨ www.amazon.com/exec/obidos/ASIN/0596004478/
> ref%3Dnosim/researchbuz03-20/102-1651225-2500151).

In the meantime, meta search utility Copernic, which already has this ability, is leading the way in this new and important frontier. For more information on this topic: ⇨ Chapter 5: Post-processing of findings.

Key takeaway: Take advantage of search tools that post-process your findings, saving you valuable time when doing complex searches.

External References & Links: Chapter 2

You will find these items, to which the above numbers in square brackets refer, at ⇨ www.searchhelpcenter.com/refchap2.htm.

3: SEARCH ENTRY BASICS

In this chapter:

- Introduction to parameters.
- Use of parameters for effective searches.
- Features common to most search engine interfaces.
- Basic types of search entry interfaces.

Using reference materials in the Reference Manual sections

To enhance your learning experience, use the examples and exercises in Chapters 3 to 6 in conjunction with materials from the Reference Manual. This will familiarize you with our extensive reference materials and also encourage you to browse within the book.

Refining Search Results

What are parameters?

They are words, phrases and/or symbols that provide guidelines or constraints directing the search engine how to conduct a search so you receive the most relevant and authoritative information.

Some search engines allow you to use natural language (informal language as spoken). However, targeted search results require more exact terminology.

Formal parameters allow you to search with greater precision, thereby decreasing your unwanted results. Of course, their effective use requires more knowledge of precise syntax (rules for constructing terms), as well as the use of particular boxes and choices on the structured forms provided by search interfaces.

Why use parameters?

Their basic function is to control the scope of search results, as well as how they are presented.

Hmmm! I think Mel needs some parameter-setting. Yikes! What an ugly picture of me!

Parameters can be used either to expand or contract a search, to produce more or fewer findings, as desired. Of course, your choice will vary with each new topic.

To increase the number of findings:

1. Use more search terms, separated by OR — or enter the terms in a text box labeled "any of these words" or its equivalent.

   ⚙ cat OR dog will produce more findings than simply dog.

   ⚙ For even wider searches, use OR more than once; e.g., cat OR dog OR pet.

2. Use more general, non-specific, less specialized terms.

   ⚙ pet instead of dog, since a dog is a special type of pet.

3. Use wildcards (sometimes called **truncation operators**) to allow variations of strings of characters to be found.

   ⚙ employ* as a term with the asterisk (the wildcard character) will cause matches to be made by many search engines on any words that start with employ, e.g., employee, employer, employment.

   > 💡 When a wildcard is placed at the end of a word, some people refer to this as **stemming** or **word stubbing**. Although it sometimes means the same thing, stemming also has a more general and complex meaning, (⇨ Chapter 6: Term variation filters).

4. Try to search for related terms or topics presented along with the findings. Many search engines maintain organized subject directories, which point you from the findings page to a broader topic that contains the topic specified in your search.

   ⚙ If you search for dog, the subject category "pets" might be presented as a link for further investigation.

5. Only use the above parameters and the search terms themselves. By default, if you do not specify the parameter, the search engine will assume the widest and least constrained possible setting.

🔍 Do not use parameters such as document age, document location, file type, or any others, which will confine the search. However, you could expand the document age parameter to look for documents in the past 5 years, as opposed to, say, documents that are just one week old.

To decrease the number of findings:

1. Use terms that have a more precise, specialized, and specific meaning.

   🔍 Use dog instead of pet, since the class "dog" is a narrower sub-class (specific type, variety, kind, category, flavor, genre, and so on) of the "pet" class.

2. Search within findings using an additional parameter, possibly a further search term or a type of file.

   🔍 Search for *pictures* of dogs instead of just dogs by indicating that only image files are to be sought.

3. Use more terms separated by either AND or NOT.

   🔍 cat AND dog require both these words occur within a document for it to be included in the findings, while cat NOT dog excludes documents that contain dog even though they also contain cat.

   🔍 Using AND is the most common way to narrow a search to a manageable number of hits. So to narrow your search results even more, use AND or NOT more than once; e.g., cat AND dog AND pet, or cat AND dog NOT horse.

4. Require terms be ordered in a particular way by using phrases.

   🔍 dog catcher as a phrase is treated as a single term, with the word dog immediately preceding the word catcher.

5. Enter values for your selected parameters or use them in a more restrictive way. This works, because, **by default, most parameters limit the scope of a search**.

⚠ This does not, of course, apply to the OR parameter, which *expands* rather than contracts the scope of the findings.

🔂 Instead of limiting your search to documents aged less than a year, restrict the time frame even further.

Parameter types

To help you better understand the concept of parameters, it is useful to think of them in different ways.

Parameter Type Summary			
Term	**Also Known As**	**Definition**	**Examples**
Parameters	Constraints	Indicators of how searches are to be conducted.	See below.
Primary parameters		Search terms themselves and catalogs to be used; also terms entered when user seeks help.	Words, word particles, phrases forming character strings.
Non-primary parameters	Secondary, tertiary, etc. parameters	Refine search requirements provided by primary parameters; used to further narrow or broaden search scope.	See next table.

Primary versus non-primary parameter types:

- **Primary parameters** are the search terms themselves; words, word particles, phrases, which form character *strings,* as well as indicators to the catalog or specialized topic within which to search. In other words, you use primary parameters to limit your search by specifying both the search terms and catalogs to be used.
- **Non-primary parameters** are the secondary, tertiary, or additional requirements used to further refine the search requirements.

🖙 If the primary parameter is the term kangaroo, a secondary parameter could be the geographical region of the servers hosting documents having that term. Thus, a secondary parameter could be used to restrict the search for kangaroo to web servers located in North America. Of course, this is different than typing the search terms kangaroo and North America (as a phrase). The latter would look for these two textual strings in the same document, as opposed to restricting the web server for the document to only those located in North America.

Search control versus search support parameter types:

1. **Search control** parameters are the ones used in an individual search. Another way of saying this is that these parameters are dynamically entered one search at a time, as opposed to being set as defaults or otherwise applying to many searches. There are two kinds used in this book — those for search entry and those for findings presentation. The ones for searching refine the scope of what is found. Most search engines commonly refer to them as **filters**, the term which will now be used in balance of this book.

   There are two types of filters: term-based and metadata-based.

   - **Term-based filters**, also known as *word filters:* Control variations and relationships of search terms. They include wildcards and Boolean logic relationship specifications such as AND, OR, and NOT. They are also used to narrow or broaden the scope of the findings.
   - **Metadata-based filters**, or simply *filters:* Narrow down or sometimes expand search scope by controlling acceptable values for particular fields of metadata in search engine catalogs. They are used to conduct *fielded searches.*

	Non-primary Parameter Summary		
Term	**Also Known As**	**Definition**	**Examples**
Search control parameters:			
Search parameters: Term-based filters	Word filters	Control variations and relationships of search terms.	Wildcards, AND, OR, NOT, greater than.
Search parameters: Metadata-based filters	Filters	Control acceptable values for particular fields of metadata in search engine catalogs.	File age, file type, filters to block offensive content, author, relationships to other findings, physical location of file, etc.
Findings display parameters	Display options	Control the way results are displayed in a given search.	Way of sequencing findings, number of findings per page, fields to display for each result.
Search support parameters:			
Search engine help parameters	Assistance	Control how user obtains help to use search engine.	Branches provided in help menus.
Search engine customization parameters	Settings, user preferences	Control the way the search engine works in general.	Look and feel of search engine interface; default settings for filters or findings display parameters.

[G] Restrictions by: file age, file type (document, multi-media, etc.), filters to block offensive content, restrictions of term location to particular sections or embedded features of documents, geographical region of the Internet host (server), characteristics of the Internet address (URL), and relationships between search terms.

2. **Search support** parameters permit you to organize the search engine over more than one search.

   [G] You might:

   - Set the default values for filter parameters.
   - Choose to have certain optional boxes appear on your search forms.
   - Set which of certain optional fields show on your findings page for each search result.
   - Establish your own search engine categories for use with a meta-search utility search engine.

   Chapter 6 discusses filter, findings display, and search engine customization parameters in greater depth.

Operator versus non-operator parameter types:

Non-primary parameters may be entered using extra boxes on search forms, separate from those used to enter the primary ones. Alternatively, you can often enter them as "operators."

1. **Operators** are embedded as extra characters in the character strings forming the primary parameters. They allow you to specify searches using ordinary text rather than graphical interfaces, providing a convenient, compact, and direct way of specifying searches. They can also generate sophisticated searches with a fairly simple interface using a single text box.

   In practice, operators are generally only ever used to specify filter parameters, and so may be divided into:

   a. **Term-based operators:** Many operator parameters are **term-based filters**; that is, they produce term variations or specify relationships between them.

      [G] Suppose you wanted to conduct a search related to employment in a dog kennel; you enter the search string (employ* OR dog) AND kennel. Here the primary parameters are employ, dog, and kennel; the term relationship operator parameters are OR and AND; the term variation operator is the wildcard asterisk * ; the brackets are also operator parameters.

Search Engine Parameter Entry			
Term	**Also Known As**	**Definition**	**Examples**
Operators: term-based filters		Parameters entered in the same text string as the search terms; i.e., inline commands or command line entries.	AND, OR, and wildcards for term-based filters.
Operators: metadata-based filters	Meta-words; field operators		Inserted as prefixes to search terms; e.g., title:, url:.
Non-operators		Parameters entered other than in the same text string as the search terms; i. e., "out-of-line" commands, "non-command line" entries.	Choices made with checkboxes, radio buttons or drop-down menu boxes on forms; text entered in boxes on forms other than those for the search terms.

Entering ~fast ~food in Google causes Google to search not only on the keywords fast and food, but also on synonyms of these keywords (both of which are required in this case). Note the use of the tilde (~) operator in front of the keywords.

b. **Metadata-based operators** (field operators): These are often inserted as prefixes to search terms. Field operators apply **metadata-based filters** to restrict or sometimes expand the search in particular metadata fields.

The operator "title" in front of the search string kangaroo, in the format title:kangaroo, restricts the search engine to finding the term kangaroo in the title section of a document, shown here using AltaVista's advanced Web search interface.

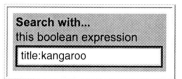

Search with...
this boolean expression
title:kangaroo

The operator "url" in front of the search string kangaroo, in the format url:kangaroo, restricts the search to web servers that have the string kangaroo embedded in their Internet address (URL).

In both the above examples, the operators (title: and url:) act as filters indicating how to apply a primary parameter, the term kangaroo, against the data collected in the search engine database.

A search string that contains both metadata-based field operators along with some term-based operator parameters, all in a single text entry box for specifying the search requirements:

employment OR (url:dog AND title:kennel)

In this example, the document must contain at least one instance of (dog in the URL and kennel in the title) and employment. A document that simply contains the word employment will satisfy the search. If employment is not present in the document, however, then the search can only be satisfied if the document has both dog in the URL and kennel in the title.

In the above search string, OR and AND are secondary parameters, and the brackets are an example of a tertiary parameter. The brackets, which in this case provide "distribution" of the OR over another expression having two terms separated by AND, work in some search engines and not in others. They do not work, for instance, with Google and Yahoo, the two most popular search engines.

In general, our featured search engines restrict the syntax for field operators to lowercase letters. Also, with Google at least, some field operators may not work if you put a space between the term and the colon.

VERY IMPORTANT! Apparently because of the need to keep things simple for most users, our featured search engines tend not to document their operator parameters at an advanced level in their help screens. For instance, Google, AlltheWeb, and AltaVista do not mention using brackets with Boolean expressions to control which operators to apply first (similar to use of brackets in mathematical formulas). More importantly, it appears only some of the field operators available for use are mentioned. Further, it is left to the user to find external documentation on these, or to experiment with various possibilities to determine what works and what does not.

This problem takes on a particular twist with AltaVista and AlltheWeb, which appear to have changed their field and Boolean operator sets since their Yahoo takeover. Boolean operators have been simplified (e.g., ANDNOT or AND NOT are now simply NOT or still AND NOT for repetition of negation). In addition, many of the field operators formerly documented in the help screens of these two search engines are no longer so. Since Google may also have dropped this kind of documentation (see ⇨ www.google.com/help/operators.html), it is difficult to tell whether these operators no longer exist or are now simply no longer documented.

Regardless, very recently updated websites still document the complex sets of, for example, Google field operators, which we presume still exist. The following are Google field operators, all or almost all of which are covered in this book's Reference Manual:

For sections or parts of a document:

- **allinanchor** and **inanchor:** in the hyperlink text
- **allintext** and **intext:** in the body section of the document
- **allintitle** and **intitle:** in the title of the document

Related to Internet address (URL):

- **allinurl** and **inurl:** in the URL of the file
- **link:** URL's of pages that point to a URL (Internet address)
- **site:** website identifier part of URL, i.e., domain
- **id** and **info:** followed by a URL, is the same as simply typing that URL as a search term

For discussion groups searches:

- **author:** creator of message
- **group:** discussion group identifier
- **insubject:** in the subject line of a message
- **msgid:** message identifier

Phone number database look-ups:

- **bphonebook:** yellow page entries
- **rphonebook:** residential white pages entries
- **phonebook:** white pages in general, business and residential

Other database look-ups:

- **define:** term definitions
- **stocks:** financial information about a stock

Related to News search:

- **location:** place where news originated, for News search
- **source:** organization that originated the news item

Other:

- **daterange:** range of Julian dates
- **cache:** version of the file when it was last detected on the Internet by the Google webcrawler
- **store:** restricts your search to a particular store in shopping search
- **ext** and **filetype:** file formats
- **related:** similar pages to the one in a specified URL

We go into the details of the above in various sections of our book. Some complexities using these operators are:

- Some operators cannot be used in the same query as others, or may cancel out the effect of another operator when used improperly in the same query.
- Some operators only work in particular Google search entry interfaces, but not in all.
- In future, Google may change how undocumented operators work, or even eliminate them entirely.

In this book, Google operators are documented within each applicable search engine feature. Within these, various incompatibilities or other usage restraints or dangers may be noted. You may find out more information about the above located in one centralized presentation, with the parameters and their properties arranged into various tabular structures: ⇨ www.google.com/help/operators.html, or www.googleguide.com/advanced_operators.html. Among other things, you will also find a table specifying which field operators work in Google's various kinds of searches (Web, Image, Groups, Froogle, News, Directory).

Key takeaway: Although they may not be user-friendly, the availability of a rich set of both field (metadata-based) and term-based operators in a search engine permits the composition of complex queries. Otherwise, they could only be achieved by using complex search entry forms.

2. **Non-operators**. Except for filters, non-primary parameters are seldom, if ever, entered as operators in most search engines. But, as interface design becomes simpler for inexperienced users, even filters are being employed more frequently as non-operator parameters.

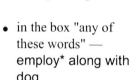 For the above search involving employment in a dog kennel, you might enter:

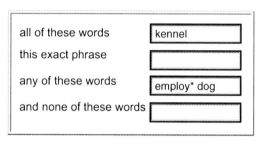

- in the box "any of these words" — employ* along with dog
- in the box "all these words" — kennel

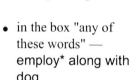 For the search involving the term kangaroo, here is how it might be entered using AlltheWeb's advanced Web search interface.

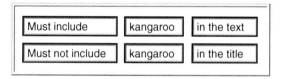

Parameter application

Search engines may implement parameters at different times and locations in the search process.

Localities:

- On the user's local computer (the client computer, called **client-side** processing).
- On the server computer at the search engine's website (using **server-side** processing).

Times:

- When the findings are first extracted from the search engine's catalog, called **pre-processing results**.
- At some point after the findings have been extracted, known as **post-processing results**.

Most search engines concentrate on pre-processing of findings, that is, filtering them up front before they are listed for users. This is generally achieved using server-side programs.

The meta-search utility Copernic is a notable exception. Almost all of its filtering is executed client-side, using programs you purchase. As search results are compiled for their initial display to users, dead links are checked by actually visiting websites hosting the referenced files. In addition, duplicate findings from different sources are eliminated, keyword summaries extracted, document language detected, and metadata-based filters applied.

The basic reason Copernic works this way is that it sources many search engines, of which it tries to take the highest common denominator. However, that denominator is limited, so only limited kinds of filters (phrases and Boolean ones, in this case) can be applied in common to all sources. More sophisticated Boolean and other searches are then applied to the findings once they have been obtained and are ready for further, client-side filtering. In other words, Copernic applies its filters in two basic stages, first collecting many more findings than will eventually be reported to the user.

Copernic also has extensive post-processing abilities. It can search within the previous round of search findings, as well as manage or summarize them in ways the major Internet search engines can't.

> ⇨ For more on this topic, consult Chapter 5: Post-processing of findings.

Search Interfaces and Filter Entry

Simple search interfaces

Most search engines include simple search interfaces. Regardless of their simplicity, some user knowledge can produce fairly sophisticated searches, nonetheless.

As the name suggests, simple search interfaces have relatively uncomplicated forms on their screens including:

- A single text box for entering search terms and perhaps some operator parameters.
- A limited ability to select options for parameters, other than operators.
- A button to start the search.
- Various links and general information for making further use of the search engine.

For an example of a simple search entry interface, see AltaVista's (www.altavista.com) or AlltheWeb's (www.alltheweb.com).

Simple search interfaces also serve as control centers for the more complex interfaces, essentially playing two important roles.

1. **Parameter entry:** Even though only a single text box is provided for entering search terms, if the search engine allows operator parameters and you know how to use them, sophisticated searches are then possible (described later in the book).

   However, not all operator parameters will work in all the various search entry interfaces of any given search engine:

   - Often, the Boolean operators you can enter in a simple search must be entered in a different way (perhaps with a different syntax) in an advanced search interface: ⇨ Reference Section 6.1: AND, OR, and NOT.
   - Many field operators usable in Web search will not work in other search entry interfaces.

     🔳 Google has many field operators for fielded search that will not function in a directory search, where only the intitle: and inurl: operators will work.

   - Some specialized search interfaces have their own kinds of field operators.

     🔳 The group: and author: field operators are unique in Google to its groups search entry interface.

   In some cases, you may not even have to know operator parameters to enter complex logic. This occurs when the search interface supports natural language interpretation or other similarly intelligent features that anticipate what the user means (⇨ Reference Section 3: Intelligent avoidance of formal parameter entry).

   Examples of intelligent features:

   - Google's display of a company's current stock price when the company stock symbol is typed in, or display of a company's telephone number and address when the company name is entered.
   - AltaVista's shortcuts: e.g., when you enter map as a search term, it will present an interface for finding a map.

- Spelling assistance: provided either automatically or with user participation.

- Automatic word stemming: The stem of a word is the starting stub of the word. This stub is used in various word variations.

  🔲 If, for instance, in Google you enter the query big hat, Google might find pages that contain bigger hat, big hatter, big hats, biggest hats, and the like. Of course, without other interpretation, such as that involved in concept search (see next point), it might also find pages with irrelevant words like big-time hater, etc.

- Concept search: if you request a search for synonymous keywords, search engines may search for words using synonyms from a glossary, which in this case, provides the necessary metadata.

  Concept search might also include automatic translation of a search term into another language *before* searching to find documents using a term with a similar meaning in that other language. It might also include treating hyphenated words either as two words or as one word without a hyphen, as in part-time, part time, and parttime.

  > 🔨 Similarity of meaning is the most important aspect of a very complex area, sometimes referred to as the **theory of thesaurus relationship types**, as covered under "Discussion Topics" on our website: ⇨ Search Engine Evolution, Part 3: Toward the use of semantics on the Web.

- Search personalization: takes into account your history of previous searches when interpreting the meaning of your search keywords.

  🔲 By keeping a record of your former searches, a search engine may be able to distinguish between whether you meant the planet or the make of car for the keyword Saturn.

2. **Control center:** Simple search interfaces can also act as control centers from which you may branch in several different directions to other search or user tool interfaces (⇨ Chapter 5: Other user tools). The latter provide services for:

End users — with tools for:

Post-processing of findings, language translation, and tasks completed by meta-search utilities.

Setting user preferences, i.e., customization settings for search entry screens and findings display screens.

Blocking data from websites having potentially offensive content.

Maintaining user accounts (to pay for certain documents that are unavailable for free).

Webmasters — with tools for:

Submitting websites to search engines for indexing.

Finding sites linking to the webmaster's website.

Other users — with tools for:

Help on how to use search engines.

Doing business with search engines, e.g., advertisers.

> ⇨ See Reference Section 3: Control center, for more information.

Medium complexity interfaces

The distinction between simple and advanced search interfaces can sometimes be misleading, because one or more levels of interface can exist between the most simple and the most advanced. And, sometimes even the so-called simple interface is already fairly complex.

Advanced search interfaces

All search engines included in this book offer advanced search interface screens. They have at least one text box for entering the search terms (including operator parameters), along with a "go" button. Other boxes allow parameterizing the search in more sophisticated or alternative ways.

Advanced search entry interfaces have more complex forms, often including the following kinds of boxes and buttons.

1. **Text entry boxes:** These allow you to enter search terms, perhaps along with operator parameters. Whereas the simple search entry interface has just a single text box, the advanced interfaces may have several. Text boxes may be either:

   a. **Simple text boxes:** Placed on a single line, in which the text may possibly scroll horizontally.

      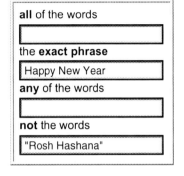 Google's multiple text entry boxes, as shown here.

   b. **Multi-line text boxes:** They may also scroll vertically.

      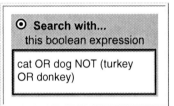 Here is AltaVista's scroll text box to enter a Boolean search string.

2. **Selection boxes or buttons:** These allow you to make choices without having to use operator parameters. The three basic types are:

   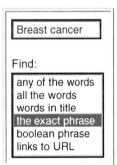

   a. **Drop-down menu lists:** These only permit you to make a single choice from a pre-defined set of options. The default choice is the one at the top.

      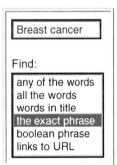 Here is the MSN Search drop-down menu with "any of the words" at the top. Moving the arrow downward reveals all the available choices, one of which must be selected.

   b. **Check boxes:** They allow you to check off any number of choices from those provided. Default values (checked or unchecked) may be pre-set for some.

   c. **Radio buttons:** These allow you to select from alternatives. Activating one radio button will deactivate the other, since the choices are mutually exclusive. Usually, one of the buttons is pre-activated as the default choice, such as AltaVista's scroll text box above.

⇨ For screenshots of advanced search entry interfaces, look at:

- AlltheWeb's advanced Web search interface in the next section of this chapter.
- Reference Section 3: Advanced Web search interfaces, for the search engines featured in this book.
- Chapter 5: Links from findings display (to switch to other catalogs), showing Hotbot's advanced search interfaces.

Primary Search Entry Interfaces

Simple Web search interfaces

⇨ For more information, consult Reference Section 3: Simple Web Search Interfaces.

Below is an example of a simple general web document search (Web search) interface from AlltheWeb.

AlltheWeb Simple Web Search Entry Interface (www.alltheweb.com)
Reprinted by permission from FAST

AlltheWeb Simple Web Search Interface	
Location	**Functions**
Top row: Logos	Contains search engine and company logos. Click on search engine logo for simple general web document search (Web search) page; considered the "home" page of most search engines.
Second line: Link Tabs	Contains links for various simple search interfaces. "Web" tab highlighted on left indicates use of "Web" Interface, i.e., simple general web document search (Web search) interface for search engine; de-emphasized link tabs can be used for News, Pictures, Videos, and Audio specialty searches.
Third line: Search Parameters Entry Text Box	Used to enter search terms and operator parameters.
To right of third line: Links	Contains links for: • Advanced Search: for advanced general web document search (Web search). • Customize Preferences: for user tools to customize search interfaces.
Bottom lines: More Links	Contain interface language setting buttons and links, and additional links to user tools (Submit Site, Help); also search engine information and ownership (Privacy Policy, About Us).

Advanced Web search interfaces

Compare AlltheWeb's advanced general web document search (Web search) interface on the next page with its simple interface shown on the previous page. The advanced one has more boxes and buttons for parameter entry, replacing many of the control center features of the simple one. These include additional text entry and selection boxes or buttons (drop-down menus, radio buttons, and checkboxes).

For additional information, ➪ Reference Section 3: Advanced Web Search Interfaces.

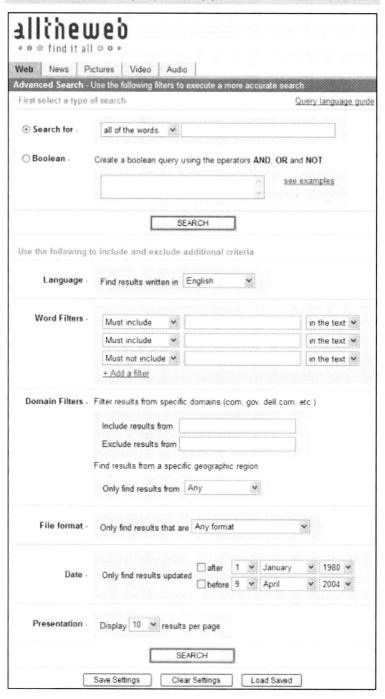

Subject directory search interfaces

Subject directories have several pre-defined topic categories as well as levels of sub-categories. Editors review and select sites for inclusion in their directories on the basis of previously determined selection criteria.

To appreciate the size and sophistication of various subject directories, you first need to know which company supplies it with directory data. This has previously been addressed (⇨ Chapter 1: Catalog types and origins).

Subject directories now on the Web tend to follow a roughly similar pattern from one search engine or tool to another. Our Search Tool Guide is organized along similar lines: ⇨ Search Tool Guide: Search by Topic and Search Tool Guide: Search Other than by Topic.

Notwithstanding the similarities, the difference between the Microsoft directory and those of Google and AltaVista is noteworthy. In comparison, the MSN directory is:

- More commercially oriented.
- Sleeker in look and feel.
- Accompanied by numerous specialized search interfaces tailored to the various subject categories.

All of this is probably a result of the MSN directory's being based largely on paid listings, including those of Microsoft Itself. This approach contrasts with:

- The free listings from the ODP (Open Directory Project), on which the other mentioned directories are based.
- The lesser degree to which the others are founded on a general Internet portal business model.

Below is an example of the high-level entries from the "Health" branch of the Google version of the ODP (Open Directory Project).

Subject directories also include interfaces to other pre-organized lists of links, often referred to as "Web resources" or "search resources." In effect, these are search tool directories, much like but far less elaborate than our own Search Tool Guide.

Addictions (5586)
Aging (148)
Alternative (6938)
Animal (3267)
Beauty (657)
Child Health (1005)
Conditions and Diseases (17478)
Dentistry (567)

Directories (17)
Disabilities (1395)
Education (200)
Employment (587)
Environmental Health (410)
Fitness (2116)
Healthcare Industry (6896)
History (7)
Home Health (413)

Insurance (175)
Medicine (14182)
Men's Health (460)
Mental Health (7113)
Nursing (1823)
Nutrition (663)
Occupational Health and Safety (819)
Organizations (184)
Pharmacy (6551)
Products and Shopping (61)

Professions (1418)
Public Health and Safety (4063)
Publications (158)
Regional (11)
Reproductive Health (2697)
Resources (264)
Search Engines (9)
Senior Health

(1185)
Senses (494)
Services (100)
Support Groups (547)
Teen Health (89)
Weight Loss (454)
Women's Health (940)

Related Categories:
Business > Business Services > Consulting > Medical and Life Sciences (221)
Kids and Teens > Health (604)
Recreation > Humor > Medical (41)
Science > Social Sciences > Communication > Health Communication (7)
Society > Issues > Health (1807)

Local application interfaces

⇨ For more on Copernic, see www.freep.com/money/tech/mwend24_20020924.htm.

The interfaces discussed so far involve the use of forms on webpages, hosted on a server.

However, some search engine interfaces place application programs directly on your personal computer. The meta search utility (or "toolbar"), Copernic, is one such case, with its "home" screen layout shown on the next page. (To see the screenshot in full resolution, go to ⇨ www.SearchHelpCenter.com/effective-internet-search-copernic-screenshots.html, "Main application screen.")

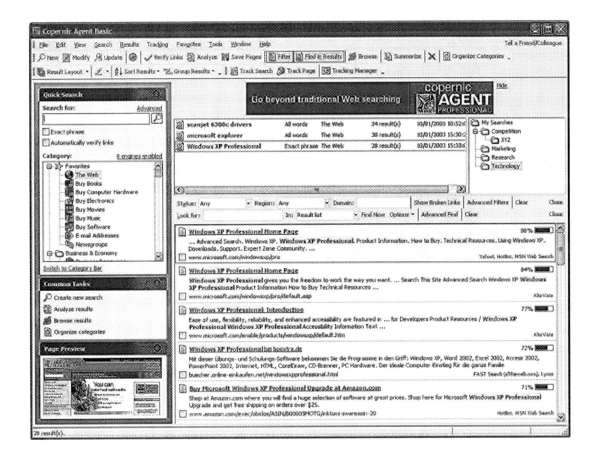

The following table briefly explains the main areas of Copernic's search interface screen.

⇨ For details on customizing the various commands and toolbars, and selecting screen panes, see Reference Section 6.4: Interfaces options made available.

Copernic Home Interface	
Location-Pane	**Functions**
Left column of panes: Command Bar	Consists of the following panes: search (Quick Search with Categories areas), common tasks, and page preview, as described below in this table.

Location-Pane	Functions
Upper left: Quick Search	To enter a new, simple search; includes box to enter terms, category, and other search filter items.
Bottom left: Page Preview	For thumbnails of files referenced in the search results pane when the cursor is placed over them.
Above Page Preview Pane: Common tasks	For context-dependent tasks. 📇 If "Browse results" chosen, new browser window opens; results shown in different format than above.
Top middle: Search History (for selected history folder)	To select and view past searches; if new folder chosen, a different set of searches previously completed searches will appear.
Upper right: Search History Folders	To select a folder containing a particular kind of search you have or will perform; is scrollable if necessary.
Bottom right: Results Display	A large scrollable window to view, annotate, and manipulate search results; can select any result for viewing in a new window.

Other Controls	Functions
Top: Menu & associated toolbars	To enter commands. Top line is menu bar, second is Standard toolbar, and third a composite of Results and Tracking toolbars.
Above results pane: Control panel boxes & buttons	To enter "Find in results" commands, generally referred to as "search within findings" in this book; consists of two lines for entering filters and search terms.

4: SAMPLE SEARCH PROJECTS

In this chapter:

- Application of search techniques to real-life search problems.
- Practical mini-courses on the use of numerous search engines and the meta search utility, Copernic.
- Differences in search engine databases and subsequent search results produced.
- Superiority of particular engines for conducting certain kinds of searches.
- Quirks, technical problems and software bugs in search engines, and how to investigate and, hopefully, solve them.

Introduction

> ⚠ You are strongly advised to read the cases sequentially to learn how to effectively use the many features of Copernic.

The investment and media cases were completed in late 2002; the health-related case was mostly done in the fall of 2004 (with the exception of the Copernic materials, which didn't change in a way that materially affected the results); and the "industrial-strength search" case, was completed in mid-summer 2005. Thus:

- Certain features of the search engines involved may have changed; e.g., some screenshots may no longer be identical to the ones you see here. Some rules for Boolean operators have also changed, except in Google and Copernic.
- Some data, from which results were derived, have changed, particularly those involving AltaVista and AlltheWeb, which now rely on Yahoo crawler catalogs.
- Certain limitations of search engines, such a restrictions on the number of words allowed in a query string, are no longer present.

Regardless, the principles taught in this chapter remain the same, and any differences are fairly trivial. We simply wanted to alert you to these changes, which will continue to occur as the search engine industry evolves.

Case #1: Stock Investment Search

Turbo-Genset is a company listed on the Toronto Stock Exchange in Canada and the London Stock Exchange in the United Kingdom. It designs new alternator technology that can be used to distribute power generation systems; the alternator itself can also be reversed to form a very high-speed electrical motor.

Let's say you wanted to research Turbo-Genset for potential investment purposes. Finding information on the Web about innovative small companies can be difficult. Here's one way you might approach this search.

MSN Search

Your first step does not require a complex search interface since its primary purpose is to find the company website and anything else it can locate by chance. You enter the company name in MSN Search.

You located the company web address in some of the findings seen below. You also found there useful company information, including links to "About Us," "Corporate Information," "Investor Relations," and its most recent annual report. "Career Opportunities," which could also provide valuable insights into hiring levels and requirements.

Partof an MSN Search Findings Page: Reprinted by permission from Microsoft

Web Results
1-10 of 296 containing **Turbogenset** (0.19 seconds)

The Business - XF-Section
... London shares - midday features UK small caps higher midday as contract news lifts Stanelco, **TurboGenset** Hong Kong's Hutchison Harbour Ring H1 net profit 44.04 mln hkd vs 32.78 mln Wall Street outlook ...
thebusinessonline.com/modules/xfsection/index.php Cached page

Turbo Genset & I-Power : Distributed Generation and Power Electronics
Technical innovation and engineering excellence underpin the products offered by **Turbo Genset** ...
Turbo Genset's innovative range of power generation systems utilise the company's patented ...
www.turbogenset.com Cached page 2/10/2005

Special publications search engine

Your next step might be to look for financial statements and measures, as well as stock market analyst reports on Turbo-Genset. These can be found at financial sites such as Yahoo Finance, Fool.com, FreeEdgar, Factiva, Multex, Morningstar, SmartMoney, SEDAR (Canada) and Dun and Bradstreet's Zapdata. Unfortunately, not all reports or services are free of charge. In this case, you located a paid report on Turbo-Genset from HSBC Securities (Europe), written by K. Campbell, dated 01/24/2002.

Copernic

Next, you used the Copernic meta search utility to:

- Scour many different search engines for recent documents about Turbo-Genset.
- Try to find the above HSBC Securities report by other means than paying for it.
- Set up tracking for Turbo-Genset so any new findings are reported daily.

Following is your actual search using Copernic, which you could model for your future stock investment searches.

1. You configured Copernic to conduct a general Web search using 18 different search engines and to find up to 700 documents per search engine, using a screen like the one shown next.

2. You then entered the phrase **Turbo-Genset** into the "Search for" box in the Quick Search panel; you chose "The Web" as a category and the two checkboxes are selected, as shown here.

3. You clicked the hyperlink to conduct an advanced, new search, where you specified further search parameters for optimal analysis along with extraction of key concepts, as shown on the below screenshot.

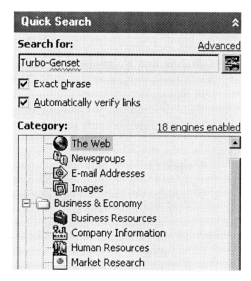

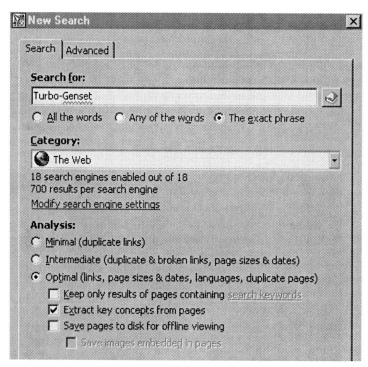

4. The search proceeded, as seen in these messages from the partially shown search progress bar. From this you obtained an idea of the search engines used and the comparative number of findings derived from each.

Based on your previously established settings for analysis of search findings, 249 unworkable web links were eliminated and 245 findings were skipped due to excessive file size for local retrieval, duplication of findings between search engines and different websites, and so on. Conceptual summaries of each retained document were extracted and document languages also detected.

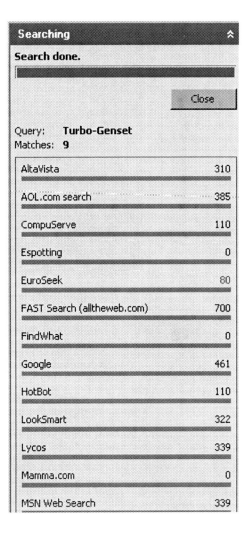

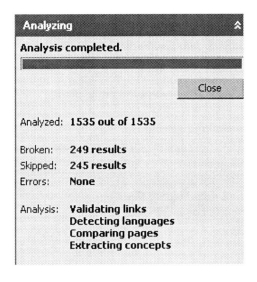

5. Search specifications were automatically saved for later actions such as updating of results and duplication or modification of search requirements. The "Search Properties" screenshot below shows the general properties you used for this particular search.

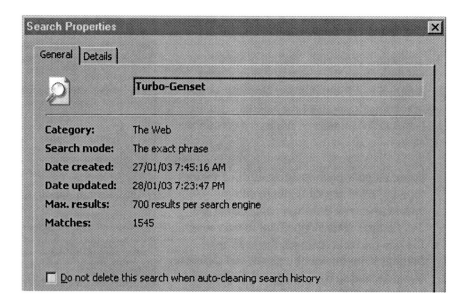

6. Once the results were listed, you used the controls near the top of the interface to group results by "date modified." This was one of several different ways to organize the findings, but you found it particularly relevant here, because your purpose was to obtain the most recent company information.

As it turned out, date modified was more misleading than helpful here. Because webcrawlers do not yet have an accurate way of determining the most recent version of a document, they tend to detect file changes since the last crawl against the website. And further, the file change may be irrelevant to the information sought. In this particular case, the following time groupings were created. (To see the screenshot in full resolution, go to ⇨ www. SearchHelpCenter.com/effective-internet-search-copernic-screenshots. html, "Results date groupings.")

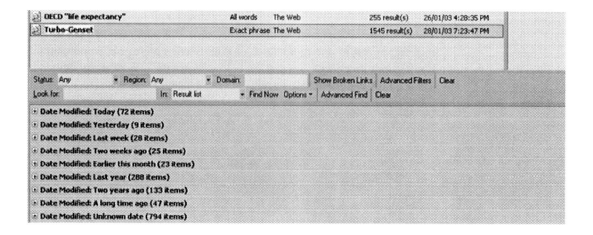

The screen below shows the nine findings modified "yesterday." You had set your "view" choices to show only one line per finding. The details shown below appeared when you clicked the plus sign to the left of "Date Modified Yesterday (9 items)" line. (To see the screenshot in full resolution, go to ⇨ www. SearchHelpCenter.com/effective-internet-search-copernic-screenshots. html, "Results date groupings expanded.")

> 🔍 The degree to which the far right rectangles are filled indicates their comparative relevance.

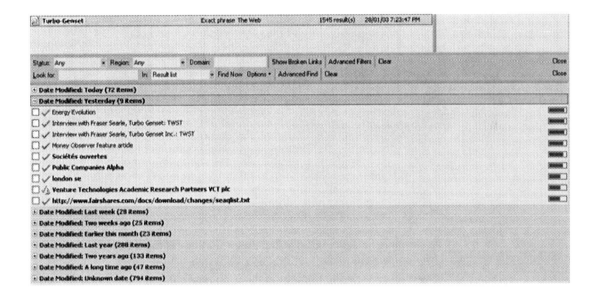

You also clicked the "Show Broken Links" button above the findings list, which caused these to appear, marked with an "X," as seen on the next screenshot.

- ✓ Employment- Oil, Gas, Petroleum Industry
- ✗ **Forecast International/DMS: Online Store**
- ✓ Hoover's Online - Manufacturing - Turbines, Transformers & Other Electrical ...
- ✓ Price Reports - Quotes
- ✓ ROB Magazine - Top1000: Big Swinging Caps - July 2000
- ✓ Stock Markets - TSE 300 alphabetically - CANOE Money
- ✓ Stock Markets - TSE 300 by sector - CANOE Money
- ✓ Track Record : Mergers and Acquisitions transactions 2000 - European Investm...
- ✓ UK-Wire
- ✓ www.backuptoserver.com symbol1

Note: Next to the last finding above (previous page), there is a gray checkmark followed by a yellow triangle with small exclamation mark inside it. These icons indicate that the website was accessed, but the document was not checked during the analysis phase because it was over your file size limits.

7. Although you chose to show only one line per finding, you were able find out more by simply floating your mouse above the findings individually. The "View Properties" display below illustrates the kind of metadata you obtained for each finding.

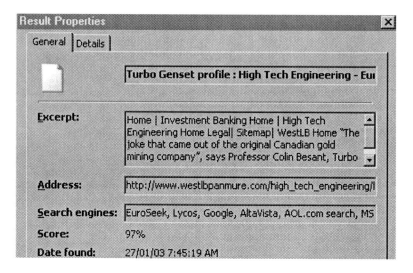

To see more in-depth information about findings without floating your mouse over individual findings, your then set the result properties to view the findings at the most detailed level, as shown below. (To see the screenshot in full resolution, go to ⇨ www. searchhelpcenter.com/effective-internet-search-copernic-screenshots. html#Results detailed view, "Results detailed view.")

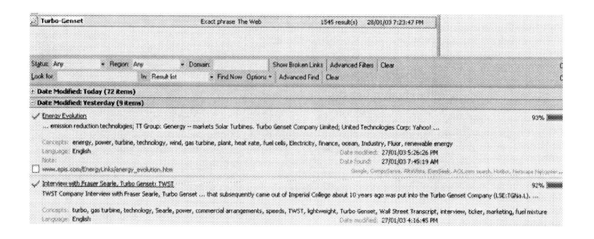

8. You now wanted to continue your search for the specific analyst report from HSBC found earlier. You began by looking for the term HSBC in the "Result list," without actually looking inside each individual document. As seen below, only three findings occurred, none containing the desired item. (To see the screenshot in full resolution, go to ➪ www. SearchHelpCenter.com/effective-internet-search-copernic-screenshots.html, "Results compact view.")

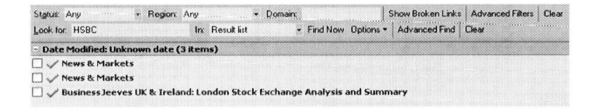

Using the "Advanced Find" button, you looked for both the word HSBC and the phrase K. CAMPBELL (the document author) in the documents themselves ("Find in each page contents").

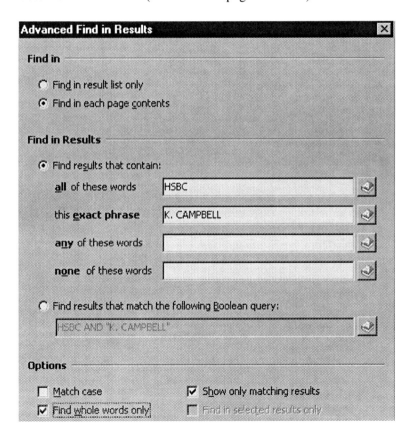

The search took a few minutes while websites were rechecked for broken links and the entire analysis redone. As shown here, 1,045 (1,535 - 240 - 250) items were inspected. However, none contained the illusive analyst report. It may simply have meant that reports like these were only available for a fee, requiring a specialized search engine to handle the billing,

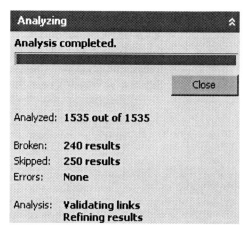

not accessible to Copernic. (To see the screenshot in full resolution, go to ⇨ www.SearchHelpCenter.com/effective-internet-search-copernic-screenshots.html, "Results date groupings #2.")

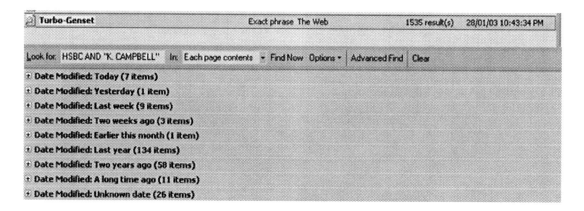

9. You then set up search tracking to assist you in obtaining regular information about Turbo-Genset. This caused

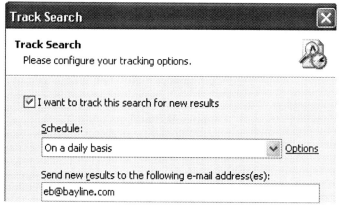

Copernic to do automatic daily updates of your search and e-mail you links to new findings. The top part of the dialog box you used to track the search as a whole is shown here.

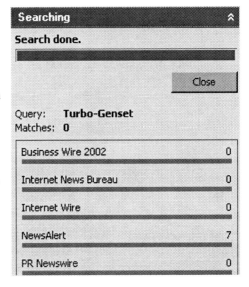

Search tracking only reports new pages. To track changes to individual pages, use Copernic's page tracking functions.

10. To further advance your investment search, you tried some final strategies.

- You used Copernic to investigate the "Press Releases" category using news search engines such as those associated with individual newspapers or from news catalogs of the large search engines. This may not always be useful, since the general Web search engines already pick up press releases, while at the same time producing a more comprehensive set of new daily findings.

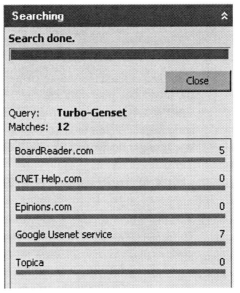

- You used Copernic to find postings on stock message boards pertaining to Turbo-Genset. In this case, a search on the company name in the category "Forums & Communities" in "Encyclopedia & Reference" found nothing. "Newsgroups" was another possibility; its progress bar is seen here. This time some postings were located from the Stockhouse discussion board as well as from Google Groups.

- You consulted articles in current and archived issues of financial periodicals such as The Economist.

Case #2: Multi-Media File Search

Your grandmother's 75th birthday was coming up. True to form, she pretended she did not want anyone to bother with a big party. But she was amenable to a celebration of some sort. Unbeknownst to her, you came up with the brilliant idea of throwing her an "**un**birthday party" instead. You decided first to locate sound tracks, video, and images related to the Unbirthday Party scene in Disney's production of "Alice in Wonderland," starring the Mad Hatter and gang.

AltaVista

Since AltaVista had a particularly good multi-media search facility, you decided to use it to find a sound file for the "Happy Unbirthday" song. To get to the simple audio search from AltaVista's homepage, you clicked the "MP3/Audio" tab at the top of the screen. This switched the search entry interface from a Web to an MP3/Audio search, as seen below.

You then entered the search string song:"Happy Unbirthday" and checked all the media and play duration checkboxes, thereby doing a "fielded search" (⇨ Chapter 3: Parameter types) on the song title field. Unfortunately, you fpund no song matches. You then attempted a similar query, but without the specified field operator parameter (song:). Still no luck.

Index of multi-media search engines

You decided to try a new approach. You used the various audio, image, and video file specialty searches obtainable at www.freeality.com, an index of many general-purpose and specialty search engines. All these searches failed too. You concluded something was wrong. Perhaps the song name was incorrect or it was unavailable for download via the Internet because of Disney's copyright protection.

Google Web search

You next decided to try a simple general web document search ("Web" search) using Google's search engine, seen below. You entered the search string "Happy Unbirthday" AND (Disney OR "mad hatter" OR "tea party"). This looked for the song title along with one or more of the other terms enclosed in brackets.

> 🔨 The AND and OR are called "Boolean operators," and specify relationships between the words and phrases.
>
> ⇨ For more information, refer to Chapter 6: Term relationships using Boolean logic, as well as to Chapter 3: Parameter types.

Google Simple Web Search Entry Interface: (www.google.ca/)
Reprinted by permission from Google

Google was able to detect the search entry is made from someone in Canada and automatically switched the browser to a Canadian site. Approximately 750 matches were found, a few of which are shown on the next page. Some even lead to musical renditions of the song, albeit without words.

In addition to the MIDI format sound file (composed from musical notes using software), many listings were found for places selling CD's of the song, as well. Unfortunately, you were unable to download the recording track directly from the Web, at least not for free.

You had now located the song. You also found links to images and text fitting the unbirthday theme, including a text file including part of the Mad Hatter's birthday party scene from Lewis Carroll's original book, Alice in Wonderland (⇨ www-2.cs.cmu.edu/People/rgs/alice-VII.html).

~*~*~**Disney** Music~*~*~
... **Disney** Midis. Arabian Nights A **Happy UnBirthday** Everybody Wants To Be A Cat Bambi
Shower Song I Just Can't Wait to Be King I Know You Someday My Prince Will ...
www.geocities.com/hullabaloo_228/disneymusic.html - 10k - Cached - Similar pages

    Disney Midis
    ... o0 Bibbity Bobity Bo!(Cinderella) 0o0 Cool **Disney** Melody 0o0 We are Siamese,
    Lady and the Tramp 0o0 Bella Notte 0o0 A Very **Happy UnBirthday** Alice in ...
    www.geocities.com/disneysmouse/Disney_Music/ - 44k - Cached - Similar pages
    [More results from www.geocities.com]

Disney's Midi 2
... **Disney** Melody, When you Wish... Grand **Disney** Melody. Cool **Disney** Melody. We are
Siamese, (Lady and the Tramp). A Very **Happy UnBirthday** (Alice in Wonderland). ...
www.ginevra2000.it/Disney/Midi/allmidi2.htm - 26k - Cached - Similar pages

Other searches with general-purpose search engines

You decided to repeat the same search to see what else you coul find, this time
using AltaVista and MSN Search. Many fewer findings resulted and were a lot
less relevant to boot. As seen on the next screenshot, a video search using
AlltheWeb produced some findings from the Web catalog ("Web Results"),
although none from the video catalog.

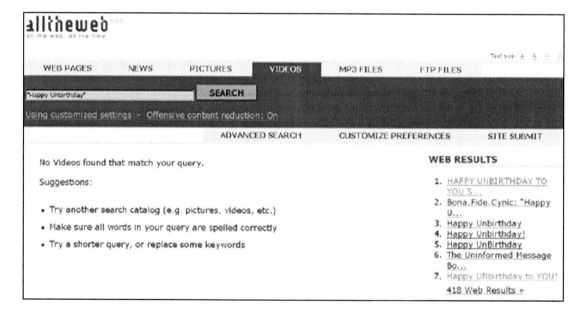

Copernic meta search engine

You were still not satisfied with your results. It seemed to have taken a long time to produce the few good hits you had obtained so far. You decided on a different tack using the meta search engine, Copernic.

1. You began with a "Quick Search" on the phrase Happy Unbirthday against the "Audio & Video Files" category. To minimize time delays, you decided not to check "Automatically verify links."

   Note the link labeled "13 search engines enabled." You clicked on it to see the various search engines to be used, as seen next.

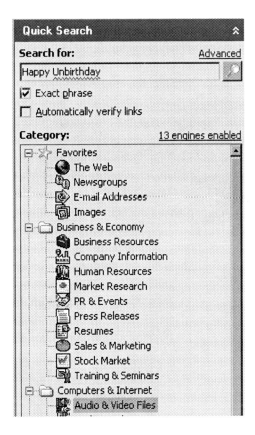

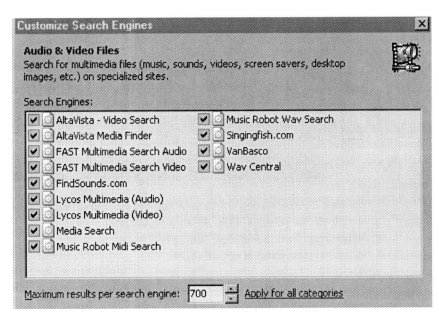

Only one match resulted, viewed below. (To see the screenshot in full resolution, go to ⇨ www.SearchHelpCenter.com/effective-internet-search-copernic-screenshots.html, "Results compact view #2.")

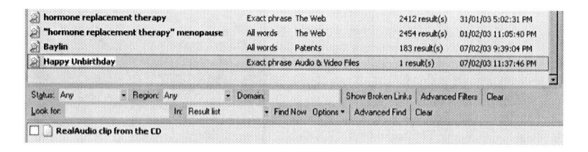

2. Next, you decided on a general web document search (Web search). You right-clicked on the "Happy Unbirthday" result on the previous screenshot, then chose "Modify" from the context menu. In the dialog box below, you chose "The Web" category from the drop-down menu list, along with the "Minimal" analysis radio button.

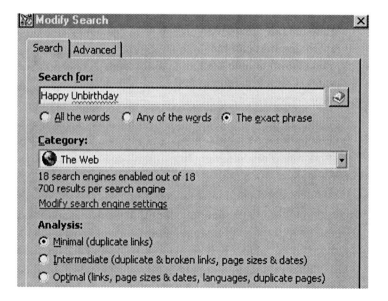

To view the search engines to be used, you clicked on the "Modify search engine settings" link. As seen on the next page, the "Customize Search Engines" dialog box appeared, which you closed without making any changes.

Copernic sources over 1,000 search engines. These are organized into categories by Copernic, depending on the type of search engine specialization, if any. At this point, you can change to any sub-set of the available search engines by selecting the appropriate checkboxes.

Say your search engine category is "The Web." If you prefer the relevancy rankings of Yahoo to sequence the findings, you can simply choose Yahoo alone, if it is available, or one of the other search engines that use the same data sources as Yahoo. If desired, Copernic can then post-process up to 700 Yahoo findings. (To see the screenshot in full resolution, go to ➪ www.SearchHelpCenter.com/effective-internet-search-copernic-screenshots.html, "Search engine customization.")

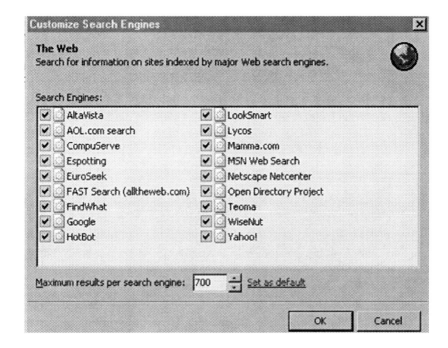

3. Your search produced 1,000 matches after eliminating duplicates from the different search engines. The search progress tracking bar, shown here, indicates the number of findings from each search engine prior to elimination of duplicates.

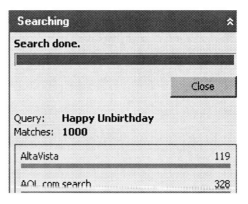

Below you can see Copernic's top findings with the view setting of one line per finding:

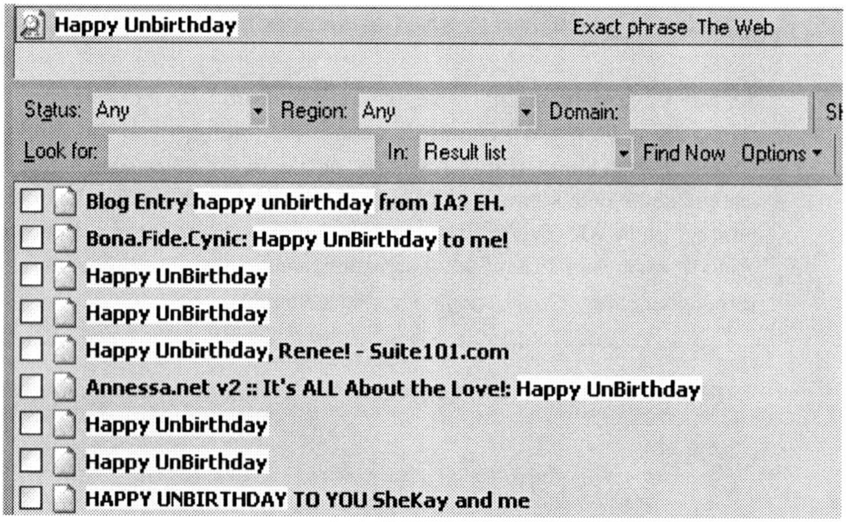

Happy Unbirthday   Exact phrase The Web

Status: Any   ▼   Region: Any   ▼   Domain: SI

Look for: In: Result list   ▼   Find Now   Options ▼

- ☐ ▢ **Blog Entry happy unbirthday from IA? EH.**
- ☐ ▢ **Bona.Fide.Cynic: Happy UnBirthday to me!**
- ☐ ▢ **Happy UnBirthday**
- ☐ ▢ **Happy UnBirthday**
- ☐ ▢ **Happy Unbirthday, Renee! - Suite101.com**
- ☐ ▢ **Annessa.net v2 :: It's ALL About the Love!: Happy UnBirthday**
- ☐ ▢ **Happy Unbirthday**
- ☐ ▢ **Happy UnBirthday**
- ☐ ▢ **HAPPY UNBIRTHDAY TO YOU SheKay and me**

4. Because you wished to browse the individual findings, you simply clicked on each one in order, starting from the most relevant findings at the top. They opened up in a new window. In each case, the search terms were highlighted, making it easy to see where they occurred in the text.

Another way to browse the findings is to choose the "Browse results" option located in the lower left of the screenshot on the next page. This will show the finding identifiers in a left panel and the findings pages on the right (similar to doing a search with Internet Explorer). (To see the screenshot in full resolution, go to ⇨ www.SearchHelpCenter.com/effective-internet-search-copernic-screenshots.html, "Browse results link.")

Finally, you also can take advantage of Copernic's various options available for displaying findings. There are three possible levels of viewing detail: standard, compact (the ones seen above and on the next page), and detailed. The latter shows all metadata for the finding, either downloaded or extracted by Copernic from the referenced page. You can also control the number of lines of text displayed in the detailed view through customization settings.

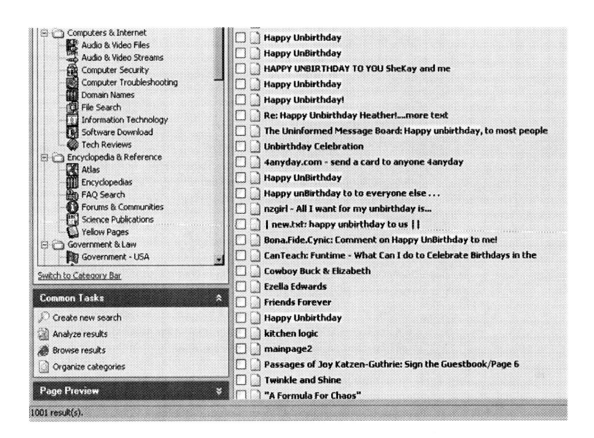

Your search continued. You placed a check mark in the box to the left of the two findings of interest (one of which is shown in the screenshot on the next page).

5. To only see findings you were interested in, you chose "Checkmarked" from the "Status" dropdown menu

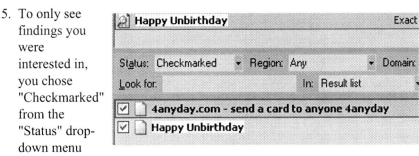

box seen here. Then you executed a "Find within results" with the "Results List" option.

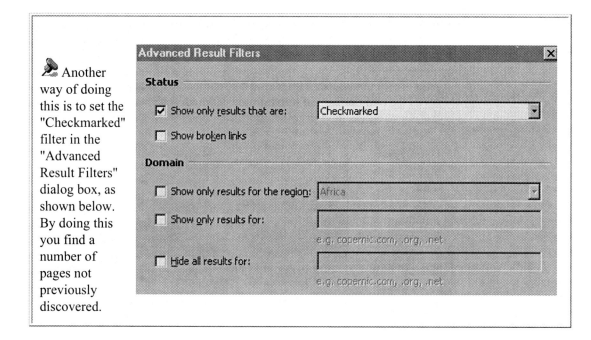

Happy Unbirthday	Exact phrase The Web

Status: Any ▾   Region: Any ▾   Domain:

Look for: [   ]   In: Result list ▾   Find Now   Option

- ☐ 📄 **Blog Entry happy unbirthday from IA? EH.**
- ☐ 📄 **Bona.Fide.Cynic: Happy UnBirthday to me!**
- ☐ 📄 **Happy UnBirthday**
- ☐ 📄 **Happy Unbirthday, Renee! - Suite101.com**
- ☐ 📄 **Annessa.net v2 :: It's ALL About the Love!: Happy UnBirthday**
- ☐ 📄 **Happy Unbirthday**
- ☐ 📄 **Happy UnBirthday**
- ☐ 📄 **Happy UnBirthday**
- ☐ 📄 **HAPPY UNBIRTHDAY TO YOU SheKay and me**
- ☐ 📄 **Happy Unbirthday!**
- ☐ 📄 **Re: Happy Unbirthday Heather!....more text**
- ☐ 📄 **The Uninformed Message Board: Happy unbirthday, to most people**
- ☑ 📄 **4anyday.com - send a card to anyone 4anyday**

🔍 Another way of doing this is to set the "Checkmarked" filter in the "Advanced Result Filters" dialog box, as shown below. By doing this you find a number of pages not previously discovered.

Advanced Result Filters ☒

Status

☑ Show only results that are: [Checkmarked ▾]

☐ Show broken links

Domain

☐ Show only results for the region: [Africa ▾]

☐ Show only results for: [   ]
   e.g. copernic.com, .org, .net

☐ Hide all results for: [   ]
   e.g. copernic.com, .org, .net

6. Your next step was to look within the "Images" category, using specialized image search engines or search engine interfaces. Here you can see the "Modify Search" dialog box you used, followed by another screen image displaying the set of search engines used.

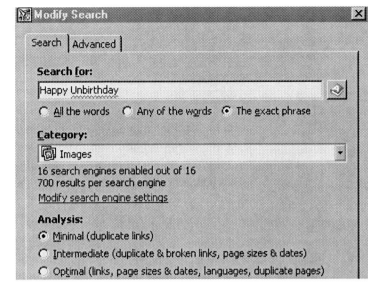

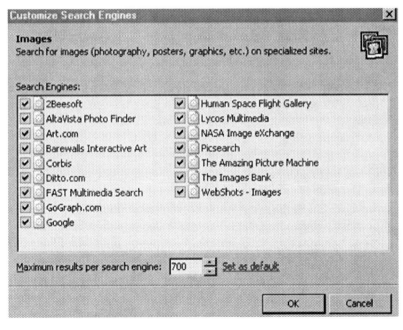

(To see this screenshot in full resolution, go to ⇨ www. Search HelpCenter. com/effective-internet-search-copernic-screenshots. html, "Search engine customization #2.")

Here you see the search progress bar for the search, from which you found the four matches shown in the screenshot below.

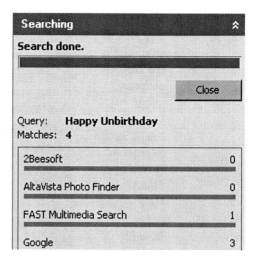

7. You browsed the four results and discovered a new finding, but decided it wasn't what you were looking for.

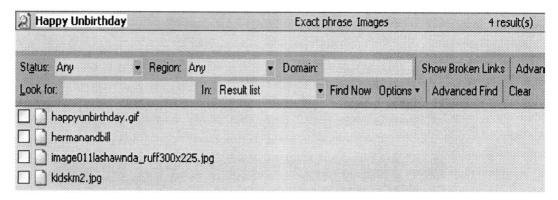

Copernic did not have a special display format for images or special filters for image files. Therefore, when it did a specialized search, it often displayed the findings in the context of the search engine from which the findings originated.

The finding shown below was made by the FAST Multimedia Search engine (prior to its purchase by Yahoo). The whole FAST findings page was displayed. Using that, your were able to further filter the findings based on specialized image file filters. You could also display your findings in the format native to that search engine. Thus, when you entered the word Unbirthday (without Happy in front of it to make a phrase) into the following interface, a grid of images displayed.

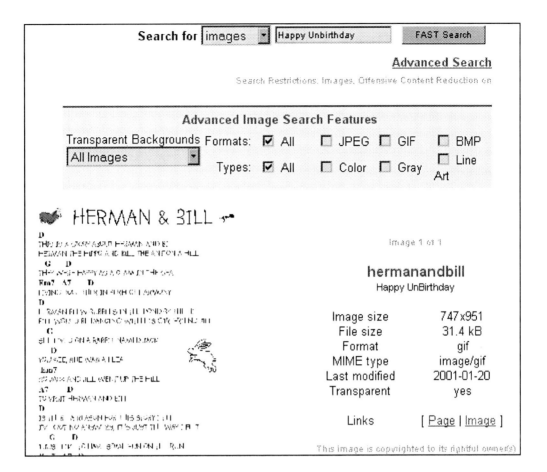

8. From the above list, you decided to use the MIDI file, which gave you the tune to accompany you in singing. In addition, you kept one of the document files containing some text and graphics to make your grandmother a birthday card.

9. Belatedly, you took one more look at the deep web search tool sets provided by Copernic, just in case you missed something. Lo and behold, Copernic had a category for "music lyrics" to accompany the melody you have uncovered! You found this using our Search Tool Guide, where Copernic's various deep web search tool sources are listed (⇨ Search Tool Guide: Entertainment, transportation, travel). Alas, this too failed to produce the desired lyrics!

Case #3: Health-Related Search

This single case serves as a mini-course for all our featured search engines. It was first completed in late 2002, and then revised in November 2004. It was then repeated for MSN Search in February 2005, shortly after MSN came out with its new search engine.

Copernic: Few changes were noted in its interface and program logic. The main difference seems to be in the data catalogs it was able to source. Google, for instance, no longer makes its catalog directly available to Copernic. However, AOL Search was accessed, and this is known to be based on the Google catalog. Therefore, they may have been accessed indirectly.

AlltheWeb, AltaVista, Google: Between November 2002 and November 2004, the following changes were noted:

- Certain of their features changed; e.g., AltaVista no longer supports wildcards at the ends of words, and some screens have changed.
- Their syntaxes used for Boolean operators are also different, with the exception of Google (for the most part) and Copernic.
- Some data, from which results were derived, have changed, particularly those involving AltaVista and AlltheWeb, which now rely on Yahoo crawler catalogs.

Thus, the health-related case that follows was revised for all our featured search engines, with the exception of Copernic.

MSN Search: Between November 2002 and February 2005, the syntactical rules for Boolean and field operators changed. Also, MSN Search was now relying on catalogs of its own, collected by Microsoft's own webcrawler, rather than on data supplied by Inktomi and others.

Search requirements and approach

Menopause and hormone replacement therapy are much found in the news lately. You decided to conduct a search project on this controversial subject using the five search engines featured in this book: AlltheWeb, AltaVista, Copernic, Google, and MSN Search. You saw it as a golden opportunity to:

- Try out all the search engines in a real life search situation.
- Learn to make the best possible use of each one's abilities.

- Weigh their relative strengths and weaknesses.
- Discover many of the useful tools and resources provided in the book.
- Learn to effectively use the many features in the Reference Manual.

To fairly compare the search engines, you decided to use their advanced general web document search (Web search) entry screens and specify the same search requirements as much as possible.

To avoid being inundated with too much data, you decided to restrict your search to information for women who have had their uteruses removed (hysterectomy), but not their ovaries (i.e., not an oophorectomy). Your search began with this strategy in mind.

Term-based filters

You began by imposing the following requirements for terms and term-based filters (⇨ Chapter 3: Parameter types).

- The phrase hormone replacement therapy and the word menopause must be present in the found document.
- One or both of hysterectomy (a word) and uterus removal (a phrase) must be present in the found document.
- The word oophorectomy and the phrase ovary removal must be absent from the found document. This can be phrased as "not both oophorectomy and ovary removal," or alternatively as "not oophorectomy and not ovary removal." Theoretically both formulations of the Boolean logic should produce the same results. Practically speaking, some search engines cannot implement the first one correctly.

Metadata-based filters

You also attempted to limit your search using certain metadata-based filters (⇨ Chapter 3: Parameter types) and record individual search engine responses, as follows.

1. Restrict findings to documents whose age is reported as being in a specified time period (⇨ Chapter 6: File content characteristics).
    - **AlltheWeb, AltaVista, Google and Copernic:** Had document age filtering options.
    - **MSN Search:** Did not permit this kind of filtering.
2. Require the presence of the phrase hormone replacement in the document title (⇨ Chapter 6: File structure characteristics). In theory all search engines were able to handle this restriction. However:
    - **MSN Search:** Could not do this.
    - **Copernic:** Was only able to apply it in an approximate way.

3. Limit findings to a maximum of just one or two findings per website ("domain"). By default:

- **AlltheWeb:** Listed only one finding per website.
- **AltaVista, Google, and MSN Search:** Showed a maximum of two findings per website. Note: This could have been set to one, two, or three in MSN Search.
- **Copernic:** Has no direct control over this feature; it relies on other search engines whose results it integrates.

Search strategy

The following discussion is organized into sections for each search engine, followed by our conclusions. The discussion for each search engine is further broken down into sub-sections for:

1. **Search entry with minimal operator parameters:** How to correctly enter the search while minimizing the use of operator parameters — the way most people tend to conduct searches. Such an approach involves using various kinds of selection boxes and designated text entry boxes.

2. **Search entry with maximal operator parameters:** How to correctly enter the search while maximizing the use of operator parameters — the way people with more expertise tend to conduct searches. Such an approach involves integrating all terms and parameters together into a single Boolean search string.

3. **Preliminary conclusion:** How to do the search, if possible, based on the preceding.

4. **Variations tested:** What happens when you vary your method of entering the search, to test the effects of using:

- **Search within findings features, if any:** used to overcome limits in the allowed lengths of search strings expressed in number of words or words plus operator parameters of certain kinds. Is there such a feature and does work to solve the problem?

- **No date range restriction filters:** Does this increase the number of findings, as would be expected if they really work?

- **No title restriction filters:** Does this increase the number of findings, as would be expected if they really work?

- **Wildcards and word stemming:** e.g., as applied to the word stub menopaus. Do these work, and thereby increase the number of findings?

- **Different field operator orders:** e.g., using title: in the middle of the search string rather than at the start. Are there any restrictions on that order? Do these change the ordering of the findings on the results display?

- **Different ordering of entered terms:** Does this change the ordering of findings on the results display by making the earlier terms more relevant?

- **Factoring out term relationships:** such as entering the string menopause NOT oophorectomy AND NOT "ovary removal" as opposed to the logically equivalent menopause NOT (oophorectomy OR "ovary removal"). What works and what doesn't? What is the difference in results?

- **Boolean search strings in simple Web search:** use in simple search text entry boxes as opposed to their use in those for advanced Web search. Do the operators also work in the simple search interface?

The differences in the findings produced, and whether the features actually worked, are noted in each case. The same set of tests was applied as much as possible to all the search engines, and documented in a similar structure except in the case of Copernic. In the latter case, these factors are documented, but as part of the flow of the two basic options, rather than in a list at the end of the Copernic description.

5. **Notes, tips & warnings:** Other interesting and useful features of various search engines are documented, including:

- Whether they do spellchecking of some kind.
- How to revise a search string from the results listing.
- Special quirks, such as using certain field operators in certain text entry boxes, use of the minus sign instead of NOT in certain cases, need to use uppercase or lowercase for certain operator parameters, and so on.

AlltheWeb

Search entry with minimal operator parameters

In the AlltheWeb advanced Web search screen (see next page), you entered the search strings you see in the text boxes.

Word Filters			
Must include	homone replacement	in the title	
Must include	menopause	in the text	
Must include	hormone replacement therapy	in the text	
Must not include	oophorectomy	in the text	
Must not include	ovary removal	in the text	

Date - ☑ after 25 November 2003 ☑ before 25 November 2004

Based on these entries, AlltheWeb produced 220,000 findings; the first two are shown below. However, there was no way of specifying OR, so the inclusion of hysterectomy OR ovary removal logic was not possible using these boxes.

Results 1 - 10 of 220,000 Advanced Search results

Web Results   (What's this?)

MedlinePlus: **Hormone Replacement Therapy**
... List of All Topics. **Hormone Replacement Therapy** ... articles on **Hormone Replacement Therapy**: • Estrogen **Replacement Therapy** ... Medicine) **Hormone Therapy** for **Menopause**: Who Should Take ...
more hits from: http://www.nlm.nih.gov/medlineplus/hormonereplacementtherapy.html - 34 KB

Amazon.com: Books: **Hormone Replacement Therapy** Yes or No?: How to Make an Informed Decision About Estrogen, ...
Hormone Replacement Therapy Yes or No?: How to Make an Informed Decision About Estrogen, Progesterone, & Other Strategies for Dealing With Pms, **Menopause**, & Osteoporosis, Betty Kamen ... **Menopause** Survival Guide: Surviving the Change of Life in addition to **Hormone Replacement Therapy** ... progesterone, PMS, **menopause**, and osteoporosis ... as a **hormone replacement therapy** ... more hits from: http://www.amazon.com/exec/obidos/ASIN/0944501109 - 65 KB

Search entry with maximal operator parameters

In the AlltheWeb advanced Web search screen, you entered the following string in the Boolean search text entry box at the top of the screen in the screen, shown here.

> ⊙ Boolean - Create a boolean query using the operators **AND**, **OR** and **NOT**.
>
> title:"hormone replacement" AND menopause AND "hormone replacement therapy" AND (hysterectomy OR "uterus removal") NOT oophorectomy NOT "ovary removal"

title:"hormone replacement" AND menopause AND "hormone replacement therapy" AND (hysterectomy OR "uterus removal") NOT oophorectomy NOT "ovary removal"

At the same time, you set the same date restrictions through the boxes shown above. AlltheWeb reported that it had found nothing for the above. However, when you shortened the query string to 10 words (including words within phrases, but not including operator parameters), by dropping the NOT "ovary removal", AlltheWeb reported 30,600 findings, of which the first couple are shown here.

Results 1 - 10 of 30,600 Advanced Search results for

Web Results   (What's this?)

FertilityRX.com: Completing The Picture About Uterine Fibroid Therapy
... estrogen, while **menopause** causes a ... a total **hysterectomy** in which ... **uterus. Removal** of the ovaries results in a permanent state of **menopause** and may require **hormone replacement therapy** ...
http://www.fertilityrx.com/infertilityinfo/fibroids - 35 KB

MayoClinic.com - Uterine Fibroids Health Decision Guide
Learn about uterine fibroids and explore the pros and cons of your treatment options. Hear the insights of a Mayo Clinic doctor and read the stories of four women who chose different courses of treatment. ... **hysterectomy** leads to urinary incontinence — a tendency to leak urine. Because the same muscles and ligaments support both your bladder and **uterus, removal** ... changes after **menopause** ...
http://www.mayoclinic.com/invoke.cfm?objectID=802ED1C5-492...-ACA0D4AC3566D98E&page=12
 - 42 KB

You then selected "Search within results," and entered -"ovary removal" in the text box that appeared. Now AlltheWeb reported just 875 findings, of which the first couple appear below (next page).

Some conclusions: AlltheWeb had a "Search within findings" feature that was able to extend the number of words used in your search beyond the initial limit of 10. To have all the terms in this complex search used in AlltheWeb, you needed to make use of this feature, since the Boolean box option appeared to have a maximum of 10 words. Also, the entry route that avoided using operator parameters was very restrictive, because it did not support OR logic.

When "Search Within Results" was used, the NOT in front of the added NOT "ovary removal" did not work, but -"ovary removal" did. Thus, the negation operator at the start of a search string could only be entered with a minus sign.

Search variations tested

- It appeared that AlltheWeb had a 10-word limit, not including operator parameters. However, you tried another variation in the Boolean text box: title:"hormone replacement" AND menopause AND "hormone replacement therapy" AND (hysterectomy OR "uterus removal") NOT oophorectomy **AND** NOT "ovary removal", along with the same date restrictions. Now, with the AND inserted before the second NOT, the search produced 30,000 findings, slightly less than the 30,600 that occurred when you truncated the string after the word oophorectomy. Also, the first few findings were similar. So, it still appeared that there was truncation, but that it might have worked somewhat differently with this search string variation.

  You then applied the "Search within results," and entered -"ovary removal" in the text box that appeared, you received 779 results, compared to the 875 findings with the "Search within results" first tried.

  Just how to interpret all this was unclear, as it was not documented in any AlltheWeb Help.

- You then removed the range of dates restriction. Strangely, this did not seem to affect the number of results. Indeed, 779 results were obtained this way, actually fewer than the 875 findings obtained *with* the date restriction in place. If anything, the date restriction seemed to you to have backfired.

  Why didn't the date restriction work in this case? Was it dropped because of the limit on the length of the search string? To find out, you entered the simpler phrase hormone replacement with and without the date restriction. Indeed, AlltheWeb reported 515,000 findings with the restriction, and 613,000 ones without it. So, you concluded that the date restriction in the search had been dropped from the search because of the limit.

- Next, you also removed the restriction of the phrase hormone replacement having to be in the title section of the document. As anticipated, the number of findings increased. With both date and title restrictions off, the number of findings rose dramatically, to 35,700, mainly due to the removal of the title restriction.

- You then typed menopaus*, thinking that the asterisk might act as a wildcard. AlltheWeb returned the same number of findings as if you typed the word stub menopaus. Apparently, the asterisk was ignored, and the greatly reduced number of findings showed that word stemming is not done automatically. That is, the exact spelling, without the letter e, was apparently required.

- You typed the field identifier title in the middle of the search string in the advanced Boolean search, and moved some of the other terms around as well: (hysterectomy OR "uterus removal") AND "hormone replacement therapy" AND **title:**"hormone replacement" AND menopause NOT oophorectomy AND NOT "ovary removal". It made no significant difference in the findings produced, although they decreased slightly from 30,000 to 29,900. Thus, you concluded that this field operator can be used anywhere in the search string. Notwithstanding, you speculated that the order in which you enter terms can be significant in AlltheWeb: ⇨ Reference Section 6.3: Overall ordering.

- You experimented with factoring out brackets. For example, you tried menopause NOT oophorectomy AND NOT "ovary removal", and compared the results from that with those from the logically equivalent menopause NOT (oophorectomy OR "ovary removal"). The results were almost the same. So, you concluded that factoring out brackets basically appears to work, at least to one level of brackets.

- You dropped the AND field operator from the Boolean text box, and the results changed drastically. You concluded that entering an explicit Boolean operator is required to produce correct results in the Boolean search string. That is, leaving a blank between search terms in a Boolean phrase is not equivalent to any Boolean operator. The only acceptable Boolean ones in the Boolean text box are AND, NOT, and OR.

- You tried out the Boolean expression in the text box for the simple Web search. When the same initial search string was placed in the simple Web search text box, but without the date range restriction (not available in the simple Web search, even by a field parameter), 803 findings were obtained, as opposed to the 30,800 shown above with the date range restriction. However, by adding -"ovary removal" to search within results, the same 901 findings were obtained. Obviously, the Boolean logic didn't work straight from the simple search interface, probably because operators such as OR and NOT were interpreted as search terms. However, at the point where you reached the modification of the results, and re-entered the same search, your search string seemed to be interpreted as if you had arrived at the search using the advanced search entry route.

AlltheWeb: Notes, tips & warnings

⚠ Syntactical constraints:

- All field operators must be in lowercase text, followed by a colon. The operator value must follow the colon directly, with no space in between.
- AND, OR, and NOT Boolean operators must be in uppercase. Minus and plus sign variety of Boolean operators must have no spaces after them.

💡 To edit the previous search, simply choose "edit your advanced search" near the top of the findings page.

🔨 AlltheWeb has automatic spelling correction suggestion. Thus, when the word oophorectomy is spelled with an "e" instead of an "o" in the fifth character position, a spelling change or error is indicated.

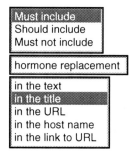

🔨 When AlltheWeb, in the days was owned by FAST, a more flexible and functional set of drop-down menu choices was available, as you see here. This was a prime selling point of AlltheWeb compared to other search engines, which for some reason was lost when AlltheWeb was sold to Yahoo.

Search entry with minimal operator parameters

In the AltaVista advanced Web search screen below, you entered the search strings you see in the text boxes:

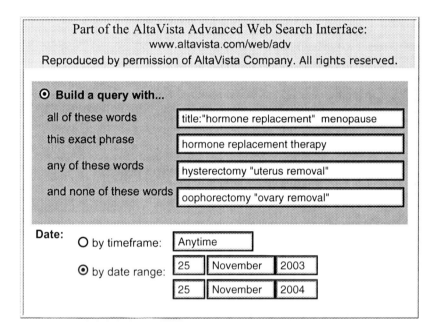

Note that certain operator parameters cannot be avoided in these text boxes. Specifically:

- The quotes around hormone replacement, uterus removal, and ovary removal indicate phrases.
- The title: before the phrase hormone replacement is a field operator that instructs the search engine to look for the phrase in the title section of the HTML document.

AltaVista produced 680 findings; the first ones are shown on the next page.

AltaVista found 680 results About

Amazon.com: Books: Natural **Hormone Replacement** for Women over 45: For Women over 45
... Customers interested in this **title** may also be interested ... treatment of **menopause**. Conventional **hormone replacement** treatment as ... fatigue after a **hysterectomy**, and months of research ...
www.amazon.com/exec/obidos/tg/detail/-/0962741809?v=glance
More pages from amazon.com

Article: **Hormone Replacement Therapy** Is It For You - Age Page - Health Information: NIA - WrongDiagnosis.com
... **title**: **Hormone Replacement Therapy** Is It For You - Age Page - Health Information: NIA. Conditions: **menopause** ... So this is **menopause**. You are ... the cervix, removed (by **hysterectomy**
www.wrongdiagnosis.com/artic/hormone_replacement_therapy_i...ealth_information_nia.htm
More pages from wrongdiagnosis.com

Search entry with maximal operator parameters

In the AltaVista advanced Web search screen, you entered the following string in the "Boolean expression" text box:

> **title:"hormone replacement" AND menopause AND "hormone replacement therapy" AND (hysterectomy OR "uterus removal") NOT oophorectomy NOT "ovary removal"**

You also selected "by date range" in the below to restrict the search to finding documents aged for the period under study.

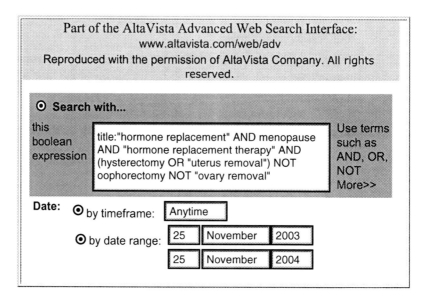

In the Boolean expression:

- The quotes around groups of words in four places indicate phrases.
- The title: before the phrase hormone replacement is a field operator that instructs the search engine to look for the phrase in the title section of the HTML document.

Based on these entries, AltaVista reported that it had found nothing. However, when you shortened the query string to 10 words (including words within phrases, but not including operator parameters), by dropping the NOT "ovary removal", AltaVista reported 32,600 findings. The first two are shown below.

Part of the Findingson a First AltaVista Findings Page:

AltaVista found 32,600 results About

FertilityRX.com: Completing The Picture About Uterine Fibroid Therapy
... estrogen, while **menopause** causes a ... a total **hysterectomy** in which ... **uterus. Removal** of the ovaries results in a permanent state of **menopause** and may require **hormone replacement therapy** ...
www.fertilityrx.com/infertilityinfo/fibroids
More pages from fertilityrx.com

MayoClinic.com - Uterine Fibroids Health Decision Guide
Learn about uterine fibroids and explore the pros and cons of your treatment options. Hear the insights of a Mayo Clinic doctor and read the stories of four women who chose different courses of treatment. ... **hysterectomy** leads to urinary incontinence — a tendency to leak urine. Because the same muscles and ligaments support both your bladder and **uterus, removal** ... changes after **menopause** ...
www.mayoclinic.com/invoke.cfm?objectID=802ED1C5-492F-4D34-ACA0D4AC3566D98E&page=12
More pages from mayoclinic.com

Unfortunately, you were not able to find a way to search within results, so the NOT "ovary removal" restriction could not be added by this route.

Some conclusions: AltaVista did not have a "Search within findings" feature. To have all the terms in this complex search used in AltaVista, you needed to use the set of boxes for entering search terms, since the Boolean box option *appeared* to have a maximum of 10 words.

Search variations tested

- It appeared that AltaVista had a 10-word limit, not including operator parameters. However, you tried another variation in the Boolean text box: (hysterectomy OR "uterus removal") AND "hormone replacement therapy" AND title:"hormone replacement" AND monopause

AND NOT oophorectomy **AND** NOT "ovary removal", along with the same date restrictions. Now, with the AND inserted before the second NOT, the search produced 31,600 findings, slightly more than the 30,800 that occurred when you truncated the string after the word oophorectomy. Also, the first few findings were similar. So, it still appeared that there was truncation, but that it might have worked a bit differently with this search string variation. But, just how to interpret all this was unclear, as it was not documented in AltaVista Help.

- You then removed the range of dates restriction. This did not have a very significant effect on the number of results. 831 results were obtained this way, compared to the 680 findings obtained *with* the date restriction in place. You had expected a much larger increase.

- Next, you also removed the restriction of the phrase hormone replacement having to be in the title section of the document. As anticipated, the number of findings increased. With both date and title restrictions off, the number of findings rose dramatically, to 37,900, quite a jump from the 831 with the restriction in place. With no title restriction but a date restriction, the number of results decreased to 32,000.

- You then typed menopaus*, thinking that the asterisk might act as a wildcard. AltaVista returned the same number of findings as if you typed the word stub menopaus. Apparently, the asterisk was ignored, and the greatly reduced number of findings showed that word stemming was not done automatically. That is, the exact spelling, without the letter e, was apparently required.

- You typed the field identifier title in the middle of the search string in the advanced Boolean search and moved other terms around a little as well: (hysterectomy OR "uterus removal") AND "hormone replacement therapy" AND **title:**"hormone replacement" AND menopause NOT oophorectomy AND NOT "ovary removal". It made no significant difference in the findings produced. Thus, you concluded that this field operator can be used anywhere in the search string. Notwithstanding, you speculated that the order in which you enter terms can be significant in AltaVista: ➪ Reference Section 6.3: Overall ordering.

- You played around with factoring out brackets. For example, you tried menopause NOT oophorectomy AND NOT "ovary removal", and compared the results from that with those from the logically equivalent menopause NOT (oophorectomy OR "ovary removal"). The results were almost the same. So, you concluded that factoring out brackets basically worked, at least to one level of brackets.

- You dropped the AND field operator from the Boolean text box, and the results changed dramatically. You concluded that entering an explicit Boolean operator was required to produce correct results in the Boolean search string. That is, leaving a blank between search terms in a Boolean phrase was not equivalent to any Boolean operator. The only acceptable Boolean ones in the Boolean text box were AND, NOT, and OR.

Thus, the string (hysterectomy OR "uterus removal") - (oophorectomy OR "ovary removal") produced 30,200 findings, as opposed to the 429,000 when you used NOT instead of the minus sign.

- You tried out the Boolean expression in the text box for the simple Web search. When the same initial search string was placed in the simple Web search text box, without the date range restriction (for which AltaVista appeared not to have a field operator), 874 findings were obtained, as opposed to the 32,600 shown above with the date range restriction. Obviously, the Boolean logic didn't work in the simple search interface, probably because operators such as OR and NOT were interpreted as search terms.

AltaVista: Notes, tips & warnings

⚠ Syntactical constraints:

- All field operators must be in lowercase text, followed by a colon. The operator value must follow the colon directly, with no space in between.
- AND, OR, and NOT Boolean operators must be in uppercase. Minus and plus sign variety of Boolean operators must have no spaces between them and the terms to which they apply.

⚠ A problem occurs when the field type identifier title: is entered into the "this exact phrase" text box; in this case, it appears, title: is taken to be part of the phrase.

Copernic

Overview

Copernic was limited in the number of findings it was able to report. To begin with, it had a maximum of 700 results collected from any one of the 18 search engines it made available for the general web document search (Web search).

In this search, using a simple set of term-based filter requirements, 13 search engines produced around 4.5

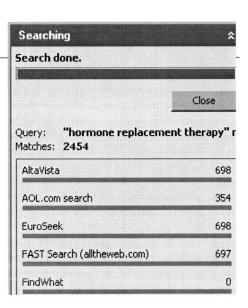

Searching	Close
Search done.	

Query:	"hormone replacement therapy" r
Matches:	2454

AltaVista	698
AOL.com search	354
EuroSeek	698
FAST Search (alltheweb.com)	697
FindWhat	0

thousand findings. Only when all findings were identified did Copernic apply its and your filtration requirements using client-side processing (conducted on your personal computer). This ultimately reduced the original 4.5 thousand findings to a much more manageable 100.

Overall, here's how it worked:

1. First, at the search front-end, you entered the highest denominator of term-based constraints common to all the search engines sourced. The filters could not be made more complex at this stage, which was Copernic's way of recognizing that not all the sourced search engines were able accept the same level of complexity and the same syntax for Boolean and other filters.

   You required the phrase hormone replacement therapy along with the word menopause, but did not yet add the various *other* Boolean constraints needed in this search. Note that you placed the phrase hormone replacement therapy before the word menopause, because the most important terms should always go first to achieve the most relevant results.

2. The approximately 4.5 thousand results were then automatically consolidated by Copernic through elimination of duplicate findings across search engines. This left you with 2,454 results.

3. Next, 204 broken (dead) links were removed, and 48 other findings were filtered out based on criteria such as access timeouts and detecting identical pages coming from different websites. This reduced the number of findings to 2,202.

4. The remaining reductions in findings resulted from your requiring Copernic to apply various filters: (1) date range; (2) more Boolean logic; and (3) restriction to the title section of the document. This ultimately reduced Copernic's final number of findings from 2,202 to 100.

Detailed steps

Here are the details of the steps summarized above:

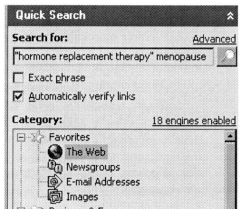

1. You chose the "Advanced" hyperlink in the "Quick Search" part of the screen shown here. When the "New Search" dialog box (see next page) appeared, you:

   a. Filled in the "Search for" text box with the search terms to be sent by Copernic to the various search engines as both being required.

   b. Chose "The Web" category from the drop-down menu box.

c. Selected the "Optimal" radio button to provide the best filtering out of irrelevant results.

d. Under that radio button, checked the now activated checkboxes for "Extract key concepts from pages," and "Keep only results of pages matching."

e. Selected the hyperlink to the right of the "Keep only results of pages matching" checkbox, seen below.

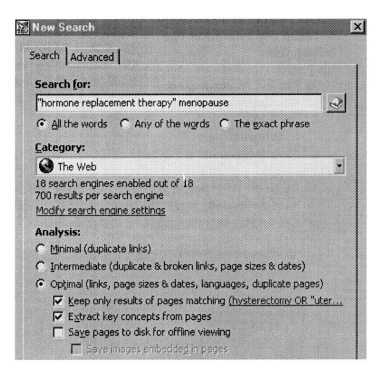

At this point, it is important to note some limitations of Copernic, based on you checking the box "Keep only results of pages matching." If you select this option:

- Skipped files are excluded from the findings. These are files designated as being too large, according to the user-controllable options for file size. Adobe Acrobat (PDF) files are often skipped for this reason.

- The search will skip all files other than ones directly readable by your browser. In addition to PDF files, this includes file types such as Word (DOC) and Excel (XLS). Therefore, your findings only consist of files with name extensions such as HTM, HTML, XHTML, SHTML, ASP, CFM, and TXT, i.e., ordinary ASCII text files.

The first part of the search string you see in the above screenshot (namely, hysterectomy OR "uter...) initially reads "Search keywords" until you go to the next dialog box (see "Refine Parameters" dialog box screenshot on next page) to enter those keywords. You get to that dialog box by clicking on the "Search keywords" link.

2. Copernic then responded with another level of dialog box, entitled "Refine Parameters." You selected the radio button labeled "Keep only results of pages matching the following Boolean query." In the text entry box under that radio button (see below), you:

   a. Entered: **(hysterectomy OR "uterus removal") AND NOT (oophorectomy OR "ovary removal")**.

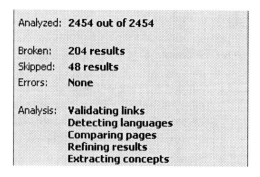
You did not repeat the "hormone replacement therapy" AND menopause part of the Boolean search string in the above box, because they had already been used to filter the findings at the source search engines when the search was first done. Rather, you just entered the **(hysterectomy OR "uterus removal") AND NOT (oophorectomy OR "ovary removal")** part of the string.

   b. Chose the "OK" button to return to the "New Search" dialog box (see previous page). The hyperlink label (hysterectomy OR "uter.... only then appeared in that dialog box.

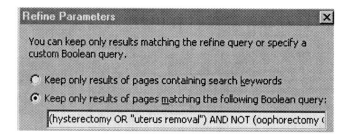

3. You then clicked the "Go" button to start the search. After collecting its initial 4.5 thousand results, Copernic began the analysis phase, to check for broken links, and do other filtering tasks associated with your earlier choice of optimal analysis. The analysis phase took several minutes.

Analyzed:	**2454 out of 2454**
Broken:	**204 results**
Skipped:	**48 results**
Errors:	**None**
Analysis:	**Validating links**
	Detecting languages
	Comparing pages
	Refining results
	Extracting concepts

4. Next, you set the date restriction filter, starting by clicking the "Filters" button above the findings list to display the following dialog box (only part of which is displayed):

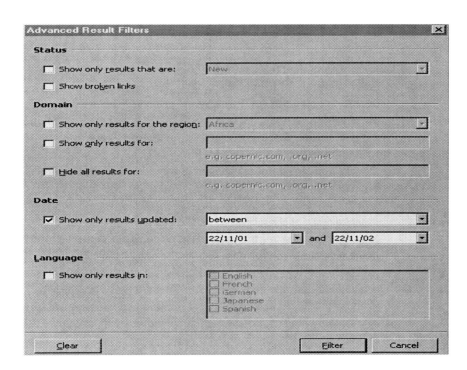

Copernic's status bar, in the bottom left of the screen, now reported "114 results (plus 2340 filtered)." This accounted for most of the filtering needed to satisfy the requirements of this search, including the extra filtering unique to Copernic.

The first several findings in the findings list appeared on the page as follows:

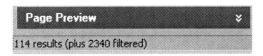

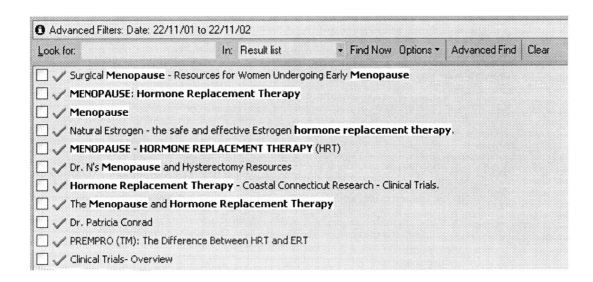

5. Next, you applied the final filter in order to search for the phrase hormone replacement therapy in the page title. While Copernic does not have a filter for this, a search within the results **list** (as opposed to the **whole page contents**) seemed to provide an approximation. This is because the results list contains only metadata (see frame on next page).

> In this search, Copernic compiled some of the metadata itself, because you chose "Optimal analysis," which extracts keywords.

Thus, to apply the final filter, you executed a find in results procedure, to look for the phrase hormone replacement therapy in the results list (all the data seen in the two "Result Properties" panels on the next page). The search executed quickly, because the actual document file on the Internet did not have to be accessed. (This would have been necessary if the find had been applied against the whole document with the "Find in each page contents" option.)

The screen for the first few findings that showed after this further filtering (with the view set to an intermediate detail level) was as follows. (To see the screenshot in full resolution, go to ⇨ www.searchhelpcenter.com/effective-internet-search-copernic-screenshots.html#Results medium view, "Results medium view.")

After all filters had been applied, the final result of 100 findings now appeared in the status bar.

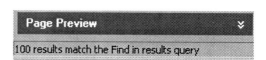

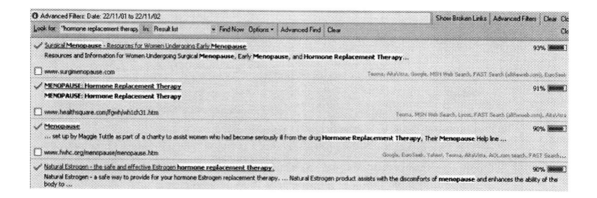

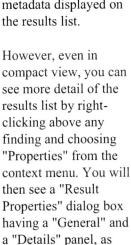 **Metadata for each finding:**

While some listings of findings shows only one line per finding (usually the document title), Copernic actually retains much more metadata for each finding. You have the choice of three levels of detail for showing each finding; the least detailed is shown above. ⇨ Chapter 4: Case #1: Stock Investment Search, to see all findings metadata displayed on the results list.

However, even in compact view, you can see more detail of the results list by right-clicking above any finding and choosing "Properties" from the context menu. You will then see a "Result Properties" dialog box having a "General" and a "Details" panel, as shown here.

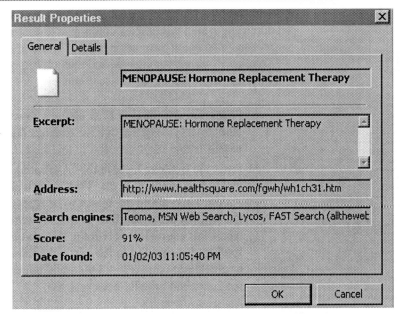

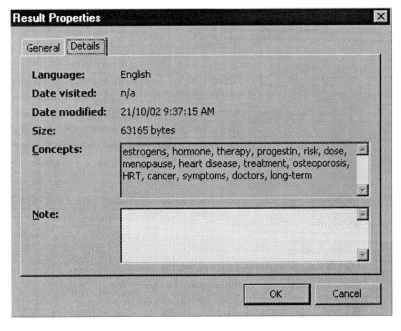

6. Next, to collect some of the other statistics needed to compare the various search engines in this case example, you re-entered the search with no date filtering. You could have achieved this by using either the "Modify" or "Duplicate" search commands, and then changing the search filters. However, what you did in this case was to:

   a. First eliminate the date filter settings, using the button to clear filters (located above the findings display on the right of that button bar).

   b. Enter the Boolean logic in the "Advanced Find In Results" dialog box, along with the "Find in each page contents" option. This caused the search to be repeated with access to the original document files from their websites. So, the time taken was equivalent to redoing the search on the 2,454 findings (as opposed to the minus the time taken to find the original approximately 4.5 thousand documents from which the 2,454 had initially been selected).

As expected, the search "within results" procedure resulted in **re-expanding** the number of findings, since the date filter was gone. Now, the search reports 468 results after filtering.

Below are the first several findings and the area of the screen above the findings obtained by you. (To see the screenshot in full resolution, go to ⇨ www. SearchHelpCenter.com/effective-internet-search-copernic-screenshots.html, "Results compact view #3.")

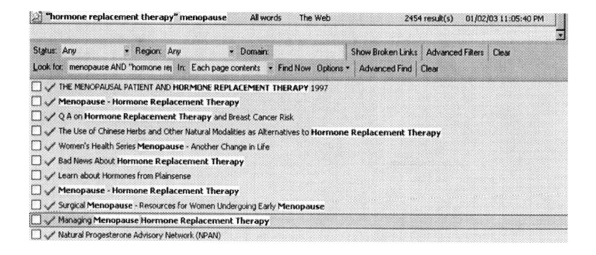

7. Finally, you once again *refined* the search in the direction of limiting the

latest round of findings, to require that the term hormone replacement therapy be present in the results list for the latest 468 results — rendering 435 findings. No new access to the findings on the Internet was needed, since you were finding what you needed in the results list (rather than in "each page's contents")

At last, you have produced all the statistics needed to compare Copernic with the other search engines selected for this case example.

Search variations tested

You didn't have to enter the extra Boolean logic filters with you original search, but could have applied those filters later. So, to see what the differences would be, you also did an equivalent "Find in results" procedure after redoing the search with just the highest common denominator terms (see above). After that, you used the following dialog to apply the further Boolean logic filters:

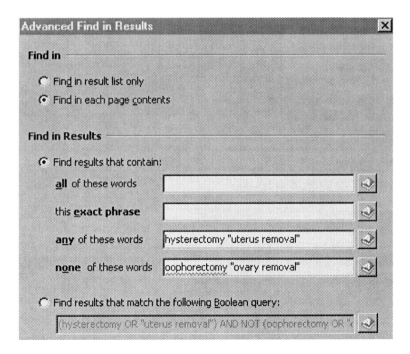

But this was not a simple find within results. Since you chose "Find in each page contents," Copernic repeated the whole analysis phase to check for broken links, etc. The actual pages on the Internet were then accessed; thus, the filtering took several minutes.

Operator parameter equivalence: As you filled out the text boxes in the above dialog box, an equivalent search string with Boolean operator parameters built in gray in the text box below the radio button labeled "Find results that match the following Boolean query." If you had clicked the radio button after entering all the data shown above, you would have switched to the approach of maximizing the entry of operator parameters. In effect, you could have simply chosen the radio button directly and typed in the whole Boolean search string yourself, as you see here.

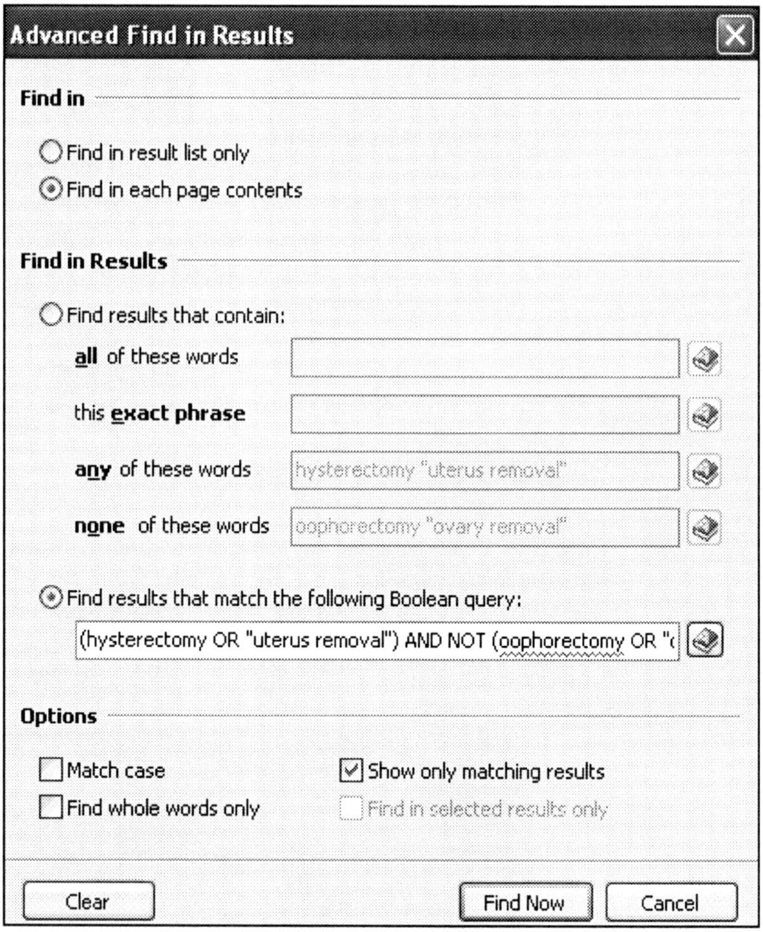

Advanced Find in Results

Find in
- ○ Find in result list only
- ● Find in each page contents

Find in Results
- ○ Find results that contain:
  - **all** of these words [   ]
  - this **exact phrase** [   ]
  - **any** of these words [hysterectomy "uterus removal"]
  - **none** of these words [oophorectomy "ovary removal"]
- ● Find results that match the following Boolean query:
  - [(hysterectomy OR "uterus removal") AND NOT (oophorectomy OR "( ]

Options
- ☐ Match case
- ☐ Find whole words only
- ☑ Show only matching results
- ☐ Find in selected results only

[Clear]   [Find Now] [Cancel]

Copernic: Notes, tips & warnings

It appears that Copernic has no problems with different ways of stating Boolean logic using operator parameters. It can nest brackets within brackets and handle all the standard variations. As well, all the different notations normally used for Boolean operators are supported in a consistent fashion.

Copernic has spell checking, and warns you of search terms not found in its dictionary. Its spellchecker is in its client-side application, rather than on the Web. So, you receive notification of spelling errors in terms as you enter them, rather than after you press the button to do the search.

Google

Search entry with minimal operator parameters

In the Google advanced Web search screen (see below), you:

- Selected "past year" in the "Date" drop-down menu box to restrict the search to finding documents aged less than a year. You could also have selected file age in a more precise fashion by using Google's **daterange:** field operator. However, in this case, since the date was November 26th, 2004, just one day different from that used in the case examples done for the other search engines, you felt that the past year would be sufficiently accurate to produce a reasonable comparison.

  Also, the **daterange:** field operator works in terms of Julian dates, which you would have needed to calculate first, using certain mathematical functions (⇨ Reference Section 6.2: File age). Here's an example: **daterange:2452389-2522450.**

- Entered **intitle:"hormone replacement" menopause (hysterectomy OR "uterus removal") -"ovary removal".**

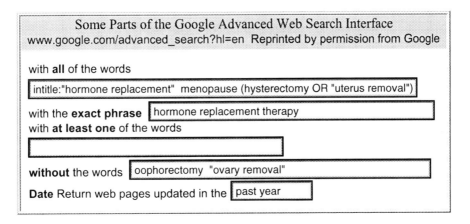

Google could not handle the full query, because, at the time the search was done, it had a maximum of ten words per query, not including operator parameters (but including individual words within phrases). Since the query was 12 words long, Google truncated two words. You arranged that to be the words in the phrase ovary removal, based on the fact that Google parsed the words from the above boxes from left to right and from top to bottom.

Certain operator parameters cannot be avoided in these text boxes. Specifically:

- In a Boolean expression, which you enter with Google in the "with **all** the words" text entry box, leaving nothing between terms, gives the same result as placing either AND between the term of + sign in front of the second term.
- The quotes around hormone replacement, uterus removal, and ovary removal indicate phrases.
- The intitle: before the phrase hormone replacement is a field operator that instructs the search engine to look for the phrase in the title section of the HTML document.

Google showed the parsed search string near the top of the results page, as you can see below. (Note: The word removal below has a minus sign added in front by Google, and was not entered that way by you.) Based on these reduced entries, Google produced 2,650 findings; the first two of these in each category (regular versus sponsored listings) are shown below.

Part of the Findings on a First Google Findings Page:
Reproduced with the permission of Google

Web Results 1 - 10 of about 2,650 over the past year for
intitle:"hormone replacement" menopause (hysterectomy OR "uterus removal") "hormone replacement therapy" -oophorectomy -"ovary -removal"

hormone replacement therapy

Hormone Replacement Therapy is the substituion of naturally occuring hormones ... woman has had a **hysterectomy** that removes ... begin with the onset of the **menopause**. ...
www.**hysterectomy**-association.org.uk/learn/hrt/hrt.htm - 10k - Cached - Similar pages

Hormone Replacement Therapy

... surgery due to a complete **hysterectomy**, all women ... at **menopause** as they did before **menopause**. ... on how estrogen and progestin **hormone replacement therapy** is used ...
www.**hormone-replacement-therapy**.com/ - Similar pages

Sponsored Links

Hysterectomy ?
Pre-Op decisions, Post-Op Support
Hyster Sisters for live help now
www.hystersisters.com

Hysterectomy Fears?
The Worried Woman's Guide to a
Happy **Hysterectomy**. Stay positive.
www.happyhysterectomy.com

You then selected "Search within results" at the bottom of Google's results page, but it still would not add the last negation condition because of the total number of words being over Google's limit.

You then discovered another way to add three more words to the query terms by using Google's "Search within results" link at the bottom of the screen. It appears next to a text box containing the integrated search string generated by Google. You clicked that link, bringing you to a new, empty text entry box to add to the search string. You typed -"ovary removal" into that box. However, when you clicked the search button once again, Google returned a message indicating that the search string was still too long.

So, search within results feature did not work as you had hoped. In effect, the feature simply adds more to the search string or to a revision thereof, rather than generating an entirely new one for search within results. That being the case, the feature would more correctly be labeled as "Revise search" than "Search within results."

Another feature that did not work as well as you would have liked is the range of dates. Since you could not specify exact dates without the complex daterange: field operator, you simply chose the "Past Year" option. This was one day after the same range of dates as used for the other search engines in this case example.

Search entry with maximal operator parameters

In the Google advanced Web search screen, you entered the following string in the "with **all** the words" text box:

> intitle:"hormone replacement" menopause
> (hysterectomy OR "uterus removal") "hormone
> replacement therapy" -oophorectomy -"ovary removal"

As before, you also selected "year" in the "Date" drop-down menu box to restrict the search to finding documents aged less than a year.

In the Boolean expression:

- You did not place AND before any terms, because this is the default. (If you had done so, Google would have reminded you of this when it listed the findings.)
- The quotes around groups of words in four places indicate phrases.
- The intitle: before the phrase hormone replacement is a field operator that instructs the search engine to look for the phrase in the title section of the HTML document.

Based on these entries, Google again produced the error message that the search string was too long. As before, Google dropped the last two words, so the -"ovary removal" negation was not executed in producing the list of findings. This time Google reported the same 2,980 results, even without the date restriction. You wondered why the date restriction had not played a role in selecting results.

So, you decided to to use Google's daterange: field operator. Would it be counted in the 10-word limit? To find out, you entered the string: daterange:2452968-2453334 intitle:"hormone replacement" menopause (hysterectomy OR "uterus removal") "hormone replacement therapy" -oophorectomy -"ovary removal". (This date range is equivalent to Nov. 25th 2003 to Nov. 25th 2004.)

This time, the search produced just 956 findings, and the first few findings were a bit different. Google also ended the search string from the word oophorectomy, indicating that the two Julian date numbers counted for two words. The number of results was beginning to approximate that found by AlltheWeb and AltaVista. You concluded that the "Past year" limitation you had entered above did not have any effect, but that the daterange: field operator did.

In sum, without both the range of dates restriction and elimination of results having the phrase ovary removal, you obtained 2,650 findings with Google. With the date restriction present, but with both negation conditions absent, your received just 956 results. Presumably, the number of results would have been a few hundred lower had you been able to get Google to apply all your conditions.

Some conclusions: Google does not have a "Search within findings" feature that would be effective in this case. And with its 10-word limit, there is no way to have it use all the search terms.

In addition, Google does not itself seem to limit by file age unless you use its not too user-friendly Julian dates field operator. However, some third-party software, based on Google's catalog, can limit by date using conventional date formats: ⇨ Reference Section 6.2: File age, the Fagan Finder.

Search variations tested

- As witnessed, *Google at the time* was not able to fully handle a query of more than 10 words. Although the impact was reduced in this particular search, this kind of limitation can pose a serious problem in some complex searches. And this is particularly true now that it no longer has the ability to search within the previous round of findings. One way to get around this is to use Google's wildcard character, the asterisk (*), to replace whole words either within a phrase or in any search string: ⇨ Reference Section 6.1: Wildcards, substrings, stemming.

In this search, being over the limit by two words, you tried to substitute the two occurrences of the word removal with this wildcard, as follows: intitle:"hormone replacement" "hormone replacement therapy" menopause (hysterectomy OR "uterus *") -oophorectomy -"ovary *". This time 4,030 findings were reported for the past year, almost twice as many as before the asterisks were inserted.

- As seen above, you were able to significantly increase the number of findings by not using the date range restriction. The two negation conditions seemed less important. However, you could not quantify the latter due to Google's 10-word limit (currently a 32-word limit). You wondered if the reason the date restriction did not work, when chosen from the drop-down menu box, was that it brought Google over its word limit. So, you entered the simpler phrase hormone replacement with and without the "Past year" selection. Indeed, Google reported 1,990,000 findings with the restriction, and 2,270,000 ones without it. So, you concluded that the date restriction in the initial search had been dropped because of the word limit.

- Next, you also removed the restriction of the phrase hormone replacement having to be in the title section of the document. As anticipated, the number of findings increased, namely, from 2,650 to 49,100. Clearly, the title restriction was very important.

- You then typed menopaus*, thinking that the asterisk might act as a wildcard. Google returned the same number of findings as if you typed the word stub menopaus. Apparently, the asterisk was ignored, and the greatly reduced number of findings showed that word stemming was not done automatically. That is, the exact spelling, without the letter e, was apparently required. This is despite the fact that other sources you checked indicated that Google does automatic stemming: ⇨ Reference Section 6.1: Wildcards, substrings, stemming. So, you were unsure what happened here.

  However, you did check another search string to test for automatic stemming. This feature can be suppressed by entering a plus sign in front of a word. So, you compared effective internet search with +effective internet +search, and found that the former produced more findings than the latter. So, although there was no significant effect of automatic stemming evident in your health-related search, you could see that it worked in other searches.

- You typed the field identifier intitle: at a location other than the front of the search string: (hysterectomy OR "uterus removal") menopause "hormone replacement therapy" intitle:"hormone replacement" -oophorectomy -"ovary removal". It made no apparent significant difference in the findings produced. Thus, you concluded that this field operator can be used anywhere in the search string. Notwithstanding, you speculated that the order in which you enter terms can be significant in Google: ⇨ Reference Section 6.3: Overall ordering.

Google: Notes, tips & warnings

⚠ Google's documentation did not warn you that you cannot handle phrases or field operators in any but the first text box. If you used any box other than this one to enter phrases or field operators, you would have concluded that the following kinds of problems occur:

- All the words in the "with the exact phrase" box are taken to form a single phrase. Any field operators, such as intitle, are also taken to be words.
- The phrase negation -"ovary removal", when entered in the "**without** the words" text box, is parsed by Google into -"ovary - removal" instead of -"ovary removal", which is not the same logic.
- Similarly, the expression (hysterectomy OR "uterus removal") cannot be entered in the "with **at least one** of the words" text box. Only individual words can be used there without causing an error. If you do put hysterectomy "uterus removal" inside that text box, Google will generate the Boolean string hysterectomy OR "uterus OR removal", which is not used by Google for the same logic.

⚠ You needed to use intitle rather than allintitle as the field operator in this case example, because the latter requires all words and phrases to the right of it to be in the title. However, the intitle field indicator can be placed anywhere in the Boolean search string.

⚠ All field operators must be in lowercase text, followed by a colon. The operator value must follow the colon directly, with no space in between.

⚠ AND, OR, and NOT Boolean operators must be in uppercase. Minus and plus sign variety of Boolean operators must have no spaces between them and the terms after.

💡 Google has spelling assistance. When you spelled the word oophorectomy with an "e" instead of an "o" in the fifth character position, it suggested a spelling change.

💡 In essence, Google provided you with the ability to edit previous search parameters, since a new text box was presented on the findings page, containing the various terms and parameters (expressed as operator parameters, whenever possible, even if not entered as such). All you had to do was revise the information in the text box and resubmit the search.

- You experimented with using NOT instead of the minus sign in front of a term. The number of findings were reduced in such a way that you had to conclude that NOT was taken to be another search term rather than a Boolean operator.

- You played around with factoring out brackets. For example, you tried menopause -oophorectomy -"ovary removal", and compared the results from that with those from the logically equivalent menopause - (oophorectomy OR "ovary removal"). The results were 2,590,000 in the former case, and just 32,300 findings in the latter. So, you concluded that factoring out brackets does not work with Google.

- You also tried donkey (cat OR dog), donkey cat OR dog, and (donkey cat) OR dog, but received no difference in the number of findings. You therefore concluded that Google probably does not handle prioritization of Boolean operator application based on brackets.

- You tried out the Boolean expression in the text box for the simple Web search. When the same initial search string was placed in the simple Web search text box, without the date range restriction. You received 2,990 results, as before. So, you concluded that operator parameters appear to work in simple search as in the advanced search interface.

MSN Search

Search entry with minimal operator parameters

MSN Search provides a "Search Builder" option that helps you to avoid direct entry of operator parameters. In the procedure you used, you clicked the "Add to search" button to generate the following search terms in the given order to search string near the top of the search entry form:

1. The "hormone replacement": by typing in the words without the quotes in conjunction with selecting "The exact phrase" in the drop-down menu.
2. The word menopause: by typing in the word in conjunction with choosing "All of these terms."
3. The quotes around "hormone replacement therapy": as in #1.
4. The brackets around and the OR between the word hysterectomy and the phrase uterus removal, to give (hysterectomy or "ovary removal"): by typing both each of these terms into the generator text box. However, you yourself were forced to type the quotes around the phrase, instead of having these phrase operators being automatically generated. In conjunction with your typing, you selected "Any of these terms." Unfortunately, when you clicked the "Add to search" button, the "Search Builder" generated three or for OR's, instead of just one, so you had to manually delete the extra OR's from the generated search string.
5. The -oophorectomy (which is equivalent to NOT oophorectomy): by typing in the word in connection with choosing "None of these terms."

6. The -"ovary removal" (which is equivalent to NOT "ovary removal"): by typing in the term, with quotes around the phrase having to be manually entered by you, in conjunction with choosing "None of these terms."

As you can see, the "Search Builder" was unable to automatically generate strings involving phrases mixed with individual words in connection with "Any of these terms" and "None of these terms" options. As well, even when you put the quotes around the phrase yourself, #4 above actually resulted in an error that had to be manually corrected by you in the generated search string.

Search entry with maximal operator parameters

Following the specifications for Boolean operator parameters given in MSN Search Help, you entered the following string in its advanced (Web) search text box:

> **"hormone replacement" menopause "hormone replacement therapy" (hysterectomy OR "uterus removal") NOT oophorectomy NOT "ovary removal"**

In the Boolean expression:

- The quotes around groups of words in four places indicate phrases.
- There is no field operator available to indicate that the phrase hormone replacement must occur in the document title, so you were unable to constrain the search in this way.
- You were also unable to restrict the findings by date range.

MSN Search produced 36,661 findings. The first couple of matches are shown below.

List of Findings on MSN Search Findings Page: Reprinted with permission from Microsoft

Web Results
1-10 of 36,661 containing **"hormone replacement" menopause "hormone replacement therapy" (hysterectomy OR "uterus removal") NOT oophorectomy NOT "ovary removal"** (0.18 seconds)

Questions Regarding **Menopause Hysterectomy** And HRT
... Poison? Part 2: **Hormone Replacement Therapy** Is A Personal Choice Part 3: What Is Optimum **Hormone Replacement**? How To Find A HRT ... altered by their **menopause, hysterectomy,** or both. This ... menopausehysterectomy.com/askdr2.htm Cached page

Questions Regarding **Menopause Hysterectomy** And HRT
... Poison? Part 2: **Hormone Replacement Therapy** Is A Personal Choice Part 3: What Is Optimum **Hormone Replacement**? How To Find A HRT ... altered by their **menopause, hysterectomy,** or both. This ... www.menopausehysterectomy.com/askdr.htm Cached page

---

From the number of findings, it appeared that the number of findings was comparable to those of the other search engines (Copernic aside), once the restrictions of document title and date range had been removed.

Search variations tested

- MSN Help [search.msn.com/docs/help.aspx? t=SEARCH_GS_ABCsOfFindingInformation.htm] indicated that MSN Search was able to handle only 150 characters in a search string, presumably not including any of the operator parameters. Fortunately, your search string was well within that limit, being only 103 characters long.

- You wanted to see if MSN Search could handle wildcards and whether using the stemming checkbox would produce the same kind of effect as a wildcard at the end of a word. To do so, you typed menopaus* as part of the above search string, thinking that the asterisk might act as a wildcard. MSN Search returned only 230 findings. The same occurred when you entered menopaus instead of menopause. Apparently, the asterisk was ignored.

  However, it was unclear whether MSN Search stemmed words. This was because one of the sliders (⇨ Reference Section 6.3: Overall ordering) available for sequencing the findings allowed different degrees of approximate term matches. Thus, it was likely that some form of word stemming was automatic.

- You were also unable to restrict the findings by date range. However, MSN search had one way of sorting findings (see below) that may be partially similar to sorting them by age. In fact, MSN Search provides a few ways of prioritizing the findings display (⇨ Reference Section 6.3: Overall ordering). Thus, you moved the "degree of update frequency" slider to from mid-way between "static" to "updated recently" to the latter, and left the other two sliders (degree of result popularity and degree to which the match is approximate) in the middle of their ranges. This changed the order of the display of results, although the degree to which this was similar to sorting the findings by their age was still unclear to you.

- You then experimented with moving the various terms into different locations in the search string. You tried: (hysterectomy OR "uterus removal") -oophorectomy -"ovary removal" menopause "hormone replacement therapy" "hormone replacement". It made no apparent significant difference in the *quantity* of findings produced. However, the results were displayed in a very different order. This indicated that the order of entry of the terms was significant.

- You played around with factoring out brackets. For example, you tried menopause -oophorectomy -"ovary removal", and compared the results from that with those from the logically equivalent menopause -(oophorectomy OR "ovary removal"). The former produced 2,989,694 results, as opposed to the 5,231,624 results rendered when brackets were used. However, at least the first pages of findings were the same. How to interpret this was unclear to you.

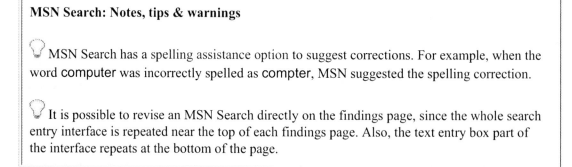

MSN Search: Notes, tips & warnings

MSN Search has a spelling assistance option to suggest corrections. For example, when the word computer was incorrectly spelled as compter, MSN suggested the spelling correction.

It is possible to revise an MSN Search directly on the findings page, since the whole search entry interface is repeated near the top of each findings page. Also, the text entry box part of the interface repeats at the bottom of the page.

Comparative analysis

Statistics

Constraining Parameters - Table 1: Search engines varied in their abilities to handle the requested parameters in the health-related search problem. Table 1, shown on the next page, summarizes these findings.

In Table 1, column number:

1. Contains the names of the search engines.
2. Demonstrates all search engines, except for Google, were able to handle the entire set of words used in the search string. Google truncated the string by two words. As a result, less restrictions were placed on its scope of findings. In this particular query, it probably did not make much difference to the results obtained. However, in other kinds of queries, this kind of limitation could prove to be serious.

   Nor does Google's "Search within results" feature circumvent the problem, as previously explained. But Google's single word wildcard is sometimes useful in handling the word-limit problem.

3. Indicates a factor that may affect the number of findings reported, depending on how they are summarized. Copernic derives its results from other search engines, so between one and two findings per site is likely a fair guess.
4. Shows all the search engines were able to implement the logic requiring at least one of the terms hysterectomy and uterus removal be found in any matched document.

Table 1: Constraining Parameters

(1) SEARCH ENGINE	Primary Parameters	Term-Based Filters				Metadata-Based Filters	
	(2) All of the search terms used?	(3) Max. of just 1 match per website?	(4) "At least one," or "any of these" interpretation?	(5) Negation (must not have term)?	(6) Wildcards or stemming?	(7) Must occur in title?	(8) Date range (past year)?
AlltheWeb	Yes	1 or 2	Yes	Yes	No	Yes	Yes
AltaVista	Yes	1 or 2	Yes	Yes	No	Yes	Yes
Copernic	Yes	Likely 1 to 2	Yes	Yes	No	Roughly	Yes
Google	No; 2 words truncated due to 10 word limit	No, up to 2 is the way it works	Yes	Yes	Whole word replacement & stemming	Yes	Yes
MSN Search	Yes	Up to 2 is the default	Yes	Yes	Likely has stemming	No	No

5. Demonstrates all of the search engines were able to implement the requirement that oophorectomy and ovary removal not be present in any matched document.

6. Indicates only Google was used to expand the scope of the findings *in a controlled way* using wildcards.

7. Establishes that only MSN Search was unable to limit the scope of the findings based on the requirement that hormone replacement be present in the result's title, as previously explained.

8. Shows all the search engines, except for MSN Search, were able to exclude findings aged more than a year before the date of the search.

Findings per Search Engine - Table 2: The number of findings from each search engine are compared, based on various combinations and restrictions of operator parameters.

In the table on the next page, two rows are provided per search engine in columns 9 to 12:

- **Minimum** — indicates the number of finds made on the basis of minimizing the number of operator parameters.
- **Maximum** — indicates the number of finds made on the basis of maximizing the number of operator parameters.

Comparisons: In theory, if both approaches — minimum and maximum use of operator parameters — are equivalent, the top and bottom figure in each column for each search engine should be identical.

Table 2: Findings Per Search Engine					
(1) **SEARCH ENGINE**	**Result based on minimum or maximum usage of operator parameters**	**(9)** **With all filters, any automatic stemming "on," and noted filters absent**	**(10)** **Same as (9), plus date filter explicitly removed**	**(11)** **Same as (10), plus title filter removed (only term-based filters)**	**(12)** **Same as (11), plus stemming actively turned "on" by a switch**
AlltheWeb	Minimum:	N/A by this route			
	Maximum:	875		35,700	N/A
AltaVista	Minimum:	680	831	37,900	
	Maximum:	N/A by this route			
Copernic	Minimum:	100	435	Situation cannot be compared with those of the other search engines	
	Maximum:				
Google	Minimum:	956; but without two negation filters working	2,650; but without one negation filter working	49,100; but without one negation filter working; automatic stemming still "on," as in columns 8 and 9	
	Maximum:				
MSN Search	Minimum:	N/A: Date & title filters not available.		36,661	
	Maximum:				

In the above table, column number:

9. Contains the number of search results with all filters working. This applies except for:

  - Google having to drop some term-based filters, namely two negation (NOT) conditions, because of the 10-word limit (now increased to 32) it had at the time of this study.
  - AlltheWeb apparently not being able to use one of its metadata-based filters, namely its date filter, because of the query string size.

  With regards to term-based filters, Google's automatic stemming appears to have had no effect on the results. It is unclear whether AlltheWeb and AltaVista had any automatic stemming features.

10. Contains the number of findings made by the search engines when one of the metadata-based filters, the date criterion, was dropped. Google also had to drop one of its term-based filters, namely one negation (NOT) condition, because of its 10-word limit.

11. Contains the number of findings made by the search engine when both the date and title section metadata-based filters were eliminated. Again, the last negation condition was dropped by Google because of its 10-word limit.

12. Contains the maximum number of findings, with both metadata-based filters dropped, and any automatic word stemming. Again, the last negation condition was dropped by Google, because of its 10-word limit.

Statistical summary

As you can see in the last column of Table 2:

- Except for wildcards, only AltaVista and Copernic appeared to have been able to implement all the filters. However, Copernic's application of the title filter was less exact, since it does not have a precise method for that.
- Google and apparently AlltheWeb could not apply all the filters due to ceilings on the number of words possible in a search string. Google had to drop both negation conditions when date filtering was applied, and one of those conditions even when date filtering was not applied. AlltheWeb apparently could not make use of its date filters in this case, probably due to the search string length.
- MSN Search does not have date and title section filters.
- Copernic has the fewest matches in each comparable column, but they are more filtered in each case, based on:
  - A limitation of extracting just 700 findings per source search engine.

> › Dropping of websites that could not be accessed when rechecked at the time of the search.
> › Discarding of certain documents due to their format or length.

These items reflect the restrictions used by Copernic (⇨ Chapter 4: Search requirements and approach, for the health-related search).

While the other search engines report a greater base of documents from which to discover pertinent findings, honors for the largest number of **relevant** documents explored may well belong to Copernic. This is because it refers to all the above search engines and others to extract the most relevant documents from each, integrating the best into a more targeted set of results. It also has the unique ability to filter out dead links and duplicate files, again improving its overall quality.

Some conclusions

No amount of knowledge or experience can prepare you for all the problems and quirks you may encounter using search engines. Here are conclusions about each search engine's ease of use.

Search Engine Usability Comparison	
Search Engine	**User-Friendliness**
AlltheWeb	In the 2002 version of this study, AlltheWeb provided well-designed text entry boxes allowing inexperienced users to bypass complex Boolean phrases, if so desired, placing focus on search problems rather than on learning complicated syntax. We are amazed to find that this stand-out feature and excellent selling point has now been simplified to the point that avoidance of the maximal operator parameter entry route is possible. Given the above and the complexity of our health-related case, AlltheWeb now has to rely on users being completely familiar with syntax of Boolean expressions because operator parameter use cannot be minimized in a relatively complex search; all term-based filters must be entered in a single Boolean phrase; the greater the complexity of Boolean expression, the more problems people unfamiliar with syntax will have.
AltaVista	Works well if user is familiar with some Boolean logic syntax; if so, very few quirks encountered related to usage of text entry boxes and operator parameters. However, certain quirks occur, as documented earlier.

Copernic	Has unique, sophisticated post-processing abilities. Has no major quirks; user help messages could be improved to explain its unconventional series of dialog boxes to enter Boolean logic in conjunction with choice of optimal search analysis. Speed of results compilation is fine if broken links are not checked, more sophisticated analyses are not specified, and maximum number of findings per source search engine is restricted to a "reasonable" quantity; otherwise, may have to wait several minutes. Under certain circumstances, all non-ASCII text files (Adobe Acrobat-PDF, Microsoft Word-DOC, Microsoft Excel-XLS, etc.) may be skipped or dropped when complex Boolean filters are applied; problem can be avoided by use of "Find in Results" procedure, i.e., filters applied on a post-processing basis.
Google	Use of boxes and syntax can be quirky, compounded by lack of documentation in user Help. However, if you understand Boolean syntax, composite Boolean strings, generated by integrating contents of text entry boxes ("query rewrite"), are shown on each findings page; this facilitates understanding of what search engine has done with entries placed in various text boxes.
MSN Search	Requires users to be familiar with syntax of Boolean expressions because operator parameter use cannot be fully eliminated in this kind of relatively complex search; the greater the complexity of expression, the more problems people unfamiliar with Boolean syntax will have.

Final conclusion: Based upon all of the preceding analysis, Copernic first and AltaVista second appeared best able to conduct a search of this complexity. AltaVista was simpler to use, but did not draw upon the data cataloged by Yahoo and other major data suppliers.

Case #4: Industrial-Strength Search

You wanted to find all people on the Web named Judy (or Judith or Judi) Gill, possibly with a middle initial or name, along with their work telephone numbers, if possible. At first, this looked like it might be a rather simple search problem. But, as you did it, you realized that the problem was actually rather intractable, without anything close to a perfect solution. In fact, you realized that this was an "industrial-strength" problem, in that collecting your data could take many days of your precious time.

Following the search strategy outlined in Chapter 2 of this book, you experimented with a few different search tools, in the hope of finding the appropriate set of search tools specialized in finding persons.

Specialized person-finder tools

Based on the Search Tool Guide at toolguide.searchhelpcenter.com, you noticed a few all-in-one search tools for finding people. You linked to the one at www. freeality.com/findi.htm. You tried out some of these tools, including the ones at international.addresses.com/directory/U.html, www.whitepages.com/10692, and the advanced searches at ZoomInfo (www.zoominfo.com).

Except for the tool at ZoomInfo, none of these person-finder tools appeared to you to be appropriate candidates for the job at hand. For one thing, these tools only located people's home addresses, whereas you wanted their work phone numbers, if possible. Second, even the international ones only appeared to cover certain countries, whereas you wanted to extend your search over the whole world and the whole Internet.

The tool at ZoomInfo, though, was specially designed to produce information from all over the world about people, their jobs, and their places of work. Also, when you searched on Judy, the tool also pulled out names like Judith and Judi, thereby showing that it automatically considered variations of popular names. Also, it automatically included middle initials and names. The first few results are shown next.

Results Ranked by Web Popularity	
1.	Judith I. Gill at Commonwealth Corporation **Judith I. Gill** - Chancellor, **Board of Higher Education** Summary automatically generated using 163 references found on the web
2.	Judi Gill at Amsterdam Digital City Speakers | Eric Kearley | Robert Fahle | **Judi Gill** | Attila Gazdag | Ion Valaskakis | Robert Leach | John Curtis | Mike Short ...... (more) Summary automatically generated using 12 references found on the web
3.	Judith Gill at Allen & Overy LLP **Judith Gill** is a partner in **Allen & Overy LLP**. **Judith** has been a partner in the litigation department since 1992. **She**... (more) Summary automatically generated using 9 references found on the web

This seemed like a very good tool for the job, although business phone numbers were not shown directly. However, you did notice a couple of inter-related problems after experimenting with the tool a little more:

- You tried searching on the name of someone you knew. The name and the right person were in the ZoomInfo database, but her place of work was about five years out of date, despite the fact that many pages were on the web having her name and indicating her latest place of work. Why had ZoomInfo not been able to obtain the correct data?

- Certain people at your own place of work were not visible in the results when you searched on their name, despite the fact that their names were obtainable via the web when you did a search on the staff directory at you own place of work. The problem was clearly that ZoomInfo had scraped its database from the surface web only, whereas a dynamic query against the *structured* database at your place of work had to be generated to obtain the missing staff members. In other words, ZoomInfo's database was missing deep web data, and only pulling data off of webpages.

Even more importantly, ZoomInfo had no post-processing abilities, e.g., for making annotations and keeping organized records of findings after you had explored them. In this kind of search, most of your time would be needed to post-process the results. Finding the results would only take a few minutes, in contrast.

So, the ZoomInfo tool was pretty good, but it was obviously far from perfect. Therefore, you continued searching with other tools, trying to find an even better match for your needs.

Mainstream search engines

You next tried the search using MSN Search, AltaVista, and Google. You entered the following search string into all three:

> "Judy Gill" OR "Judith Gill" OR "Judi Gill" OR "Judy * Gill" OR "Judith * Gill" OR "Judi * Gill" OR "Gill, Judy" OR "Gill, Judith" OR "Gill, Judi"

The asterisk was intended as a single word replacement wildcard, to pick up a single middle initial or name.

MSN Search: Based on the number of results not changing when the phrases with asterisks were removed, you could tell that MSN Search ignored the asterisk. In other words, it was treated as a stop word.

AltaVista: Although not documented in AltaVista Help, the asterisk appears to have worked as expected, increasing the number of findings to include those with a middle initial or name. You were not able to tell whether the asterisk in AltaVista stands for zero to one words/initials, or exactly one word/initial, but that was of no consequence in this case.

So, AltaVista could find your data pretty well. But, AltaVista, like ZoomInfo, did not have the needed post-processing abilities.

Google: In Google, because you had read some books on it, you knew that the asterisk was a wildcard to replace exactly one word/initial. So, the search worked as you needed, as it had with AltaVista. Nevertheless, the number of findings was not identical to that with AltaVista, because AltaVista sources the Yahoo Web catalog, while Google sources its own.

So, Google too could find your data pretty well. Also, Google had some very primitive post-processing abilities, which allowed you to keeping your search history online, with the single other post-processing ability of allowing deletion of selected items found by your search.

You speculated that, by using Google, AltaVista, ZoomInfo, and perhaps MSN Search (which accesses the Microsoft Web catalog) in tandem, and by eliminating duplicates, you should able to obtain a fairly complete set of findings of webpages on the surface web. With ZoomInfo, the legwork of associating the person with the place of work had been done for you, albeit with some inaccuracies, so you figured you might also take advantage of that.

But, the problems remained of how to:

- Integrate the results from your different sources.
- Bring the results all together into some *shared* post-processing database, for you to peruse and annotate at your leisure.
- Obtain more comprehensive findings by accessing deep web sources.

So, you moved on to try out a meta search tool that could not only integrate data from the different source catalogs, but also effectively and efficiently handle the needed post-processing task. The one that seemed to be the most appropriate was Copernic Agent (or, specifically, Copernic Agent Professional).

Copernic Agent Professional meta search tool

Using the advanced search interface (see next page), you selected the "any of these words" radio button, along with the search string:

> "Judy Gill" "Judith Gill" "Judi Gill" "Gill, Judy" "Gill, Judith"
> "Gill, Judi"

Unfortunately, you could not find a way of picking up names with a middle name or initial, since Copernic did not do single word wildcards.

You selected "The Web" as your search category, and all the different search sources available. You also set a ceiling of 700 findings per sourced search engine, which was the maximum supported by Copernic.

It was not necessary to do a "Find in Results" with Copernic, since everything you needed except names having middle initials or names was already obtained in the Analysis phase.

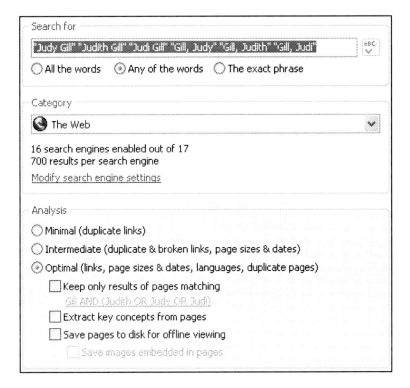

You then ran the search. As expected, since Copernic integrates the data from all of Google (via AOL Search), Yahoo, Microsoft, and other search catalogs, Copernic produced about forty percent more results than the other search tools. It also dropped dead links (inactive web sources). Unfortunately, Copernic likely did not pick up deep web data, because none of the search tools sourced in "The Web" category had the needed deep web data in their Web catalog.

Final decision on how to proceed

You concluded that the best solution was to use Copernic to find all names not having a middle initial or name, and to use Google to find only the ones having a middle initial or name. Both Copernic and Google had post-processing abilities, although those of Copernic were infinitely more sophisticated. You also decided to audit your end results against the list produced by ZoomInfo, just to see if you could make any further refinements or additions.

5: MORE SEARCH INTERFACES

In this chapter:

- **User interface features to handle:**
  - ᵒ Specialized search requirements entry.
  - ᵒ Findings display.
  - ᵒ Findings handling.
  - ᵒ Search support tools.

Specialized Search Entry Interfaces [1]

Multi-media file search interfaces [2]

These may include separate search interfaces for the following file types:

- Image (picture, graphics);

- Audio (music or other sound);

- Video (movie, possibly incorporating image and audio files).

🔲 The following is the advanced image search interface from Google.

Google™
Image Search

Images Help | All About Google

Advanced Image Search

Find results

related to **all** of the words [   ]   [Google Search]

related to the **exact phrase** [Happy New Year   ]

related to **any** of the words [   ]

not related to the words ["Rosh Hashana"   ]

Size   Return images that are

- any size
- small
- medium
- large

Filetypes   Return only image files formatted as

- any filetype
- JPG files
- GIF files

Coloration   Return only images in

- any colors
- black and white
- grayscale
- full color

Domain   Return images from the site or domain [   ]

SafeSearch   O No filtering   O Use moderate filtering   O Use strict filtering

---

Internal Book Cross-Links

1. Cross-link for this section: Reference Section 5.1: Specialized Search Entry Interfaces
2. Links for multi-media file search interfaces:

- Search Tool Guide: File format
- Reference Section 5.1: Multi-media file search interfaces

Non-Web Internet application interfaces

The idea of an **Internet application** was discussed earlier (⇨ Chapter 1: Catalog types and origins). To be exact, it actually refers to the **communications protocol** used at the **application layer** of the well-known conceptual multi-level telecommunications hierarchy. This idea does not have quite the same in meaning as "computer applications," in general. Nevertheless, as explained in Chapter 1, in this book, we will refer to email, news, and discussion boards as separate "Internet" applications whether or not they are web-based. Hopefully, this will not be too confusing to you.

It is a common error to equate the Internet with the World Wide Web, often referred to as simply the Web. Today, almost all parts of the Internet can be accessed via the Web, but it was not always so.

Until 1992, the Internet was a network that was only accessible if you knew how to invoke it using a complex set of commands. The Web, a subset of the Internet, changed this, providing an entirely new way of interacting with information online using hypertext. **HTTP — Hypertext Transfer Protocol**, is used by Web browsers to connect information items to one another, transferring webpages from a web server to your computer.

There are a number of important non-Web Internet applications still in use today, including news, e-mail, chat, Telnet, and FTP (file transfer protocol). However, employing the latter to manage files on servers has generally been replaced by using the Web, which indirectly accesses the FTP protocol.

Besides HTTP, search engines can extract data to create their databases from many of these non-Web Internet applications, including:

> ⇨ Also consult Chapter 6: Hosting site characteristics, distinguishing between websites, news sites, FTP sites, and so on.

- News [1];
- Newsgroups (USENET discussion boards) [2];
- Other kinds of discussion or chat boards;
- FTP [3].

🔳 Two screenshots follow of specialized interfaces for searching non-Web Internet applications. The first is a USENET discussion board search interface from Google (somewhat altered to save space). Google has cataloged USENET discussions all the way back to 1981, before the era of the Internet. Lately Google has also developed web-based discussion boards that are more sophisticated that its old USENET ones.

Google™
Groups

Advanced Groups Search

Find messages with **all** of the words `[          ]`

with the **exact phrase** `[          ]`

with **at least one** of the words `[          ]`

without the words `[          ]`

`[ 10 messages ]`
`[ Sort by relevance ]`
`[ Google Search ]`

`[          ]`

Group   Return only messages from the **group**   (Examples: Google-SMS, comp.os.*)

Subject   Return only messages where the **subject** contains `[          ]`

Author   Return only messages where the **author** is `[          ]`

Language   Return messages written in `[ any language ]`

Message Dates   ⊙ Return messages posted: `[ anytime ]`

○ Return messages posted between `[ 12 ]` `[ May ]` `[ 1981 ]`

and `[ 30 ]` `[ Jul ]` `[ 2002 ]`

SafeSearch   ⊙ No filtering   ○ Filter using SafeSearch

Message ID   Find the message with **message ID** `[          ]`

(Example: moderated-ng-faq-1-983174581@swcp.com)

The second interface, shown on the next page, is a sophisticated interface for FTP file search from AlltheWeb as it used to be when owned by FAST. Although it is no longer in operation, this provides a sophisticated example of search against a catalog of this kind of Internet application.

Search for	[ ]
Search type	[multiple substrings search ▼] ?
Exact hits first	☐ Try exact hits first ?
Limit to domain	Limit to domain [ ] ?
Limit to path	Limit to path [ ] ?
Limit size	Minimum size: [ ] ? Maximum size: [ ]
Date	☐ from [1 ▼] [January ▼] [1980 ▼] ? ☐ to [10 ▼] [March ▼] [2003 ▼]

AlltheWeb Advanced FTP Search Interface: Reprinted by permission from FAST (now part of Yahoo)

Hits	Max hits: [15] ? Max matches: [ ] Max hits/match: [ ]	Hide	☐ Packages ☐ Distfiles ? ☐ FreeBSD ☐ OpenBSD ☐ NetBSD ☐ Linux

[SEARCH]

Internal Book Cross-Links

1. Links for news interfaces:

- Search Tool Guide: Country, language, audience, Internet application
- Reference Section 5.1: News document search interfaces

2. Links for discussion groups:

- Search Tool Guide: Country, language, audience, Internet application
- Reference Section 5.1: Other non-Web Internet application interfaces

3. Links for FTP interfaces:

- Search Tool Guide: Country, language, audience, Internet application

---

Specialized topic search interfaces [1]

Search engines have interfaces for finding information on other specialized subjects, based on subject categories like you can find in our search tool guide (⇨ Search Tool Guide: Search by Topic). The following are a couple of examples of specialized topic search interfaces.

Example 1: Locating people, organizations, places [3]

Topic-specialized interfaces are most often used to find maps, people, businesses, and addresses (of streets, e-mail, phone numbers, etc.). They are often interrelated, as follows:

- Businesses and people;
- Locations and businesses or people;
- Addresses and businesses or people;
- Maps and locations of businesses or people.

People, for example, may be found by their phone numbers, their names, their addresses, and/or their employers. On the other hand, people, once found, may point to phone numbers, and street and e-mail addresses. Maps and street addresses are also frequently associated.

Example 2: Shopping [2]

Google's advanced Froogle interface helps people locate business products (see next page).

Internal Book Cross-Links

1. Links for specialized topic search interfaces:

- Chapter 2: Specialized search engines
- Search Tool Guide: Search by Topic

2. Links for shopping search interfaces:

- Search Tool Guide: Shopping: Other

- Reference Section 5.1: Other specialized topic search interfaces

3. Links for people/business/map search interfaces:

- Search Tool Guide: Locating people, organizations, places
- Reference Section 5.1: People, business, and map search interfaces

---

Google's Froogle Advanced Search Interface
http://images.google.com/froogle_advanced_search   Reprinted by permission from Google

Froogle BETA

Advanced Froogle Search

Find products	with **all** of the words	[ ]	[10 results] [Froogle Search]
	with the **exact phrase**	[ ]	Sort by best match
	with **at least one** of the words	[ ]	Sort by price: low to high
	without the words	[ ]	Sort by price: high to low

Price — Display products whose typical price is — Between $[   ] and $[   ]

Occurrences — Return products where my words occur —
in the product name or description
only in the product name
only in the product description

Category — Return products from the category —
Any Category
Apparel & Accessories
Arts & Entertainment
Auto & Vehicles
Baby
Books, Music & Video
Computers

Stores — ⦿ Group by store   ○ Show all products

View — ⦿ List view   ○ Grid view

SafeSearch — ⦿ No filtering   ○ Filter using SafeSearch

Findings Display & Handling Interfaces

Organization of findings display

There are two major issues of concern to users:

1. Overall ordering of findings.
2. Page organization.

Overall ordering of findings [2]

This feature is critical for all search engines. By default, they automatically sequence findings by relevance and/or website authoritativeness, both obviously complex to determine. Relevance usually involves factors such as:

- Mention of the search term in the document title (⇨ Chapter 6: Document file section or location).
- Occurrence of the search term in the metadata added to a document by the document creators — invisible to the user (⇨ Chapter 6: Metadata and metatags).
- Number of search term mentions in a document, and how close they are to the start. Also, when more than one keyword is entered, documents having these search terms closer together may sort closer to the top of the results list.
- Frequency by which sites are chosen when similar terms are used.
- Sequencing parameters entered by users (⇨ Chapter 6: Organization of the findings display). Even if no formal parameters are available, the order you use to enter search keywords usually plays a role in how findings are prioritized.
- Number of links to a page from other sites, along with the importance of the sites from which the links derive.

How Google determines relevance [Google Help]:

PageRank™ relies on the uniquely democratic nature of the web by using its vast link structure as an indicator of an individual page's value. In essence, Google interprets a link from page A to page B as a vote, by page A, for page B. But, Google looks at more than the sheer volume of votes, or links a page receives; it also analyzes the page that casts the vote. Votes cast by pages that are themselves "important" weigh more heavily and help to make other pages "important."

Important, high-quality sites receive a higher PageRank™, which Google remembers each time it conducts a search. Of course, important pages mean nothing to you if they don't match your query. So, Google combines PageRank™ with sophisticated text-matching techniques to find pages that are both important and relevant to your search. Google goes far beyond the number of times a term appears on a page and examines all aspects of the page's content (and the content of the pages linking to it) to determine if it's a good match for your query.

For more about how search engines rank findings, ⇨ refer to the following articles from SearchEngineWatch.com:

- "How search engines rank web pages:" www.searchenginewatch. com/webmasters/article.php/2167961
- "The quest for search engine relevancy:" www. searchenginewatch.com/searchday/article.php/2161801
- "Inktomi, Google Win In Recent Relevancy Test:" www. searchenginewatch.com/searchday/article.php/2192401

Some search engines can also cluster findings into various topic categories (⇨ Chapter 5: Post-processing of findings — Grouping and sorting). One of the most interesting produces "on-the-fly" subject directories that organize findings at various levels into topics. The metacrawler, Vivisimo's Clusty (clusty.com), can cluster this way, as can the popular Dogpile meta search engine, which has licensed Vivisimo technology.

For more on Vivisimo's clustering abilities, ⇨ see the following articles from SearchEngineWatch.com:

- www.searchenginewatch.com/searchday/article.php/2226841
- www.searchenginewatch.com/searchday/article.php/3070811

Page organization [3]

This refers to the organization of findings on a page. The easiest way to explain this feature is by dividing the findings page into top, middle, and bottom sections:

1. **Top section of findings page:** This typically contains materials to:
   - Repeat what is being sought.
   - Summarize what has been found.
   - Enable further refinement of your search by editing, searching within findings, or using the same search string in other interfaces.

   Links to additional information may also be provided.

A Google search on the word cat contains the following details.

Web   Results **1** - **10** of about **48,800,000** for **cat** [definition]. (**0.09** seconds)

News results for **cat** - View all the latest headlines

Fat **cat** squeezed into German animal home - Reuters - 2 Apr 2004
Cat caught in a flap - ic Wales - 2 Apr 2004
Rough ride for grumpy **cat** - News24 - 1 Apr 2004

Show stock quotes for
CAT (Caterpillar Inc.)

In the above:

- **Statistics Bar** describes the search, indicating the number of results returned and the amount of time it took. Clicking on the definition link will take you to a dictionary to define the word cat.

- **News results** is the current news found for the word cat. (Chapter 5: Links from findings display — Related entries from other catalogs).

- **Stock quotes** are presented here because Google recognizes the search term cat as a stock symbol, when it is capitalized (Reference Section 3: Intelligent avoidance of formal parameter entry).

2. **Middle section of findings page:** Individual findings are generally located here.

    Findings from the same Internet website may be indented under the first finding for that particular site.

    Further sub-organization may also occur. Most often, search engines divide their findings into two groups: sponsored matches (paid listings) and regular findings.

    Some search engines have more variety than others in the middle section of the findings page. In addition to paid entries and regular findings, they may also group search results by:

    - Clickthrough or popularity statistics: the frequency of clicking on particular findings by other users who entered the same search terms are used as a basis for findings.
    - Findings from other catalogs: the search engine distinguishes the different catalogs from which it pulls results.

🔲 Besides general web document files, search engines may cross-reference separate catalogs for news, pictures, audio, and video files.

Results coming from multi-media files are often displayed in a grid that has more than one column.

🔲 Image files from image file catalogs can be arranged in a 5 row X 3 column grid, with each cell filled by a thumbnail (reduced-size representation) of the image, along with certain fields of textual information. This gives the effect of a photo album.

🔲 Below you see sound files found from a search of an audio file catalog. Each row represents one sound file; columns provide various descriptors for each one.

1-15 of **108** results

Title		Size	Date
LadyMadonna.mp3	see other files in this folder	994 KB	2000-01-04
madonnaclp.mp3	see other files in this folder	436 KB	2000-03-02
trailofdead madonna02.mp3	see other files in this folder	235 KB	2002-03-11

3. **Bottom section of findings page:** It may contain materials similar to those in the top section, as well as links to other pages of findings such as AltaVista's shown below.

Another very different way of organizing the findings display is to show links to individual results in a pane to the left of the screen. When you click on one of them, more details appear in the right pane.

Result Pages: 1 2 3 4 5 6 7 8 9 10   [Next >>]

🔲 You may already be familiar with this if you use the search interface embedded in the Internet Explorer browser. Some people call an interface of this kind "Sidesearch." Copernic's version can be seen on the next page. The controls allow you a number of advanced and efficient ways of reviewing search results in its browser results display mode. (To see the screenshot in full resolution, go to ⇨ www.SearchHelpCenter.com/effective-internet-search-copernic-screenshots.html, "Browser results view.")

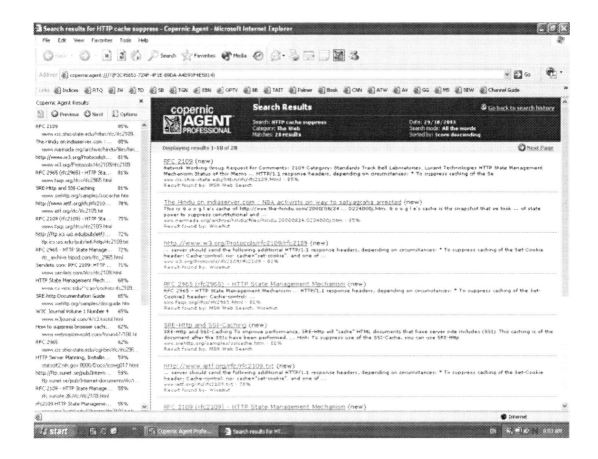

Internal Book Cross-Links

1. Cross-links for this section:

- Chapter 6: Findings Display & Handling Parameters
- Reference Section 5.2: Organization & Detailing of Findings
- Reference Section 6.3: Findings Display & Handling Parameters

2. Cross-links with: Reference Section 5.2: Overall ordering
3. Cross-links with: Reference Section 5.2: Page organization

Presentation of individual findings [1]

There are two areas of importance to users.

1. **Fields shown for each finding:**

   a. **Document files:** The fields displayed usually consist of the document title, followed by some descriptive text from the finding, derived as follows:

   - Text created by subject matter experts for the document when it was cataloged into the search engine's subject directory.
   - A document description, perhaps taken from metadata "description" tags near the front of the document source text (invisible to the user).
   - Text near the front of the document body, and/or an excerpt from a part of the text containing the highlighted search terms.

   Google highlights search terms in the results, as shown here.

   b. **Multi-media files:** The file name is displayed along with technical information such as the resolution of an image file, its format, size, the frame rate of a video file, and so on.

   > **Discovery School** - Spokane, WA
   > ... New Building for **Discovery School**. copyright May 18,1998, **Discovery School**.
   > Revised September 21, 2003, **Discovery School**. All rights reserved.
   > www.**discovery-school**.org/ - 5k - 3 Apr 2004 - Cached - Similar pages

   More free-form descriptive text, used to describe the multi-media file, often comes from associated document files. These contain "alternative descriptions," employed by Web creators to handle cases where a browser cannot manage the multi-media file format (so-called "ALT" HTML tags). Text is also included near the place in the document where the reference to the multi-media file is embedded.

2. **Language translation of findings:**

   Results of the search are translated into:

   - The language of the interface employed by the user; or

- Another target language selected by the user, regardless of the language of the search engine interface.

Our featured search engines in this book do not automatically translate findings pages. However, AltaVista and Google have translation abilities that can be linked to from the findings page.

Internal Book Cross-Links

1. Cross-links for this section:

- Reference Section 5.2: Presentation of individual findings
- Chapter 5: Links from findings display

Findings Handling [1]

Links from findings display [2]

Findings pages always contain links for further searching, but these differ from one search engine to the next. Here is a brief summary.

The different kinds of links from the findings display screens include:

1. **Links to further refine searches [3]:** They help users:

- Revise the existing search in the same search entry interface by adding new constraints or following a directory or other hierarchy downwards.

  If you search on the term canine with AlltheWeb's simple Web search interface, you might obtain the following list of "Related Searches." If you click one, it will add it as a required term to your search string, thereby narrowing your search. Select as many as you like at the same time, and see additional ones by clicking "Show more."

Refine your search:
(click "+" or "-" to include or exclude terms, and then click the "SEARCH" button)   show more >>>

| ⊞ ⊟ arctic **cat** | ⊞ ⊟ **cat** stevens | ⊞ ⊟ **cat** costume | ⊞ ⊟ dog **cat** | ⊞ ⊟ **cat** 5 |
| ⊞ ⊟ black **cat** | ⊞ ⊟ **cat** pictures | ⊞ ⊟ **cat** food | ⊞ ⊟ **cat** names | ⊞ ⊟ **cat** hat |

- Use other interfaces for the same catalog in which the same search string may be added to or refined.

  🔏 a switch from simple to advanced search.

- Search within the previous round of findings; considered part of post-processing user tools (➪ Chapter 5: Post-processing of findings).

2. **Links to switch to other catalogs [4]:** They allow you to carry the same search parameters to the other catalogs (as much as is feasible).

  🔏 You do a document (Web) search on **dog** and then want to switch to pictures of dogs. This link will allow you to quickly change to the image search interface, carrying the term **dog** there. The findings will usually appear once you click the link to switch to that catalog.

Hotbot allows you to seamlessly switch your search parameters from one data catalog to another by simply clicking radio buttons at the top of the screen. Its interface is designed to maximize use of parameters available in the advanced general web document searches (Web searches) against data catalogs from:

- Google;
- Teoma (Ask Jeeves).

Hotbot makes all its search interfaces appear as similar as possible: Teoma's (Ask Jeeve's) is a sub-set of Google's. The Ask Jeeves and Google versions of Hotbot's search screens are pictured on the next two pages.

> **🔨** Hotbot specializes in general Web document searches, but cannot search non-document files such as multi-media ones, or directory, specialized topic, and specialized Internet application catalogs.

3. **Links to more same-site findings [5]:** Our selected search engines generally display only one or two findings per site. This feature is sometimes known as "site collapse" or a form of "clustering" (www.searchenginewatch.com/facts/article.php/2155971#clustering).

If you want to obtain all the pages from a given site, search engines provide:

- A link next to a finding to further pages from the same site. In the case of multi-media files (linked by a reference embedded in a document file), this link finds more multi-media files within the same document (instead of the same site).

- A text box for entering a specific website (domain, host part of URL) as a search parameter (⇨ Chapter 6: Hosting site characteristics — discussion of URL).

4. **Links to related pages or terms** [6]**:** Either for each finding or for all findings on a page as a group. These links are usually at the level of the individual finding.

 Google displays a " Similar Pages" link next to each finding, as seen here.

> **Whatever** ~ By Eliot Lucas ... Today's Episode: #99 "He had it coming", Make with the clicky! Vote for **Whatever!** Chartruesse ...www. geocities.com/red_today/ - 15k - Cached - Similar pages

Search engines may suggest other search terms or pages related to your original terms, as well as listing individual findings — such as:

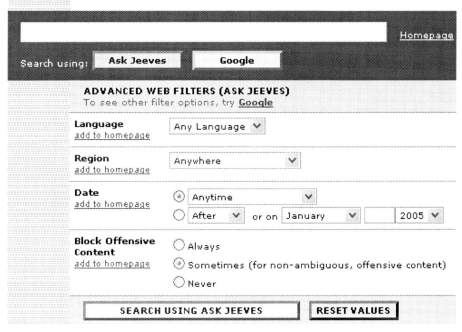

Hotbot Advanced Search Entry Form, Ask Jeeves Web Catalog
www.hotbot.com/adv.asp?prov=Inktomi&tab=web

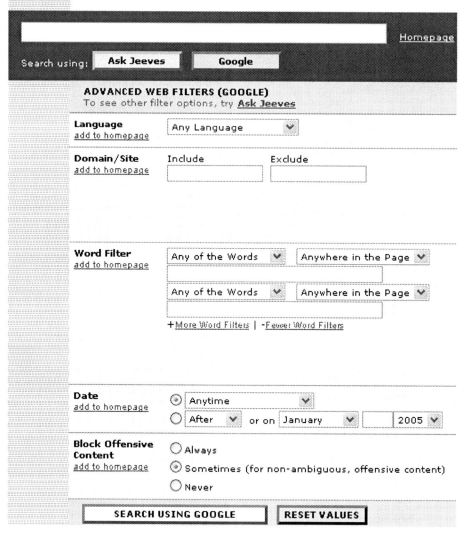

- **Clickthrough statistics**. Based on the particular search terms you used, these statistics point to webpages that were the most frequently linked to from the findings pages that resulted.
- **Dynamically established topic categories** (as opposed to pre-established ones in subject directories), based on clustering around the most relevant terms found by a search.

5. **Links to related entries from other catalogs [7]:** Either for each finding or for all findings on a page as a group, depending on which catalog your search first addressed.

   If you search the webcrawler-gathered document catalog, links to other catalogs might include:

   - Clickthrough links to the most popular sites associated with the search term;
   - Links to catalogs from other Internet applications such as news, FTP, or discussion board;
   - Links to paid (sponsored) websites associated with the search term;
   - Links to multi-media file catalogs;
   - Links to entries in a subject directory.

6. **Links to language translation interfaces [8]:** To translate your findings to and from different languages. This is an example of linking to an end user tool designed to post-process findings (⇨ Chapter 5: Post-processing of findings).

   AltaVista's language translation link is seen here.

We found 110,787 results:
Welcome To Teledyne Electronic Technologies   Teledyne Electronic Technologies is a major developer and producer of microelectronic ... **TET**'s extensive research and development result in a continual flow of new technology that we provide as standard ...www.tet.com/ • Related pages • Translate   More pages from www.tet.com

7. **Additional links [9]:** These include links to:

- **Dictionary definitions of terms**;
- **Cached webpages**, i.e., versions of webpages as they existed when they were indexed by the search engine, useful when they can no longer be located on the Internet (⇨ Chapter 1: Catalogs and indexes);
- **Translate pages from non-HTML format to HTML format,** e.g., from Word to HTML;
- **Commercial links,** such as ones to yellow pages or various shopping sites.

Internal Book Cross-Links

1. Cross-links for this section:

- Reference Section 5.2: Organization & Detailing of Findings
- Chapter 6: Findings Display & Handling Parameters
- Reference Section 6.3: Findings Display & Handling Parameters

2. Cross-links with: Reference Section 5.2: Links from Findings Display
3. Cross-links with: Reference Section 5.2: Links for refining searches
4. Cross-links with: Reference Section 5.2: Switching to other catalogs
5. Cross-links with: Reference Section 5.2: More same-site findings
6. Cross-links with: Reference Section 5.2: Related pages or terms
7. Cross-links with: Reference Section 5.2: Related entries from other catalogs
8. Cross-links with: Reference Section 5.2: Language translation links
9. Cross-links with: Reference Section 5.2: Additional links

Post-processing of findings [1]

Enhanced search functionality, such as post-processing of findings, is considered by some to be a futuristic topic. Perhaps this is because today's major search engines don't have sophisticated functionality in this area, and users are generally unfamiliar with it. They are also unaware of how much simpler complex search projects could be made and how much time they could save with this kind of search engine feature.

What is post-processing?

Post-processing was introduced in Chapter 2: Post-processing of findings. It includes tools for:

1. **Reviewing search results**, including:

- Automatically eliminating certain findings from consideration (e.g., dead links or duplicate documents).
- Grouping and sorting.
- Annotating findings and whole searches, sifting through results in a systematic way, producing document excerpts or translations, and so on.

- Searching within results, perhaps even back to the original files, including backtracking based on previous actions or annotations made against findings, referencing the original files on the Internet, and so on.

2. **Reviewing, reworking or updating previous searches**, including:

- Resubmitting variations of a search.
- Going back to previous searches for updating, following up and tracking, or simply to refer once again to their results.

Which search engines post-process findings?

Several tools specifically designed for findings post-processing are incorporated within the five search engines featured in this book. But the meta search utility Copernic encompasses a particularly sophisticated and comprehensive set of post-processing tools, based on processing the files themselves rather than just the metadata in catalogs. In other words, with Copernic, post-processing occurs using the **thick-client method** (as opposed to doing the processing server-side, using the **thin-client method**). With client-side (thick-client) processing, once the files themselves are downloaded to the user's computer, further consolidation then occurs by:

- Elimination of duplicate findings from different sources, when the same file resides at different URL's (e.g., mirror websites, that is, sites that are duplicates of one another), in addition to removal of the same finding for the same URL from different search engines.
- Deletion of findings having broken (dead) links.

Post-processing features

The following is a list of post-processing features, along with illustrations of their implementation in Copernic and other search engines treated in this book.

1. **Search within findings** [2]: Some search engines provide a "Search within results" link on their findings pages. This generally means searching within the set of catalog entries corresponding to the previous set of findings. In the case of a meta search utility such as Copernic, this can potentially be done in a more sophisticated way because of having the referenced files themselves on hand.

2. **Grouping and sorting of findings** [3]: Post-processing findings from downloaded files permits much more exhaustive and powerful methods of grouping and sorting, such as by domain, page status, and page last modified date; and perhaps even by duplication of contents between pages that contain apparently different files, but with exactly the same contents.

KG Copernic is known for its ability to sort findings and group them according to pre-established criteria; however, it does not cluster findings based on topic or keyword.

Grouping and sorting also includes dynamic clustering into subject categories.

> ⇨ For more examples of search tools that can cluster findings by topic, refer to the appropriate section of Search Tool Guide: Search tool abilities.

KG Vivisimo's futuristic knowledge-management functionality allows dynamic, on-the-fly organization of findings into multiple levels of folders based on topic. It produces a kind of "subject directory" that is unknown until the actual contents of document files have been examined, using the contents of the files themselves to detect key terms and concepts. For more information: ⇨ vivisimo.com/products/Content_Integrator/ Introduction/Integrated_Content_-__One_Unified_View.html.

3. **Language translation or page summary** [4]:

   a. **Language translation:** Some search engines provide interfaces for translating found webpages to or from another language.

   > ♡ Translation usually works best when English is either the source or target language. Even so, the results are just rough approximations.

   Our search tool guide (⇨ Search Tool Guide: Language tools) provides a list of language translation tools you might like to try out.

   KG AltaVista provides the language translation interface shown on the next page:

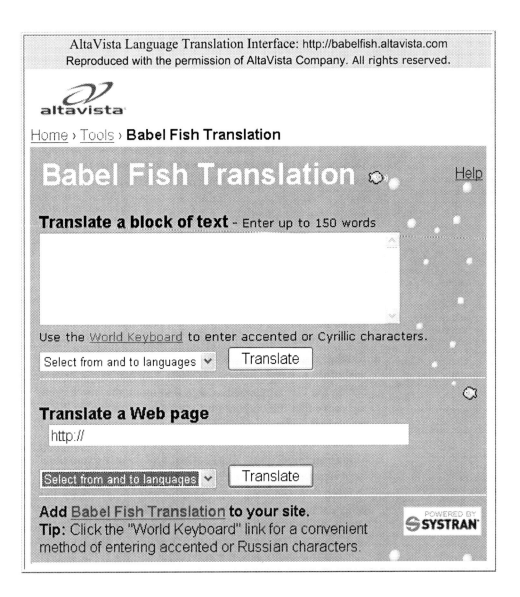

b. **Production of page summaries:** This involves extraction of key concepts, files sizes, modification dates, and other metadata from found pages by either a webcrawler or by software that processes data collected by a webcrawler. Even more exhaustive and potent methods become possible by post-processing of findings once the files themselves have been downloaded.

[C] Copernic extracts key concepts from found pages using its Summarizer, which is integrated into Copernic Agent Professional. In this way, a more extensive set of metadata can be created using post-processing.

4. **Search follow-up** [5]:

   a. **Keeping records of searches and their findings:** This includes:

   - **Organizing the search history:** You begin by organizing automatically-kept searches into hierarchical search-history folders. You can make or remove folders, rename them, move records of searches from one folder to another, and so on.
   - **Managing search history details:** In addition to managing each search in the history as a whole, you can manage the history of the individual findings, which are kept along with the overall data about the search.

   🔢 You can delete individual findings kept for a search, annotate them, and so on.

   - **Saving of individual files referenced from findings metadata to user's local computer:** You can have Copernic access the file corresponding to a finding on the Internet, and then save that file on your own computer. You can do this for individual findings or for all of them.

   b. **Updating, modifying, duplicating, and deleting searches kept in search history:** You can update a search, causing it to rerun from the start, employing the same set of filters and other parameters originally used. You can also modify the search parameters and then rerun it, thereby replacing the earlier search. Or, you can simply duplicate it. Finally, you can delete a whole search from the search history, including all its findings.

   c. **Sharing search findings:** That is, importing and exporting findings with other users.

   d. **Setting up user alerts:** User alerts are standing orders to the search engine to continue to track searches or particular search results on your behalf.

   🔢 You can have the search engine notify you by e-mail (or a message sent to a web site interface you are using) when:

   - New files conforming to your tracked search parameters are detected on the Internet.
   - Crawlers detect that a designated file found by your search has been modified since your last alert.

For more information on Copernic, ⇨ refer to:

- Product overview: www.copernic.com/desktop/products/index.html
- Flash tutorial — discusses Copernic's ability to search the deep web, in addition to being able to parallel process and integrate the results found by more than a hundred other search engines on the web: www.copernic.com/desktop/products/agent/tour.html

---

Internal Book Cross-Links

1. Cross-links for this section:

- Search Tool Guide: Language tools
- Search Tool Guide: Search tool abilities (with respect to post-processing your findings)
- Reference Section 5.2: Post-Processing of Findings
- Chapter 6: Post-processing of findings
- Reference Section 6.3: Other Post-Processing of Findings

2. Cross-links with: Reference Section 5.2: Search within finding
3. Cross-links with: Reference Section 5.2: Grouping and sorting
4. Cross-links with: Reference Section 5.2: Language translation or page summary
5. Cross-links with: Reference Section 5.2: Search follow-up

Search Support: User Tool Interfaces [1]

Setting user preferences

These settings permit you to customize or personalize the search engines you employ.

Included in this category of tools are:

1. **Filter default value preferences** [2] allow you, for example, to set default values for document language and to block the display of materials from potentially offensive websites.

> You can change many of the setting items *dynamically,* that is, override the default setting by entering parameter values applicable to an individual search. But to change the default itself, you must usually change the value in the preference setting interface.

2. **Findings display and handling preferences** [3] permit you, for instance, to allocate the number of fields to display for each finding and the number of findings to display per page.

3. **Interface screens features preferences** [4] enable you, for example, to designate the interface screen initially displayed when you enter the search engine, the screen "look and feel," and the language of the controls shown on the screen (e.g., French for French Quebec, Spanish for much of South America).

4. **Software integration and efficiency preferences** [5] can be used, for instance, to allow easy search engine access in a user's browser through search toolbars and the like.

AlltheWeb provides a sophisticated set of user preference setting interface screens for "Basic Settings," "Advanced Settings," "Language," and "Look and Feel." Below are some examples with quotes from text on the AlltheWeb "Customize Preferences" screen.

- Offensive content reduction: Sets the default value for a metadata-based search filter. To quote: The Offensive Content Reduction filter reduces the amount of offensive material displayed in the search results. Please note that the filter is not 100% accurate, and offensive material will in some cases slip through the filter and be displayed in the search results. Some pages that are not offensive may also be incorrectly filtered out. The filter only supports English documents.

Offensive content filter	⦿ On ◯ Off

- **Default search catalog:** Sets the default value for an interface screen feature. To quote: AlltheWeb can perform six different search types, and does by default a basic web search. By changing this default setting, AlltheWeb will automatically perform your chosen type of search the next time you enter AlltheWeb.

Default catalog
⦿ Web
◯ News
◯ Pictures
◯ Video
◯ Audio
◯ FTP files

- **Search results per page:** Sets the default value for a findings display parameter. To quote: This option controls the number of results displayed per page.

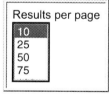

Results per page
10
25
50
75

- **Highlight search terms:** Sets the default value for a findings display parameter. To quote: Search terms can be highlighted in the search result, if the document summary contains the terms used in the search. You will see cases

Highlight search terms	◯ On ⦿ Off

where your search terms are not found within the document summary but are found in the document. AlltheWeb searches the full HTML document, not only the document summary presented in the search result.

Internal Book Cross-Links

1. Cross-links for this section:

- Chapter 6: User Preference Setting Parameters
- Reference Section 5.3:

  › Preference settings

  › Additional end user-specific tools

  › Other user tools

- Reference Section 6.4: User Preference Setting Parameters

2. Cross-links with: Reference Section 6.4: Filter Default Value Preferences
3. Cross-links with: Reference Section 6.4: Findings Display & Handling Preferences
4. Cross-links with: Reference Section 6.4: Interface Screens Features Preferences
5. Cross-links with: Reference Section 6.4: Software Integration & Efficiency Preferences

Other user tools [1]

Included in this category are tools for:

1. **End users:**

- **Maintaining user accounts** to pay for documents that are not free of charge.
- **Setting "text-only" search mode** for users whose Internet access is very slow or for browsers having limited graphics capabilities.

2. **Webmasters:**

- **Submitting a website** for indexing by a search engine or, alternatively, to prevent search engine robots from indexing a website.
- **Incorporating a search engine link into a user's website**.
- **Determining what other sites are cross-referencing (linking to) your website** (see below).

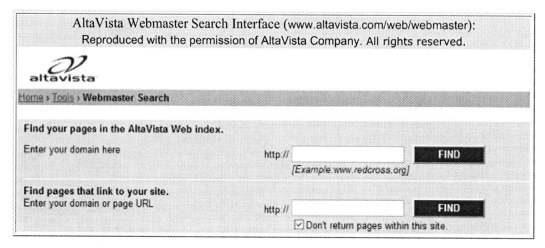

3. **All users:**

- **Providing help to users** with various search engine features and so on.
- **Viewing popular queries and reviewing recent search trends** for a particular engine.
- **Contacting the search engine company** concerning business matters (e. g., advertising), problems in using the search engine, or other.

Internal Book Cross-Links

1. Cross-links for this section: Reference Section 5.3: Other user tools

6: ADVANCED SEARCH OPTIONS

In this chapter:

- Advanced searching techniques, particularly the effective use of parameters and filters for various search engine interfaces including:
  - › Term-based filters.
  - › Metadata-based filters.
  - › Parameters to display and handle search results.
  - › Parameters to customize search engine user preferences.

Introduction

This chapter is the heart of the book. It provides an overview of the different parameters that can be entered with the various search engine interfaces to help you get better, more targeted search results.

As discussed in Chapter 3, the major types of parameters are as follows:

1. **Search filters:** These parameters are used to define the scope of your search. There are two different types:
   a. **Term-based search filters** [1].
   b. **Metadata-based search filters** [2]

Search filters may or may not be entered as operator parameters. Search engines vary widely in their ability to mix certain kinds of operator parameters.

The kinds of operator parameter mixes that do and don't work in particular search engines are found in ⇨ Reference Section 3: Support for operator parameters.

Suppose you want to mix Boolean OR logic with a fielded search for pages having the word kangaroo in them at websites having addresses in either Australia (code au) or Spain (code es). Also, suppose that the field name for country code in a fielded search is "domain." The search string kangaroo (domain:au OR domain:es) may work in a particular search engine. However, the string kangaroo domain:(au OR es), where the domain field distributes over the two country codes, may fail. It all depends on the limitations of the search engine involved.

2. **Findings display and handling parameters** [3]: These tell the search engine how to manipulate and present the found data to the user, such as by specifying how to determine relevancy for sorting the results.

3. **Search engine customization parameters** [4]: These instruct the search engine how to generally behave with respect to searching, displaying findings, user tools, and so on.

Real, substantive search projects generally involve using combinations of several parameters, often in more than one search engine. With this in mind, when trying out the numerous search examples provided in this chapter, you are encouraged to do the same. The exercises and solutions have also been specifically devised for you to experience a variety of combinations of the parameters in different search engines. This will permit you to simulate real search situations.

⇨ This chapter provides many examples that you can practice on your own. For some **interactive online tutorials** using filter parameters with several search engines (including AlltheWeb, AltaVista, and Google), ⇨ Debbie Flanagan's tutorial pages at: www.learnwebskills. com/search/main.html

For simplicity's sake, each exercise in Chapter 6 has only one solution. However, alternate ones are offered in the Reference Manual.

Internal Book Cross-Links

1. Cross-links with Reference Section 6.2
2. Cross-links with Reference Section 6.1
3. Cross-links with Reference Section 6.3
4. Cross-links with Reference Section 6.4

Term-Based Search Filters [1]

These filters, many of which have been touched upon in earlier chapters, are essential for entering complex search requirements in a concise and efficient way. They provide the rules to determine how search terms:

- Vary, while still allowing a match to occur based on a particular variation of the term.
- Relate to one another.

As explained earlier (⇨ Chapter 3: Parameter types), term-based filters are based on the search terms themselves, rather than metadata. They may be divided into two types: term variation and term relationship filters. These are further sub-classified in the following sub-sections. But, before we go there, a couple of further thoughts are in order:

- Filters to cause synonyms of words or similar concepts to be automatically looked up and searched on are not included by us as term-based filters. That's despite the fact that these filters are based on the terms themselves. However, metadata, such as that found in a thesaurus, is needed for this kind of similarity search. That's why we decided to include such filters in the later section of this chapter dealing with metadata-based filters.
- The term variation filters are sub-classified below in our own way, although others may have easily to chosen to sub-classify them somewhat differently.
- At the end of the following sub-section on term variation filters, we discuss the use of **regular expressions**. These form an advanced programming technique able to handle almost all the different kinds of term variation filters, by providing complex rules for matching patterns of characters.
- There is a certain area where the ideas of term variation and term relationship filters overlap. Note that regular expressions can also be used to some extent to specify term relationship filters, in addition to term variation ones.

Term variation filters [2]

Computer programmers will associate term variation operators with **regular expressions** in programming languages. In general, Internet search engines do not yet have the ability to handle most of the kinds of term variations that can be handled by regular expressions. (More on regular expressions: ⇨ www.regular-expressions.info .)

1. **Wildcards, substrings, stemming** [3]:

    a. **Wildcards:** are operators that act as placeholders for yet-to-be-determined characters or groups of characters in a word.

    🎲 An asterisk (*) placed at the end of a word can find from 0 to a certain number of characters in place of the asterisk. Thus, in various search engines, the term sound* will correspond to terms such as sounding, soundproof, sounded, and so on.

    In certain search engines, the asterisk can be used in the middle of a word, for, say, any 0 to 3 characters in that position in the string of characters.

    🎲 Sp*l will match words such as spoil, spill, and spool.

    > 🔨 The Find commands of word processors have many more sophisticated wildcard options than those found in most of today's Internet search engines.

    In some search engines, a single character, such as the question mark (?) or the percent (%) character, can be used as a wildcard that corresponds to an individual character in a specific place in a word string.

    🎲 In the string so??d, any characters can be used in the third and fourth positions. Possible matches include solid and sowed.

    You can place wild cards anywhere in the search string, and you can use multiple wild cards in a single word.

    > 🔨 Typing the asterisk at the end of the word is also known as **stubbing**, which is a particular kind of wildcarding. The word **stemming** may also be used, in its more restrictive usage. **Truncation** is another word used to indicate wildcarding.

    🎲 Type an asterisk at the start or end of a word particle to obtain words that either end with or start with the specified characters. Thus, the query *man returns documents containing the words man, woman, Spiderman, Oman, and so on.

🔎 Type ? (question mark) to match a single positional character. Thus, the query car? will return documents containing words like cart, card, care, and Cary.

b. **Substrings:** are like wildcards before and/or after a particular part of a word because the match is made on a subset of the characters in a word.

🔎 The substring oma occurs inside the word woman. Using wildcards, with the asterisk taking the place of 0 to n characters, this same substring could be represented as *oma*.

c. **Stemming:** Stemming operators are somewhat similar to wildcards at the ends of words. In fact, this is how some search engines appear to define stemming, in which case the term **stubbing** also finds some usage.

In a broader sense, however, stemming allows finding other kinds of variations on the same word, due to differences in tense or mood, or a word being the verb equivalent of a particular noun.

🔨 Of our featured search engines, only Google, and perhaps MSN Search, have automatic stemming, in the sense of word stubbing.

🔎 When the word think is entered as the search term, stemming will cause the search engine to find various connected nouns and verbs, such as thought, thinker, and thoughtless, as well.

🔎 You will get the word flew when searching for the word fly, along with flies, flying, flight, and so on.

2. **Different spellings or phonetic matching** [4]:

a. **Different spellings**: The ability to automatically suggest and even automatically include different spellings of the same word helps to increase the number of relevant findings in some cases.

🔎 Type matherboard into an appropriate text box, and the Google findings page will respond with: "Did you mean: motherboard?"

▊ Convert between American and British English spellings, as in behavior vs. behaviour, or humor vs. humour.

> ▊ This type of spelling assistance to different versions of English was not noticed in any of our featured search engines.

For more on spelling assistance, ➪ www.brightplanet. com/deepcontent/tutorials/Search/part7.asp#topic27

b. **Phonetic matching:** This is matching based on the sound of the word, rather than on the spelling, based on some dialect or pronunciation. Our featured search engines do not support phonetic matching, except perhaps when it is connected with spelling correction.

▊ Entering Baylin with phonetic matching will cause the like-sounding words Bailin and Beilin to give rise to findings as well.

▊ Exalead has a filter that lets the user choose one of the options in the drop-down menu shown here. Note that you can choose only one of these, although in theory the last three could all be implemented at the same time in the same search.

Search Method
Exact search
Automatic word stemming
Phonetic search
Approximate spelling

3. **Formatting masks** [5]: Formats are often used in programs to cause data to be displayed to the user in a way that enhances readability. Formatting masks refer to the "superficial" appearance characteristics of terms.

▊ A North American phone number consists of ten digits, in the form "(999) 999-9999", where '9' is a placeholder for any of the digits 0 to 9. In theory, this formatting mask could be used to select data on the Internet, where only documents containing a string of text consisting of exactly ten successive digits formatted with brackets, space, and dash, as in this example, would be found.

Entering a word in quotes, like a phrase, will cause certain search engines to become case sensitive and thereby distinguish between uppercase and lowercase letters.

▊ Entering "Idea" as opposed to idea will result in matches to documents only when the "I" is capitalized.

In practical terms, formats are seldom used when searching for text in document files. They are basically absent from all search engines, except perhaps to find uppercase letters when required in certain positions of a search term.

Some search engines also respect the usage of diacritical marks (symbols placed above or below individual letters in a word) for letters from certain alphabets (non-English ones, of course). They use the same characters as in English, but add diacritical marks (signs, accents, cedillas, etc.) to indicate different sounds or values of a letter, or to add a particular vowel before or after a consonant. These marks could be considered as special letter formats, selected using "formatting masks."

However, formatting or appearance is sometimes used to find matches for multi-media files.

Advanced image search interfaces generally allow matches to be made by image color, background pattern, or screen resolution (pixel density).

Practice Exercise:

The word satellite must occur with an uppercase "S," as in Satellite.

AlltheWeb	Case sensitivity is unavailable.
AltaVista	It is unclear whether case sensitivity is available.
Copernic	Check case sensitivity when searching within results.
Google	Case sensitivity is unavailable.
MSN Search	Case sensitivity is unavailable.

4. **Ignored words or characters** [6]: Often called **stop words**, they are words that are ignored when matching terms to documents. They usually include articles - a, the; prepositions - at, to, in; various forms of the verb "to be" - been, is; other parts of speech - how, which, if, la, de, on, who, where, and single letter words.

In addition to stop words, one can refer to **stop punctuation**, or, more generally, to **stop characters**. They cause certain words, punctuation with special keyboard characters, or numerical digits to be ignored during the match process.

The colon (:) and digit in the phrase overview: conclusion 2, may be ignored, and treated as if they did not exist. Thus, the search is really just against the phrase overview conclusion, without the : and the 2.

Search engines often do not allow you to control these features, although they are automatically applied. Many do not list their stop characters or words either, such as the search engines featured in this book. However, this is easily verified by entering the word as a search filter.

Some search engines allow you to override the disregard of stop words by placing a plus sign (+) in front of the stop word.

+the in Google will cause the search engine to include the word the when making matches.

If of and the are stop words in a given search engine, and punctuation characters and digits are ignored, then the phrase hello world will be treated as equivalent to the phrase hello to the world, in +/-2020. This occurs, since the following will all be ignored:

- preposition: to
- article: the
- special characters: comma (,), plus (+), slash (/), and minus (-)
- digits: 2020

Once you remove the above from hello to the world, in +/-2020, you end up reducing the string to just hello world.

5. **Regular expressions:** These have been referred to as "wildcards on steroids." They provide complex matching patterns that can be used for most of the preceding kinds of term variation, taking the possibilities for

such term variation to a much more sophisticated level. Note, however, that regular expressions do not cover the following kinds of word variation: phonetic matching, automatic lookup of different spellings, and the type of word stemming requiring lookup of words belonging to the same family but not having the same stub.

Despite their power, few Internet search engines have made use of regular expressions to this time. A major reason for this is, of course, that a great deal of expertise is needed to use them. In fact, the only two search engine examples we know of that support(ed) regular expressions are:

- The former FTP search interface of AlltheWeb: ⇨ Reference Section 5.1: Other non-Web Internet application interfaces.
- The new Exalead search engine: ⇨ www.exalead.com.

It takes a programmer about a week to fully master regular expressions, although learning the basics may take you only an hour or two. Following are a couple of fairly trivial examples, which apply regular expression rules to just single words:

🔢 The search string mpe?g[123] will find documents containing any one of the following words: mpg1, mpg2, mpg3, mpeg1, mpeg2, or mpeg3. As you can deduce:

- The question mark (?) after the letter e makes that letter optional.
- You can chose only one of the three digits, since they form a set of single-character choices. The set is indicated by the square brackets.

Note: Depending on the regular expression implementation in any given piece of software, it may also find varieties of the word having one or more of the three letters, m, p, and g, capitalized.

🔢 The search string Jud(y|ith|i) will find documents containing any one of the following words: Judy, Judith, or Judi. As you can tell:

- The rounded brackets contain strings of characters (each string having one or more characters). Exactly one of these strings must follow the string Jud.
- The bars (|) separating the three letter strings in the rounded brackets separate the different alternatives.

Regular expressions can also match entire phrases, i.e., extend across word boundaries. In fact, they can find patterns that go across entire documents, as opposed to just a few words forming a phrase. As you can guess, they can also provide patterns that include the logic of AND, OR, and NOT, and so also cover a territory similar to that provide by Boolean operators for term relationships (covered in the next sub-section). More about this will be said in the following section.

Internal Book Cross-Links

1. Cross-links for this section:

- Reference Section 6.1: further explains how the five featured search engines apply concepts from this section
- Chapter 5: provides a high-level explanation of the search filter entry interfaces

2. Cross-links with: Reference Section 6.1: Term variation filters
3. Links for wildcards or substrings or stemming:

- Cross-links with: Reference Section 6.1: Wildcards, substrings, stemming
- More on wildcards: www.brightplanet.com/deepcontent/tutorials/ Search/part3.asp#topic9

4. Cross-links with: Reference Section 6.1: Different spellings or phonetic matching
5. Cross-links with: Reference Section 6.1: Formatting masks
6. Cross-links with: Reference Section 6.1: Ignored words or characters

Term relationship filters [1]

Whether expressed through operator parameters or by using designated text boxes or the like, relationships between terms are usually made through the following kinds of techniques:

1. **Making larger terms through phrases** [2]: Phrases consist of multiple words separated by a space treated as a single term. In a phrase, the individual words must be in the specified order.

    Most search engines allow phrases, but they are entered into their search interfaces in a different ways, by:

- Enclosing words inside quotation marks (" ").

🔍 Google allows phrases inside the following box.

with **all** of the words | "Breast cancer"

- Placing your search words in a text box designated for phrases.

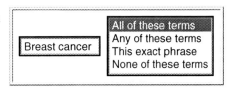

🔍 Google has an "exact phrase" box.

with the **exact phrase** | Breast cancer

- Using radio buttons, checkboxes, or drop-down menu selections that accompany the text box.

🔍 MSN Search provides a drop-down menu.

Breast cancer

All of these terms
Any of these terms
This exact phrase
None of these terms

More on phrases: ⇨ www. brightplanet.com/deepcontent/ tutorials/Search/part3.asp#topic12

2. **Using Boolean logic:** This is usually expressed by inserting connectives before or between search terms to express the ideas of negation (NOT), conjunction (AND), and inclusion (OR).

Boolean logic can be explained in terms of Venn diagrams of **crisp (non-fuzzy)** sets, as shown here. In this diagram, each circle represents a set of elements. Intersections (overlaps) between the circles represent the idea of conjunction.

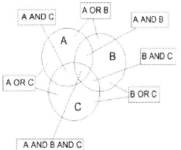

3. **Using fuzzy logic:** Most search engines do not allow users to specify fuzzy logic truth-values for relating terms, in which something can be partially true to different degrees. Thus, SHOULD HAVE taken as a kind of fuzzy operator contrasts with the crisp operator MUST HAVE, which is implied by the Boolean AND.

Despite the use of **crisp logic**, rather than a more qualitative and rich **fuzzy logic**, the latter usually more accurately reflects the real world around us. Thus, we might well expect more fuzzy logic applications as search engines become more sophisticated in the future.

MSN Search uses the prefer: field operator in a search string for the "should have" idea. If you entered the string shopping prefer: center into its Boolean search text box, the results must contain the word shopping and preferably also the word center.

Exalead, the same new search engine that offers regular expressions, also offers a fuzzy OR ability, as you see in the "preferably containing" option of the drop-down menu in the following screenshot.

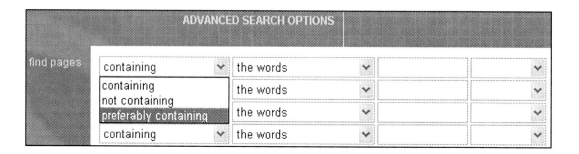

4. **Making range comparisons:** This involves testing for whether one term is greater than (>), less than (<), or equal to (=) another term. None of the search engines featured in this book have this kind of ability, let alone the ability to make fuzzy range comparisons.

5. **Regular expressions and term relationships:** As stated earlier, the different kinds of term relationships can also be made using regular expressions. Although this subject is a little too programmer-oriented for a book of this kind, what we can usefully discuss here is how to combine Boolean and fuzzy logic operators with regular expressions for individual words. This achieves much of the same effect, and is simpler to discuss here. Some examples of this will be provided below in this discussion of term relationship filters.

Internal Book Cross-Links

1. Cross-links with Reference Section 6.1: Term Relationship
2. Cross-links with: Reference Section 6.1: Phrases

Term relationships using Boolean logic [1]

Here are the basics you need to know to understand how to effectively use Boolean logic and related operators.

Negation

NOT or **AND NOT** in search engines restricts the scope of the findings; **OR NOT** expands findings. These can often be specified as follows:

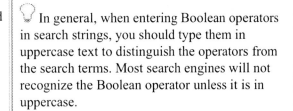 In general, when entering Boolean operators in search strings, you should type them in uppercase text to distinguish the operators from the search terms. Most search engines will not recognize the Boolean operator unless it is in uppercase.

The syntax for inclusion of Boolean operators in search strings not only varies by search engine, but sometimes according to the different boxes or search entry interfaces of the same search engine.

1. NOT is used between terms (as opposed to being in front of the first term, in which case a minus sign is often used).

    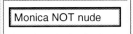 MSN Search can use NOT to express negation. The AND is implied.

    > Monica NOT nude

2. A minus (-) sign operator is placed in front of individual terms, in which case no space is allowed between the minus sign and the term.

    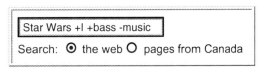 Google expresses negation as an operator parameter using a minus sign.

    > Star Wars +I +bass -music
    >
    > Search: ⦿ the web ○ pages from Canada

3. An indicator from a drop-down menu or a radio button or a checkbox is used to say how to treat the terms entered in an associated text box.

    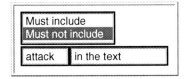 AlltheWeb has the option of using a drop-down menu to express negation.

    > Must include
    > Must not include
    >
    > attack | in the text

4. A text box indicates terms to be excluded, such as using "None of these terms."

    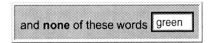 AltaVista uses a text box to express negation in one of its interfaces.

    > and **none** of these words | green

Conjunction

AND, like NOT, restricts the scope of findings. It is placed between two terms in a search engine indicating both terms are required. Search engines allow AND to be specified in a number of different ways:

1. Placement of the AND operator between terms.

    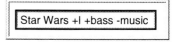 AltaVista in its "Boolean expression" textbox on its advance search form requires the use of AND, or the successive words may be interpreted as a phrase.

2. Use of a plus (+) sign operator in front of a term, where no space is allowed between the plus sign and the term.

    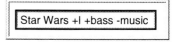 Google expresses conjunction by either blank spaces between terms or by a plus sign as seen here.

    Star Wars +I +bass -music

3. Selection of a radio button or a checkbox to say how to treat the terms entered in an associated text box.

4. Choice from a drop-down menu to indicate how to treat the terms entered in an associated text box.

    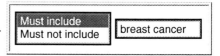 AlltheWeb has an option for expressing conjunction using a drop-down menu, as seen here.

    Must include
    Must not include   breast cancer

    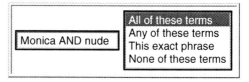 Use the drop-down menu choices shown here

    Monica AND nude

    All of these terms
    Any of these terms
    This exact phrase
    None of these terms

5. Use of a text box for terms designated to be included.

    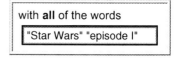 The text box seen here labeled "All of these terms" is found in Google's advanced search interfaces.

    with **all** of the words
    "Star Wars" "episode I"

Proximity variation of conjunction

The conjunction operator can have sub-types (specialized kinds), generally called **proximity** or **adjacency** operators — such as NEAR — to find terms before or after a term within a specified number of words. This conjunction operator not only makes the term required, but also makes it required within a certain word limit. Sometimes the exact size of the word limit can be controlled by an argument to the operator.

> ⚒ In Copernic, NEAR, as in bacon NEAR pork, means the terms are within a certain number of words of each other. More sophisticated search software allows the user to indicate whether the nearness occurs before or after the term.

Phrases, although discussed above as if they were separate from Boolean logic, are actually an even more specialized case of this, as a special case of proximity filter that requires one word to be directly before or after another.

> ⚒ In fact, Exalead has one such proximity operator, although one that does not specify whether one term is before or after another. This is the NEXT operator. Thus, Judy NEXT Gill as a search string will find documents having the phrase Judy Gill, as well as those with the phrases Gill, Judy or Gill Judy.

> 🔨 Although proximity operators may not be supported by a search engine, search keywords being near one another may be used to give higher priority to a finding in the search results.

Inclusion

OR between terms means that at least one of the terms (any of these terms) is required. Use of OR tends to expand the number of findings made by the search because only one of the terms is required. Many search engines allow OR to be specified by:

1. Use of the OR operator between terms, as in the below Copernic screen.

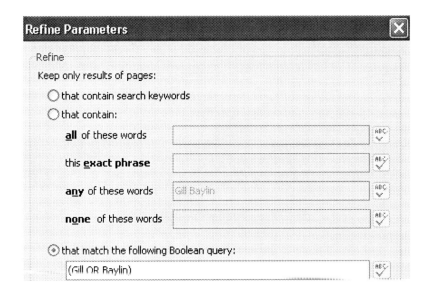

An OR placed between two words can act as a weak and clumsy substitute wildcard, if two variations of the word are thereby accommodated.

> The search string teacher OR teaching picks up two variations based on the word stub teach.

As well, OR can in certain restricted cases find practical use as a substitute for range comparison operators.

> If looking for words greater than or equal to words starting with capital M and less than words starting with capital Q, a whole range of word variations is, in effect, sought. Thus, in some syntaxes, the following are equivalent: 1) > "M" AND < "Q"; 2) "N" OR "O" OR "P".

2. Placement of search terms into a text box designated for alternative terms.

> Two common labels for such a text box are shown here.

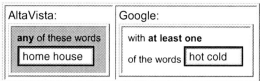

3. Selection of an indicator from a drop-down menu, checkbox, or set of radio buttons to specify how the search terms in an associated text box are to be interpreted.

Boolean operators mixed with regular expressions for words

Regular expressions to match individual words can be usefully combined.

> In Exalead's implementation of regular expressions and Boolean syntax, the search string
>
> /Jud(y|ith|i)/ NEXT Gill OR /Jud(y|ith|i)/ NEXT /.{1}/ NEXT Gill OR "Gill," NEXT /Jud(y|ith|i)/
>
> will find webpages that contains the phrases Judy Gill, or Gill, Judy, or Judy Gill having a one-character initial between Judy and Gill. Also, Judy can be spelled as one of Judy, Judi, or Judith.
>
> The components of this expression include:
>
> - **The matching pairs of forward slashes (/):** These tell Exalead that what is between them is to be treated as a word-level regular expression.

> ### 🔨 Important notes on using Boolean logic:
>
> 1. In text boxes designed explicitly for Boolean search strings (usually designated by a label or some option that converts the box for this use), most search engines ask that you explicitly enter the Boolean operators between terms. Thus, blanks between terms will cause your logic to malfunction.
> 2. No explicit Boolean operator is used before the first term in a search string unless it is a negation operator. Otherwise, it is generally assumed that the first term is required.
> 3. In an undesignated text box, AND is generally the default Boolean operator. Thus, a space between terms defaults to an implied conjunction of terms. Note: undesignated text boxes include those found on simple search entry interfaces.
>
> ⚠ Depending on the search engine, the operator itself may be interpreted as a search term. For example, in a text entry box designated for "none of these terms," "any of these terms," "with the exact phrase," or "all of these terms," no Boolean operator may be accepted.
>
> > 🔣 Google and certain other search engines do not explicitly designate a particular text box in their advanced search entry interfaces for Boolean search strings. In addition, Boolean operators and phrases will not be correctly interpreted in advanced search text entry boxes labeled "With the exact phrase," "Any of these Terms," "None of these words," or the like. They will, however, work in boxes labeled "With all of the words" (a more accurate label for which might be "With all of the terms," since phrases are accepted).
>
> ⇨ For more on the conventions for entry boxes and syntax used on the simple and advanced interfaces of our featured search engines, refer to the explanation in Reference Section 6.1: AND, OR, and NOT.

- **/Jud(y|ith|i)/ NEXT Gill:** This string will find documents having at least one of the phrases Judy Gill, Judith Gill, or Judi Gill.
- **/Jud(y|ith|i)/ NEXT /.{1}/ NEXT Gill:** This will find documents as in the preceding item, but with a one-character "word" in the middle of Judy/i/ith and Gill. The period (dot) means any character, although more precise regular expression syntax could indicate a letter of the alphabet as the kind of required character. The {1} after the period

indicates exactly one character is required. **Note:** If you wanted 1 to 8 characters to be required, you would write {1,8} for this.

- **"Gill," NEXT /Jud(y|ith|i)/:** This will find documents having at least one of the phrases Gill, Judy, Gill, Judith, or Gill, Judi.
- **The quotes around "Gill,":** These are needed so that the comma (,) will not be ignored in the matching process. In Exalead, as in other search engines, quotes usually indicate a phrase. But, they can also be used by some search engines to prevent dropping of stop words and punctuation from being required before a match can occur.

Practice Exercise:

The document must contain a term (a word) that begins with either one or both of the stubs ineffect or defect.

🔢 The words ineffective or ineffectiveness or defection or defective will satisfy this requirement.

AlltheWeb	Wildcards are unavailable; OR may be used.
AltaVista	Wildcards are unavailable at word endings; OR may be used.
Copernic	Although you can search on word particles, wildcards for word stubbing are unavailable; OR may be used.
Google	Although wildcards are unavailable at ends of words (for whole word replacement only), word stemming is automatic. OR may be used. Type ineffect OR defect.
MSN Search	Although wildcards are unavailable at ends of words (for whole word replacement only), word stemming may be automatic. OR may be used, as in ineffect OR defect.

For more readings on Boolean logic and proximity operators: ⇨

- SearchEngineWatch.com: www.searchenginewatch.com/facts/article.php/2155991
- BrightPlanet.com:
  - ⟩ www.brightplanet.com/deepcontent/tutorials/Search/part4.asp
  - ⟩ www.brightplanet.com/deepcontent/tutorials/Search/part5.asp
  - ⟩ www.brightplanet.com/deepcontent/tutorials/Search/part6.asp#topic19

Internal Book Cross-Links

1. Cross-links for this section: Reference Section 6.1: AND, OR, and NOT

Prioritizing term relationship operators [1]

Complex Boolean expressions usually involve the use of precedence operators, which are tertiary parameters. In general, search engines use brackets to prioritize Boolean operator application, and many allow brackets to be nested to one or more levels. The expressions within brackets are evaluated first, from innermost to outermost bracket levels.

Precedence operators used in Boolean expressions can be very useful when conducting your searches, as seen in the examples below.

In Boolean logic, when no brackets are present:

- NOT has precedence over AND
- AND has precedence over OR

- (video AND Sony) OR Hitachi does not render the same search results as video AND (Sony OR Hitachi).
- (video AND Sony) OR Hitachi is equivalent to video AND Sony OR Hitachi.

Explanation: The brackets are needed in the video AND (Sony OR Hitachi) expression, since the OR has a lower priority than the AND. The brackets cause the OR to be evaluated first, with entirely different consequences than if it were evaluated second.

Often, it is possible to restate a Boolean expression so it is not necessary to prioritize relationships.

🔓 You can restate NOT (cat OR dog) as NOT cat NOT dog.

🔓 To express the idea of football or baseball, but not both in the same document, an expression such as (football NOT baseball) OR (baseball NOT football) is needed,

📎 In this example, the idea being expressed is either/or (the mutually exclusive use of the word OR), as opposed to the and/or (the so-called "inclusive" OR) that means at least one of these terms is required, but not necessarily both.

although the brackets here are not necessary since the NOT is evaluated before the OR by default.

💡 You can use Boolean operators in conjunction with field operators, as in kangaroo site:es OR site:au, to find the word kangaroo in a website having a domain suffix in its address for either Spain (es) or Australia (au).

⚠️ However, you may not be able to represent the above logic with, say, site:(es OR au). Depending on the search engine, various mixes of operator parameters and nesting levels may or may not work as expected due to implementation limitations.

With nesting, Boolean expression can become very complex. In fact, few of the search engines can handle the necessary degree of complexity.

🔓 The expression:

```
(ineffective OR defective) NOT
((ineffective AND (satellite OR "dish specifications"))
OR (defective AND (satellite OR "dish specifications")))
```

— has three levels of nesting of brackets, and can be parsed as follows:

(ineffective OR defective): This expression causes the search engine to look for a document that has the words ineffective and/or the word defective.

However, even if the preceding turns out to be true, either one or both of the following cannot be true for a match to be made. The NOT is like a "common factor," applicable to both of the expressions in brackets covered by it. The two expressions over which the NOT distributes are:

- **ineffective AND (satellite OR "dish specifications"):**
  The word ineffective must not occur in conjunction with either the word satellite or of the phrase dish specifications. The AND here is distributed over the expression within brackets following it.
- **defective AND (satellite OR "dish specifications"):**
  The word defective must not occur in conjunction with either the word satellite or the phrase dish specifications. Again, the AND applies to the whole of the expression within brackets that follows it.

Here are some additional examples of prioritizing term relationship operators:

- **Phrase:** Entering "Adapter card" as a phrase, as opposed to two individual words, will require that the search engine find the words next to one another in the specified order (adapter before card). In effect, the quotes serve as operators to indicate a phrase.
- **And/or (inclusion):** Entering ice OR cream will require that the documents found have either one or both words anywhere in them. This will result in more matches and more search engine findings as compared to AND, since it expands rather than restricts the scope of the search.
- **Conjunction:** Entering ice AND cream will require that the documents returned have both words, regardless of which one comes first or how far apart these words are.
- **Negation:** Entering ice NOT cream will require that the documents have the word ice, but lack the word cream. Similar to AND, this restricts the scope of what will be found.
- **Phrases with relationships:** Entering +"ice cream" -"I scream" will cause the phrase ice cream, consisting of two words in a particular order, to be found. On the other hand, documents containing the phrase I scream will be ignored.
- **Inclusion and conjunction:** Entering ice AND (nice OR "ice cream") will cause the OR condition to be evaluated before the AND condition. Otherwise, by default, the AND operator is normally applied to the search terms involved before OR (since it is not simply a matter of evaluating the expression from left to right). Different search engine findings will be returned if brackets are not included in the expression. This is similar to the idea of using brackets to establish priorities between the operations of exponentiation, multiplication, division, addition, and subtraction, when doing mathematics by computer.
- **Range comparison:** Entering > Bailin AND < Bailout as a search parameter will cause matches to occur on all names that start with Bail and have small alphabetic characters between in and out. If searching for peoples' family names in a particular phone book, this would be like starting with the name Bailin and using all names up to Bailout as search terms.

Practice Exercises:

1. The word satellite must be near the phrase dish specifications, within a proximity of 10 words on either side.

AlltheWeb	Explicit word proximity option is unavailable.
AltaVista	Explicit word proximity option is unavailable.
Copernic	Type satellite NEAR "dish specifications" in the appropriate Boolean expression text box.
Google	Explicit word proximity option is unavailable. However, Google does automatic stemming, and you can use its single word wildcard (the asterisk) character to achieve nearness up to 2 or 3 words (⇨ Reference Section 6.1: Wildcards, substrings, stemming).
MSN Search	Explicit word proximity option is unavailable.

2. The word satellite must occur with any of the words beginning with iron and/or copper and/or the word satellite must not occur along with the word unused. Once the preceding condition is satisfied, words beginning with ineffect and/or defect must also be present.

AlltheWeb	Wildcards at the ends of words and stemming are unavailable. However, enter (satellite AND (iron OR copper) OR satellite NOT unused) AND (ineffective OR defective) for the Boolean logic to obtain some of the results intended.
AltaVista	
Copernic	
Google	Although wildcards are unavailable at ends of words (for whole word replacements only), word stemming is automatic. Entering (satellite (iron OR copper) OR satellite -unused) (ineffect OR defect) would, in theory, work. Unfortunately, brackets do not work to prioritize the application of Boolean operators, so the logic cannot be implemented.
MSN Search	Although wildcards are unavailable at ends of words (for whole word replacements only), word stemming may be automatic if you choose to adjust the "Approximate Match" slider when entering a search. Enter (satellite (iron OR copper) OR satellite -unused) (ineffect OR defect).

3. The words ineffective and/or the word defective must occur, but the word ineffective must not occur along with the word satellite and/or the phrase dish specifications. Regardless of the preceding result, finding the word defective along with the word satellite and/or along with the phrase dish specifications also satisfies the search conditions.

AlltheWeb	In the "Boolean" text box, type (ineffective OR defective) NOT (ineffective AND (satellite OR "dish specifications")) OR defective AND (satellite OR "dish specifications").
AltaVista	In the "Search with this Boolean expression" text box, type (ineffective OR defective) NOT (ineffective AND (satellite OR "dish specifications")) OR defective AND (satellite OR "dish specifications").
Copernic	In an appropriate search text entry box, type (ineffective OR defective) NOT (ineffective AND (satellite OR "dish specifications")) OR defective AND (satellite OR "dish specifications").
Google	Typing (ineffective OR defective) -(ineffective (satellite OR "dish specifications")) OR defective (satellite OR "dish specifications") does not work, since the brackets to prioritize Boolean operations have no effect.
MSN Search	Enter (ineffective OR defective) -(ineffective (satellite OR "dish specifications")) OR defective (satellite OR "dish specifications").

A better interface for entering term-based filters

We have already seen parts of the Exalead search entry interface above, along with an examples of Exalead's ability to use fuzzy logic and to match word patterns using regular expressions. But, Exalead's advanced Web search interface has even more of the best kind of features for making it easy to enter term-based filters without typing in your own operator parameters. This interface is the best we have noticed so far for term-based filters among Internet search engines.

The top rows on this interface contain two drop-down menus (expanded as you see below for the first row), followed by a text box for term entry, and another drop-down menu box (not shown below) for certain metadata-based filters associated with the terms entered on that row. You use one row for each sub-set of terms. In addition, a last drop-down menu box provides a further level of choices for term variation filters.

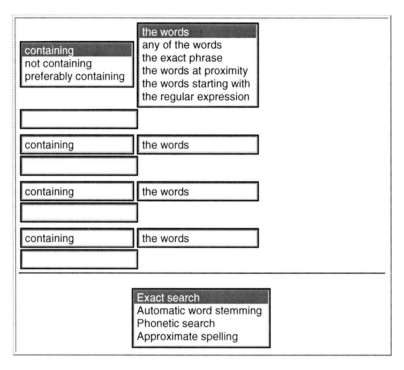

 Along with entering your terms in the text box on each row, you can enter:

- Fuzzy OR logic by choosing "preferably containing" in the first box, and "any of the words" in the second box.
- The proximity refinement of the Boolean AND by choosing "containing" in the first box, and "the words at proximity" in the second box. **Note:** Exalead's NEXT proximity operator, exemplified earlier, for some reason does not appear as a choice in the second drop-down menu. Perhaps this is an omission that will be corrected later.
- Stemming for all words in your search terms box by choosing "Automatic word stemming" from the shown drop-down menu box under all the rows where you enter your terms.

You cannot, however, enter certain combinations unless you use operator parameters, or operator parameters in conjunction with the choices from the various menu boxes.

> 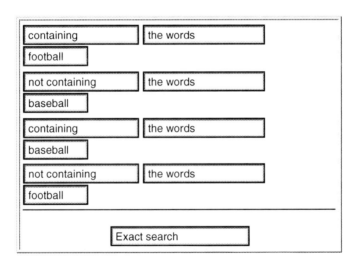 Thus, if you choose "containing" from the first box, and want both the phrase good dog and the word Bumper as your terms, you yourself need to type the quotes in the text box around the good dog part of the search string to indicate that it is a phrase rather than two separate words.

If you want to enter a complex expression, in which you prioritize your term sets with anything other than a Boolean AND (the implied Boolean operator), you need to enter the entire search string manually.

> (football NOT baseball) OR (baseball NOT football) must be entered manually, by typing the operator parameters yourself. The following entries, in other words, will not work, because you would need an OR between the first two rows (as a set) and the third and fourth rows (as a second set).

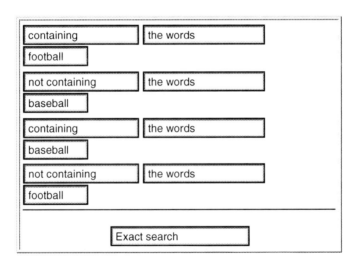

Perhaps in some future edition of this interface, Exalead will add a further level of choices to implement the logic provided by brackets. With this, certain choices would become available, inserted between the different sets of rows in the above. Such choices might include:

- AND, i.e., "must contain," which is the default, as mentioned.
- NOT, i.e., "must not contain."
- OR, i.e., "any of these words."
- Fuzzy OR, i.e., "preferably containing."
- The proximity refinement of AND, i.e., "the words at proximity."

You might get something that looks like the following:

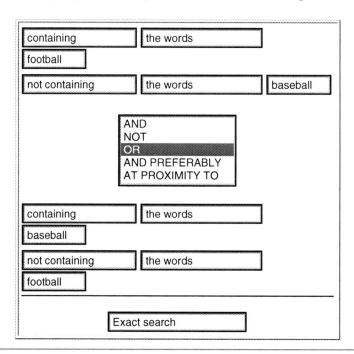

Internal Book Cross-Links

1. Cross-links for this section: Reference Section 6.1: AND, OR, and NOT

Metadata-Based Search Filters [1]

This section describes the basic ideas of metadata-based filter features. Metadata-based filters are organized here into three sub-classes:

- File content characteristics.
- Hosting site characteristics.
- Related documents or sites.

Metadata and metatags

Search engine catalogs contain metadata (⇨ Chapter 1: Catalogs and indexes, on how catalogs work). When the metadata is gathered by metacrawlers (spiders, robots), it is automatically detected based on information either inside the

Internet files themselves or accompanying the files on websites (e.g., entries in file directories kept for all files on a given website).

The metadata kept *inside* HTML document files can be found in the document title, or in other so-called **metatags** near the front of the document. These are the second most important source of metadata, after the document title. WebMonkey has an entertaining and informative article on metatags (hotwired.lycos.com/webmonkey/html/96/51/index2a.html).

New metatags are being developed every day to characterize the contents of files.

🎵 For a file that contains music, a "genre" metatag to describe the type of music, e.g., classical or jazz.

By convention, the most important metatag after the title for webcrawlers is the one named DESCRIPTION, meant to summarize a document file's contents. Some webcrawlers also use the KEYWORDS metatag. An example is: <META NAME="KEYWORDS" CONTENT="computer, parts, kits">.

Note that the "NAME=" attribute in the metatag element identifies the field, e.g., author, company, program that generated the document, reference number, and so on. The "CONTENT=" attribute gives the value(s) of the field. In the above example, the values are the keywords "computer, parts, kits."

Since much of the metadata available on the Internet is either missing or not provided in a standardized form, at present, many or even most of the metatag field types are not provided as pre-defined choices (formal filters) by search engines.

> ⇨ For more discussion of this problem, refer to "Discussion Topics" on our website: ⇨ Search Engine Evolution, Part 4: Infrastructure of the semantic web.

Following are some examples of metatags from various documents:

- <META NAME="Abstract" CONTENT="The IBM corporate home page, entry point to information about IBM products and services"/>
- <META NAME="address" CONTENT="123 Sunshine Road">
- <META NAME="AUTHOR" CONTENT="John F.Peterson.">
- <META NAME="CATEGORY" CONTENT="home page" />
- <META NAME="CONTENT_OWNER" CONTENT=" "/>
- <META NAME="Copyright" CONTENT="Copyright (c) 2001 by IBM Corporation"/>
- <META NAME="DC.contributors" CONTENT="http://www.nomex.net">
- <META NAME="DC.coverage" CONTENT="all">
- <META NAME="DC.creator" CONTENT="http://www.nomex.net">
- <META NAME="description" CONTENT="Family Spiegl's Homepage">
- <META NAME="DOCUMENTCOUNTRYCODE" CONTENT="us">
- <META NAME="generator" CONTENT="Adobe GoLive 4">

- <META NAME="KEYWORDS" CONTENT="computer, parts, kits">
- <META NAME="MS.LOCALE" CONTENT="EN-US" />
- <META NAME="Owner" CONTENT="webmaster@www.xyz.com"/>
- <META NAME="package" TYPE="end" CONTENT="Dublin Core">
- <META NAME="PRODCAT" CONTENT="Home">
- <META NAME="PROGRAMMER" CONTENT=" "/>
- <META NAME="rating" CONTENT="General">
- <META NAME="REVISIT-AFTER" CONTENT="1 day">
- <META NAME="ROBOTS" CONTENT="INDEX,FOLLOW">
- <META NAME="Security" CONTENT="public"/>
- <META NAME="SEGMENT" CONTENT="dhs">
- <META NAME="Source" CONTENT="Franklin/IPC"/>
- <META NAME="TEMPLATE" CONTENT="3com v5 Sample Template version 2.0"/>

Internal Book Cross-Links

1. Cross-links for this section:

- Reference Section 6.2: explains how the concepts here apply to our featured search engines.
- Chapter 5: provides a high-level explanation of search filter entry interfaces.

File structure characteristics [1]

These may be used as convenient filters when conducting searches, and may be divided as follows:

1. **File format or type** [2]: is usually identified by extensions to the file name.

   The file "Happy_Unbirthday.WAV" is a sound file in the WAV format.

   The file format extension is usually 3 or 4 characters long, as seen in the table on the next page.

File Types	File Format Extensions
Document Files	HTM or HTML - Hypertext Markup Language; PDF - Adobe Acrobat files; DOC - Microsoft Word; TXT - ASCII text
Dynamic vector graphics	SWF files produced with Flash
Image - pictures, static graphics	GIF; JPG; PNG
Audio	MP3; AU; WAV
Video - movies	AVI; MPEG

To use file format as a search filter: Select particular kinds of files (e.g., image, audio, video, PDF, RTF, Word) via their file name extensions, which will restrict the search findings to these kinds of files.

Here are some file formats used by AlltheWeb.

Document and dynamic vector graphic files:

Use the drop-down menu box in the advanced Web search to choose either "Any format" (which includes HTML files), or any other format shown here.

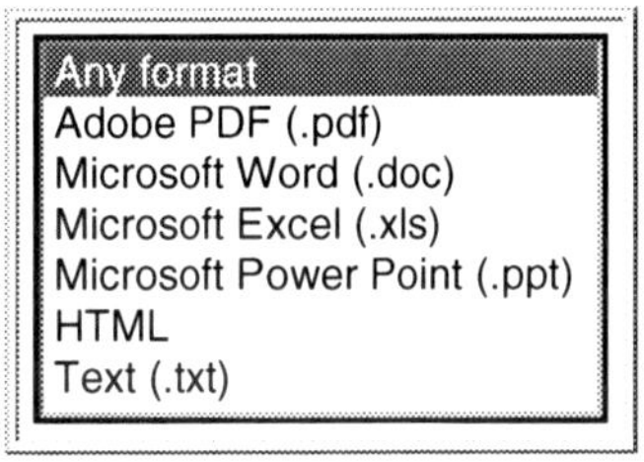

Any format
Adobe PDF (.pdf)
Microsoft Word (.doc)
Microsoft Excel (.xls)
Microsoft Power Point (.ppt)
HTML
Text (.txt)

Multi-media files:

- In the advanced Pictures search interface:

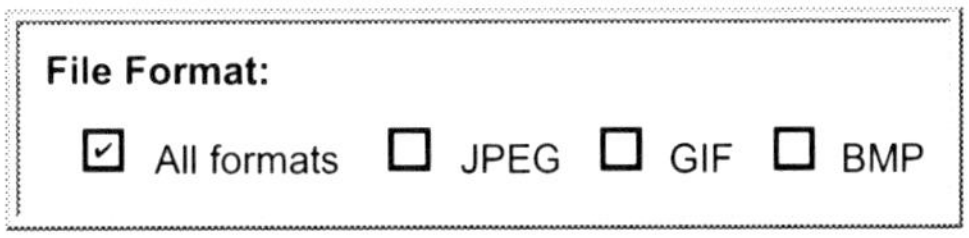

  File Format:
  ☑ All formats   ☐ JPEG   ☐ GIF   ☐ BMP

- In the advanced Video search interface:

  Formats: ☑ All   ☐ AVI   ☐ AVI/DivX   ☐ MPEG   ☐ Real   ☐ QuickTime

2. **Embedded content or embedded feature** [3]: Occurs when a document file contains a link to a multi-media file that is to display on the webpage along with the text. Embedded content also includes programs inside the document file, including those in VBScript, JavaScript, or ActiveX, as well as Java applets and the like.

🔞 Filtering by embedded content no longer appears to be supported by most mainstream search engines. However, MSN Search does support it to an extent. Here is an example.

Results are restricted to those that contain links to files of all the selected extensions.

☐ Image(.jpg, .gif, etc)   ☐ Audio(.wav, .aiff)   ☐ Video(.avi, .mpeg)
☑ MP3 Audio(.mp3)   ☐ ActiveX(.ocx)   ☐ VBScript(.vbs)
☐ Shockwave(.dcr)   ☐ PDF/Adobe Acrobat(.pdf)   ☐ JavaScript(.js)
☐ Java applets   Other extensions: [＿＿＿＿] (e.g. .doc)

To use embedded content as a search filter: Select only HTML document files with lines of Javascript inside or having a link to display an image in JPG format from an accompanying JPG file.

3. **Document file section or location** [4]:

File section: Most of the document files on the Web are encoded in a format known as HTML. This encoding divides the document hierarchically into two major sections, the **header** and the **body**.

Inside the header, most documents have a particular pair of HTML tags delimiting the **title** to print in the bar at the very top of the web browser screen. **The document title is vital because it is the single most important element used by search engines to index a document.**

The remaining screen content is contained in the "body" section, often referred to as the **text** of the document. You can direct the search engine to search only within the text (body) section, or only within the title of the document.

To use document section as a search filter: Choose the "title only" option, which will limit the search engine to inspecting only this part of the document in making a match.

Enter title:goldfish in a search box to restrict the search to documents that have a title with the word "goldfish" in them. This is an example of a field search operator embedded along with the primary parameter, the search term itself.

Document location: In addition to file section, you can often choose particular locations within the document file where these are demarcated using HTML tags. Such tags identify, for example, tables, scripts, frames, anchors (places for hyperlinks), and so on. Certain search engines can look for text inside such tags or detect the presence of these tags as a document feature.

Google is able to find text restricted to anchor tags, i.e., hyperlink text displayed on a webpage. Thus, inside the HTML code, a hyperlink whose text is John McPherson might be coded as **<a href="http://www.johnmcpherson.com>John McPherson</a>**. Thus, entering inanchor: "John McPherson" as a search term would be used by Google to look for the specified term in the hyperlinks on a webpage.

To restrict the search to the title section with Google:

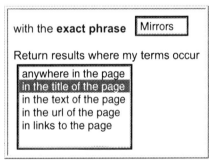

- Type the search query in an appropriate text box.
  e.g., enter Mirrors.
- Select "in the title of the page" in the "Occurrences: Return results where my terms occur" drop-down menu box.

Internal Book Cross-Links

1. Cross-links with: Reference Section 6.2: File structure characteristics
2. Cross-links with: Reference Section 6.2: File format
3. Cross-links with: Reference Section 6.2: Embedded content
4. Cross-links with: Reference Section 6.2: Document file section or location

---

Practice Exercises:

1. The word defective must appear in the document text (body section), while the word ineffective must not occur in its title.

AlltheWeb	In the "Word Filters" section: Select "Must include" along with "in the text," and enter defective in the accompanying text box. In the next set of choices, select "Must not include" along with "in the title," and enter ineffective in the accompanying text box.
AltaVista	In the "Search with this Boolean expression" text box, type defective NOT title:ineffective. However, this does not ensure that defective occurs in the document body (it might be only in the title).
Copernic	It cannot handle this problem in an exact way. However, you can roughly confirm that the word ineffective is not an important term in the document as follows: Do a "Find in results" procedure against the "Results list" (i.e., against the metadata about the documents) such that the word ineffective is disallowed. This provides a rough equivalent for the not-in-title condition, because the document metadata always includes the terms in the document title (along with keywords, for example).
Google	Enter intext:defective -intitle:ineffective defective in the "with all the words" text box.
MSN Search	Enter inbody:defective -intitle:ineffective defective in the text box.

2. The word defective must be found in the text of a hyperlink (anchor HTML tag).

At present, this option is available only in Google and MSN Search, where you enter inanchor:defective.

3. The document must contain the word satellite and have a table inside of it.

At present, this option is unavailable in any of our featured search engines.

File content characteristics [1]

File characteristics are among the most important metadata-based filters. They can be divided as follows:

1. **File age** [2]: The date and time of creation or last modification of a file usually indicates the date a webcrawler detects a new file or a file change. This is because, contrary to what you might expect, the information contained in metatags or in file directory tables on the servers where the files are stored is ignored.

   Thus, it is difficult to obtain the accurate file age from a search engine because it is often simply based on when the crawler detected the file on the Internet (www.searchenginewatch.com/searchday/article.php/2160061).

   > One exception: if you do a discussion board search, such as one on USENET groups, the message posting dates are exact.

   AlltheWeb advanced Web search provides the following file age filter selections.

Date	Only find results updated	after	1	January	1980
		before	9	March	2003

2. **Document language** [3]: Even if there is no metatag for document language, webcrawlers or analysis programs have ways of detecting the language used. Search engines will often default to searching for documents in all languages, unless otherwise told. Thus, the language setting's use is to restrict the scope of what the search finds.

   > △ To use language search in some search engines, the switch that screens out potentially offensive material must first be "off."
   >
   > Some search engines also have language translation abilities, although this generally applies more to presenting findings than to searching for them.
   >
   > Some search engines have parameters that allow the user to customize the language of the search engine interface. This would permit French-speaking users to choose "French" as their interface language, for example.

🏁 You are looking for documents in English or Korean. Enter your search terms in an appropriate text box, and select the appropriate checkboxes in the AltaVista interface below.

Search Languages: Search only for pages written in these language(s):

☐ Albanian - Shqip	☐ German - Deutsch	☐ Polish - Polski
☐ Arabic - العربية	☐ Greek - Ελληνικά	☐ Portuguese - Português
☐ Bulgarian - български	☐ Hebrew - עברית	☐ Romanian - Română
☐ Catalan - Català	☐ Hungarian - Magyar	☐ Russian - Русский
☐ Croatian - Hrvatski	☐ Icelandic - Íslensk	☐ Simplified Chinese (China) - 汉语
☐ Czech - Český	☐ Italian - Italiano	☐ Slovak - Slovenčina
☐ Danish - Dansk	☐ Japanese - 日本語	☐ Slovenian - Slovenščina
☐ Dutch - Nederlands	☑ Korean - 한국어	☐ Spanish - Español
☑ English - English	☐ Latvian - Latviešu	☐ Swedish - Svenska
☐ Estonian - Eesti	☐ Lithuanian - Lietuvių	☐ Thai - ภาษาไทย
☐ Finnish - Suomi	☐ Norwegian - Norsk	☐ Traditional Chinese (Taiwan) - 漢語
☐ French - Français	☐ Persian - فارسی	☐ Turkish - Türkçe

⇨ Refer to Reference Section 6.2: Similarity of meaning concerning translation of search terms into another language *before* searching.

⇨ See Reference Section 6.3: Finding language translation, concerning translation of *found* documents into the user's language of choice.

Practice Exercise:

The document must be in French, and contain both of the phrases school board and panneau d'école, and be located at a URL whose domain name starts with http://www.jeanchretien.abc.

AlltheWeb	Proceed as follows in the advanced Web search:
	• Enter url:www.jeanchretien.abc "panneau d'école" "school board" in the "Boolean" text box.
	• In the language drop-down menu, choose the French language.

AltaVista	Proceed as follows:
	• Enter panneau d'école in the "this exact phrase" box. • Enter url:www.jeanchretien.abc and "school board" into the "all of these words" text box. • In the language dialog box, check French.
Copernic	Proceed as follows:

	• If applicable, choose a suitable search engine category, such as Web Search. Also, select the desired search tools from the available list, along with the maximum number of results per search tool.
	• Enter "panneau d'école" "school board" with the "All the words" option selected. Then do the search.
	• Do a "Find in results" procedure, with filters:
	   o Select the French language checkbox.
	   o In the "Domain" section of the filter form, in the "Show only results for" text entry box, enter www.jeanchretien.abc.

Google	Proceed as follows:
	• Enter inurl:www.jeanchretien.abc "panneau d'école" "school board" in the "with all the words" text box. • In the language drop-down menu, choose French.
MSN Search	Proceed as follows:
	• Enter url:www.jeanchretien.abc "panneau d'école" "school board" in the text box. • In the SearchBuilder language drop-down menu, choose French.

3. **Potentially offensive content** [4]: Many search engines have features such as "family filter" or "safe search" to exclude websites or pages having "adult-only" materials. Setting a filter can prevent the search from finding pornographic material.

[icon] In AltaVista, select the "Family Filter" link using the basic search interface. The search engine will branch to a page that specifies how AltaVista will filter out pages. There is also an option to create a password to prevent changing these settings by unauthorized users, such as underage children. When done, click the "Save Settings" button.

Choose your Family Filter preference.

⦿ **Multimedia Only** - filters image, video and audio search only.

○ **All** - filters all searches: web pages, images, audio and video. **Note:** With the Family Filter set to "All", you can perform Web searches in only English, French, German and Spanish.

○ **None** - will not filter any search

Password Protection (Optional):
Makes it necessary to enter a password to change your Family Filter preferences.

Enter Optional Password: [_____]

Re-enter Optional Password: [_____]

4. **Additional document file content characteristics** [5]: Examples include the name of the publication, publisher, author, company or its stock symbol, and message identifier.

[icon] In Google, entering stocks:intc will locate the latest stock quotation at the Yahoo finance site for Intel (stock symbol INTC).

5. **Additional multi-media file content characteristics** [6]: Examples include the name of the artist and/or song, duration of play, and audio or video files.

[icon] Google's advanced image search allows you to make selections based on image size and/or coloration.

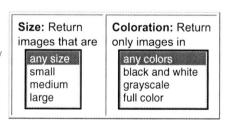

Size: Return images that are	**Coloration:** Return only images in
any size small medium large	any colors black and white grayscale full color

Practice Exercises:

1. The file must not contain potentially offensive material, be in MP3 audio format, contain the song Me and Mister Blackster, and have a play duration of less than 1 minute.

AlltheWeb	While it has an offensive content filter and a simple Audio file search, you cannot specify which audio file format to choose; nor can you limit play duration of an audio file. You can use title:"Me and Mister Blackster" to search for song with that title.
AltaVista	On the simple MP3/Audio search interface, choose the link for "family filter," and turn the filter "on." Click on the "advanced search" link to go to the advanced MP3/Audio search. Then: • Select the checkbox only for MP3 files. • Type title:"Me and Mister Blackster" in the search terms text box. • Choose the radio button for under one minute play duration.
Copernic	It has no offensive material filter, or one to limit play duration, to select specific audio file formats, or to restrict the search term to a song title. However, to locate audio files, search categories are available to use only search engines or only search engine interfaces. These will take you to specific search engine interfaces that may allow continued searching.
Google	It does not have a filter for play duration. It does have an offensive content filter, intitle: and filetype: fielded searches for limiting the search to the file title and audio file formats, respectively.
MSN Search	It does not have a filter for play duration. It does have an offensive content filter, intitle: and filetype: fielded searches for limiting the search to the file title and audio file formats, respectively.

2. The document must contain the word satellite and be a press release.

AlltheWeb AltaVista Google MSN Search	Options are not all available in a straightforward manner. However, you can enter the phrase Press Release as a search term along with the term satellite.
Copernic	Do a search on the term satellite using the "Business & Economy>Press Releases" search engine category.

3. The query on **satellite** must be restricted to documents published in Forbes Magazine, and the company involved must be Worldgate Communications.

AlltheWeb AltaVista Google MSN Search	Options are not all available in a straightforward manner. However, you can enter Forbes as a search term along with the terms satellite and Worldgate Communications.
Copernic	Choose the "Business & Economy>Company Information" search engine category. Uncheck all the search engines except for Forbes.com. Enter the phrase Worldgate Communications in the search terms box.

Internal Book Cross-Links

1. Cross-links with: Reference Section 6.2: File Content Characteristics
2. Cross-links with: Reference Section 6.2: File age
3. Cross-links with: Reference Section 6.2: Document language
4. Cross-links with: Reference Section 6.2: Potentially offensive content
5. Cross-links with: Reference Section 6.2: Additional document file content characteristics
6. Cross-links with: Reference Section 6.2: Additional multi-media file content characteristics

Hosting site characteristics [1]

These parameters include:

1. **Geographical region of server** [2]: This restricts the findings to files located on servers in particular continents, countries, states, provinces, or cities, etc. Although the Internet is very international, being able to restrict access to servers in particular parts of the world is still valuable for many kinds of searches.

   The **domain suffix** of the URL (the last characters after the last period of Internet addresses) often indicates the country, if located outside the United States. However, this is becoming less true as many countries adopt the U.S. conventions for domain suffixes.

In theory, a more accurate and comprehensive method of finding servers by geographical region is to use search engines providing choices not based on domain suffix. Most of our featured search engines provide drop-down menus with options for the different continents of the world, i.e., North America, Europe, and so on. In practice, the search engines generally use the domain suffix to determine the region or country for websites.

Although seldom employed, there is a domain suffix for the United States (.us). Most domain suffixes used in the U.S. are as follows:

org: non-profit organization
mil: military
gov: government
com: commercial
edu: education
net: network operation
int: international organization

Additional domain names were added in 2001:

aero: air-transport industry
biz: businesses
coop: cooperatives
info: any use
museum: museums
name: individuals
pro: professionals such as physicians, lawyers.

AlltheWeb Help states: The **Limit to region** option will limit your search to a geographical region, based on the top level domain names for that region.

⇨ Domain names are explained in more detail below in URL (resource) or site Internet address.

In the example here, the search term is typed in the appropriate text box and then the "region" is selected from the drop-down menu.

Choosing "New Zealand" from a list of options will cause the search engine to restrict its search to websites in that country.

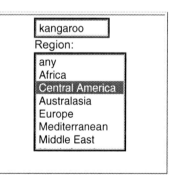

Enter the phrase primary school and choose servers from Australia to receive only webpages on that topic that are hosted in that region of the world.

🔠 Entering kangaroo domain:ca in certain search engines will restrict the search for the word "kangaroo" to servers located in domain "ca," i.e., in Canada, but only for those Canadian servers using the "ca" domain name. (This is an example of the syntax of a "fielded search," using operator parameters. In addition, a search engine might indicate a domain restriction using perhaps a text box devoted to domain or an options drop-down list box.)

Practice Exercise:

The document must have a word that starts with the stub deb followed by any characters, and ends in the letters ect. In addition, the document must be written in Spanish and be hosted (located) on a server in North America.

AlltheWeb	It does not have wildcard selection features. It does have a filter for region. Choose "North America" from the appropriate "Domain Filters" drop-down menu box, along with the Spanish language from the document language drop-down menu.
AltaVista	It does not have wildcard selection features. Nor does it have a filter for region. You can, however, choose the Spanish language option.
Copernic	It does not have wildcard selection features. For the rest, perform a "Find within results" procedure using the "Advanced Filters" dialog box. In the latter, choose: "North America" from the appropriate drop-down menu box and the Spanish language, using the appropriate checkboxes.
Google	It does not have wildcard selection features for parts of words. It does have country selection, but only in one of its less well-known interfaces — its "Language Tools" interface. Use the latter to select both language and region. To find North America, you will need to run the search 3 times; once for each North American country (Canada, United States, Mexico).
MSN Search	It does not have wildcard selection features for parts of words; nor can enabling stemming handle a wildcard in the middle of a word. You can, however, choose the Spanish language and Country/Location options with SearchBuilder, or simply directly enter the search string language:sp (loc:US OR loc:CA OR loc:MX) for these.

2. **URL (resource) or site Internet address** [3]: A URL (Uniform Resource Locator, or Internet address) consists of:

- **Protocol identifier**, identifying the type of Internet application, such as http:// (Hypertext Transfer Protocol) for the Web, or ftp:// (File Transfer Protocol), or mailto: (for e-mail).

- **Site (full domain) name**, including the domain suffix.

- **Resource identifier**, the part of the URL following the first single forward slash ("/") character. This provides the name of the **resource** (file) identified at the end of the string, which may also include the

> The IP (Internet Protocol) address is not the same thing as the domain name in most cases, but some search engines can search on this. One server can have 1 to many network interface cards, each of which can have 1 to many IP addresses, each of which can have from 0 to many associated domain names. For example, IP address 24.120.45.3 can hold up to 256 full domain names.
>
> Some search engines, such as MSN Search, can filter according to IP address.

directory path to that resource on the server.

In the URL http://www.abbott.ca/ab/schedule.htm:

- http:// is the **protocol identifier**.
- www.abbott.ca is the **site/full domain name**. The ca is the domain suffix, and stands for Canada.
- /ab/schedule.htm is the **resource identifier**; /ab/ gives the **directory path** to the file schedule.htm.

A full URL as a search parameter may seem illogical, since web browsers can simply go to a specified URL. However, search engines allow searching on *parts* of URL's, such as domain only.

In Google, enter the search term kangaroo in one of the appropriate text boxes. Then, in the "Domains" text box, type the domain suffix es for Spain.

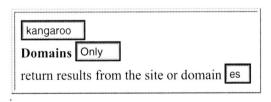

Make sure that "Only" is selected in the drop-down menu box.

▓ Entering quicksolve in, say, a "URL" text box will restrict the search to data on servers that have "quicksolve" as part of their name. (If a fielded search syntax is available, the same restriction might be specified by entering **url:** quicksolve as part of the search term.)

> ▲ The "only" value in the above drop-down box can be used to exclude rather than to include a specific domain.

▓ In Google, to find the word house in any part of the URL string, enter inurl:house in an appropriate text box. This will find the string house somewhere in the URL.

> with **all** of the words
> | inurl:house |

In some search engines, combining the URL with wildcards can locate many different URLs having a string of characters that is common to them all.

> ▲ Do not enter URL search logic that is self-canceling.
>
> ▓ In Google, if you enter site:www. house.com -inurl:house.com, you will receive no results. This is because the site/domain, which is part of the URL, must contain house.com, but house.com is not allowed in the URL (since the minus sign means negation).

▓ To find all URL's having john in them, enter *john* in the URL box on a search form, where the asterisks represent wildcard characters before and/or after john.

Practice Exercises:

1. The URL of the found documents must have the words ineffective and/or defective in it, and the word satellite must be somewhere in the document. Also, the document must be aged less than two years prior to the query's date. Finally, the findings must be sorted for display by the word satellite.

AlltheWeb	Enter satellite AND (url:ineffective OR url:defective) in the Boolean search text box. In the "Date" area, check "Date after" and choose the day, month, and year of the starting date from the drop-down menu boxes. Note: AlltheWeb does not have a way of sorting the findings by keyword.

AltaVista	Enter satellite AND (url:ineffective OR url:defective) in the "Search with this Boolean expression" text box. Enter the range of dates in the date range area. Note: AltaVista does not have a way of sorting the findings by keyword.
Copernic	Not all of this is possible with Copernic. You can do a search on the single word satellite, using optimal search filtering to extract the dates associated with the findings. Then do a "Find in results" procedure using the "Advanced Filters" dialog box to filter by a range of dates. The best you can do from that point on is to search for ineffective OR defective. You will then have to scan the findings one by one to determine whether these words are embedded in the URL's for particular findings. Once you have removed all findings not having the required URL, you can sort what remains by result title, if that helps to sort by the word satellite.
Google	These options are not fully available, because there is no direct equivalent of this particular kind of "sort by" feature. However: • You can choose dates by Julian date range with the daterange: fielded search operator. (Google has various date ranges through a drop-down menu, but only going back one year for date filtering.) • Google provides sophisticated URL search, using the fielded searches with allinurl: and inurl: fields. Thus, you can enter satellite inurl:ineffective OR inurl:defective in the "With all of the words" text box to help you in the direction of your search requirements.
MSN Search	Filtering by document age is unavailable, except in the sense that you can order findings according to frequency of change. While MSN Search has certain ways of sorting the findings display, sorting according to the text in the title is not possible. As for filtering by URL, you can do the following fielded search: satellite inurl:ineffective OR inurl:defective.

2. The document must contain the word satellite, but all webpages that are on servers in the .com (for-profit company) domain must be excluded from your search result.

AlltheWeb	In the "Word Filters" section, select "Must include" and "in the text" to accompany entry of the word satellite. In the "Domain Filters" section, enter .com in the "Exclude results from" text box.
AltaVista	In the "Search with this Boolean expression" text box, type satellite NOT domain:com.
Copernic	Do a search on the word satellite in the "Web" category. Then do a "Find in results" using the "Advanced Filters" dialog box. In the latter, check the "Hide all results for" in the "Domain" section, and enter .com in the appropriate text box.
Google	Type satellite in the "all these words" text box. In the "domain" area, select "DON'T" from the drop-down menu, and enter com in the domain text box.
MSN Search	Choose "Site/Domain" in "Search Builder" view, select the radio button to exclude the domain, and enter com in the text box. Enter satellite as your search term.

3. **Findings shown per site [4]:** Many websites have hundreds, if not thousands of different pages, interlinked in an assortment of different ways. One way to restrict the number of findings might be to set a maximum number of findings according to some category, such as per domain or per URL.

By default, most of our featured search engines will display a maximum of one to two findings per domain (site). However, you can cause some of them to display all findings for a particular site by restricting the search to it alone (see #2 above), or or by selecting a particular link on the findings display (⇨ Chapter 5: Links from findings display — More same-site findings).

Two other methods used to control the number of findings per website are as follows:

- Some search engines can restrict a search to only a certain number of top levels of pages on a website, e.g., the homepage plus one or two levels down.

	URL	Depth	Document
			directory
🔆 Shown		top level	depth:
here are	http://www.fbay.com/	(home	
are		page)	any
different	http://www.fbay.com/sat.htm	1st	1
levels	http://www.fbay.com/hlp/	1st	2
potentially	http://www.fbay.com/hlp/inst.htm	2nd	3
found on a	http://www.fbay.com/hlp/faqs/	2nd	
website.			

You can specify how deeply to search any website, using the drop-down menu you see here. Choosing the number of levels of pages to search down in a hierarchically-organized website will control the extent to which the more detailed levels of pages are searched to find the desired results. results. results.

- It may be possible for a search engine to restrict findings to particular kinds of pages, when they are classified in some recognizable way (e.g., a personal page, about the website creator or administrator).

Internal Book Cross-Links

1. Cross-links with: Reference Section 6.2: Hosting Site Characteristics
2. Cross-links with: Reference Section 6.2: Geographical region of server
3. Cross-links with: Reference Section 6.2: URL (Internet address)
4. Cross-links with: Reference Section 6.2: Findings shown per site

---

Related documents or sites [1]

These filters include:

1. **Similarity of meaning [2]:** Phrases such as **related terms** or **related documents** are used along with terms such as **concept search** or **similarity search** to refer to various kinds of relationships between search terms (⇨ Chapter 3: Simple search interfaces — intelligent features to avoid formal parameter entry). As well, they may refer to relationships between documents and their files. These, in turn, may be used as a basis for suggesting the user look at additional files or websites to satisfy a given search.

Entering the fielded search related: www.teachers.com will cause Google to look for websites similar in subject matter to that particular website. In the same way, related:www.abebooks.com will find webpages of other booksellers, similar to Abe Books, that specialize in rare and used books.

Google has a special box for similarity searches, namely, the "Page Specific Search" > "Similar" box. Just type in the URL into the "Find pages similar to the page" text box.

Page-Specific Search Find pages similar to the page

www.google.com/help.html

This is the most important aspect of a very complex area, sometimes referred to as the **theory of thesaurus relationship types**, as covered under "Discussion Topics" on our website: ⇨ Search Engine Evolution, Part 3: Toward the use of semantics on the Web.

Practice Exercises:

1. The websites must deal with a topic or theme similar to that dealt with by http://www.whatever.com.

AlltheWeb	Feature is unavailable.
AltaVista	Feature is unavailable.
Copernic	Feature is unavailable.
Google	Type related:www.whatever.com into an appropriate box.
MSN Search	Feature is unavailable.

2. The webpages must deal with a topic similar to that dealt with by the website at URL http://www.dishspecifications.com/, unless the host (server) name is http://www.johnabbott.qc.ca/.

AlltheWeb	A host can be excluded using the "Exclude results from" text entry box in the "Domain Filters," but there is no similarity search ability.

AltaVista	Enter -host:www.johnabbott.qc.ca/ in the Boolean search text entry box. However, there is no similarity search ability.
Copernic	A host can be excluded, but there is no similarity search ability. To hide the host, do a "Find in results" using the "Advanced Filters" dialog box. In the latter, check the "Hide all results for" in the "Domain" section, and enter the full domain name in the appropriate text box.
Google	Type related:www.dishspecifications.com/ -site:www.johnabbott.qc.ca/.
MSN Search	It does not provide a similarity search from the search parameters entry interface. However, you can enter -site:www.johnabbott.qc. ca.

2. **Inverse page links** [3]: This involves finding documents that link *to* a particular URL, rather than *from* it. This feature would be particularly useful to webmasters who want to know about webpages that point to their websites.

   If entered along with a search term, this feature finds other websites pointing to the website of interest that also contain the specified search term.

   Entering the fielded search link:www.johnabbott.qc.ca in MSN Search will cause the search engine to find the pages of all websites that link *to* (rather than *from*) the specified URL, which in this case is the Home page. If you want to find all the individual pages from other websites linking to any individual URL (any webpage) on this site, enter link**domain**:www.johnabbott.qc.ca.

Practice Exercise:

The found webpages must link to www.johnabbott.qc.ca.

AlltheWeb	Type link:www.johnabbott.qc.ca in any appropriate text box.
AltaVista	Type link:www.johnabbott.qc.ca in any appropriate text box.
Copernic	Feature is unavailable.

Google	In the "Page Specific Search" > "Links" section of the search form, type **www.johnabbott.qc.ca** into the "Find pages that link to the page" text box.
MSN Search	Type link:www.johnabbott.qc.ca.

Internal Book Cross-Links

1. Cross-links with: Reference Section 6.2: Related Documents or Sites
2. Cross-links with: Reference Section 6.2: Similarity of meaning
3. Cross-links with: Reference Section 6.2: Inverse page links

Findings Display & Handling Parameters [1]

Organization of findings display [2]

This takes place at two different levels: (1) overall ordering and (2) page organization.

1. **Overall ordering of findings** [3]: Search findings may be sorted in a number of different ways:

   a. **By relevance or importance:** Findings are usually sorted according to the relevancy of the file's contents to what is sought and/or the authority ranking of the website. However, the user sometimes has other choices.

   b. **By date:** News items would perhaps more logically be sorted this way. You can do it by selecting a link on the findings display, which will then post-process your results by date. It may also be possible to sort by both date and time of file creation or last change.

   c. **By keyword or other filtering criteria:** Some sort criteria may be entered on the search entry interface itself, prior to doing the search. This may include date, keywords (words or terms entered by the user), or other filtering criteria (e.g., document title).

In general, you activate this sorting activity by selecting a link on the findings display, and therefore, the sorting is done on a post-processing basis (⇨ Chapter 6: Post-processing of findings).

🔍 Google can sort Directory findings by relevance or alphabetically by page title.

2. **Page organization** [4]: This refers to how the search findings are organized into pages and within pages. There are a number of choices available.

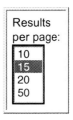

a. **Number of findings per page:** This determines how long the webpage will be.

🔍 Use the drop-down list shown here seen here.

b. **Indenting of findings from a single website after showing the first finding:** This feature is called to as **site collapse**.

Internal Book Cross-Links

1. Cross-links for this section:

- Chapter 5: provides a high-level explanation of findings display and handling interfaces.
- Reference Section 6.3: elaborates on concepts in this section, applying them to our five featured search engines.
- Reference Section, findings display and handling section.

2. Cross-links for this section:

- Chapter 5: Organization of findings display
- Reference Section 6.3: Organization of findings display

3. Cross-links for this section:

- Reference Section 6.3: Overall ordering
- Reference Section 5.2: Overall ordering

4. Cross-links for this section:

- Reference Section 6.3: Page organization
- Reference Section 5.2: Page organization

Presentation of individual findings [1]

Search engines will often allow you to customize the internal presentation of each finding. Parameters available to do this include:

1. **Finding fields to display** [2]: Metadata displayed for each finding usually include document title, description, keywords, URL, and other links. Some search engines provide parameters to control which fields are displayed, as well as perhaps their contents and formatting.

2. **Finding language translation** [3]: This means translating your search results back into the language of the user interface employed or another target language. Our five featured search engines do not automatically translate findings. However, AltaVista and Google do provide language translation abilities that can be selected from each finding.

Internal Book Cross-Links

1. Cross-links for this section:

- Reference Section 6.3: Presentation of Individual Findings
- Chapter 5: Presentation of individual findings
- Reference Section 5.2: Presentation of individual findings

2. Cross-links with: Reference Section 6.3: Finding fields to display

3. Cross-links for this section:

- Reference Section 6.3: Finding language translation
- Chapter 5: Links to language translation interfaces

Post-processing of findings [1]

Interfaces for post-processing your search results have already been discussed (⇨ Chapter 5: Post-processing of findings). But in many cases, you can also use parameters to post-process your findings as follows.

1. **Search within findings** [2]: Ideally, you should be able to use any of the filters available from your original search to search within your findings. If you can download the actual files from the Internet, in addition to downloading their metadata from search engine catalogs, further criteria maybe employed.

If your search engine can keep the history of previous post-processing of a particular search, you may be able to further filter your findings based on these actions.

> 🏆 Copernic provides you with the option of using saved pages (document files) when searching within results, in case you have already saved certain files found by your search.

🔲 Your search engine may be able to filter findings based on whether you have previously accessed them (visited their pages), annotated them, or other actions. In Copernic, this is called filtering according to the **status** of the result.

2. **Grouping and sorting of findings** [3]: Post-processing can be used to group and sort your findings (⮞ Chapter 6: Organization of findings display).

   🔲 Of our featured search engines, Copernic provides by far the most powerful parameters for grouping and sorting of results through post-processing:

   - If you apply both grouping and sorting criteria, you are actually sorting at two levels, where the group, in effect, becomes the primary sort criterion.
   - You can use the various metadata-based search filters as criteria for grouping or sorting.
   - You can also use the **status** of the result (see #1 above).

3. **Language translation or page summary** [4]: They allow the text of findings to be altered as follows:

   a. **Language translation:** Parameters used to translate a document file may permit stipulating the program you wish to employ or how those programs are to work. None of our featured search engines allow this, except entering the text to be translated.

   b. **Page summary:** Copernic allows you to choose the maximum length of page content summaries.

4. **Search follow-up** [5]:

   a. **Keeping records of searches and their findings:** involves the following kinds of functions:

   - **Organizing the search history:** An example is a parameter to control the naming conventions for search history folders. None of our featured search engines presently do this.

- **Managing search history details:** An example is a parameter to control the details kept in search history folders. None of our search engines presently do this.
- **Saving of individual files referenced from findings metadata to the user's local computer:** Copernic has a parameter to save image files linked to a document file along with the file itself. It also has one to refresh already saved files when updating the search.

b. **Updating, modifying, duplicating, and deleting searches kept in the search history:** Copernic has a parameter to revise search filters when modifying a search.

c. **Sharing search findings:** Copernic provides a parameter to choose different file formats for exporting a search, including DOC, TXT, XML, HTML, and others.

d. **Setting up user alerts:** Examples of these kinds of parameters are ones stipulating how often you want the search engine to monitor a page or track a search for changes, and the e-mail address to which you want the tracking results sent.

Internal Book Cross-Links

1. Cross-links for this section:

- Reference Section 6.3: Other Post-processing of findings
- Chapter 5: Post-processing of findings

2. Cross-links with: Reference Section 6.3: Search within findings
3. Cross-links with: Reference Section 6.3: Overall ordering
4. Cross-links with: Reference Section 6.3: Language translation or page summary
5. Cross-links with: Reference Section 6.3: Search follow-up

User Preference Setting Parameters [1]

Filter default value preferences

Any of the filters discussed earlier in this chapter can be pre-set to preferred values that you can be override as needed at the time of individual searches. Document language and screening potentially offensive content are the two most frequently used.

> ⚠ Most search engines store your preferences in cookies on your computer, so you won't be able to save preferences if they are turned off. However, if you have some programming knowledge, there are some workarounds, such as making customized search forms.

1. **Document language** [2]**:** This permits you to choose documents in a particular subset of available languages. Some search engines employ your settings for country and site to control language.

    🔎 AlltheWeb uses a form filled with checkboxes to set preferences for document language.

2. **Potentially offensive content** [3]**:** You can set this filter "on" or "off." Some search engines may allow you to apply this filter selectively, for say, only multi-media files.

    > ⚠ You might miss something valuable as a result of setting potentially offensive content filters.
    >
    > 🔎 If you are doing a look-up on breast cancer, the filter may malfunction and not allow certain pages to be reported due to the word breast.

    🔎 Google allows an intermediate setting between a simple "on" and "off," as you can see here.

> **SafeSearch Filtering:** Google's SafeSearch blocks webpages containing explicit sexual content from appearing in search results.
> ○ Use strict filtering (Filter both explicit text and explicit images)
> ◉ Use moderate filtering (Filter explicit images only - default behavior)
> ○ Do not filter my search results.

3. **Other filter setting preferences** [4]**:** Other common default filter preferences include the spelling dictionary or settings that filter search terms. Copernic allows you to set the level of findings analysis, using the dialog box seen on the next page.

Internal Book Cross-Links

1. Cross-links for this section:

- Reference Section 6.4: Filter Default Value Preferences: elaborates on concepts in this section, applying them to our five featured search engines.
- Chapter 5: Setting user preferences: provides a high-level explanation of user preference setting entry interfaces.

2. Cross-links with: Reference Section 6.4: Document language
3. Cross-links with: Reference Section 6.4: Potentially offensive content
4. Cross-links with: Reference Section 6.4: Other filter setting preferences

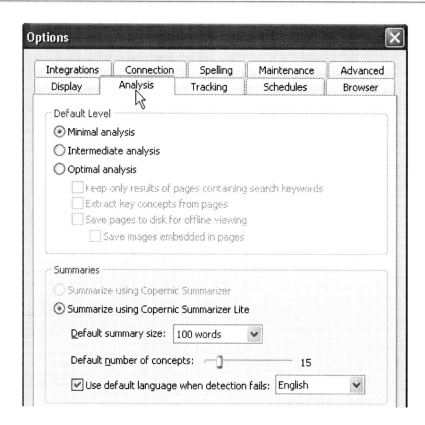

Findings display and handling preferences [1]

1. **Findings page organization** [2]: Some of the most commonly-used parameters are used to:

   - Set a limit on the number of results reported per website.
   - Display findings in a new browser window — helpful in keeping your place in a findings list as you investigate each result.

> 💡 Setting the number of search results per page generally applies only to textual listings of findings. For findings pages with thumbnail images, it doesn't pay to reduce the page size by showing fewer findings. Even if you have a slow Internet connection, the difference in speed is negligible.

   - "Flash in" news items above Web catalog findings — allowing you to show the findings from more than one catalog, if so desired.

2. **Individual findings detail** [3]: Parameter choices include the fields of information to display for each finding, the level of detail shown, and options for highlighting search terms in the result.

   AltaVista preferences allow some control over the fields displayed with each finding. From the basic search interface, select "Search Settings." A number of options are provided including:

   - **Description:** of the finding;
   - **URL:** its web address;
   - **Page size:** its size in terms of number of bytes or characters;
   - **Page language:** language of the found document;
   - **Translation link:** to translate the found document into the language of the interface;

Display of web results:
Check the elements you want to include in your results.

Web page information
- ☑ Description
- ☑ URL
- ☐ Page size
- ☐ Page language

Useful links: ☑ Translate

Results page format
- ☑ Bold the search term in the results

   - **Results page format:** includes options to bold print (highlight) search terms in the description and the number of results to display on each findings page.

Other field options you can choose to display:

- **Links to other information:** Tells the search engine to display links next to each finding for related pages, subject categories, or language translation.
- **File information:** Specifies the language, file format or size of found documents.
- **Description length:** Controls the maximum description length for each finding.
- **Description type:** Determines whether the finding description will consist of an excerpt including your search term or simply the first part of the text contained in the document.

3. **Handling of findings** [4]:

🔳 As seen on the next page, Copernic allows you to set preferences for scheduling result tracking to alert you to new or updated information as a follow-up to a search.

Internal Book Cross-Links

1. Cross-links for this section:

- Reference Section 6.4: Findings Display & Handling Preferences
- Chapter 5: Post-Processing of Findings
- Chapter 5: Setting user preferences

2. Cross-links with: Reference Section 6.4: Findings page organization
3. Cross-links with: Reference Section 6.4: Individual findings detail
4. Cross-links with: Reference Section 6.4: Handling of findings

---

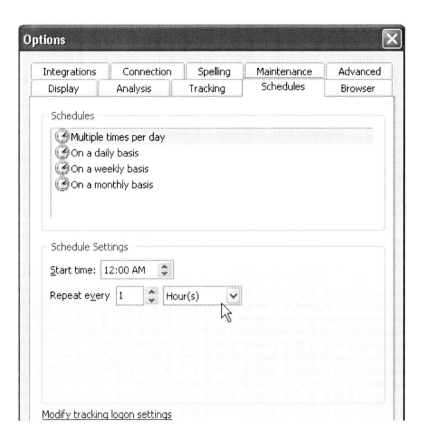

Interface screen features preferences [1]

1. **Interface options made available** [2]: These parameters control the boxes, menu choices, and toolbars to be displayed on certain screens, and choices provided in certain selection boxes or box sets.

    🔍 Copernic has a complex set of preference setting interfaces to control the categories of search engines furnished to the user.

    🔍 AlltheWeb gives you the option of displaying certain drop-down menu boxes on their simple search interfaces.

2. **Interface style or language** [3]: Interface style refers to the cosmetics of the search engine website, including choices of screen text size, colors, and themes displayed on the search entry form. Interface language allows you to select your own language for communicating with the search engine. Some will automatically default to your geographical location.

    🔍 If you are located in Ontario, Canada, AltaVista will initially set your interface language to English.

Internal Book Cross-Links

1. Cross-links for this section: Reference Section 6.4: Interface Screen Features Preferences
2. Cross-links with: Reference Section 6.4: Interface options made available
3. Cross-links with: Reference Section 6.4: Interface language or style

Software integration and efficiency preferences [1]

1. **Software integration** [2]: The most common parameters here have the ability to integrate a search engine with an Internet browser, with other kinds of applications (word processors, e-mail), and/or with an operating system (Windows).

   You can integrate the Google toolbar into your browser for easy access to its functions at any time, without having to enter Google's URL.

2. **Software efficiency** [3]: This applies especially to client-side search software, and includes functions such as getting rid of files no longer needed, setting options related to tradeoffs between search speed and other factors, and updating client-side software with newer versions or with the latest settings.

Internal Book Cross-Links

1. Cross-links for this section:

- Chapter 5: Setting user preferences
- Reference Section 6.4: Software Integration & Efficiency Preferences

2. Cross-links with: Reference Section 6.4: Software integration
3. Cross-links with: Reference Section 6.4: Software efficiency

Effective Internet Search

E-Searching Made Easy!

Skills & Strategies for Improved Search Engine Results

Features

Control

Center

FEATURES CONTROL CENTER

In the control center you can:

- Experiment with summary, multi-level matrices of comparative search engine features.
- Compare and evaluate the relative strengths and weaknesses of various features of our five featured search engines.
- Explore cross-links between Chapters 3, 5, and 6 and Reference Manual sections 3, 5, and 6.

Introduction to Features Matrices

It is difficult to make broad generalizations about the best search engines to use in specific situations. But to assist you in making these kinds of comparisons, we have provided you with this unique features control center.

Once you look at it, the set-up is fairly self-evident. But in case you are unclear, the features matrices are organized as follows:

- **Left column (bolded text) - major search engine features:** links to book chapters, providing a more conceptual discussion of search engine features.
- **Left column (small text) - specific types or breakdowns of major search engine features:** links to explanations for specific search engine features.
- **Search engine columns:** link directly to the Reference Manual section — to the selected feature for a particular search engine. Links to related material found throughout the book are also provided here.

Note: Book hyperlinks are also explained in the Introduction: Book hyperlinking.

User Interface Features Matrices

Search entry interfaces

 Cross-links:

- Chapter 3 & Reference Section 3
- First section of Chapter 5 & Reference Section 5.1

FEATURE	SEARCH ENGINE				
Simple Web Search Interfaces	**AlltheWeb**	**AltaVista**	**Copernic**	**Google**	**MSN**
Control center	Present on all simple search interfaces	Present on all simple search interfaces	Not applicable - only has one starting interface	Present on all simple search interfaces	Present on various search interfaces
Support for operator parameters	Has some limitations in simple search	Has some limitations in simple search	Basic Boolean operators only	Same as in advanced search	Yes
Intelligent avoidance of formal parameter entry	Spelling, conversion calculator	Spelling, various structured database lookups, etc.	Spelling	Sophisticated, incl. linguistic assistance, structured database lookups, etc.	Spelling and other language assistance, calculator, lookups

Advanced Web Search Interfaces	**AlltheWeb**	**AltaVista**	**Copernic**	**Google**	**MSN**
	Yes	Yes	Yes	Yes	Yes, Search Builder

Subject Directory Search Interfaces	AlltheWeb	AltaVista	Copernic	Google	MSN
	No	Yes, via Yahoo	Indirectly through search categories	Yes	Yes, via MSN

Specialized Search Entry Interfaces	AlltheWeb	AltaVista	Copernic	Google	MSN
Multi-media file search interfaces	Yes, for all media types	Yes, for all media types	Indirectly through categories	For image files mainly; also video files	Yes, some indirectly via directory
News document search interfaces	Yes	Yes	Indirectly through categories	Yes	Yes, and indirectly MSNBC
Other non-Web Internet application interfaces	No	No	Indirectly through categories	News & other discussion groups	E-mail, chat, etc. via MSN
People, business, & map search interfaces	No	Yellow pages, people finder, maps	Indirectly through categories	Yes, via intelligent features & local search	Yes, via intelligent features & local search
Other specialized topic search interfaces	No	No	Indirectly through categories	Several	Yes, many via MSN directory

Findings display and handling interfaces

Cross-links: Chapter 5 and Reference Section 5.2: Findings Display & Handling and Findings Display sections

FEATURE	SEARCH ENGINE				
Organization & Detailing of Findings	**AlltheWeb**	**AltaVista**	**Copernic**	**Google**	**MSN**
Overall ordering	By relevance	By relevance	Mainly by relevance of sourced engines	By relevance	By relevance
Page organization	Varies by type of search	Varies by type of search	Application & browser formats	Varies by type of search	Varies by type of search
Presentation of individual findings	Varies by type of search	Varies by type of search	Application & browser formats	Varies by type of search	Varies by type of search

Links from Findings Display	**AlltheWeb**	**AltaVista**	**Copernic**	**Google**	**MSN**
Links for refining searches	Yes	Yes	Yes, very elaborate	Yes	Yes, but minimal
Switching to other catalogs	Yes	Yes, from simple interfaces	Yes	Yes, from simple interfaces	Yes
More same-site findings	Yes	Yes	Yes	Yes	Yes

Related pages or terms	Related searches - to narrow search	No	Document summarizer keywords	Similar pages, topics, groups	No
Related entries from other catalogs	Yes - incl. news & paid listings	Yes - incl. paid listings	Not applicable	Yes - incl. news & paid listings	Yes - incl. news & paid listings
Language translation	No	Yes	No	Yes	No
Other kinds of links	Yes, dictionary definitions	No	Yes, document summarizer	Yes, incl. dictionary, cached pages	Yes, cached pages

Post-Processing of Findings	AlltheWeb	AltaVista	Copernic	Google	MSN
Search within findings	Yes, but simplistic	No	Yes, elaborate	Yes, but simplistic	No
Grouping and sorting	For news	For news	Yes, many criteria	For news, groups, directory	No, not on a post-processing basis
Language translation or page summary	No	Language translation	Page summary	Language translation	No
Search follow-up	No	No	Yes	Yes	Yes, via an MSN

Search support: user tool interfaces

> **Cross-links:** Chapter 5 and Reference Section 5.3: Search Support: User Tool Interfaces sections

FEATURE	SEARCH ENGINE				
Search Support: User Tool Interfaces	**AlltheWeb**	**AltaVista**	**Copernic**	**Google**	**MSN**
Preference settings	Yes, relatively elaborate	Yes	Yes, extremely elaborate	Yes	Yes
Additional end user-specific tools	Yes	Yes	Yes	Yes	Yes
Other user tools	Yes	Yes	Yes	Yes, several	Yes

Search Filter Features Matrices

Term-based search filters

> **Cross-links:** Chapter 6 and Reference Section 6.1: Term-Based Search Filters sections

FEATURE	SEARCH ENGINE				
Term Variation	**AlltheWeb**	**AltaVista**	**Copernic**	**Google**	**MSN**
Wildcards or substrings or stemming	No	Wildcards for whole words	Substrings	For whole words; automatic stemming	Stemming
Different spellings or phonetic matching	Perhaps done during spell-checking	Perhaps done during spell-checking	No	Perhaps done during spell-checking	Perhaps done during spell-checking

Formatting masks	No	Unknown if has case-sensitive matching	Has case-sensitive matching	No, unless include diacritical marks	No
Ignored words or characters	No	Option to search on ignored words	Option to search on ignored words	Option to search on ignored words	Option to search on ignored words

Term Relationship	AlltheWeb	AltaVista	Copernic	Google	MSN
Phrases	Yes	Yes	Yes	Yes	Yes
AND, OR, and NOT	Yes	Yes	Yes	Yes	Yes
Proximity	No	No	Yes	Partially	No
Prioritizing term relationship operators	Unsure if works beyond one level of brackets	Unsure if works beyond one level of brackets	Unsure if works beyond one level of brackets	No	Yes
Other kinds of term relationships	No	No	No	No	Yes, fuzzy conjunction

Metadata-based search filters

> 🔨 **Cross-links:** Chapter 6 and Reference Section 6.2: Metadata-Based Search Filters sections

FEATURE	SEARCH ENGINE				
File Structure Characteristics	AlltheWeb	AltaVista	Copernic	Google	MSN
File format	Various document & multi-media	Various document & multi-media	Various document & multi-media	Various document & image	Various document & multi-media

Embedded content	Yes	No	No	No	Yes
Document file section or location	Yes, HTML document section	Yes, HTML document section	Yes, but indirectly	Yes, HTML document section; in hyperlink text	Yes

File Content Characteristics	AlltheWeb	AltaVista	Copernic	Google	MSN
File age	Yes	Yes	Yes	Yes	No, but has ordering by frequency of change
Document language	Yes	Yes	Yes, but limited	Yes	Yes
Potentially offensive content	Yes	Yes	No	Yes	Yes
Other document file content characteristics	News source	No	Finding handling status; in results list or source	Database lookup: e. g., phone no., stock code	Provides a rich assortment via MSN subject directory searches, as well as locality filter
Other multi-media file content characteristics	Image type, stream or download	Duration, color, source	Finding handling status; in results list	Size, coloration	Yes

Hosting Site Characteristics	AlltheWeb	AltaVista	Copernic	Google	MSN
Geographical region of server	Yes	Yes	Yes	Only in language search	Yes
URL (resource) or site Internet address	Yes	Yes	Yes	Yes	Yes
Findings shown per site	Yes	Yes	N/A	Yes	Set through preferences

Related Documents or Sites	AlltheWeb	AltaVista	Copernic	Google	MSN
Similarity of meaning	No	No	No	Yes	No
Inverse page links	Yes	Yes	No	Yes	Yes

Non-Filter Parameter Features Matrices

Findings display and handling parameters

> 🔨 **Cross-links:** Chapter 6 & Reference Section 6.3: Findings Display & Handling sections

FEATURE	SEARCH ENGINE				
Organization of Findings Display	AlltheWeb	AltaVista	Copernic	Google	MSN
Overall ordering	News by date	News by date	Multiple sort & grouping criteria	News by date	Has a few different ordering parameters
Page organization	Findings per page	Findings per page; findings per site	Application vs. browser view; findings per page	Findings per page	Controlled by setting preferences

Presentation of Individual Findings	AlltheWeb	AltaVista	Copernic	Google	MSN
Finding fields to display	No	No, but can set preferences	Yes, has a few options	No, except for file type	No
Finding language translation	No	No, but has a link to translator	No	No, but has a link to translator	No

Other Post-Processing of Findings	AlltheWeb	AltaVista	Copernic	Google	MSN
Search within findings	Yes, but trivial	No	Yes, elaborate	Yes	No
Language translation or page summary	No	Language translation	Page summary	Language translation	No
Search follow-up	No	No	Yes, elaborate	Yes	Yes, via MSN

User preference setting parameters

> **Cross-links:** Chapter 6 & Reference Section 6.4: User Preference Setting Parameters sections

FEATURE	SEARCH ENGINE				
Filter Default Value Preferences	AlltheWeb	AltaVista	Copernic	Google	MSN
Document language	Yes	Yes	No	Yes	Yes

	AlltheWeb	AltaVista	Copernic	Google	MSN
Potentially offensive content	Yes	Yes	No	Yes	Yes
Other filter setting preferences	Findings per site	Site country	Analysis & spelling options	No	Searcher's location

Findings Display & Handling Preferences	AlltheWeb	AltaVista	Copernic	Google	MSN
Findings page organization	Results per page; new window; no. of news results to show	Results per page	Results per browser page	Results per page; new window	Results per page; new window; no. of findings per site
Individual findings detail	Highlight terms	Highlight terms & detail level	Highlight terms & detail level	No	No
Handling of findings	No	No	Summarizer & search tracking	No	No

Interface Screen Features Preferences	AlltheWeb	AltaVista	Copernic	Google	MSN
Interface options made available	Default catalog on simple search	No	Engine categories; panes & controls; others	No	No
Interface language or style	Style & text size	Interface language	Yes, some	Interface language	Yes, language & country

Software Integration & Efficiency Preferences	AlltheWeb	AltaVista	Copernic	Google	MSN
Software integration	Browser integration	Browser integration, incl. toolbar	Browser, e-mail, & other integration	Browser integration, incl. toolbar	Toolbar suite
Software efficiency	No	No	Several options	No	No

Effective Internet Search

E-Searching Made Easy!

Skills & Strategies for Improved Search Engine Results

Reference Manual: Search Engine Features

REFERENCE MANUAL: SEARCH ENGINE FEATURES

Reference Manual Use

The following hyperlinks have been provided for your convenience:

Reference Manual	Chapter
3	3
5.1 - 5.3	5
6.1 - 6.4	6

- Internal links to related book materials, as shown here.
- An internal navigation bar to facilitate testing of features within our featured search engines.
- External links to related materials on the Internet.

Disclaimers

- Search engines continue to evolve quickly, periodically changing their interfaces and inner workings. This book reflects the state of the search engines at the time of its writing. Moreover, the case studies documented in Chapter 4 depict the search engine features as they existed at the time the case studies were conducted.
- Individual search engines provided the descriptions of their features. Although tested, this is no guaranty they always work exactly as described.
- Due to differences in search engines, it is sometimes difficult to verify the existence of certain features, particularly when they are not documented by the search engines.
- Although every attempt has been made to be thorough, some search engine features may have been inadvertently overlooked.
- **Important note:** When depicting small portions of search engine screens such as placement of particular boxes on a form, the box and its labeling have often been adapted to the formatting constraints of this book.

Reference Manual
Section 3: Primary
Search Entry Interfaces

⇨ This section cross-links with Chapter 3.

Simple Web Search Interfaces

Control center

⇨ For more explanation, consult Chapter 3: Simple search interfaces.

One of the roles of simple search interfaces is to act as a control center, from which you may branch in several different directions to other search or user tool interfaces.

All the search engines featured in this book work in this manner with the exception of Copernic, whose "Quick Search" interface serves as a kind of stand-in. An explanation of how the control center functions for each search engine follows.

General	AlltheWeb	AltaVista	Copernic	Google	MSN

AlltheWeb

Has a very simple general web document search (Web search) interface. It links to specialized interfaces for news and image (picture), audio, and video files. These searches each have a similar set of tabs linking to various interfaces, highlighted below (next page) for "Web" search.

There is a link to an advanced version of this Web search [1]. In addition, Pictures, Video, and News searches (but not Audio) each have links to their own advanced level searches [2], as well as to help screens and various other user tools located at the bottom of the screen image.

Another AlltheWeb feature seen on the screenshot (next page) is the **language of documents**. This defaults to English, but by using the Preferences link, you can set any combination of supported languages, e.g., English and French. Regardless of your preferences, a radio button can be selected to receive results in any language. Also, you can change your languages dynamically, that is, for an individual search [3].

Reference Manual Section 3:
Primary Search
Entry Interfaces

266

Simple Web
Search Interfaces

As well, using preference settings [4], an **"Exact phrase"** checkbox link can be activated. This provides a checkbox next to the search terms entry box if you prefer to indicate that your term is a phrase without having to place quotes around it. Alternatively, settings can be customized create a drop-down menu box with choices **"any"** (of these terms), **"all"** (of these terms), **"phrase,"** or **"boolean"** (to allow correct interpretation of Boolean operators).

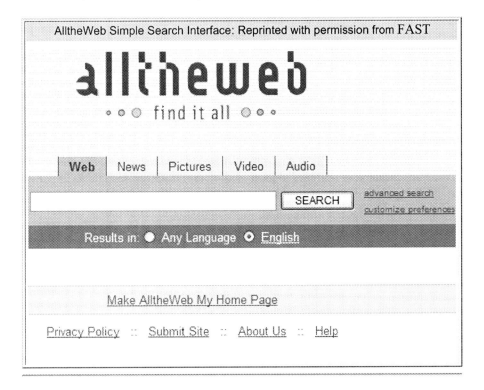

AlltheWeb Simple Search Interface: Reprinted with permission from FAST

AltaVista

Provides links from its simple Web search interface to its directory and specialized ones. The latter include searches for multi-media files and news items [1]. Each of these has a similar set of links, like the one highlighted in the screenshot on the next page for "Web" search. Clicking "More" in this list provides still further tools and specialty interfaces [2] including [www.altavista.com/web/tools]:

- Webmaster Search: Find your site's pages in the AltaVista index, or find pages that link to your site.
- Text-Only Search: Search the Web with a faster, graphics-free version of AltaVista's Web search.
- Converter: A simple conversion calculator for units of length, time, speed, temperature, weight, area, and volume.

Reference Manual Section 3:
Primary Search
Entry Interfaces
267
Simple Web
Search Interfaces

- Quick Search: Place Quick Search on any site for one-click searching of webpages, images, video, or news.
- Maps: Find maps within Canada (in this example) and other countries with the Yahoo! Maps service.
- Business Finder: Find business listings with this tool offered in alliance with Verizon Super Pages.
- People Finder: Find White Pages listings with this tool offered in alliance with Verizon Super Pages.

The above are covered in more detail in various places in this book.

AltaVista is very international, and has interfaces for various countries, each associated with a particular set of languages. The link in the upper right-hand corner of the screenshot below takes you to an interface to select a country-language(s) combination, such as U.S. (English-Spanish), Canada (English), or Canada (French). The two pairs of radio buttons seen in the screenshot allow you to restrict your searches to particular countries and to documents in particular languages, at your discretion.

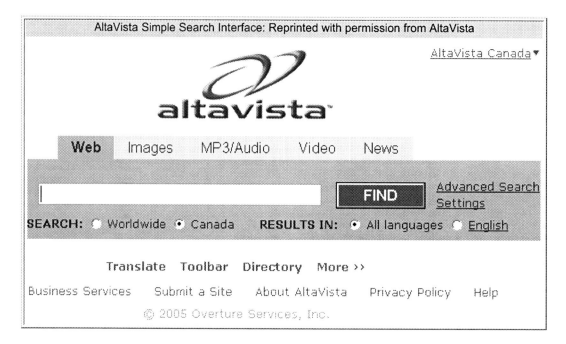

Reference Manual Section 3:
Primary Search
Entry Interfaces
268
Simple Web
Search Interfaces

Copernic

Its "Quick Search" pane approximates a "simple" search

⇨ For a specific example, consult Chapter 4: Case #1: Stock Investment Search. For a screenshot of Copernic's main application interface, ⇨ Chapter 3: Local application interfaces.

interface. A text box is provided for entering a series of search terms (phrases or words) without Boolean operators. Checkboxes are also available to look for broken links and to treat all words in the text box as a single phrase. Under these boxes in the pane is a two-level list of categories for various kinds of searches, each invoking an appropriate set of search engines.

Google

As seen here in the top navigation bar,

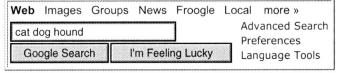

Google provides links from the simple Web Search interface to its specialized searches [1]. A similar bar appears on all its simple search interfaces and results pages.

💡 The "I'm Feeling Lucky™" button seen in the above takes you directly to the first web page Google returned for your query. You will not see the other search results at all.

The simple search entry interfaces also contain other links to Preferences and, in the case of simple Web search, to language translation tools. You can also link from simple Web, Image, News, and Groups

🔨 Directory search only has a single, simple interface, so a link to a more advanced interface is not available.

search interfaces to correspondingly more advanced search interfaces against the same catalog [2].

Links, such as those seen at the bottom of the screenshot (on the next page) for doing business with Google, and so on, vary somewhat by interface, and for the simple Web search interface by country.

Reference Manual Section 3:
Primary Search
Entry Interfaces
269
Simple Web
Search Interfaces

Google is very international, and will by default set certain interface screen features based on detected country and language. For instance, by default, a Canadian working in English sees the screen below, allowing the person to work in particular languages and to restrict the search by geography.

MSN Search

In addition to providing a way of obtaining a user-selectable drop-down list for advanced search (the "+Search Builder" hotspot on the form), and a link for setting search preferences [1], the main MSN search interface provides links to the larger MSN environment. You can branch to Hotmail, Chat, specialty interfaces for shopping, music, and movies, and various other MSN Search branches. These selections can be made from the links always shown, or from the links in the drop-down list shown here.

By choosing "MSN Home" in the search entry form, you branch to a page have a variety of further subjects, as well as links to a general subject directory (see Reference Section 3: Subject directory search interfaces for more detail).

General	AlltheWeb	AltaVista	Copernic	Google	MSN

Internal Book Cross-Links

AlltheWeb:

1. Reference Section 3: Advanced Web Search Interfaces
2. Reference Section 5.1: Multi-media file search interfaces
3. Reference Section 6.2: Document language
4. Reference Section 6.4: Interface options made available

AltaVista:

1. Directory and specialized search entry interface links from simple Web search entry interface:

- To find image, MP3/audio and video files: Reference Section 5.1: Multi-media file search interfaces
- Reference Section 3: Subject Directory Search Interfaces
- Reference Section 5.1: News document search interfaces

2. Other links from simple Web search entry interface:

- For advanced Web search entry interface: Reference Section 3: Advanced search interfaces
- Reference Section 6.2: Document language

Reference Manual Section 3:
Primary Search
Entry Interfaces

271

Simple Web
Search Interfaces

Google:

1. Links to specialized searches from Simple Web Search:

- For images: Reference Section 5.1: Multi-media file search interfaces
- For discussion groups: Reference Section 5.1: Other non-Web Internet application interfaces
- For subject directory search entry interface: Reference Section 3: Subject Directory Search Interfaces

2. Other simple search interface links:

- Reference Section 3: Advanced Web search interfaces
- Reference Section 5.3: Preference settings

MSN Search:

1. Additional links:

- Reference Section 3: Advanced Web search interfaces
- Reference Section 5.3: Preference settings

2. Reference Section 3: Subject Directory Search Interfaces

Support for operator parameters

> ⇨ For more explanation, see Chapter 3: Simple search interfaces.

A single text box is provided for entering search terms in most simple search interfaces. If the search engine allows operator parameters, and you know how to use them, sophisticated searches are also possible.

Only some of our featured search engines permit entry of operator parameters as parts of the search strings in their simple or basic interfaces. Such operator parameters may include field identifiers (e.g., title:), as well as Boolean operators (e.g., AND, OR, NOT).

> 🔨 More on Boolean search: ⇨ Reference Section 6.1: AND, OR, and NOT. For more details about quirks and exceptions associated with using operator parameters in simple search text boxes, refer to ⇨ Chapter 4: Case #3: Health-Related Search.

General	AlltheWeb	AltaVista	Copernic	Google	MSN

Reference Manual Section 3:
Primary Search
Entry Interfaces

272

Simple Web
Search Interfaces

AlltheWeb

Boolean searches must be entered using the advanced search interface, using the appropriate boxes. For expressions that include operator parameters to work, the search strings must be in the specialized text box for Boolean searches. That applies to both Boolean and field operator parameters.

By default, when no operator parameters are placed between the entries in the simple search text box, a Boolean AND is assumed between these terms. However, if AND itself is entered, it is taken to be one of the search terms.

AltaVista

Same as for AlltheWeb.

Copernic

The single text box in its "Quick Search" interface allows entry of a composite of words and phrases (in quotes) separated by blanks. Boolean operator parameters are disallowed because they will be treated as search terms. Rather, a space between terms is equivalent to an AND operator.

Alternatively, you can enter a series of words in the "Quick Search" text box, which is interpreted as a phrase by checking the "Exact phrase" box.

You can also run Copernic Agent as a Web search tool in your browser or in other applications. That's because Copernic, like most of the mainstream search engines,

> From the search toolbar, you are provided with a limited number of choices for Boolean logic including OR, which is unavailable in the "Quick Search" interface.

offers a search toolbar you can insert to integrate Copernic into other programs. In such cases, the larger Copernic client-side application is not opened up, although the search is recorded in your search history and also viewable in the Copernic application proper. Your results appear in a pane to the left of your browser screen, which looks like the screen you get when you choose "Browse Results" in the Copernic application proper. For more details on this intermediate level kind of Copernic search entry interface, see ⇨ Appendix 6.4: Software integration.

Reference Manual Section 3:
Primary Search
Entry Interfaces
273
Simple Web
Search Interfaces

Google

If no operators are entered between terms in its simple search interface, AND is assumed. Both Boolean and field operators will work when entered here.

⚠ When brackets are used in conjunction with field operators and Boolean operators, certain combinations do not work (⇨ Reference Section 6.1: Prioritizing term relationship operators).

⚠ Certain field operators (link: and the phonebook: ones) must not be mixed in searches with other field operators: ⇨ Reference Section 6.2: Additional document file content characteristics.

⚠ Not all field operators will work in all search entry interfaces:

- In directory search, only intitle: and inurl: work: ⇨ Reference Section 3: Subject Directory Search Interfaces.
- In news search, only intitle: and site: work: ⇨ Reference Section 5.1: News document search interfaces.
- In image search, only intitle:, inurl:, site:, and filetype: work: ⇨ Reference Section 5.1: Multi-media file search interfaces. Note: filetype: only works with the file types displayed in the drop-down menu list found in Reference Section 5.1.
- In groups search, only intitle: works, and is equivalent to the topic of any posting. As well, groups search has the group: and author: field operators, which are unique to that search interface: ⇨ Reference Section 6.2: Additional document file content characteristics.

Note: intitle: works in all interfaces.

For more details on the complexities of using various Google field operators, refer to ⇨ Chapter 3: Parameter types.

MSN Search

If no operators are entered between terms in its simple search interface, AND is assumed. Both Boolean and field operators will work when entered here.

General	AlltheWeb	AltaVista	Copernic	Google	MSN

Intelligent avoidance of formal parameter entry

⇨ For more explanation, refer to Chapter 3: Simple search interfaces.

It is not always necessary to use operator parameters to enter complex logic in a simple search interface. Natural language interpretation or other similarly intelligent features, if available, can anticipate what the user means.

None of our featured search engines claim to have natural language search ability. However, our featured search engines all have a number of intelligent features that automatically anticipate what the user might be looking for, based on the search terms entered. In particular, all engines provide spelling correction assistance, with or without user participation in changing the spelling.

General	AlltheWeb	AltaVista	Copernic	Google	MSN

AlltheWeb

1. **Provides spelling assistance on search terms**. To quote [AlltheWeb Help]: AlltheWeb checks all the query terms entered into the search box on AlltheWeb against a dictionary and common search terms. If AlltheWeb detects a misspelling in your query, you'll see a suggested spelling correction at the top of the results page.

   For example:

   Clicking the underlined term or phrase will execute a query with the corrected spelling.

2. **Provides a special conversion calculator utility**. To quote: You may or may not have noticed that AlltheWeb offers a simple conversion calculator. The conversion calculator is accessed by prefacing any of the

   🔨 The calculator does not support common fractions (1/2, 3/4, etc.), so you must use whole (3, 5, 100, etc.) or decimal notation (3.5, 5.25, 100.3, etc.).

   ⇨ For more details on its features, see AlltheWeb Help.

   following supported units of measure with **"convert:"** in the query field. Length Conversions; Time Conversions; Speed Conversions; Temperature Conversions; Weight Conversions; Area Conversions; Cooking/Volume Conversions.

Reference Manual Section 3:
Primary Search
Entry Interfaces

275

Simple Web
Search Interfaces

AltaVista

1. **Provides something called "shortcuts,"** defined by AltaVista Help as follows:

   For popular searches such as maps and weather, AltaVista provides relevant results from sources that are not normally available to search engines.

   Depending on how specific your search is, we either provide shortcuts directly to your goal, or we provide tools or interfaces to help you narrow your search. For example, a search for "san francisco map" produces a link to a map of San Francisco. A search for "map" produces a form in which you can type "San Francisco".

   We currently provide shortcuts in these areas:

Area Codes (Shortcuts Answers)	Maps
Conversions Calculator (Shortcuts Answers)	Movies
Directions	News
Exchange Rates (Shortcuts Answers)	Shopping
Finance	Time Zones (Shortcuts Answers)
Images	Weather (Shortcuts Answers) (Shortcuts Answers)
Local Information	ZIP Codes (Shortcuts Answers)

   We choose sources that are accurate, reliable and thorough. While we access most of these sources for free, some sources pay us. For a list of all shortcut sources, with paying partners indicated, please see our Shortcut Cheat Sheet.

   To distinguish them from other AltaVista results, shortcuts are labeled with a small icon. Clicking on the icon provides a pop-up window describing each shortcut. Here is how shortcut results appear:

   Search: san francisco map

   > ☑ Get a map of San Francisco Yahoo Maps
   > Get directions. MapQuest

   Being owned by Yahoo,
   AltaVista also has access to the richer set of shortcuts found in Yahoo search (➪ help.yahoo.com/help/us/ysearch/tips/tips-01.html), namely:

Airport Information	Hotel Finder	Stock Quotes
Airline Registration Info	ISBN Numbers	Synonym Finder
Area Codes	Local Search	Time Zones
Calculator	Maps	Traffic
Dictionary Definitions	Movie Showtimes	UPC Codes
Encyclopedia Lookup	News	VIN Number
Exchange Rates	Packages	Weights, Measures & Temperatures
Flight Tracker	Patents	Weather
Gas Prices	Sports Scores	Zip Codes

2. **Provides spelling assistance for search terms:** If AltaVista cannot match a word to anything, it may automatically look for the correct spelling.

   🔲 Type matherboard into an appropriate text box, and the AltaVista findings page will still find many entries for motherboard. It will also ask you whether you intended to enter motherboard [1].

Copernic

Has a sophisticated spellchecker, customizable in several ways [1].

Google

Has various features described in its Help section, under "Google Web Search Features" (➪ www.google.com/help/features.html). Some of these apply only to the United States, or only to the U.S. and Canada. Other countries have their own sets of features, described in the corresponding Google Help section for that particular country. Such features, often referred to as "shortcuts" (➪ www.googleguide.com/shortcuts.html), more often than not involve automatic "deep web" lookups in structured databases, include:

1. **Language assistance, including:**
   a. **Similarity of term meaning:** Placing the tilde (~) operator before your search keywords will cause Google to search against synonymous words in addition to the search keyword you actually enter.

Reference Manual Section 3:
Primary Search
Entry Interfaces

277

Simple Web
Search Interfaces

ఃG ... to search for food facts as well as nutrition and cooking information, use: ~food ~facts [Google Help].

More: ⇨ www.googleguide.com/crafting_queries.html

b. **Spelling correction for search terms:** Google checks each of your keywords to verify whether you are using the most common version of a word's spelling. If your spelling of a term produced at least one finding, but Google estimates that more relevant search results would likely be obtained using an alternative spelling, you will be prompted with: "Did you mean: *more common spelling*?". Then you click on the alternative presented if you like it.

> 🔍 Because Google's spell check dictionary takes into account actual spelling usage on the Internet, it is able to suggest common spellings further to those that might appear in a standard dictionary. This includes spellings for proper nouns (names of people, organizations, and places).

If, on the other hand, your original query produces no results at all, Google will automatically search again, using the closest alternative spelling.

More: ⇨ www.googleguide.com/spelling_corrections.html

c. **Variations of hyphenated terms:** For example, if you enter decision-making, Google will also search on decision making, and on decisionmaking.

d. **Variations of words having the same starting characters (automatic stemming):** Google will do this unless you deliberately suppress it: ⇨ Reference Section 6.1: Wildcards, substrings, stemming.

e. **Glossary lookup:** Finds definitions for words, phrases, and acronyms. Simply begin your search term with the word **Define**, followed by what you want to define.

More: ⇨ www.googleguide.com/dictionary.html

2. **Assistance in locating people, businesses, and places, including:**

a. **Street maps:** To quote Google Help:

Reference Manual Section 3:
Primary Search
Entry Interfaces
278
Simple Web
Search Interfaces

To use Google to find street maps, enter a U. S. street address, including zip code or city/state (e.g. 165 University Ave Palo Alto CA), in the Google search box. Often, the street address and city name will be enough.

When Google recognizes your query as a map request, it will return links from high quality map providers that will lead you directly to the relevant map. These map providers have been selected solely on the basis of their quality.

More: ⇨ www.googleguide.com/maps.html

b. **Telephone Area Codes:** example search: 650.

More: ⇨ www.googleguide.com/search_by_number.html

c. **Phone book:** To quote Google Help:

Google has added the convenience of US street address and phone number lookup to the information we provide through our search box. You'll see publicly listed phone numbers and addresses at the top of results pages for searches that contain specific kinds of keywords.

To find listings for a **US business**, type the business name into the Google search box, along with the city and state. Or type the business name and zip code. Entering the phone number with area code will also return a complete business listing.

To find listings for a **US residence**, type any of the following combinations into the Google search box: first name (or first initial), last name, city (state is optional); first name (or first initial), last name, state; first name (or first initial), last name, area code; first name (or first initial), last name, zip; phone number, including area code; last name, city, state; last name, zip code.

> Google has fielded searches that allow you to choose between residential and business phone numbers, as well as to do reverse phone number lookup [1].

More: ⇨ www.googleguide.com/phonebook.html

Reference Manual Section 3:
Primary Search
Entry Interfaces

279

Simple Web
Search Interfaces

3. **Search by Number:**

    a. **Flight Numbers:** Enter an airline name or code and a flight number (e.g., UA 92, or united 92, or UAL 92) to receive links to flight information from Travelocity and fboweb.com for major airlines.

    b. **Courier Parcel Delivery Tracking Numbers:**

- **UPS:** example search: 1Z9999W999
- **FedEX:** search entry mask: 99999999999
- **USPS:** search entry mask: 9999 9999 99

    c. **FAA (Federal Aviation Authority) Airplane Registration Numbers:** Example search: n199ua.

    d. **FCC (Federal Communications Commission) Equipment ID's:** Example search: fcc B4Z-34009-PIR.

    e. **Patent Numbers:** Example search: patent 5123123.

    f. **Universal Product Codes:** Enter the number on the bottom of a bar code displayed on product packaging, such as 06680923580. You will receive a link to the UPC database, if the code produces a match.

    g. **Vehicle ID Numbers:** Entering a VIN (Vehicle ID number), e.g., 2T1BR12EXXC757565, returns to you a link from carfax.com. The latter provides more information about the make, model, and year of a specific vehicle.

More: ⇨ www.googleguide.com/search_by_number.html

4. **Other:**

    a. **Calculator:** A built-in calculator to solve both simple and more complex math problems, do unit conversions, and more.

More: ⇨ www.googleguide.com/calculator.html

    b. **Airports and Travel Information:** If you enter the airport's three letter code followed by the word airport, you will receive weather and other travel information.

More: ⇨ www.googleguide.com/travel_conditions.html

    c. **Stock quotes:** To quote Google Help:

To use Google to get stock and mutual fund information, just enter one or more NYSE, NASDAQ,

Reference Manual Section 3:
Primary Search
Entry Interfaces

280

Simple Web
Search Interfaces

AMEX, or mutual fund ticker symbols, or the name of a corporation traded on one of the stock indices. If Google recognizes your query as a stock or mutual fund, it will return a link that leads directly to stock and mutual fund information from high quality financial information providers.

🔎 Look for the link for the desired ticker symbol query (e.g., "SUNW") at the top of your search results. If you search on a company name (e.g., "Sun Microsystems"), look for the "Stock Quote" link on the final line of Google's result for that company's homepage (e.g., www.sun.com).

| intc sunw nuan | Google Search |

Show stock quotes for
INTC (Intel Corporation) - SUNW (Sun Microsystems Inc.) - NUAN (Nuance Communications Inc.)

More: ⇨ www.googleguide.com/stock_quotes.html

MSN Search

MSN Search has various features described in its Help section, under "Find facts, look up words, calculate, convert" (⇨ search.msn.com/docs/help.aspx? t=SEARCH_PROC_FindFactsNStatistics.htm). Such features more often than not involve automatic "deep web" lookups in structured databases, include:

1. **Language assistance, including:**

    a. **Spelling correction for search terms:** MSN Search checks each of your keywords to verify whether you are using the most common version of a word's spelling. If your spelling is not in the search engine's dictionary, MSN Search will suggest an alternative spelling, if it finds a match. In such a case, you will be prompted with: "This may give better results: ," followed by a suggestion. Click on the alternative presented if you like.

    When the search engine is unable to interpret one or more search terms, it checks for alternate spellings, and, if possible, prompts you with "This may give better results: ," followed by a suggestion. Click the suggestion to search using the alternate spelling or phrasing. If no suitable alternatives are found, MSN

Reference Manual Section 3:
Primary Search
Entry Interfaces

281

Simple Web
Search Interfaces

Search informs you that "No results were found containing [search term]."

b. **Glossary/dictionary lookup:** Finds definitions for words, phrases, and acronyms. Simply begin your search term with the word **Define**, followed by what you want to define. You can also phrase the question in other ways, such as: What is the definition of handbook?; What is a black fly?; Black fly definition.

2. **Calculator/Unit Converter/Equation Solver:** A built-in calculator to solve both simple and more complex math problems, do unit conversions, and more. The relevant MSN Search Help page provides a complete list of mathematical symbols you can use. To quote: The Encarta Calculator and Equation Solver uses basic mathematical operators, exponents, and roots, factorials, modulo, percentages, logarithms, trig functions, and mathematical constants. Here are some examples: 5+3/1-(6*2); sqrt 9; sin 100 * 50; 32% of 54; 4x=19; 2y^2 + 5y + 10 = 40. For a complete list of mathematical operators and mathematical syntax rules, see the URL given above.

In addition, MSN Search can perform unit conversions when you enter queries such as: How many minutes in a day?; What is 40 degrees Celsius in Farenheit?; How many miles in a light year?; 15 inches in meters. It will also provide health unit conversion answers, when you enter queries such as: How many calories in spinach?; potassium in a banana; carbohydrates in bread; vitamin C in a grapefruit.

3. **Lookup of non-quantitative facts and statistics:** Encarta is a database for information about geographical locations, historical figures, animals, and more. Encarta is accessed to search for facts when you enter queries phrased like the following: What is Sigmund Freud known for?; Mount St. Bruno height; What is the population of Canada?; Rhinoceros habitat; Depth of the Pacific Ocean.

As well, you can get answers for queries on the following specialized subjects when doing a Web search, just based on the terms you enter and the way you phrase your search (see the above MSN Help page for more specifics):

- **News:** When you enter a term corresponding to a popular news topic, news items may be "flashed in" above the results from the Web catalog; e.g., enter tsunami in a Web search.
- **Financial matters:** When, for example, you enter names of companies, stock/mutual fund/exchange symbols, and so on, you will obtain stock quotes. For international stock quotes, precede the stock symbol by the country domain suffix in

capitals, as in DE:BMW, for quotes on the BMW stock on the German stock exchange.

- **"Local" answers:** To quote: Up to three business or residential listings are returned when you (1) enter a name, (2) specify a location, (3) select Web search, and (4) we have matching information in our online directory. The name you enter can be a complete or partial business or person name. The location must always correspond to a city, state, or zip code. For example: pizza San Francisco; CA; M Jones 94114.

- **Movies:** Based on certain ways of phrasing your query, you can obtain information on local movies, and movies in other cities or postal code areas. You can also filter your movie results based on genre, such as family, PG, action, horror), as well as on film ratings.

- **Music:** Entering the names of popular artists or groups will provide you with information about their music.

- **Sports:** You can get the latest or dated statistics about sporting events by entering team and player names, dates, league or type of sport identification, and so on.

| General | AlltheWeb | AltaVista | Copernic | Google | MSN |

Internal Book Cross-Links

AltaVista:

1. Reference Section 6.1: Different spellings or phonetic matching

Copernic:

1. For more details on Copernic's spellchecker:

- Reference Section 6.4: Other Preferences
- Reference Section 6.1: Different spellings or phonetic matching

Google:

1. For fielded searches on different kinds of phone numbers: Reference Section 6.2: Additional document file content characteristics

Reference Manual Section 3:
Primary Search
Entry Interfaces

283

Simple Web
Search Interfaces

Advanced Web Search Interfaces

⇨ For more explanation, consult Chapter 3: Advanced search interfaces.

Advanced search interfaces have at least one text box for entering the search terms (including operator parameters), along with a "go" button. Other boxes allow parameterizing the search in more sophisticated or alternative ways.

All the search engines featured in this book have advanced non-specialized (general) Web searches, which follow.

| General | AlltheWeb | AltaVista | Copernic | Google | MSN |

AlltheWeb

⇨ For a screenshot of the AlltheWeb advanced Web search entry interface, refer to Chapter 3: Advanced Web search interfaces.

AltaVista

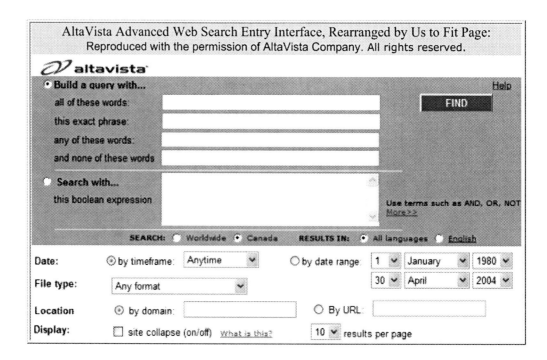

AltaVista Advanced Web Search Entry Interface, Rearranged by Us to Fit Page: Reproduced with the permission of AltaVista Company. All rights reserved.

Reference Manual Section 3:
Primary Search
Entry Interfaces

284

Advanced Web
Search Interfaces

Copernic

Collectively using the five dialog boxes below, all advanced search filters may be entered. The first two are used for obtaining the initial results from the sourced search engines, while the last three further filter the findings, based on search within results processing.

First, search results are gathered based on entries made in the following (on this and the next page) three dialog boxes:

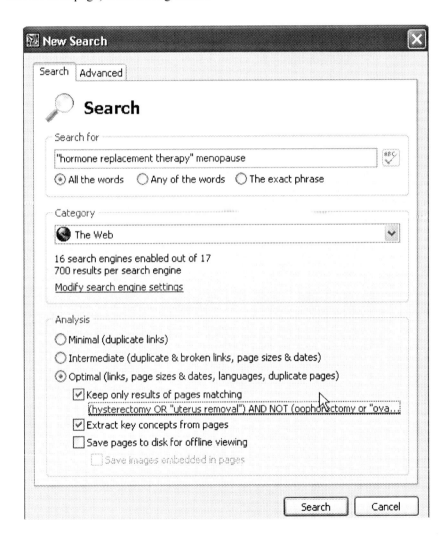

Reference Manual Section 3:
Primary Search
Entry Interfaces

285

Advanced Web
Search Interfaces

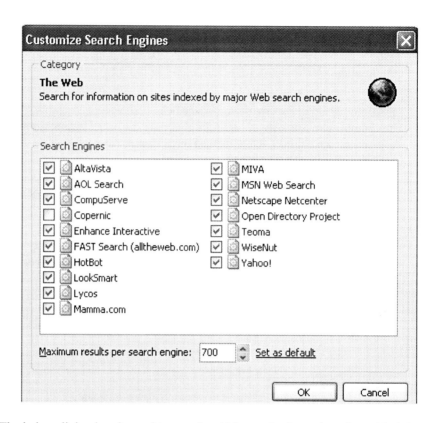

The below dialog box is used to search within results in conjunction with doing the search based on sourced search engines. That is, the refinements are applied as part of the original Analysis, based on findings that have already been placed in the findings list in the computer memory.

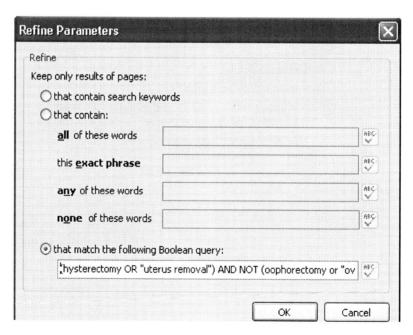

Reference Manual Section 3:
Primary Search
Entry Interfaces
286
Advanced Web
Search Interfaces

The following dialog box, along with the one shown here, are used to further refine the search, by searching within findings. Application of these two further filters at a later point (after the original search is done and the results acquired and filtered) produces temporary restrictions in the findings, which can then be expanded back to their original set of findings if you like.

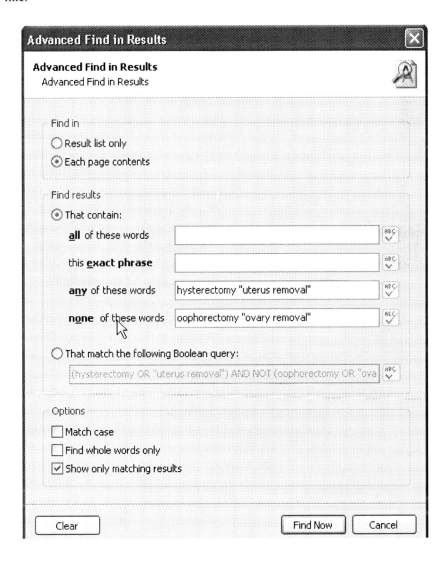

Reference Manual Section 3:
Primary Search
Entry Interfaces

287

Advanced Web
Search Interfaces

Google

Google **Advanced Search** Advanced Search Tips | About Google

Find results	with **all** of the words	[ ]	10 results ⌄
	with the **exact phrase**	[ ]	Google Search
	with **at least one** of the words	[ ]	
	without the words	[ ]	

Language Return pages written in   [any language ⌄]

File Format [Only ⌄] return results of the file format [any format ⌄]

Date Return web pages updated in the [anytime ⌄]

Occurrences Return results where my terms occur [anywhere in the page ⌄]

Domain [Only ⌄] return results from the site or domain [   ]
e.g. google.com, .org *More info*

SafeSearch ⦿ No filtering ◯ Filter using SafeSearch

Page-Specific Search

Similar Find pages similar to the page [   ] [Search]
e.g. www.google.com/help.html

Links Find pages that link to the page [   ] [Search]

Topic-Specific Searches

Google Print - Search the full text of books
Google Scholar - Search scholarly papers

Apple Macintosh - Search for all things Mac
BSD Unix - Search web pages about the BSD operating system
Linux - Search all penguin-friendly pages
Microsoft - Search Microsoft-related pages

U.S. Government - Search all .gov and .mil sites
Universities - Search a specific school's website

In addition to Google's own advanced search entry interface seen above, several third parties have developed their own variations, specializing in the following kinds of filters not found in native Google:

- **GAPS (Google API Proximity Search):** www.staggernation.com/cgi-bin/ gaps.cgi — Specializes in proximity search, with sorting of results options: ⇨ Reference Section 6.1: Proximity.
- **GooFresh:** www.freshgoo.com — Finds recently added sites: ⇨ Reference Section 6.2: File age.
- **Fagan Finder:** www.faganfinder.com/engines/google.shtml — Finds sites added between specified dates: ⇨ Reference Section 6.2: File age.
- **Google Ultimate Interface:** www.faganfinder.com/google.html:
  - ⟩ Finds sites added between specified dates: ⇨ Reference Section 6.2: File age.
  - ⟩ Provides filtering based on country and/or language for several Google search entry interfaces further to those already found in Google: ⇨ Reference Section 6.2: Geographical region of server, and Reference Section 6.2: Document language.
  - ⟩ Supplies a list of foreign language characters for you to insert into your search terms on Web, news, directory, groups, images, catalogs, Froogle, answers, translate, glossary, and sets search entry interfaces.

> **Keyboard:** à á â ã ä å æ ç è é ê ë ì í î ï ð ñ ò ó ô õ ö ø ù ú û ü ý þ

- **Soople:** www.faganfinder.com/google.html — Provides a different, perhaps more helpful, kind of presentation of Google's advanced filters.

Follow the above links to Reference Manual sections 6 for more discussion of these third-party interfaces.

MSN Search

To obtain MSN's Advanced Search options, you have to click on the "Search Builder" link on the basic search entry interface. A new box, full of extra options, then appears below the basic search form, as shown on the next pages.

Reference Manual Section 3:
Primary Search
Entry Interfaces
289
Advanced Web
Search Interfaces

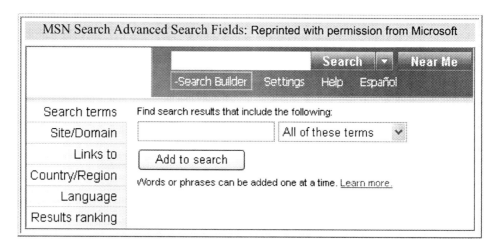

To use the advanced options, you first need to click on the row headers in the new part of the search entry form. The following partial screenshots show you what you obtain by doing this in each case:

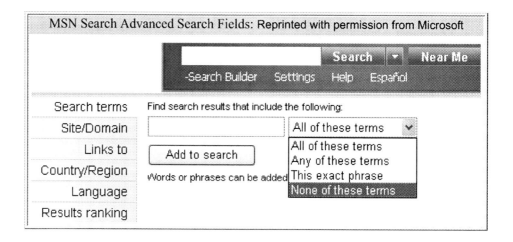

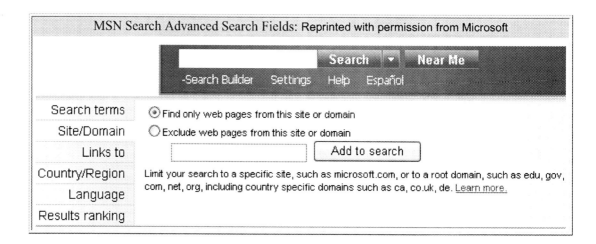

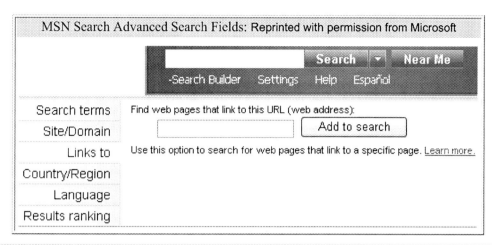

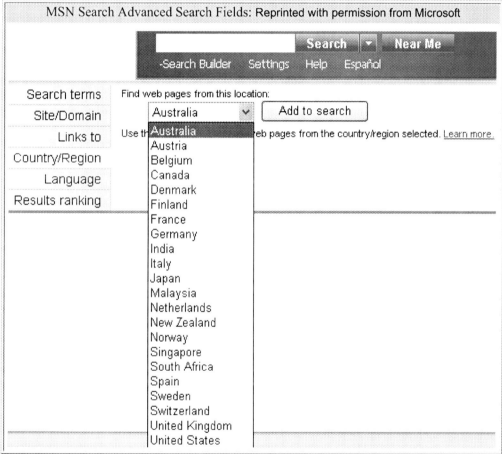

Reference Manual Section 3:
Primary Search
Entry Interfaces

291

Advanced Web
Search Interfaces

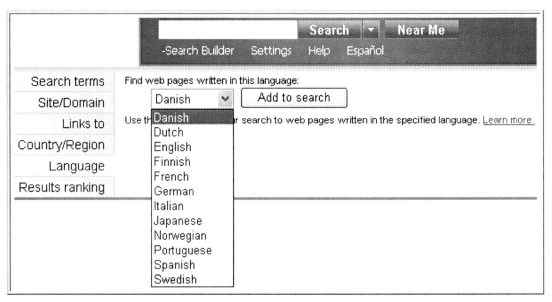

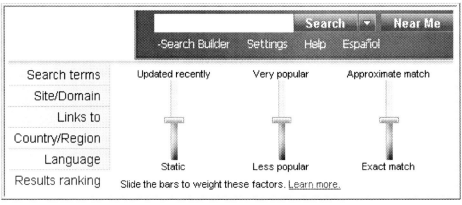

General   AlltheWeb   AltaVista   Copernic   Google   MSN

Subject Directory Search Interfaces

⇨ For more explanation, refer to Chapter 3: Subject directory search interfaces.

Subject directories have several pre-defined topic categories as well as levels of sub-categories. Editors review and select sites for inclusion in their directories on the basis of previously determined selection criteria.

The structures and topics of the subject directories of our featured search engines vary widely, as can be seen below. The difference between the Microsoft directory and those of Google and AltaVista is noteworthy, as explained in Chapter 3.

Reference Manual Section 3:
Primary Search
Entry Interfaces

292

Subject Directory
Search Interfaces

AlltheWeb

Subject directory search interface unavailable.

AltaVista

Being owned by Yahoo, AltaVista makes use of the Yahoo subject directory. Select the "Directory" link below the search term entry box to get to the subject directory. You can then choose the sites that are listed (see example below), or you can do a search within that specific category by typing the search term in the single text box.

> When using the search engine on the Web, click on the "Computers & Internet" link under the heading Web Directory, then scroll down and select a site, or type computing in an appropriate text box and select among the categories shown. On the page for the computing topic, choose a sub-category of that subject.

The subject directory interface is country-specific.

> Below is the Canadian version of the subject directory.

Arts & Humanities History, Visual Arts, Crafts, Literature...	News & Media Full Coverage, TV, Newspapers...
Business & Economy B2B, Shopping, Jobs, Finance...	Recreation & Sports Sports, Lotteries, Travel, Autos...
Computers & Internet Internet, Hardware, Software, Games...	Reference Phone Numbers, Dictionaries, Quotations...
Education Higher, Continuing, Distance, Teaching...	Regional Canada, Countries, Provinces, Cities...
Entertainment Movies, TV Shows, Music, Humour...	Science Animals, Space, Engineering, Maps...
Government Politics, Law, Immigration, Taxes...	Social Science Languages, Economics, Archaeology...
Health Medicine, Drugs, Diseases, Public...	Society & Culture People, Environment, Religion...

Copernic

Does not have a true subject directory interface, although its "categories" are somewhat similar. Instead, Copernic calls upon search engines that specialize in certain topic areas (⇨ Reference Section 5.1: Other specialized topic search interfaces).

Copernic also uses different subsets of search engines for search specialization other than by topic, e.g., by file format, kind of Internet application, audience, country, and so on.

Google

Its directory is derived from the ODP (Open Directory Project), where all submissions are free and reviewed by volunteer editors. When connected to Google on the Web using the simple search interface, click on the "More" link, then on the "Directory" link, and then select among the available subject categories.

Choose "Health" as a subject category, as shown below.

Addictions (5586)	Directories (17)	Insurance (175)	Professions (1418)	(1185)
Aging (148)	Disabilities (1395)	Medicine (14182)	Public Health and	Senses (494)
Alternative (6938)	Education (200)	Men's Health (460)	Safety (4063)	Services (100)
Animal (3267)	Employment (587)	Mental Health (7113)	Publications (158)	Support
Beauty (657)	Environmental	Nursing (1823)	Regional (11)	Groups (547)
Child Health (1005)	Health (410)	Nutrition (663)	Reproductive	Teen
Conditions and	Fitness (2116)	Occupational Health	Health (2697)	Health (89)
Diseases (17478)	Healthcare	and Safety (819)	Resources (264)	Weight
Dentistry (567)	Industry (6896)	Organizations (184)	Search Engines (9)	Loss (454)
	History (7)	Pharmacy (6551)	Senior Health	Women's
	Home Health (413)	Products and		Health (940)
		Shopping (61)		

Related Categories:
Business > Business Services > Consulting >Medical and Life Sciences (221)
Kids and Teens > Health (604)
Recreation > Humor > Medical (41)
Science > Social Sciences > Communication > Health Communication (7)
Society > Issues > Health (1807)

Reference Manual Section 3:
Primary Search
Entry Interfaces

294

Subject Directory
Search Interfaces

Below the list of categories, individual findings are listed by default in the same order of priority as for Web results.

> ⚠ In directory search, only intitle: and inurl: field operators work:
> ⇨ Reference Section 6.2: URL (resource) or site Internet address.

More on Google's subject directory: ⇨ www.googleguide.com/directory.html.

MSN Search

Provides a subject directory, which you can get to from the MSN homepage (www.msn.com). The major categories in this directory are shown on the next page.

For another kind of coverage of the more or less full subject directory, see ⇨ Reference Section 6.2: Additional document file content characteristics, where specialized metadata-based

> 🔨 Maps, white pages, yellow pages and music are discussed in this book under the heading of specialized search entry interfaces (⇨ Chapter 5: Specialized topic search interfaces).
>
> 🔨 Submitting a website and adding MSN to your site are discussed in the section dealing with user tools (⇨ Chapter 5: Other user tools).

search filters are documented in relation to each subject directory major category.

Inside MSN   MSN Next   **MSN Directory**   Specials

» View by Alphabetical

Going Places
City Guides
Hotel Deals
Maps & Directions
Local Traffic
Travel

Shop
Autos
Auctions
Books
Clothes
Real Estate
Videos/DVDs
MSN Shopping

Look it up
Dictionary
Encarta
MSN Toolbar
MSN Search Duels
White Pages
Yellow Pages

Living and Finances
Hot Stocks
Business
Buy a House
Careers and Jobs
Credit Analysis
Dating and Personals
Health & Fitness
Getting Married
House and Home
Money
Retiring
Starting a Family
Stock Quotes

News & Sports
News
Sports by Fox Sports
Slate Magazine
Weather

Technology
Downloads
Cell Phones
Microsoft.com
Online Safety & Security
Tech & Gadgets

Entertainment and Fun
Cartoons
Entertainment News
Free Games
Gossip
Greeting Cards
Horoscopes
Lottery Results
Movie Times
Photos
Radio Plus
TV Listings

Communicate
Chat Rooms
Groups & Chat
Spaces
Hotmail
MSN Messenger
Personal Domains

People
Family
Kids
Latino
MSN Member Directory
Women

MSN Video
Business on Video
Movie Previews on Video
MSN Enhanced Video
Music Videos
News on Video
Top Ten Most Watched Videos
Weather on Video

MSN Worldwide
MSN US - Latino
MSN Australia
MSN Canada
MSN China
MSN France
MSN Germany
MSN India
MSN Japan
MSN Korea
MSN Mexico
MSN Singapore
MSN UK
MSN Worldwide

From MSN
Advertise on MSN
MSN Direct Watches
MSN Internet Access
MSN Internet Software
MSN Music
MSN Member Center
MSN Mobile
MSN TV

From Microsoft
Games & Xbox
Office Outlook Live
Office Online
PC Protection
Microsoft Product Support
Microsoft Small Business Services
Windows Update

General   AlltheWeb   AltaVista   Copernic   Google   MSN

⇨ This section cross-links with Chapter 5: Specialized Search Entry Interfaces.

Specialized Search Entry Interfaces

Multi-media file search interfaces

⇨ For more explanation, refer to Chapter 5: Multi-media file search interfaces.

Interfaces to look for multi-media files may include ones for image (picture, graphic), video (movie), and sound (audio) file types.

Of the search engines featured in this book:

- AlltheWeb, AltaVista, and Google *directly* provide specialized video searches.
- AlltheWeb and Google *directly* provide specialized image searches.
- Unlike AlltheWeb, AltaVista, and Google, Copernic does not work by displaying organized grids of findings of multi-media files. However, it can search for multi-media files in a number of ways, depending on the search category and the search engines within it.
- MSN also has a music search, but with the more advanced forms provided in the form of Subject Directory topics.

General	AlltheWeb	AltaVista	Copernic	Google	MSN

AlltheWeb

Has simple specialized search interfaces for image (Pictures), sound (Audio), and video (Videos). The video and image interfaces also provide an advanced level.

Below (next page) you can see the metadata-based parameter details on the advanced video and picture search interfaces. Both provide selections for different file formats, offensive content restriction, and other details specific to a media type [1].

```
┌─────────────────────────────────────────────────────────────────────────┐
│              Advanced video search interface boxes                        │
├───────────────────────────────────────────────────────────────────────── │
│ Formats:              ☑ All  ☐ AVI ☐ AVI/DivX ☐ MPEG ☐ Real ☐ QuickTime   │
│ Streams or            ⦿ Both ○ Downloads Only  ○ Streams Only             │
│ Downloads:                                                                 │
│ Offensive Content Filter:  Turn filter [ On ]                             │
└─────────────────────────────────────────────────────────────────────────┘
```

```
┌─────────────────────────────────────────────────────────────────────────┐
│              Advanced picture search details boxes                        │
├─────────────────────────────────────────────────────────────────────────│
│ File Format:    ☑ All formats  ☐ JPEG      ☐ GIF        ☐ BMP            │
│ Image Type:     ☑ All types    ☐ Color     ☐ Grayscale  ☐ Line Art       │
│ Background:     ⦿ Both types   ○ Transparent  ○ Non-Transparent          │
│ Offensive Content Filter:  Turn filter [ On ]                            │
└─────────────────────────────────────────────────────────────────────────┘
```

AltaVista

Has intermediate (but not simple or advanced) levels of specialized searches for MP3/audio, video, and image files. In the partial and rearranged screen images below, various selections are provided based on file format and other metadata specific to the media type [1].

> There is also a link from each of these interfaces to the interface for offensive content restriction (⇨ Reference Section 6.2: Potentially offensive content).

```
┌─────────────────────────────────────────────────────────────────────────┐
│                   Image search interface boxes                            │
│         Reproduced by permission of AltaVista Company. All rights reserved.│
├─────────────────────────────────────────────────────────────────────────│
│ Find: ☑ Photos   ☑ Graphics   ☐ Buttons/Banners                          │
│                                                                            │
│ Color: [All Colors]   Sources: [All Sources]   Sizes: [All Sizes]         │
└─────────────────────────────────────────────────────────────────────────┘
```

```
┌─────────────────────────────────────────────────────────────────────────┐
│                   Video search interface boxes                            │
│         Reproduced by permission of AltaVista Company. All rights reserved.│
├─────────────────────────────────────────────────────────────────────────│
│                   The largest video search on the Web.                    │
│ Find:   ☑ Avi  ☑ MPEG  ☑ Quicktime  ☑ Windows Media  ☑ Real  ☑ Other    │
│ Duration: [All Durations]   Sources: [All Sources]                        │
└─────────────────────────────────────────────────────────────────────────┘
```

The largest audio search on the Web.

Find: ☑ MP3 ☑ WAV ☑ WindowsMedia ☑ AIFF ☑ Real ☑ Other

Duration: [All Durations]   **Sources:** [All Sources]

⇨ For another example of the above audio search interface, see the interfaces for basic and advanced "MP3/Audio" in Chapter 4: Case #2: Multi-media file search.

Copernic

Can search for multi-media files in a number of ways:

- It can make use of the search facilities of search engines that directly provide multi-media file searching. In such cases, it lands you at some level of the findings screen as seen in the context of using that search engine. Thus, you see the findings screen of a specialized multi-media search engine as it looks after the multi-media file is found.

    🔏 See last step in the search described in Chapter 4: Case #2: Multi-Media File Search.

- It may try to open the multi-media file, as in the case of sound or video files.

Copernic provides the following search engine categories for multi-media file searching:

- **Favorites:** images.
- **Computer & Internet:** audio and video files, audio and video streams.
- **Entertainment & Media:** music, music lyrics.

For details of Copernic categories, click on the category name in our Search Tool Guide, and follow the links down to the lowest category level and search sites for that category. In this instance, you can also start with the following link: ⇨ ToolGuide. SearchHelpCenter.com/search-tool-guide-for-effective-internet-search-copernic-cross-links-2.html.

Google

As seen in the screen details here, the advanced image search entry interface provides selections based on a few kinds of metadata relevant to multi-media files [1].

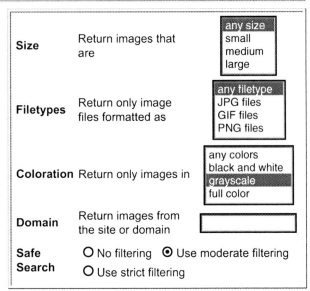

In image search, the only field operators that work are:

- intitle:, inurl:, and site: ⇨ Reference Section 6.2: URL (resource) or site Internet address.
- filetype: ⇨ Reference Section 6.2: File format.

More about Google image search: ⇨ www.googleguide.com/images.html.

Google also has a video search against a catalog derived from the closed (textual) captioning of television programs: ⇨ video.google.com. You can only see stills and transcripts from the television programming. Google's video search has been extended to include videos uploaded by those who want others on the web to be able to find their videos. You can actually play videos uploaded by users, if you also download the Google video player.

MSN Search

"MSN Web Directory" (⇨ Reference Section 3: Subject directory search interfaces), in its "Entertainment" category, provides a link to a search interface for entertainment. This is, in effect, a search for a type of sound multi-media files. Using the various interfaces, you can search by many metadata fields, such as theater, artist, movie name, song title, song album, and so on.

Search ▼
Web
News
Images
Local
Look up word
Encarta
Stock Quotes
Find Movies
Shopping
Music

You can also enter searches for images, music, and movies by making the appropriate selections from MSN Search, as you see here.

General	AlltheWeb	AltaVista	Copernic	Google	MSN

Internal Book Cross-Links

AlltheWeb:

1. Metadata-based selections on advanced Picture and Video search entry interfaces:

- Different file formats: Reference Section 6.2: File format.
- Offensive content: Reference Section 6.2: Potentially offensive content.
- Other details specific to media type: Reference Section 6.2: Additional multi-media file content characteristics.

AltaVista:

1. More on metadata-based filters on the advanced multi-media file search entry interfaces:

- Reference Section 6.2: File format
- Reference Section 6.2: Additional multi-media file content characteristics

Google:

1. More on metadata-based filters on the advanced image search entry interface:

- Reference Section 6.2: File format
- Reference Section 6.2: Potentially offensive content
- Reference Section 6.2: Additional multi-media file content characteristics

News document
search interfaces

⇨ For more explanation, see Chapter 5:
Non-Web Internet application interfaces.

People often use the terms "Internet" and "Web" interchangeably, when in fact, the Web makes up only a part of the Internet. In fact, as far as search engines are concerned, the second most important Internet application after the Web is news. All search engines featured in this book have a specialized news document search interface.

News search interfaces work a bit differently for each search engine. Copernic is the most individual, because it treats news as a search engine category, involving a set of source search engines specialized in the news Internet application.

General	AlltheWeb	AltaVista	Copernic	Google	MSN

AlltheWeb

Click on the "News" tab while in any of the search entry screens. This branches you to another screen for news. In the advanced news search screen (see boxes on next page), in addition to a text box for search terms, you will find various boxes to select or enter:

- **Location in the article text:** in the headline, URL, or elsewhere.
- **Language:** including encoding method.
- **Topic category:** Business, Finance, Technology, Sports, Traffic, Weather, Entertainment.
- **Major geographical region:** International, United States, local. ⇨ Reference Section 6.2: Geographical region of server.
- **Internet domain of the news source:** can be used to include or exclude particular sources.

    🔢 Enter cnn.com for news from CNN. Then use the domain suffix to specify the country as being the United Kingdom, i.e., domain suffix uk. ⇨ Reference Section 6.2: URL (resource) or site Internet address.

Boxes on AlltheWeb's Advanced News Search Entry Screen

Search for -

all of the words	anywhere in the article
any of the words	in the headline of the article
the exact phrase	in the URL of the article

Language -

Find results written in

Preferred	
Any Language	Unicode (UTF-8)
Afrikaans	Western European (ISO-8859-1)
Albanian	Western European (ISO-8859-15)
Arabic	

News Sources -

- ☑ All
- ☐ International
- ☐ US News
- ☐ Various Local News
- ☐ Finance
- ☐ Business
- ☐ Technology
- ☐ Sports
- ☐ Traffic
- ☐ Weather
- ☐ Entertainment

Domain Filters -

Filter results from specific domains (com, gov, dell.com, etc.)

Include results from [ ]

Exclude results from [ ]

Location -

Filter results by newpapers from a specific region (France, Colorado, San Diego)

Search articles from newspapers in [ ]

Source -

Filter results by news sources (News York Times, CNN, etc.)

Search articles from [ ]

Found -

Within

| Any time |
| Pages indexed last 2 hours |
| Pages indexed last 6 hours |
| Pages indexed last 12 hours |
| Pages indexed last 24 hours |
| Pages indexed last 2 days |
| Pages indexed last week |

Display

Presentation -

| 10 |
| 25 |
| 50 |

results per page

Sort results -
- ⦿ Relevance
- ○ Date

- **Specific geographical location:** e.g., France, Colorado, San Diego.
- **News source (creator):** e.g., CNN, New York Times.
- **News document age:** selected from a drop-down menu, using increments ranging from the last 2 hours to the last week, to "All pages" still in the news catalog. ⇨ Reference Section 6.2: File age.
- **Whether to sort findings by relevance or by date:** ⇨ Reference Section 6.3: Overall ordering.

Click on the "News" tab to go to the news search entry interface.

There, in addition to a text box for search terms, you will find various drop-down menu boxes to select:

- **Topic category:** Top Stories, Business, Finance, and so on.
- **Major geographical region:** Africa, Europe, United Kingdom, and so on.
  ⇨ Reference Section 6.2: Geographical region of server.

- **News document age:**
  selected from a drop-down
  menu, in increments ranging
  from "Today/Yesterday" to
  "Any time." You can also
  choose a specific range of
  date options in the drop-
  down menu. ⇨ Reference
  Section 6.2: File age.

  📖 Click on the "News" tab,
  choose "All Topics" in the
  drop-down menu, and type
  Bell Centre as a phrase in
  the text box.

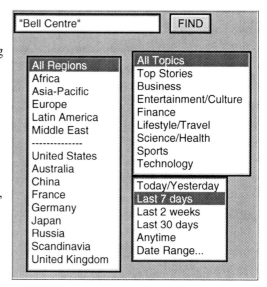

You can also select news topic categories and particular news stories from hyperlinks given at two levels on the screen. The first level of choices for AltaVista Canada is as follows:

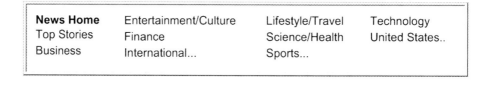

News Home	Entertainment/Culture	Lifestyle/Travel	Technology
Top Stories	Finance	Science/Health	United States..
Business	International...	Sports...	

Copernic

Has a news search engine group that has the following categories of news search engines:

- **By country:**
  Australia,
  Brazil, Canada,
  Portugal, UK.

- **By language:**
  French, German,
  Italian, Spanish.

- **By topic:**
  business, technology, sports.

> 🔨 For details of Copernic categories, click on the category name in our Search Tool Guide, and follow the links down to the lowest category level and search sites for that category. In this instance, you can also start with the following link: ⇨ ToolGuide. SearchHelpCenter.com/search-tool-guide-for-effective-internet-search-copernic-cross-links-2.html.

- **By topic and country:** sports in France, technology in France.

- **By topic and language:** technology news in Spanish.

- **By newspaper and country:** newspapers (U.S.), newspapers in Germany.

A number of the above mix search engine by Internet application with some other method of establishing search engine specialization — topic, language, and country.

In addition, Copernic provides a category called "Top News," which invokes the major Internet news search engines, such as those of AltaVista, Google, FAST (now part of Yahoo), Yahoo, MSN, ABC, and so on.

Google

> Web Images Groups **News** Froogle Local

Provides a separate "news" link on its simple search interfaces. Click on it to go to a news screen. That screen will be full of headlines. For stories not already on the page, you can:

- Enter search terms in the text box provided. Apply the search term against the news catalog, or more generally, against a wider set of catalogs. Do this by using either the "Search News" or the "Search the Web" buttons to start the search.

- Choose links to branch to various sections of the news interface page for stories:

> 🔨 Google news search entry uses a combination method of searching by both keyword and by subject category. You can customize the news categories by setting preferences: ⇨ Reference Section 6.4: Other filter setting preferences.

  - From various topic categories, namely, Business, Sci/tech, Sports, Entertainment, and Health.
  - From the single "Top stories" category.
  - From news sources all over the world or just from the United States.

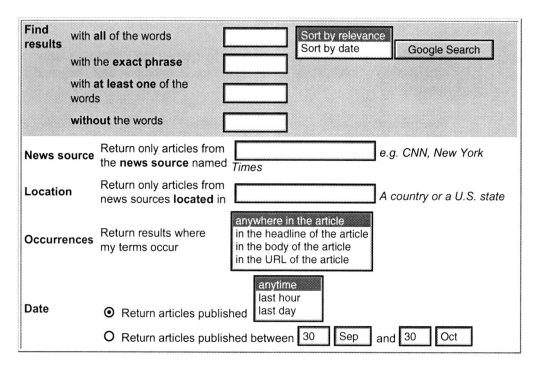

In news search, only certain field operators work:

- For intitle: and intext: field operators: ⇨ Reference Section 6.2: URL (resource) or site Internet address.
- For inurl: and site: field operators: ⇨ Reference Section 6.2: Document file section or location.

The fields on Google advanced news search entry interface are shown below.

Find results	with **all** of the words		Sort by relevance / Sort by date	Google Search
	with the **exact phrase**			
	with **at least one** of the words			
	without the words			
News source	Return only articles from the **news source** named		e.g. CNN, New York *Times*	
Location	Return only articles from news sources **located** in		A country or a U.S. state	
Occurrences	Return results where my terms occur	anywhere in the article / in the headline of the article / in the body of the article / in the URL of the article		
Date	⊙ Return articles published	anytime / last hour / last day		
	○ Return articles published between	30 Sep and 30 Oct		

More about Google news search: ⇨ www.googleguide.com/news.html.

MSN Search

Its simple search interface provides a link to a simple news search interface. Or, you can select the "News" category from the MSN's subject directory to obtain the MSNBC news search entry screen you see below. In this interface, you can search by news category, as you see down the left margin of the screenshot.

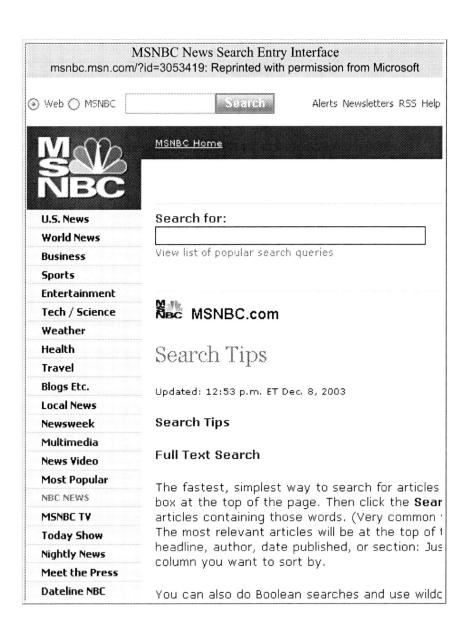

○ Web ○ MSNBC [   ] Search   Alerts Newsletters RSS Help

MSNBC Home

U.S. News
World News
Business
Sports
Entertainment
Tech / Science
Weather
Health
Travel
Blogs Etc.
Local News
Newsweek
Multimedia
News Video
Most Popular
NBC NEWS
MSNBC TV
Today Show
Nightly News
Meet the Press
Dateline NBC

Search for:

[   ]

View list of popular search queries

MSNBC.com

Search Tips

Updated: 12:53 p.m. ET Dec. 8, 2003

Search Tips

Full Text Search

The fastest, simplest way to search for articles
box at the top of the page. Then click the **Sear**
articles containing those words. (Very common
The most relevant articles will be at the top of 1
headline, author, date published, or section: Jus
column you want to sort by.

You can also do Boolean searches and use wildc

General   AlltheWeb   AltaVista   Copernic   Google   MSN

Other non-Web Internet application interfaces

⇨ For more explanation, see Chapter 5: Non-Web Internet application interfaces.

In addition to news, other major non-Web Internet applications include e-mail, FTP (file transfer protocol), chat, and Telnet. Of these, search engines often give you the ability to search discussion groups, often organized in a certain hierarchical fashion, and to search for files on FTP sites.

Search engines featured in this book provide some non-Web application interfaces, as follows:

- Google has an ability to find postings in discussion groups, the old kind of which are the USENET ones, associated with the news application.
- MSN Search has branches to MSN, which hosts community message boards and chat, among other community applications.
- Copernic has access to discussion groups (both USENET and others associated with communities) and FTP, based on categories that invoke appropriate search engines specialized in these applications.

As for FTP search, Copernic has a category for this, but none of the others do. However, before AlltheWeb was taken over by Overture and then Yahoo, it had one of the most advanced and sophisticated FTP search interfaces available. To give you an example of such an interface, we document the old AlltheWeb advanced FTP interface below. For more examples, ⇨ www.ftpsearchengines.com.

General	AlltheWeb	AltaVista	Copernic	Google	MSN

AlltheWeb

An FTP search looks for files by name. AlltheWeb's former FTP

⇨ To understand regular expressions, you will need to go beyond the scope of this book.

⇨ Also see Reference Section 6.1: Wildcards, substrings, stemming.

interface had a sophisticated way of looking for all kinds of variations in the name, by examining parts of the name, making distinctions based on whether letters are capitalized, and using wildcards. It also allowed searching for term variations using **regular expressions** (see ⇨ Chapter 6: Term variation filters). These allow all kinds of flexible pattern variations specified by algorithms.

This interface also provided many metadata-based search filters. You can find more details about these in various Reference Manual sections 6.2 or 6.3 [1].

Search for -	dog
Search type -	substring search substring search, case sensitive substring match substring match, case sensitive multiple substrings search wildcard search wildcard search, case sensitive wildcard match wildcard match, case sensitive regular expression search regular expression match exact search browse directory **?**
Exact hits first -	☐ Try exact hits first ?
Limit to domain-	Limit to domain [es] ?
Limit to path -	Limit to path [ ] ?
Limit size -	Minimum size: [ ] ? Maximum size: [1000000]
Date -	☐ from [1] [January] [1980] ? ☐ to [14] [March] [2003]
Hits -	Max hits: [15] ? Max matches: [ ] Max hits/match: [ ]
Hide -	☐ Packages ☐ Distfiles ? ☐ FreeBSD ☐ OpenBSD ☐ NetBSD ☐ Linux

The above search form is completed to look for files that:

- Have the sub-string dog embedded one or more times in the file name.
- Have a URL whose host has a domain suffix es, for Spain.
- Have a maximum size of 1,000,000 bytes.
- Are in the first 15 files on any particular FTP server.

AltaVista

Internet applications other than news are unavailable.

Copernic

Has categories for:

| For details of Copernic categories, click on the category name in our Search Tool Guide, and follow the links down to the lowest category level and search sites for that category. In this instance, you can also start with the following link: ⇨ ToolGuide. SearchHelpCenter.com/search-tool-guide-for-effective-internet-search-copernic-cross-links-2.html. |

- **Discussion groups:** Copernic generally lands you in the middle of a discussion on a discussion board. The categories are:
  - › **Favorites:** newsgroups;
  - › **Encyclopedia & Reference:** forums and communities.
- **FTP and application file download:** The various search engine categories for these include:
  - › **Computers & Internet:** file search, software download, software download in French.

Google

The advanced group search interface (available from the simple group search screen) provides many additional options, each of which further restricts the query by providing a more targeted search, as follows:

1. Type specific terms into the various text boxes at the top.

Find messages: with **all** of the words [ ] with the **exact phrase** [NHL 2002]
with **at least one** of the words [ ] **without** the words [ ]

2. Look for a more specific Newsgroup by typing its name in "**Newsgroup** Return only messages from the **newsgroup**" box.

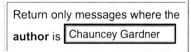
Return only messages from the **group** rec.games.misc

3. Specify a particular author.

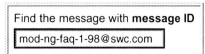
Return only messages where the **author** is Chauncey Gardner

4. Specify a particular message identifier.

Find the message with **message ID**
mod-ng-faq-1-98@swc.com

5. Search:

- In a particular language: ⇨ Reference Section 6.2: Document language.
- Between particular dates: ⇨ Reference Section 6.2: File age.

More about Google groups search: ⇨ www.googleguide.com/groups.html.

MSN Search

MSN includes other features than simply search. By going to the MSN homepage, and then following the links downward, you will find it also provides search related to Internet chat, another non-Web Internet application.

Click "People & Chat" on the MSN homepage. Then follow the links there to the advanced group search (groups.msn. com/search), where the search interface such as seen here, tailored to your country interface, will appear.

General   AlltheWeb   AltaVista   Copernic   Google   MSN

Internal Book Cross-Links

AlltheWeb:

1. More about FTP search filters:

- Exact hits first: Reference Section 6.3: Overall ordering.
- Limit to domain and/or to path: Reference Section 6.2: URL (resource) or site Internet address.
- Limit size: Reference Section 6.2: Additional document file content characteristics, or Reference Section 6.2: Additional multi-media file content characteristics.
- Date: Reference Section 6.2: File age.
- Hits: Reference Section 6.2: Findings shown per site.
- Hide: Reference Section 6.2: Additional document file content characteristics, or Reference Section 6.2: Additional multi-media file content characteristics.

People, business, and map search interfaces

⇨ For more explanation, refer to Chapter 5: Specialized topic search interfaces.

Topic-specialized types of interfaces in search engines are most often those for finding maps, people, businesses, addresses, and the like. Of course, these topics are interrelated.

Some special notes:

- With the exception of AlltheWeb, all the search engines featured in this book have interfaces to locate people, businesses, and so on.
- Google's and AltaVista's people, business, and map search are also available as "shortcuts," based on semi-natural language queries in Web search: ⇨ Reference Section 3: Intelligent avoidance of formal parameter entry.
- Copernic has access to various kinds of Internet application special searches, including ones in this area, based on categories that invoke appropriate search engines.

General	AlltheWeb	AltaVista	Copernic	Google	MSN

AlltheWeb

People, business, and map search interfaces are unavailable.

AltaVista

Lists these kinds of interfaces, accessed by choosing the "More ..." option in simple Web search. If your country preference is the U.S., links to Yahoo Yellow Pages and People Finder also appear on the simple Web search interface itself, although you have to click "More ..." to obtain the Yahoo Maps link. In each case, your search will pertain to your country-language preference settings.

AltaVista also has various so-called "shortcuts" (⇨ Reference Section 3: Intelligent avoidance of formal parameter entry) for using Web search to obtain information on topics that include area codes, maps, driving directions, zip codes, and local information, based on the entry of certain search strings related to these topics.

Copernic

Provides categories that group search engines. The categories are:

- **Favorites:** e-mail addresses.
- **Encyclopedia & Reference:** Atlas, yellow pages.

> For details of Copernic categories, click on the category name in our Search Tool Guide, and follow the links down to the lowest category level and search sites for that category. In this instance, you can also start with the following link: ⇨ ToolGuide.SearchHelpCenter.com/search-tool-guide-for-effective-internet-search-copernic-cross-links-1.html.

Google

Google has various so-called "shortcuts" (⇨ Reference Section 3: Intelligent avoidance of formal parameter entry) for using Web search to obtain information on topics that include area codes, maps, driving directions, zip codes, and local information, based on the entry of certain search strings related to these topics. Thus, Google automatically displays United States street maps and phone book information when certain strings of search parameters are typed into the Web search entry text box.

Also, local Google business search is available using a separate interface, at local. google.com. It currently handles the United States and Canada. You start by entering a type of business, such as a coffee shop, and the city or area of interest, as in the following:

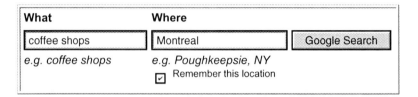

The results listing allows entry of many further choices for displaying and further investigating the results: ⇨ Reference Section 5.2: Links for refining searches; Switching to other catalogs; Related pages or terms; Related entries from other catalogs.

In the area of maps, Google goes far beyond relating them to local search and driving directions, providing satellite images and maps of the entire globe. The Google Earth application provides is a "console" with controls. The controls permit you to manipulate 3-dimensional satellite imagery of the Earth. The initial view is of the entire globe, from which you can zoom in and out on specific locations.

For more on:

- Finding local businesses and services: ⇨ Search Tool Guide: Shopping: other (ToolGuide.SearchHelpCenter.com/search-tool-guide-for-effective-internet-search-shopping-other.html).
- Google local search: ⇨ www.googleguide.com/local.html.
- Google map and satellite imagery search: ⇨ searchenginewatch.com/searchday/article.php/3516001.

MSN Search

| City Guides |
| Yellow Pages |
| White Pages |
| Map & Directions |
| Maps (Encarta) |

Has a list of "MSN Search Resources," including the ones seen here.

In addition, MSN Search allows you to localize your search, so that you can more easily find organizations and residences near your detected or chosen geographical location. Local search is one of the main choices in the menu bar. Also, you can use the "Near Me" button on this interface, which is a way of producing Web results from web servers located near you: ⇨ Appendix 6.2: Additional document file content characteristics for details.

Below is a screenshot of the top part of the local search interface.

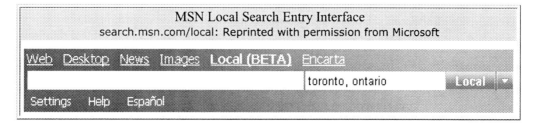

In the area of maps, the MSN Virtual Earth application provides a "console" with controls that permit you to manipulate 3-dimensional satellite imagery of the Earth, from which you can zoom in and out on specific locations. For more on this, see ⇨ searchenginewatch.com/searchday/article.php/3522476.

Other specialized topic search interfaces

⇨ For more explanation, refer to Chapter 5: Specialized topic search interfaces.

Other than people or business addresses, maps and the like, search engines often have interfaces to other specialized subjects, each with their own interface.

Note that:

- Google has several specialized topic interfaces.
- MSN has a large set of specialized topic search interfaces, most of which are accessed via its subject directory rather than through its general MSN Search screens. In effect, when fielded searching of a subject category is available, as well as tailored to that category, you can think of that subject directory branch as providing a specialized topic search interface.
- Copernic accesses various kinds of Internet application special searches through search engines specialized in searching particular topics.

General   AlltheWeb   AltaVista   Copernic   Google   MSN

AlltheWeb

Has no other specialized topic interfaces.

AltaVista

From its U.S. simple web search interface, has a link to Yahoo Shopping. Also:

- It does have various so-called "shortcuts" (⇨ Reference Section 3: Intelligent avoidance of formal parameter entry) for using Web search to obtain information on topics such as shopping, exchange rates, finance, weather, and local information, based on the entry of certain search strings related to these topics.
- Being owned by Yahoo, AltaVista also has access to shortcuts found in Yahoo search (⇨ Reference Section 3: Intelligent avoidance of formal parameter entry).

Copernic

Categories for searching other specialized topics include:

> For details of Copernic categories, click on the category name in our Search Tool Guide, and follow the links down to the lowest category level and search sites for that category. In this instance, you can also start with the following link: ⇨ToolGuide. SearchHelpCenter.com/search-tool-guide-for-effective-internet-search-copernic-cross-links-1. html.

- **Favorites:** e-mail resources.
- **Business and Economy:** business resources, company information, human resources, market research, PR and events, resumes, sales and marketing, stock market, training, and seminars.
- **Computers and Internet:** computer security, computer troubleshooting, domain names, information technology, software download, technology reviews. Also: computer security in French, desktop themes, programming (ASP and PHP, C++, Java, miscellaneous, scripting, Visual Basic), software download in French.

- **Encyclopedia and reference:** atlas, encyclopedias, science publications, yellow pages.
- **Government and law:** government (United States, Canada, United Kingdom, France), legal resources, official documents, patents, law.

> E-mail resources are under Favorites. Also, encyclopedias in French, yellow pages for France, and so on are separate items in this category.

- **Shopping:** buying books, computer hardware, electronics, and software; reviews of books, computer hardware, electronics, and software. Also: antiques and collectibles, auctions, buy books in Canada, buy movies, buy music, movie and music reviews.
- **Entertainment and media:** games, humor, movies, music, music lyrics, television.
- **Special news topics (other than news for specific countries):** sports, technology.
- **Recreation, home, and lifestyle:** cars, Christianity, drinks, educational resources, family and parenthood, genealogy, health, home and garden, jobs (Canada, United Kingdom, France, United States), pets, recipes, science, travel, wine.
- **The Web:** for kids, by country (Australia, Belgium, Brazil, Canada, Denmark, India, Netherlands, Poland, Portugal, Sweden, Switzerland, United Kingdom), by language (French, German, Italian, Spanish).

Some of the above topic specializations are mixed with those based on type of Internet application, including the Web, shopping, and news (⇨ Reference Section 5.1: Other non-Web Internet application interfaces).

Also see ⇨ Reference Section 5.1: People, business, and map search interfaces.

Overall, Copernic has categorized over 1,000 search engines into 120 different categories.

Google

Specialized topic searches are found in Google Help (www.google.ca/options/index. html) under "Services." Items not previously discussed are:

- **Answers** (answers.google.com): An open forum where researchers answer your questions for a fee. More about Google answers search: ⇨ www. googleguide.com/answers.html.

- **Catalogs** (catalogs. google.com): Search and browse mail-order catalogs online, such as shown here. The basic interface branches to more advanced searches and listings of catalogs.

| **Apparel & Accessories** J. Crew, L.L. Bean, Lands' End, ... |
| **Education** Discount School Supply, ... |
| **Computers** Dell, PC Connection, ... |
| **Sports & Outdoors** Golfsmith, West Marine, ... |

The advanced catalog search (catalogs.google.com/advanced
_catalog_search) allows you to enter further parameters to restrict
your search (⇨ Reference Section 6.2: Additional document file content
characteristics). More about Google catalogs search: ⇨ www.
googleguide.com/catalogs.html.

- **Froogle** (www.google.com/froogle): Find products for sale from across the Web; now listed at the same level as web, images, groups, and news. Froogle now takes the place of Directory search, which is demoted to the "more" category in the Google link bar seen here. More about Froogle search: ⇨ www.googleguide.com/froogle.html.

> **Web** Images Groups News Froogle Local >**more »**

- **Special Searches** (www.google.com/options/specialsearches.html): Narrow your search to a specific topic such as BSD, Apple, and Microsoft. More about Google special searches: ⇨ www.googleguide.com/special_searches. html.

🔟 Select "Linux" from Topic-Specific Search.

> **Topic-Specific Search:** Google offers specialized searches on:
> Apple Macintosh - Search for all things Mac
> BSD Unix - Search web pages about the BSD operating system
> Linux - Search all penguin-friendly pages
> Microsoft - Search Microsoft-related pages
> U.S. Government - Search all .gov and .mil sites
> Universities: Stanford, Brown, BYU, & more

Many of the above special searches were developed by **Google
Labs** (labs.google.com). Current lab projects include: Froogle
Wireless, Deskbar, Compute, Sets, Viewer, WebQuotes, Voice
Search, Web Alerts, Personalized Web Search. More about Google
labs: ⇨ www.googleguide.com/labs.html.

- **University Search** (⇨ www.google.com/options/universities.html): Narrow your search to a specific school website.
- **News alerts** (www.google.com/newsalerts): Specify a topic and receive e-mail updates when news breaks: ⇨ Reference Section 5.2: Search follow-up.
- **Academic References** (scholar.google.com): Find scholarly reference materials, including books and articles, by author, title, publisher, subject, etc., using deep web databases, including materials not normally available to Internet webcrawlers.

- **Ride Finder** (http://labs.google.com/ridefinder): Finds taxi and shuttle service locations.

> 🔨 Many third parties have also been using the Google interface to develop search applications based on it.
>
> 🔲 Social networking search, where results are refined and personalized according to a person's social network. For more, see ⇨ www. searchenginewatch.com/searchday/article.php/3302741, and www. searchenginewatch.com/searchday/article.php/3301481.
>
> 🔨 Google also provides various ways of using Web search to obtain deep web information on topics such as stocks, products, airline flights, vehicles, and mailed parcels. Search strings are entered along with relevant codes to access structured online databases on these topics: ⇨ Reference Section 3: Intelligent avoidance of formal parameter entry.

MSN Search

From the MSN simple search interface, you can branch directly to a few subject-specific searches, including Images, Movies, and Music, already dealt with above in this Reference Manual section (see the accompanying partial screenshot).

MSN Search Interface: Reprinted with permission from Microsoft

More importantly, by clicking on "MSN Home," you can indirectly access a whole slew of subject-specific search interfaces, each specialized in relation to a particular MSN directory category (⇨ Reference Section 3: Subject Directory Search Interfaces).

Many of the subjects are searchable using fielded searches appropriate

> 🔨 Dictionary and encyclopedia searches, as well as map (atlas) and several other search topics are found under "Encarta" in the MSN subject directory.

to the subject category, such as search by artist for a search within the music category. In effect, when fielded searching of a subject category is available as well as tailored to that category, you can think of that subject directory branch as providing a specialized topic search interface. Because of the extensive nature of all these specialized topic interfaces, we will not show the various search entry interfaces here. For:

- A screenshot of the major subject directory entries, see ⇨ Appendix 3: Subject directory search interfaces.
- More about the complex and varied filters available to many of these searches, refer to ⇨ Reference Section 6.2: Additional document file content characteristics.

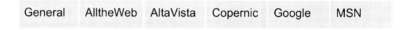

General	AlltheWeb	AltaVista	Copernic	Google	MSN

Reference Manual Section 5.2: Findings Display & Handling Interfaces

⇨ This section cross-links with Chapter 5: Findings Display & Handling Interfaces and Chapter 5: Findings Handling.

Organization & Detailing of Findings

Overall ordering

⇨ For more explanation, refer to:

- Chapter 5: Organization of findings display.
- Reference Section 6.3: Overall ordering.

By default, search engines automatically sequence findings by relevance and/or website authoritativeness. As you can imagine, actually determining these involves fairly complex processes.

Relevance in most of today's search engine catalogs is largely determined by the number and quality of links coming into a webpage from other pages, especially in the case of Google (e.g., see Google's PageRank™ system below). Yahoo (which provides the web results for AlltheWeb and AltaVista) uses a somewhat different approach.

In all our featured search engines, some kinds of search results pages usually provide options to sort by other criteria, such as date, especially in the case of news search listings. But, this is done for the most part after the results have been produced. MSN Search, in contrast, provides a system of three sliders you can use when entering the original search, by which you can provide settings for three kinds of factors usable by MSN Search in sorting your findings.

General	AlltheWeb	AltaVista	Copernic	Google	MSN

Reference Manual Section 5.2:
Findings Display &
Handling Interfaces

321

Organization &
Detailing of Findings

AlltheWeb

Findings are
ordered by
relevance.

> 🔨 Using a parameter, you can sequence news
> document search findings by date: ⇨ Reference Section
> 6.3: Overall ordering.

AltaVista

> 🔨 You can alter its news findings sequencing criteria
> with parameters: ⇨ Reference Section 6.3: Overall
> ordering.

Copernic

Uses its own
algorithms for
sequencing of
findings by
relevance.
However, those
determined by the
source search
engines are considered first.

> 💡 If you prefer the sequencing of one or two of the
> source search engines, then have Copernic simply limit
> itself to those engines. ⇨ Reference Section 3: Advanced
> Web search interfaces.
>
> 🔨 Copernic provides a comparatively rich set of
> options for regrouping and re-sequencing the list of
> findings: ⇨ Reference Section 6.3: Overall ordering.

Google

Uses its **PageRank™**
system, which includes all
the ordering criteria
described earlier in this
book: ⇨ Chapter 5:
Organization of findings
display.

> 🔨 You can alter Google's findings presentation
> ordering criteria for certain catalogs including
> news, groups, and subject directory: ⇨
> Reference Section 5.2: Grouping and sorting.
> Ordering of results also tends to follow the order
> in which you enter your search terms: ⇨
> Reference Section 6.3: Overall ordering.

MSN Search

> 🔨 You can alter its findings presentation ordering
> criteria: ⇨ Reference Section 6.3: Overall ordering.

General	AlltheWeb	AltaVista	Copernic	Google	MSN

Reference Manual Section 5.2:
Findings Display &
Handling Interfaces

322

Organization &
Detailing of Findings

Page organization

The easiest way to explain the organization of findings is to divide results pages into top, middle, and bottom sections. Available options are also discussed.

Each search engine has its own particular way of organizing its findings pages, but in general:

> All the search engines discussed here (with the exception of Copernic) allow you to control the number of findings shown per page using a search parameter. ⇨
>
> - Reference Section 6.3: Page organization.
> - Reference Section 6.4: Findings Display & Handling Preferences.

- **Top and/or bottom sections of page:** Repeat the search, give overall statistics, and provide boxes and choices for further refining it.
- **Middle part of page:** Provides finding details. Organization here may depend on the type of catalog searched against (the type of search).
- **Bottom of page:** Has links to more pages of findings.
- **Additional separate panes/areas/frames:** May, for example, show paid listings or results from other catalogs other than the main catalog searched against, using a particular search entry interface.

General	AlltheWeb	AltaVista	Copernic	Google	MSN

AlltheWeb

Its findings pages are organized as follows:

1. **Top of page:** contains:

    a. A repeat of the the top part of your completed search form, if you filled out a simple search interface screen.

    b. If you did an advanced search in addition to the above, an "edit your advanced search" link to return you to your original completed advanced search form, if so desired.

    c. After this you may find links to "Related Searches," to further refine your search by adding search terms. For more about this, see ⇨ Reference Section 5.2: Links for refining searches.

Reference Manual Section 5.2:
Findings Display &
Handling Interfaces

323

Organization &
Detailing of Findings

To carry the same search string to another interface, click on one of the links provided. You will then be taken to a findings page for the other type of catalog.

2. **Middle of page:** May be partitioned into findings from different catalogs:

> ⇨ For details of the findings display for each type of search (catalog), refer to Reference Section 5.2: Presentation of individual findings.

   a. **Web search:** Sponsored Matches for paid listings appear first, then news catalog listings, followed by Web catalog findings.

   b. **News search:** This has a simpler organization than a Web search, providing a straight listing of document finds from the news catalog.

   c. **Audio and Video searches:** These are displayed in a grid that has more than one textual column. Each row represents a particular finding. The contents in each column depends on whether it is an audio or video search.

   d. **Pictures search:** This produces a 3-row X 4-column matrix filled with thumbnails (reduced size representations) of images. Each one is accompanied by certain fields of textual information.

3. **Bottom of page:** Next come links to other pages of findings.

> Results page: 1-10 11-20 21-30 31-40 41-50 51-60 61-70   Next »

4. Final link is "Search within your results."

> ⇨ For a discussion of this, see Reference Section 5.2: Links for refining searches.

AltaVista

Its findings pages are organized as follows:

1. **Top of page:** contains your completed search form, unless you have conducted an advanced Web search. In the latter case, only the top part of the form is repeated at the top of the findings page, while the rest of the form is at the very end. The completed search form also includes tabs with links to the simple levels of AltaVista's most important search interfaces.

Reference Manual Section 5.2:
Findings Display &
Handling Interfaces

324

Organization &
Detailing of Findings

2. **Middle of page:** Individual findings. The page organization varies by type of catalog you are searching against:

    a. **Web search:** Findings are divided into two groups:

       • Sponsored matches, i. e., paid listings. These are listed above the web document (Web) catalog findings.

       • Matches from the web document (Web) catalog. These are preceded by a line that indicates the total number of such findings.

> The display of Web catalog findings may be controlled by parameters. For example, the "site collapse" parameter can be set to indent all findings from the same website under the first finding. You can also control the number of findings shown on each page. For details, ⇨ Reference Section 6.3: Page organization.

    b. **News search:** No sponsored matches occur at the top of the page; only news catalog items are shown.

    c. **Image and video searches:** They produce a 5-row X 4-column grid of image thumbnails. Each image is accompanied by certain fields of textual information. Findings for sponsored matches are in the top rows, followed by the number of regular findings, and then rows of thumbnails for those findings.

    d. **MP3/Audio search:** Each finding is specified in terms of a textual form consisting of a few well-defined fields. Sponsored matches are listed prior to the regular findings.

    e. **Directory search:** If you type a search term, AltaVista goes to the Yahoo directory. Here, the various categories related to your search terms display under the "Related Directory Categories" near the top of the findings page. For each related category, the hierarchical path levels are separated by ">" signs in "breadcrumb" fashion (e.g., Animated TV Shows > Top **Cat**, if searching on the term cat). Once you choose a path, a new page appears. The selected path is repeated at the top of that page, until you reach the bottom level of the Yahoo directory. At that level, the individual findings are displayed, as shown on the next page.

Reference Manual Section 5.2:
Findings Display &
Handling Interfaces
325
Organization &
Detailing of Findings

Animated TV Shows > Top Cat

Directory > Entertainment > Television Shows > Animation > **Top Cat**

Search [   ]   O the Web   O Canadian sites   ⊙ this category

SITE LISTINGS

- Hangin' Out With Top Cat 🖳 - interview with Arnold Strang, the voice of Top Cat.
- Top Cat Web 🖳 - find out all about TC, Benny, Spook, Brain, Choo Choo, Fancy Fancy, and Officer Dibble.

3. **Bottom of page:** Links to other pages of findings.

> **Result Pages: 1** 2 3 4 5 6 7 8 9 10 [Next >>]

4. Finally, if you have done an advanced Web search, your entire completed form is repeated, allowing you to modify your search. Otherwise, all that appears is a text entry box with your search terms and a search command button. You can use these to revise your search.

Copernic

You can view search results in either Copernic, which divides your window into panes, or in your browser, which divides your window into frames. Each page organization method is described below.

> ⇨ For more about options for findings page organization, consult Reference Section 6.3: Page organization.

Copernic pane findings display method:

Copernic displays its findings in folders, found under the search history pane, which shows the various searches you have conducted over time.

> ⇨ Consult Chapter 4: Local application interfaces for a full screenshot of all the main Copernic panes, including the ones for findings display.

From top to bottom of the findings display panes:

1. **Top pane, search history:** Somewhat similar to the top section of the other search engines. You can view the overall characteristics of a search in a few different ways including:

   a. Floating your mouse over the search history item, which pops up a box giving the overall search specifications.

Reference Manual Section 5.2:
Findings Display &
Handling Interfaces

326

Organization &
Detailing of Findings

b. Choosing to view the search details in the top pane. As you can see in the below partial screenshots, this will show you:

- **Mode:** whether the search was for an exact phrase, alternative terms, or all the terms.

  Turbo-Genset
  Mode: Exact phrase
  Matches: 1589
  Updated: 15/02/03 12:00:20 AM
  Note:

- **Matches:** how many *new* matches were made after filtering out duplicates from different search engines.

- **Updated:** when the search was completed or last repeated.

- **Note:** any annotation you added to the search history for that particular search.

- **Category:** the subject category of the search engines sourced.

  Category: The Web
  Res. per engine: 700
  Created: 27/01/03 7:45:16 AM
  Schedule: On a daily basis

- **Res. per engine:** maximum number of results allowed from each sourced search engine.

- **Created:** original date and time of this query (different from an update - if the search was rerun since).

- **Schedule:** repeat frequency, if you have search tracking selected for this search (⮕ Chapter 5: Post-processing of findings).

c. Right-clicking over the search item and then choosing "Properties" from the drop-down menu. This gives you a dialog box having the "General" and "Details" tabs seen on the next page.

> ⚠ The information about the search obtained here in part 'c' is not exactly the same as found in 'a' and 'b' above. because 1,545 is the number of matches after the search was updated a day later.

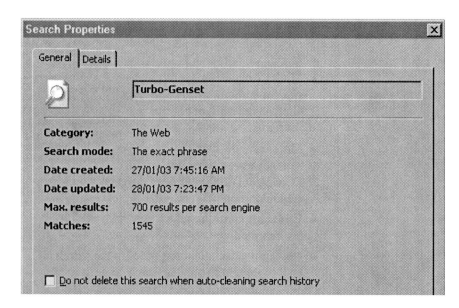

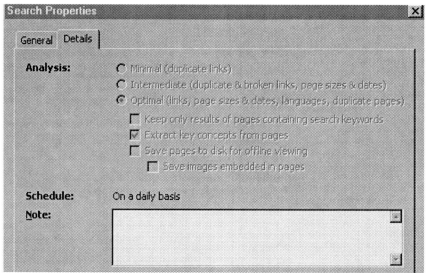

2. **Bottom of the screen:** Provides search details. Here, you can view each finding in detailed, standard, or compact modes, according to the parameters you select (⇨ Reference Section 6.3: Finding fields to display).

3. **Status bar**, located in the lower left-hand corner of the main Copernic screen: Displays the number of findings in the search after filtering, with the number of findings that have been filtered out in brackets.

Browser window findings display method:

⇨ For a detailed screenshot, see Chapter 5: Organization of findings display.

Here you choose "Browse results" to open a new window in which to view the findings.

Reference Manual Section 5.2:
Findings Display &
Handling Interfaces

328

Organization &
Detailing of Findings

In it, you will see the findings list in the left frame. As you click on each finding, it is accessed on the Internet and opened in the bigger frame to the right, below a frame that displays the overall search specifications.

Ignoring the left frame in the browser window (used to control which results are accessed), the right screen frames provide a similar top to bottom arrangement as those of our other featured search engines.

1. **Top of page:** The overall specification for the search appears in a frame above the one displaying individual results. It provides a message on the total number of findings and which sub-series of the findings you are looking at. It also displays links to any next and previous pages of findings (based on a ceiling number of findings per page). From the top of the browser page, you can also choose to view the search history list in that browser window, as you see in the screenshot below.

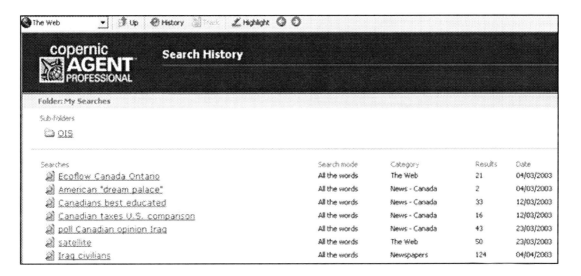

(To see the preceding screenshot in full resolution, go to ➪
www.SearchHelpCenter.com/effective-internet-search-copernic-screenshots.html,
"History view in browser.")

2. **Next frame:** Provides the search details or the individual files themselves, if you select one of the findings from the control frame on the left of your browser window.

3. **Bottom of page:** At the very bottom of the results listing, Copernic again displays the total number of findings, the sub-series of which appears on the page you now see and links to any next or previous pages of findings.

Google

Its findings pages are organized as follows:

1. **Top of page:** (see following screenshot) includes:

   a. Above the text entry box are links to the most important of Google's simple search interfaces, as well as to "More" interfaces.

   b. A text entry box shows your search string, including search terms and operator parameters. You can modify this string and then press the "Search" button to do another search.

   c. To the right of the text entry box are links to advanced search options and to Preferences.

   d. If you did a Web search for a non-American version of the Google interface, below the text entry box you will see some radio buttons to provide you with the option of limiting the geographical scope of the search, for example, to distinguish Canadian sites from the Web as a whole.

   e. Next, a statistics line indicates the catalog searched against (Web in this case), the search string, the number of results returned, and the amount of time it took to complete the search. To have Google retrieve a definition of a word search term, simply click on the word "definition" to be taken to a dictionary.

   f. Below the Statistics Bar, you may see results from other catalogs, e.g., from News if you do a Web search. (In earlier versions of Google, a breadcrumb list would often appear here giving the subject directory category attributed to the search for Web and Directory searches: ⇨ Reference Section 5.2: Related entries from other catalogs.) In the case of a Groups search, related groups are shown here. Nothing appears for Image and News searches.

   g. For a Web search, you may see some other links, such as the stock quote link on the next page, for the Web search on the word cat (⇨ Reference Section 3: Intelligent avoidance of formal parameter entry).

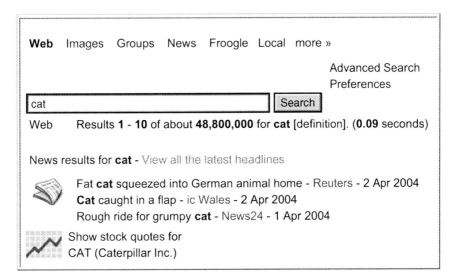

Further to the above, each type of search presents some different variations, described next.

Local search: The following is a screenshot of what you get for the term cat.

As you can see in the screenshot on the previous page, the top of the findings page is somewhat different. The business category (or other identifying keywords) and location you entered are repeated at the top of the page. Following that, but under the sponsored listings, are links for you to choose sub-categories to search within your findings. As well, there is a link for choosing the radius of your geographical search.

Groups search: Related groups are shown before the start of the individual findings in the middle part of the page. Also, some groups management links are shown in a pane to the left side of your screen. The following is a screenshot of what you get for the term cat.

Google Groups Search Results: Reprinted with permission from Google

Google Groups BETA

Web   Images   **Groups**   News   Froogle   Local   **more »**

cat   Search   Advanced Group
                                                                Preferences

Members: Sign in
New users: Join

Google Groups

✉ Groups Alerts

Create a new group

About Google Groups

Searched all groups

Related groups: LuartSound Produções e Eventos - 2640
                   Cat's Meow Movie Web Log
                   CAT Hunters Inc
                   154 more »

Picky **cat**: Friskies or Whiskas?
This is only anecdotal evidence, but my **cat** is around 15 years old. O
minor thyroid problem, my **cat** is healthy on the food I provide for her.
alt.cats - Aug 4, 6:28 pm by Shawn Hirn - 42 messages - 14 authors

the Laws of **Cat** Physics
Chip, Are you getting a **cat** for Christmas????? smiles, Elise Law of C
Motion IA **cat** at rest will tend to remain at rest, unless ...
alt.support.anxiety-panic.moderated - Dec 12 2003, 6:25 pm by w

Directory search: The first middle section of the page may contain a section called "Categories," which is divided into categories that contain your keywords and "Related categories." The following, on the next page, is a screenshot of what you get for the term cat.

Google™
Directory

[   ] [Google Search] Dire

◉ Search only in Cats ○ Search the Web

Cats

Recreation > Pets > Cats

Categories

Behavior (125)	Health (253)	Pedigree Registration (
Breeds (3813)	Humor (49)	**Personal Pages** (320)
Chats and Forums (40)	Image Galleries (83)	Products and Services
Clubs (82)	Issues (208)	**Rescues and Shelter**
Directories (19)	Loss (11)	Resources (50)
Famous Cats (38)	Magazines and E-zines (15)	Shows and Showing (2
Feline Web Graphics (13)	Names (12)	Web Rings (34)
Free Utilities (1)		

Related Categories:

Kids and Teens > Your Family > Pets > Cats (18)

Science > Biology > Flora and Fauna > Animalia > Chordata > Mammalia > Carniv

Society > Issues > Animal Welfare > Specific Animals > Cats (8)

Web Pages   Viewing in Goog

Moscow Cat Museum - http://www.moscowcatmuseum.com/eng/
A collection of facts and thoughts connected with the theme of the cat in art and life, mos

Kitty Klips - http://www.corporatevideo.com/klips/index.htm
A method to keep cats in a yard by making it impossible for them to climb fences.

2. **Middle of page:** Contains individual findings. What you see here depends on the type of search. In Web, Directory, Groups, and News searches, you will see a list of search findings.

> You can control the number of findings shown on a page using a parameter (⮕ Reference Section 6.3: Page organization).

In Web or Groups search, you may also see some paid listings ("Sponsored links") cited down the right side of the page, or, for local search, near the top of the listing.

Reference Manual Section 5.2:
Findings Display &
Handling Interfaces

333

Organization &
Detailing of Findings

In these findings lists, for Web search, a maximum of two findings per website are normally displayed. If applicable, the second finding is indented under the first. Moreover, if more than two links are found for a single website, Google provides a link to the remainder instead of showing them, as can be seen below:

Whatever ~ By Eliot Lucas
... Today's Episode: #99 "He had it coming", Make with the clicky! Vote for Whatever! Chartruesse ...
www.geocities.com/red_today/ - 15k - Cached - Similar pages

　　whatever : baby blues
　　Wednesday : 13 March 2002 Baby update. And again, not much to share with you on
　　the babyfront yet. Tomorrow. ...
　　www.geocities.com/sherlonkah2/whatever.html - 36k - Cached - Similar pages
　　[More results from www.geocities.com]

Further to the above, each type of search presents some different variations, described next.

Image search: The format for Image searches is different, displaying picture thumbnails in a 5-row X 4-column grid = 20 thumbnails per grid.

Local search: To the right of the regular findings list is a map of the locality, along with various links to control the map display.

3. **Bottom of page:** Contains a text box with the search string as generated, along with links to other pages of findings. For Web and Image searches, you will also notice a link to search within findings, as seen in the example below.

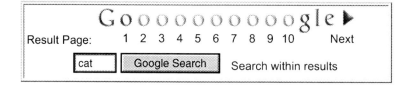

Note: Anacubis, a third-party product based on Google, has a way of displaying findings graphically: ⇨ www.anacubis.com/Products/ViewManager. This provides a very different kind of page organization.

Reference Manual Section 5.2:
Findings Display &
Handling Interfaces
334
Organization &
Detailing of Findings

MSN Search

Its findings pages are organized as follows:

1. **Top of page** displays various boxes and buttons including:

    a. A repeat of the search form, with your search string entered. You can change the contents to revise the search and try again (⇨ Reference Section 5.2: Links for refining searches).

    e. A line indicating the number of results, and the amount of time taken for retrieval of results.

    > Web Results
    > 1-9 of 120,154,595 containing **cat** (0.25 seconds)

For Local search, the top of the findings page is somewhat different. As you see below, the search terms, which also include the location you entered, are repeated at the top of the page. Following that are some links for you to choose. By choosing one of these, you can activate or suppress the display of different categories of findings, based on whether these are "Business Listings," "Residential Listings," or "Web Results." The default is to display all three of these in the middle section of the page, each under their own sub-header.

If you click on the underlined location, seen in brackets below next to "Local Results," you are taken to a screen where you can set your default location.

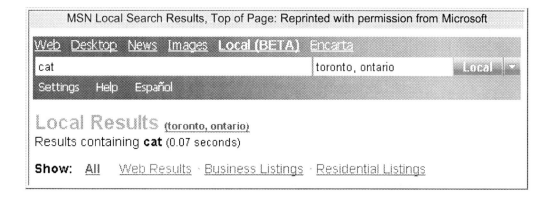

MSN Local Search Results, Top of Page: Reprinted with permission from Microsoft

Web   Desktop   News   Images   **Local (BETA)**   Encarta

cat   toronto, ontario   Local ▾

Settings   Help   Español

Local Results (toronto, ontario)
Results containing **cat** (0.07 seconds)

Show: All   Web Results · Business Listings · Residential Listings

2. Middle of page:

a. **Web search:** Regular document file findings from the Web catalog may be preceded by sponsored listings, highlighted against a different background color. Also, sponsored listings may appear down the right margin of the page.

Other listings of document file findings are in the main part of the results page. These come from the Web catalog. The sponsored listings at the top of the page may repeat under the regular listings.

b. **News, word, and Encarta searches:** Regular results are listed in the middle part of the page. No sponsored or other listings appear.

c. **Images search:** These results are displayed, preceded by certain display option buttons, in a 4-row X 5-column grid of image thumbnails. Each image is accompanied by certain fields of textual information.

d. **Local search:** The results are sub-categorized into Business, Residential, and Web groupings, each with their own sub-header. To the right of the findings list is a map of the locality, along with various links to control the map display.

e. **Other specialty searches (stock quotes, movies, shopping, music):** For more details on these, refer to ➪ Appendix 3: Subject Directory Search Interfaces, and follow the links from there to inspect the various MSN specialty searches.

3. Bottom of page:

The search string entry box and the total number of results are repeated. You may revise the search string, and

> 🖋 Result summaries and the number of findings shown on a page are features you can control using a search parameter (➪ Reference Section 6.3: Page organization).

then resubmit your search using the button next to the text entry box.

General	AlltheWeb	AltaVista	Copernic	Google	MSN

Reference Manual Section 5.2:
Findings Display &
Handling Interfaces

336

Organization &
Detailing of Findings

Presentation of individual findings

Each finding has various fields of information, presented in various formats, dependent on the type of search and the particular search engine involved. The following kinds of searches are among those available with our featured search engines:

⇨ For more explanation, see:

- Chapter 5: Presentation of individual findings.
- Reference Section 6.3: Presentation of Individual Findings.

- **Web, news, image, and video searches:** All featured search engines.
- **Audio search:** All featured search engines, except Google.
- **Directory search:** AltaVista, Google, and MSN Search.
- **Local search:** Google, MSN Search, and AltaVista via Yahoo.

Copernic displays all individual findings in the same format, although you can choose different levels of display detail. However, when linking to a particular finding, the interface to the findings screen of a source search engine may appear, depending upon the category, the particular finding, and the individual search engine involved.

Note: Although no longer available, for illustration purposes, you will find results for AlltheWeb's FTP search included below. Copernic also has an FTP search category.

General	AlltheWeb	AltaVista	Copernic	Google	MSN

AlltheWeb

1. **Web document (Web) search**. According to AlltheWeb Help:

   Each result is listed with the title of the page, a text excerpt describing it, its URL, and a file.

   To get more than one page hit from a specific site, click on the "more hits from:" link. AlltheWeb will then perform a new search with the same filters, but only within the particular site.

   🔳 On the next page are a sample findings, illustrating the above.

Reference Manual Section 5.2:
Findings Display &
Handling Interfaces

337

Organization &
Detailing of Findings

2. **News document search**. Unlike Web searches, you do not obtain fields for URL or "more hits from" links at the end of the finding. But you do get information on when the page was indexed.

   🔢 The first finding below was indexed "8 hours ago."

Sort by Relevance ▸ Sort by Date

Cat Survives Trip in Crate From China
AP via Yahoo! News - 3 KB- Found: 8 hours ago
A business owner opening a shipment of merchandise from China got an additional item he didn't expect — a severely undernourished cat.

Cat survives month in shipping crate
News Interactive - 60 KB- Found: 4 hours ago
A US business owner opening a shipment of merchandise from China got an additional item he didn't expect - a severely undernourished cat.

---

3. **Audio search**. The main part of the findings page returns a list of audio files that match your query, sorted by the reliability of the source. Search results are presented in a tabular form, with columns for title, file size, and date of each finding.

   🔢 If you search on Madonna, sample findings will look like this:

Title	Size	Date
madonna american life hollywood http://www.nhnam.com/madonna/	-	2004-03-11
Madonna Die Another Day http://mystikdragon.net/archives/000064.html	-	2004-03-11

Reference Manual Section 5.2:
Findings Display &
Handling Interfaces

338

Organization &
Detailing of Findings

4. **Video search**. The main part of the findings page returns a list of video files that match your query. Search results are presented in a tabular form, with columns for video title and nearby text, play duration (length), file size, and file format of each finding.

If you search on Britney, sample findings will look like this:

---

1 - 10 of 448 Results for Britney

Title	Length	Size	Format
 video britney spears For your viewing pleasure Britney Spears on her Nickolodeon premier I httpwwwJOHNNYBREADcom http://www.johnnybread.com/media.php	00:01:46	-	MPEG
 britney spears stronger live at ama tolerance uva Stronger xxxballoons http://minnow.cc.gatech.edu/dvfx.69	00:04:48	-	MPEG

In the above columns:

- **Title:** Click this to download it to your computer, or to play the stream.
- **Length:** Video play duration in hours, minutes, and seconds.
- **Size:** File size in megabytes (MB), if shown. Videos with larger file sizes look better, but have a longer download time.
- **Format:** e.g. AVI, QuickTime, and MPEG. Note: You may need different players to view these.

5. **Pictures search**. The details provided for each picture in the grid are: Filename, File format (i.e. GIF, JPEG, BMP, etc.), Image pixel dimensions (length x width), and file size in kilobytes (KB).

As Cute as a Koala B...
JPEG 968x671, 356 KB

If you search on koala, you might get this finding:

The details for each image are explained by AlltheWeb Help as follows:

Reference Manual Section 5.2:
Findings Display &
Handling Interfaces

339

Organization &
Detailing of Findings

- **Thumbnail:** Click the thumbnail image to go to fullsize image.
- **Filename:** In the example above, **"As Cute as a Koala B..."**. Clicking the image filename will take you to the fullsize image.
- **Image dimensions:** Displayed in pixels and in "Length x Width" format.
- **File size:** Indicated in kilobytes (KB).

Depending on the picture, clicking on its name may take you to the webpage from which it came.

6. **FTP search**. The main part of the findings page returned a list of FTP files that matched your query, sorted by the reliability of the

⚠ This search is no longer part of AlltheWeb, but is simply included here to provide an example of an FTP search.

source. Search results were presented in a tabular form, with columns for type, filename/path, file size, and date of each finding.

If you searched on winzip, sample findings would look like this:

1-15 Results			
Type	**Filename/Path**	**Size**	**Date**
	WINZIP ftp://ftp.elet.polimi.it/outgoing/Stefano.Ceri/.../WINZIP	Folder	1999-11-03
	WinZIP ftp://ftp.schools.net.au/usr/sina/customers/schnet/.../WinZIP	Folder	2002-04-22
	WinZip ftp://ftp.ablecom.net/pub/myers/WinZip	Folder	1999-10-03

The above columns were explained by AlltheWeb Help as follows:

- **Type:** Sometimes you will get results that are folders, or directories of files on a computer. Clicking the ☐ icon will allow you to view the contents of that directory.

  You can also browse the parent folder of a file by clicking on the ☐ icon. Files are marked by the ☐ icon.

- **Filename/Path:** Click on the filename to download the file.
- **Path:** The URL of the file or directory.
- **File size:** Is shown in kilobytes (KB).
- **Date:** Indicates the date at which the file was last modified.

Reference Manual Section 5.2:
Findings Display &
Handling Interfaces

340

Organization &
Detailing of Findings

AltaVista

1. **Web document (Web) search**. Individual findings look as follows:

Adventure cruise destination - Eternité Bay, Saguenay
Small ship adventure cruises to explore Eternité Bay, Saguenay Fjord, with ECOMERTOURS.
www.ecomertours.com/D_Eternite_Bay.htm • Translate   More pages from ecomertours.com

---

For each web document (webpage) finding listed, AltaVista lists:

- **Title:** Taken from TITLE metatag.
- **Description:** Displays contents of DESCRIPTION metatag in an HTML page (if coded by webpage creator) or data from first few lines of text shown in browser window. In the case of a multi-media file, descriptions are usually taken from the text of document files from which the multi-media files are cross-referenced, as well as from the file name.
- **Website's URL:** Web address.
- **Links to more information:** ⇨ Reference Section 5.2: Links from Findings Display.

2. **News document search**. The breakdown of each finding is along the same lines as for documents found using Web search. Here is an example:

News Home › Search results for iraq, page 1of 3880

AltaVista found 38,794 results - sorted by relevance | sorted by date

Kerry blasts Bush Iraq 'mistakes'
The Democrat presidential hopeful says President Bush's Iraq policy has produced a "tragedy of errors".
BBC News Found 13 minutes ago Translate • More info

---

3. **Audio search**. You obtain a breakdown into fields along different lines from a document (Web or news) search. AltaVista shows:

- **File name**.
- **File information:** Length of play or other.
- **URL of document file:** Page in which audio file link is embedded.
- **Open in new window:** Opens document in question, from which you can click the audio link to play or download it.

- **Links:** For more information.
- **Copyright notice:** If applicable.

> **IG** You
> can see
> these
> fields here.

> File Info mp3 • 00:05:21 sec
> Page URL http://www.nhnam.com/madonna/
> More info   Open in new window
> File Name madonna_hollywood_128-a.asx
>
> File Info msmedia • 00:04:24 sec
> Page URL http://www.rronline.com/gfa/epk/m...a_hollywood.htm
> More info   Open in new window
> Copyright Copyright 2003 Warner Bros. Records

4. **Video search**. Here is an example of a finding.

Koala.mpg
720x576 • 8 sec
More info

Below the image for each video are fields for the file name, pixel (screen) dimensions of the video, and play duration. If you click on the line to "More info," you obtain further technical information and details about the webpage containing the video link. Technical information specific to movies (video) includes file format, picture frame rate, and number of bits per sample. Links may include:

- **Webpage** in which video link is embedded.
- **Further media** from that page.
- **Same webpage**, but opened in a new window.
- **Tips** on how to find the video on that webpage.

IG If you click "More info" in the above example, you get the the details you see in the frame on the next page:

5. **Image search**. Here is an example of a finding. The details shown for each image include the image file name, resolution (in pixels), and file size (in kilobytes). If you click on the link for "More info," you obtain further technical information and details about the webpage containing the image link. Technical information specific to images includes file format, photometrics (whether the picture is color or black and white). Further links are to:

koala.jpg
345x291 • 10.0kB
More info.

Title: Koala
File name: Koala.mpg
Duration: 00:00:08 sec
Dimensions: 720x576 pixels
File type: mpeg

Sample Size: 16 bits/sample
Frame Rate: 25 frames/sec

Tips for finding this video on the page

Found on:
http://www.knowhowe.net/pages/australiatext.htm
Abstract: lamb and Rob still hasnt had the chance to cuddle a pudgy barrelshaped Australia content
Open in new window | All media from this page

All pages with this file:

1. **Page Title** Koala
   Page URL http://www.knowhowe.net/pages/australiatext.htm
   Abstract lamb and Rob still hasnt had the chance to cuddle a pudgy barrelshaped Australia content
   Open in new window | All media from this page

2. **Page Title** Koala
   Page URL http://www.knowhowe.net/pages/australiaitems.htm
   Abstract Australia menu
   Open in new window | All media from this page

- **Webpage** in which image link is embedded.
- **Same webpage**, but opened in a new window.
- **Tips** on how to find the image on that webpage.

If you click "More info" in the above example, you get the following details:

Title: **koala**
File name: **koala.jpg**
Dimensions: 345x291 pixels
File size: 10.0kB
File type: jpeg
Coloration: color

Tips for finding this video on the page

Found on:
http://www.autopiatours.com.au/tour4.htm
Abstract: Autopia Tours Australian Backpacker Tours of Great Ocean Rd Victoria
Open in new window | All media from this page

Reference Manual Section 5.2:
Findings Display &
Handling Interfaces

343

Organization &
Detailing of Findings

Copernic

⇨ For more about the various options for displaying findings, see Reference Section 6.3: Finding fields to display.

As explained in Copernic Help, the detailed elements for each result are:

- **Icon:** the result icon (select the Legend command from the Help menu to display the icons, other markers and their meaning — see: Result List Marker Legend).
- **Title:** the result title as a link to the local saved page or to its Internet address.

This may simply be the file name for a multi-media file search, as in the following screenshot.

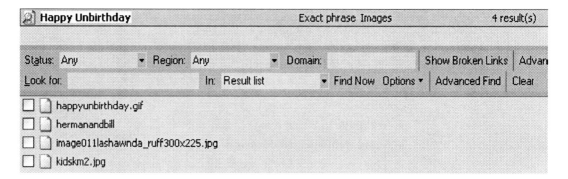

- **Excerpt:** the result excerpt.
- **Score:** score attributed to a result in terms of relevancy or degree of interest. The maximum score is 100 %; it is displayed graphically and numerically.
- **Concepts:** extracted key concepts from the result web page contents (Copernic Agent Professional required; see: Analyzing Results).
- **Languages:** the detected languages of the corresponding page (Copernic Agent Professional required; see: Analyzing Results).
- **Note:** the user note, as the case may be (Copernic Agent Professional required; see: Annotating Results).
- **Last modified:** the last date when the corresponding page was modified (Copernic Agent Professional required; see: Annotating Results).
- **Found by:** the search engines where the result was found.
- **Address:** the link to the corresponding web page address.

Copernic also calls the "icon" a "marker," explaining it this way:

Reference Manual Section 5.2:
Findings Display &
Handling Interfaces
344
Organization &
Detailing of Findings

Markers used to differentiate results and detect related information (e.g. existence of saved pages and annotations) include icons, colors, font styles and font effects. Note that you may also checkmark interesting results in order to trace them more easily. A result may have more than a marker to pinpoint it, depending on conducted operations in its case.

The markers used by Copernic, demonstrated in the screenshots on this and the next page, are as follows:

⇨ Icons versus markers: An example follows at the end of point #2 below.

1. **When the result was obtained**, based on title font:

   - **Normal result** (title font black, not bolded)**:** Result is from initial search or from a previous update of this search, but not from latest update.
   - **New result, following the last search update** (title font black and bolded).

2. **Accessibility indicator**, detected during the automatic analysis phase of a search, based on a choice of optimal analysis, whereby the actual file is accessed on the Internet:

   - **Reachable result** (green checkmark**:** Means file is accessible on the Web.
   - **Unreachable result** ("X" in red**:** Indicates broken links.

   - **Skipped result** (gray checkmark with a yellow triangle with an exclamation mark inside it**:** Generally means file was too large to have been downloaded during analysis.

   As explained in the health-related search case example (⇨ Chapter 4: Copernic): When the search is done in a certain way, all files that are not plain text or part of the HTML file format family may be skipped.

3. **Result handling status indicator**, based on your post-processing actions against the finding:

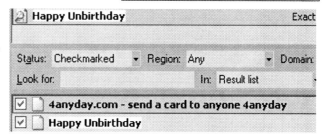

Reference Manual Section 5.2:
Findings Display &
Handling Interfaces

345

Organization &
Detailing of Findings

☐ ✗ Electricity Generating & Distributing Equipment
☐ ✓ Employment- Oil, Gas, Petroleum Industry
☐ ✗ **Forecast International/DMS: Online Store**
☐ ✓ Hoover's Online - Manufacturing - Turbines, Transformers & Other Electrical ...
☐ ✓ Price Reports - Quotes
☐ ✓ ROB Magazine - Top1000: Big Swinging Caps - July 2000
☐ ✓ Stock Markets - TSE 300 alphabetically - CANOE Money
☐ ✓ Stock Markets - TSE 300 by sector - CANOE Money
☐ ✓ Track Record : Mergers and Acquisitions transactions 2000 - European Investm...
☐ ✓ UK-Wire
☐ ✓⚠ www.backuptoserver.com symbol1
☐ ✓⚠ www.backuptoserver.com symbol2

- **Saved result page:** Icon to indicate you have saved a finding or caused it to be saved by making the appropriate choice connected with optimal analysis.

- **Checkmarked result** (green check arrow inside a square box): Provided with each finding, used to identify particular results whatever your reason.

- **Annotated result:** Icon used for this purpose.

- **Indicator of success of a "Find in Results" procedure** (title font blue): Matching result, following a search in result list or webpage contents. Blue color indicates the Find In Results procedure located this result.

(To see the screenshot in full resolution, go to ⇨ www.SearchHelpCenter.com/effective-internet-search-copernic-screenshots.html, "Results medium view.")

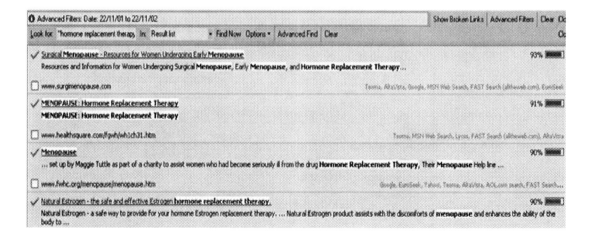

Reference Manual Section 5.2:
Findings Display &
Handling Interfaces

346

Organization &
Detailing of Findings

- **Page visitation indicator**, based on color of URL (Internet address):
  - › **Non-visited result page** — dark blue**:** URL may or may not be accessible on the Internet; you may not have accessed this file yet.
  - › **Visited result page** — violet**:** URL shows up here as a visited link, as in a normal web browser, seen in below screenshot of results presented in detail view.

(To see the screenshot in full resolution, go to ⇨ www.SearchHelpCenter.com/effective-internet-search-copernic-screenshots.html, "Results detailed view.")

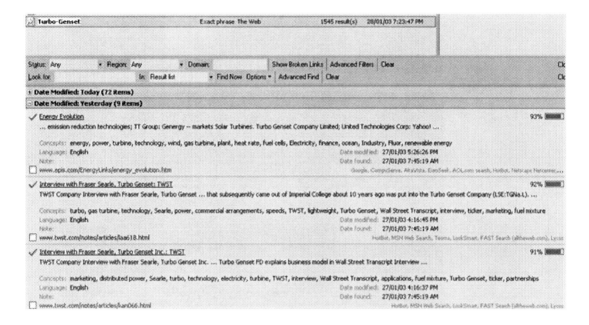

You can view Copernic's individual findings in three basic ways. Each has options controlling the viewing detail (see above screenshots). The three ways are to:

1. Look at each finding in the bottom pane in detailed, standard, or compact modes. To see details:

- Select detailed view for all results.
- Place the mouse or other pointer device over a finding, which displays a box giving details.
- Right-click the finding and then choose "Properties" from the context menu. This gives you a dialog box having two tabs, seen on the next page.

Reference Manual Section 5.2:
Findings Display &
Handling Interfaces

347

Organization &
Detailing of Findings

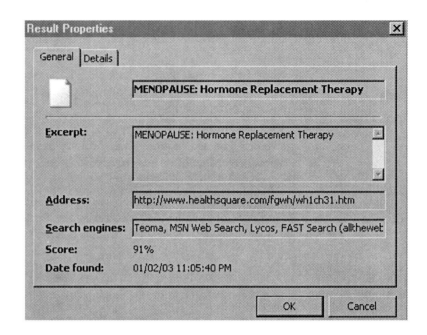

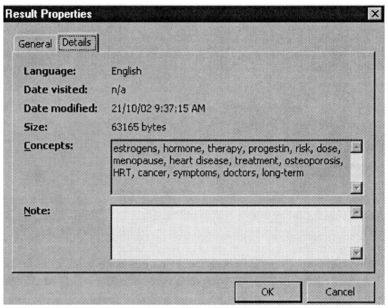

2. Examine the findings in "Browse results" mode in the left frame of a new window. In this view, as you click on each result, the corresponding download file opens in the frame to the right. Below is a partial screenshot of the browser window.

⇨ For a full screen image of the browser display of findings, refer to Chapter 5: Organization of findings display.

Reference Manual Section 5.2:
Findings Display &
Handling Interfaces

348

Organization &
Detailing of Findings

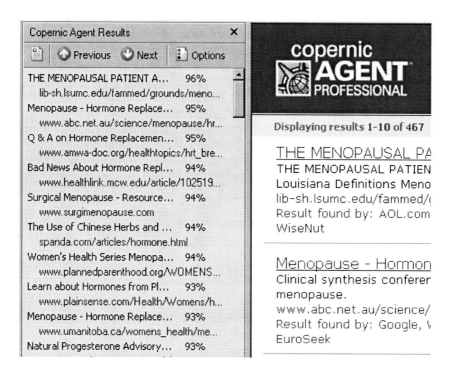

3. If so desired, as you select each result in the findings list, you can view a thumbnail in the bottom left-hand corner of the screen.

Google

1. **Web document (Web) search**. A typical Google finding looks like this:

> Lone Pine Koala Sanctuary
> At Lone Pine **Koala** Sanctuary (zoo) you can hold a **koala** , feed a kangaroo , meet a wombat and see over 100 kinds of Australian animals. ...
> www.koala.net/ - 7k - Cached - Similar pages

For each finding, Google lists:

- **Title:** Taken from TITLE metatag in an HTML document. If no such tag is found, "Untitled Document" is displayed instead.

> As stated in Google Help: The first line of the result is the title of the web page found. Sometimes, instead of a title there will be a URL, meaning that either the page has no title, or Google has not indexed the full content of that page. We still know it's a good match because of other web pages – which we have indexed – that have links to this returned page. If the text associated with these links matches your query, we may return the page as a result even though its full text has not been indexed.

- **Text below the title:** Excerpt from part of document containing search terms, in whole or in part.

> 🔨 As stated in Google Help: This text is an excerpt from the returned result page showing your query terms bolded. These excerpts let you see the context in which your search terms appear on the page, before you click on the result. If Google expanded your search using its <u>stemming technology</u> to include variations of your search terms, those words will also be bolded.

- Following the above:
  - ○ **Website URL:** Web address.
  - ○ **Page size** (in Kilobytes)**:** that is, size of text portion of found webpage.
  - ○ **Various further links to more information:** ⇨
    Reference Section 5.2: Additional links.

Optionally, the **date last detected** (of last crawl) sometimes shows for a finding, if the file was only recently detected on the Web.

2. **News document search**. Below is an example of a Google news finding.

San Diego
Union Tribune

Death set to ignite tinderbox in Iraq
Sunday Herald, UK - 2 hours ago
Iraq was last night poised on the edge of a full-scale religious uprising as the assassination of Hamas leader Abdel-Aziz al-Rantissi fed oxygen to the ...
Two Japanese Hostages Freed in Iraq, Falluja Calm - Reuters
Iraq Sunni group says it supports Shiite cleric - Sydney Morning Herald
Kidnappers free two Japanese in Iraq - Reuters
Atlanta Journal Constitution - Channel News Asia - all 212 related »

For each such finding listed, Google lists:

- **Title:** Title of news article.
- **Time:** Age of news item is, that is, how long ago it was indexed for inclusion in Google's news catalog.
- **Description:** Usually first two of lines of article below title.
- **Links to other news sources where the same news item was published:** Other versions of news item with perhaps a different title and other changes to make it more suitable for that other source.

3. **Image search**. A typical Google finding looks similar to the one here.

File name, resolution (pixels), and web URL are all listed. The latter refers to the document that embeds a reference to the picture file.

If you click on the image, Google shows it again at the top of the screen, along with the part of the document file that embeds the reference to it.

If the image can be enlarged, just click the image on this second screen, whereupon another screen containing the enlarged image will appear.

koala.jpg
287 x 288 pixels - 12k
www.mayhemarts.de/
jpg/koala.jpg

4. **Groups document search**.

For a search on cat, you get the following finding:

rec.pets.cats: Norwegian Forest Cat Breed-FAQ
... name: **cats**-faq/breeds/NFO Posting-frequency: 30 days URL: http://home.powertech.no/skogkatt/
NFOfaq.html
Last-modified: 14 Jul 2002 All the **cat** breed faqs are ...
rec.pets.cats.announce - 17 Apr 2004 by Bjorn Steensrud - View Thread (81 articles)

For each such finding listed, Google lists:

- **Group identifier:** Name of the group and hyperlink to it.
- **Message subject line:** As entered by the message creator.
- **Description:** Excerpt from text where search term sought first appears.
- **Link to discussion group:** Links to latest list of discussion topics on discussion board where finding occurred; may or may not include discussion related to your topic.
- **Link to discussion messages and corresponding discussion thread on discussion board:** Thread that deals with topic of finding; may contain one or more messages ("articles").

5. **Directory search**. In a Directory search, Google shows the directory hierarchical chain you selected under the title for each finding, in the form of a breadcrumb display (levels separated by ">" signs). Findings may be from lower levels inside your category.

Reference Manual Section 5.2:
Findings Display &
Handling Interfaces

351

Organization &
Detailing of Findings

IG If you search on the subject cat within the shopping-pets category, Google displays items in categories such as:

- Shopping > Pets > Cats.
- Shopping > Pets > Theme Merchandise > Cats.

Typical Google findings may look like this:

Cat Gallery of famous artists' funny cat art, photos, names
Category: Shopping > Pets > Theme Merchandise > Cats
Sells prints, e-cards, stationery, and jigsaw puzzles, with photographs and name suggestions.
www.thecatgallery.com/ - Cached - Similar pages

Cat Furniture, Cat Supplies, Drinkwell pet fountain, Kittypod, Cat ...
Category: Shopping > Pets > Cats
Offering drinking fountains, heated beds and toys as well as themed merchandise.
www.lovethatcat.com/ - Cached - Similar pages

For each such finding listed, Google lists:

- **Title:** Similar to title of any document.
- **Topic category:** "Breadcrumb" list from highest level of topic hierarchy down to specific topic category of finding.
- **Description of finding.**
- **Finding's URL:** Web address of document file.
- **Links to more information:** ⇨ Reference Section 5.2: Links from Findings Display.

6. **Local search**. In a Local search, Google shows:

- **Sponsored Links:** shown above the regular findings, with a title (commercial establishment name), a short ad, and a site hyperlink.
- **Regular findings:** As shown below, Google displays the title (commercial establishment name), site hyperlink, phone number, address, a link to references (inverse links pointing *to* the site from other sites), a link to directions (provided by MapQuest) for driving to the commercial establishment, and a link to more pages from the same site.

  Also provided is an image of the location, in the form of a map or an aerial view. See ⇨ Appendix 5.2: Links for refining searches for more about this.

Reference Manual Section 5.2:
Findings Display &
Handling Interfaces

352

Organization &
Detailing of Findings

A. Murchie's Tea & **Coffee** Ltd 650 41st Avenue West
   (604) 872-6930 Vancouver, BC
   1.9 km - Directions

   References: boysco.com - 475 more »

B. Laura's **Coffee Shop** 1945 Manitoba St
   (604) 876-3579 Vancouver, BC
   2.0 km N - Directions

   References: menutogo.net - 2 more »

MSN Search

1. **Web document (Web) search.** Here is an example of an MSN Search finding:

The Cat Fanciers' Association (CFA)

... insight into the world of pedigreed cats - with breeder search, breed profiles, top cat photos, cat show schedule, health articles INTRODUCING ... FANC-E-CLASSIFIEDS The purr-fect one-stop ...

www.cfainc.org   Cached page

In addition to the website's URL, for each finding, MSN Search lists:

- **Title:** Taken from TITLE metatag in HTML document.
- **Some descriptive text:** Source not explained in MSN Search Help.
- **Link to cached page**.

2. **News document search.** The simple news document search linked to from the MSN Search entry interface is a simple text listing, such as:

Shiite candidates hold wide lead over Iraq's U.S.-backed prime minister

BAGHDAD (AP) - U.S.-backed Prime Minister Ayad Allawi was trailing a Shiite ticket with ties to Iran in Iraq's historic election, according to partial returns released Friday. Four U.S. ... United Iraqi Alliance, endorsed by Iraq's top Shiite clerics, captured more than ... Macleans Online 05/02/2005

However, if you go to MSN Home and choose the news link from the MSN Directory, you arrive at a kind of news directory, in which the news items are categorized under various sub-headers.

3. **Image search.** A typical finding looks similar to the one here.

File name, resolution (pixels), and web URL are all listed. The latter refers to the document that embeds a reference to the picture file.

If you click on the image, Google shows it again at the top of the screen, along with the part of the document file that embeds the reference to it.

383 x 413: 39kb
www.giftlog.com/imag…
a/koala_backpack.jpg

If the image can be enlarged, Google allows you to click it on the second screen above, whereupon another screen containing the enlarged image appears.

4. **Local search.** As shown below, MSN Search displays the title (commercial establishment name, for commercial listings), phone number, address, distance, and a link to driving directions (provided by MSN Maps & Directions).

MSN Local Search Results, Details Text:
Reprinted with permission from Microsoft

BUSINESS LISTINGS

A **Main Street Gas & Grille**   (716) 745-1130
   311 Main St, Youngstown, NY 14174   33.8 mi - Directions

B **Destinos Pizzeria**   (716) 745-7750
   3909 Creek Rd, Youngstown, NY 14174   36.3 mi - Directions

As shown later in ⇨ Appendix 5.2: Links for refining searches, a navigable map or satellite image of the location is provided next to the text of the findings in local search.

5. **Specialty (e.g., groups, music, movies) searches.** These are usually fairly simple textual listings, in various formats.

General	AlltheWeb	AltaVista	Copernic	Google	MSN

Links from Findings Display

Links for refining searches

> ⇨ For more explanation, consult Chapter 5: Links from findings display.

These include:

- Links from a simple to an advanced interface.
- Links to search within results.
- Adding further constraints on the search by additional terms or following a directory or other hierarchy downwards.

All search engines featured in this book have some kind of ability to modify the previous search. Copernic has by far the most sophisticated set of links and abilities in this respect. AlltheWeb and Google provide links to allow searching within the previous round of findings to further restrict the search scope.

| General | AlltheWeb | AltaVista | Copernic | Google | MSN |

AlltheWeb

> ⇨ Using this feature, AlltheWeb seems to be able to expand the search beyond its regular number of words ceiling. For more details, refer to Reference Section 6.3: Search within findings.

After completing a simple search, you have several choices:

a. **Search within your results:** This link, found after the list of your findings, further refines and narrows their scope through the addition of more parameters. (You cannot use this to expand the scope of your findings, as you would with the OR Boolean operator.)

b. **Advanced search:** Clicking on this link will carry the same search terms to the advanced entry form.

> 🔨 After doing an advanced search, you can also **edit your advanced search criteria:** If you still wish to continue searching, you can then click this link at the top of the page, which will take you back to your completed search form. You can then edit your advanced search and resubmit it.

🔣 If you did a Pictures search on the word cat, choosing the advanced search link at the top of the findings page takes you to the advanced pictures search entry form, with the term cat already filled in.

Reference Manual Section 5.2:
Findings Display &
Handling Interfaces

355

Links from
Findings Display

c. **Hints for extra terms to narrow the search:** AlltheWeb helps you narrow your Web search by producing search strings on your keywords, based on related searches most frequently conducted by users. Such results appear near the top of its Web findings display page, shown here for a search on the word cat. You can select or deselect any combination of the suggestions, and obtain more by clicking the "Show more" link.

Refine your search:
(click "+" or "-" to include or exclude terms, and then click the "SEARCH" button)

show more >>>

⊞ ⊟ arctic **cat**   ⊞ ⊟ **cat** stevens   ⊞ ⊟ **cat** costume   ⊞ ⊟ dog **cat**   ⊞ ⊟ **cat** 5
⊞ ⊟ black **cat**   ⊞ ⊟ **cat** pictures   ⊞ ⊟ **cat** food   ⊞ ⊟ **cat** names   ⊞ ⊟ **cat** hat

---

AltaVista

Does not allow you to directly search within the previous round of findings. However, it does provides features at the top of the findings page, that when used in certain combinations, can make it easy to modify the parameters of a recently completed search. These features are:

- One or more text boxes containing the previously used search string(s), depending upon whether you did a simple or an advanced search.
- In the case of a Web search:

   › Two radio buttons give you the choice of searching websites in a particular country or geographical region.
   › Two radio buttons allow you either to search for documents in the language of your country or region, or in all languages.
   › A repeat of your completed search entry form found after the findings list, giving you another place to modify your search. For an advanced search, your whole form is repeated.

- A "Find" button to resubmit your search, perhaps with a modified search string or language setting.

Copernic

Has a sophisticated ability to search within findings including:

⇨ For more on refining your search with Copernic, refer to: Reference Section 5.2: Search within findings, or Reference Section 6.3: Search within findings.

Reference Manual Section 5.2:
Findings Display &
Handling Interfaces

356

Links from
Findings Display

- Redoing your search, applying further filters to the actual, downloaded files themselves.

- Searching within results based on new or changed filters — term-based and/or metadata-based.

- Searching within findings based on previous actions you took during your post-processing of findings — referred to as the "status" of findings. Term-based and metadata-based filters can also be applied.

To do the above, you simply make your selections from a control panel, which you activate when desired. (It is found between the search history pane on the top and the search results pane on the bottom.) This control panel can be seen below, divided into left and right parts.

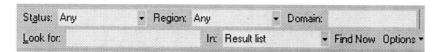

In Copernic, you can also refine your search by updating, modifying, or duplicating it (with or without duplication of the same results). These choices are available using the menu bar or by right-clicking on a search to obtain the context menu, of which a partial view is shown here.

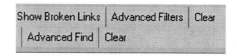

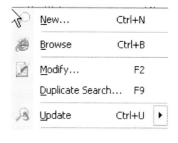 If you choose to modify the search in the search history pane, you receive the dialog box seen at the top of the next page.

New...	Ctrl+N
Browse	Ctrl+B
Modify...	F2
Duplicate Search...	F9
Update	Ctrl+U	▶

Google

Allows you to refine your searches in a number of ways:

- On its findings page, previous search terms and parameters are listed for further editing. This is the search re-expressed by Google using all operator parameters. All you have to do is revise the generated search string in the text box and resubmit the search. Alternatively, you could use the "back" button in the browser to return to the previous search entry screen to revise it.

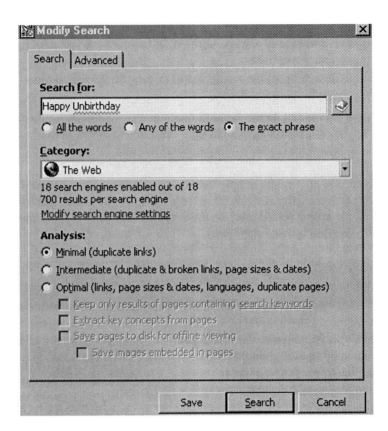

- On any search findings page produced from a simple search entry interface, simply select the advanced search link to carry the search terms to the corresponding advanced search entry interface.

- Google also repeats the generated search string at the bottom of the page, after the list of findings. To add new search requirements, select "Search within results" and

⚠ Non-additive changes to the search requirements — that is, the use of OR to expand the scope of the search — require a change to the search string from the previous round of searching, before choosing "Search within results."

Also, adding new terms doesn't work if it takes you over Google's 32-word search string limit. For more details on the limited nature of Google's search within findings, ⇨ Reference Section 6.3: Search within findings.

use the empty text box to further restrict your findings with the search string generated by the previous round of searching.

Reference Manual Section 5.2:
Findings Display &
Handling Interfaces

358

Links from
Findings Display

Local search findings pages work somewhat differently. On these, you can refine your search by choosing any sub-categories of commercial establishments, if any are listed for your category at the top of the page. Also, you can contract the local search distance from the center of the location you chose, using a set of alternatives in the form of links near the top of the page. You can see both of these kinds of choices in the following screen example:

In addition, in local search, you have options to choose between a satellite or map image (or a combination thereof), adjust the image magnification, or scroll the image in any direction, as seen on the following screenshot.

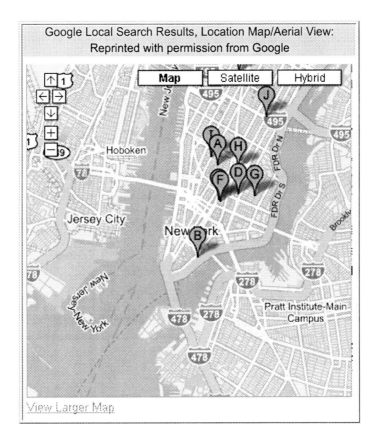

Reference Manual Section 5.2:
Findings Display &
Handling Interfaces

359

Links from
Findings Display

MSN Search

Does not provide search within findings except on its Local search. However, it is possible to revise the search without pressing the "Back" button, since the entire search entry form is repeated at the top of the findings page. As well, the search string entry box is repeated at the bottom of the page.

With Local search, you have options to choose between a satellite or map image, adjust the image magnification, or scroll the image in any direction, as seen on the following screenshot.

MSN Local Search Results, Location Map/Aerial View Screen:
Reprinted with permission from Microsoft

General   AlltheWeb   AltaVista   Copernic   Google   MSN

Reference Manual Section 5.2:
Findings Display &
Handling Interfaces
360
Links from
Findings Display

Switching to other catalogs

⇨ For more explanation, refer to Chapter 5: Links from findings display.

These are links to switch between catalogs, carrying the same search parameters from one to another.

All of our featured search engines allow easy switching. However, switching with Copernic is a matter of redoing the search using a different search engine category.

| General | AlltheWeb | AltaVista | Copernic | Google | MSN |

AlltheWeb

Your completed search entry form is repeated at the top of the findings page. To switch catalogs, simply click on one of the provided links; e.g., if you did a Web search, click on the link to Pictures search to see the images for the same search terms.

AltaVista

Tabs on the findings page are provided to easily switch between Web, Image, MP3/Audio, Video, Directory, and News searches. To carry the same search string to another interface, click on the desired link. The findings for the selected catalog will then automatically appear. The one exception is that terms cannot be transferred to the advanced Web search.

Copernic

As a meta search engine, Copernic allows you to:

- Search many different catalogs from various sources in parallel, as long as the catalogs are of the same type, e.g., they are all general web document (Web) files.
- Duplicate or modify your search, carrying all the parameters of the previous search to its advanced search interfaces.
- Switch catalogs by simply choosing a different category from the drop-down menu box.

Reference Manual Section 5.2:
Findings Display &
Handling Interfaces

361

Links from
Findings Display

- Modify the search engine settings for your new category by clicking on the appropriate link, such as seen with the "Modify Search" dialog box in the image on the previous page (four pages back).

Google

You can carry your previous or revised search string to another one of Google's simple search types by simply clicking on the desired one. The corresponding findings page appears automatically.

 If you did a Web search on the word cat, simply click on the "Images" link near the top of the findings page to produce the findings page for a simple Image search on this same term.

MSN Search

Your search terms can be carried to any of the other search interfaces, simply by clicking on the links to those.

General	AlltheWeb	AltaVista	Copernic	Google	MSN

More same-site findings

⇨ For more explanation, see Chapter 5: Links from findings display.

As a general rule, our featured search engines display only one or two findings per site. This is sometimes referred to "**site collapse**."

More pages per website may also be displayed, handled by search engines in various ways.

General	AlltheWeb	AltaVista	Copernic	Google	MSN

AlltheWeb

> A "site collapse" customization setting controls the number of listings per website (⇨ Reference Section 6.2: Findings shown per site).

For document files,
AlltheWeb will only show one finding per website, unless you restrict the search to a particular domain (website). To see the other pages from that site, click the "more hits from" link, if it appears in connection with a finding.

AltaVista

> If you set the "Site Collapse" feature to "on" when you do your search, more pages from a given website are displayed (⇨ Reference Section 6.2: Findings shown per site). If the second page is very close in ranking to the first from the same site, the second page is indented under the first.

By default,
unless you click the links provided for
more details from a given website, AltaVista restricts the number of findings per website to just one.

Multi-media files: work differently. After choosing "More info" to obtain additional details on a given finding on a new page, you can click:

- **More media from this page:** to show other files of the same media type (image, audio, video) in the same document file in which a link to the multi-media file is embedded.
- **Other pages with this file:** to show other webpages that contain this multi-media file.

Copernic

> ⚠ You can do a "find in results" procedure with Copernic to specify a particular website, but because this is simply a search within findings, it does not cause the source search engines to return all findings from that site.

Because it sources
other search engines for its
findings, Copernic relies on the default settings of those particular search engines. Thus, if it sources Google, up to two results per domain can be obtained in any one search. However, if different findings from the same domain are obtained from another search engine, you may have more than two findings for a given website after the integration of findings from different search engines.

Google

It normally reports a maximum of two findings per

> If the search is restricted to a single website, other pages from that domain conforming to the search parameters are also listed in the findings (⇨ Reference Section 6.2: Findings shown per site).

website, indenting the second one under the first. However, if you select the "More results from" link, all findings conforming to the search requirements from a particular website will be shown by Google.

See the "More results from" link below.

Yahoo!
... Entertainment - Games - Movies - Music - TV. Local **Yahoo**!s. ... US Cities: Atlanta - Boston - Chicago - Houston - LA - NYC - SF Bay - Seattle - more... More **Yahoo**! ... www.yahoo.com/ - 33k - 15 Apr 2004 - Cached - Similar pages - Stock quotes: YHOO

> Yahoo! Groups
> **Yahoo**! Groups. Sign In. New users Click here to register. ... Members: 149 Category: Florida Marlins. Yahoo! Personals - Discover great singles near you. ...
> groups.yahoo.com/ - 22k - Cached - Similar pages
> [More results from yahoo.com]

If only a few pages of results are obtained from a search, Google will not offer the "More results from ..." link in conjunction with each finding, but, rather, offer a link for more results from all the pages in the findings list.

If only 25 results are produced, spread over just three pages, you will obtain a message such as the following at the end of the third page:

> *In order to show you the most relevant results, we have omitted some entries very similar to the 25 already displayed.*
> *If you like, you can repeat the search with the omitted results included.*

In a Directory search, Google simply displays all the findings.

Note: If you enter a site's URL as your search keyword, Google not only displays a link to it, along with a brief description and the normal links to cached and similar pages for the site, but also links to pages that:

- Link to the site entered: ⇨ Reference Section 6.2: Inverse page links.
- Contain the site's URL.

Reference Manual Section 5.2:
Findings Display &
Handling Interfaces

364

Links from
Findings Display

MSN Search

⇨ For more on these parameters, see Reference Section 6.2: Findings shown per site.

By default, it displays up to two findings per website, any second result indented under the first. If there are further pages, a link to them, labeled "Show more results from ....," occurs below the second finding.

The default can be changed to one, two, or three findings per site using a Preference Setting.

General	AlltheWeb	AltaVista	Copernic	Google	MSN

Related pages or terms

⇨ For more explanation, see Chapter 5: Links from findings display.

Search engines may suggest other search terms or pages related to your search terms, or with respect to individual findings.

The abilities of our featured search engines to handle related documents varies quite substantially.

General	AlltheWeb	AltaVista	Copernic	Google	MSN

AlltheWeb

Has no further links for related pages or terms.

AltaVista

Has no further links for related pages or terms.

Reference Manual Section 5.2:
Findings Display &
Handling Interfaces

365

Links from
Findings Display

Copernic

⇨ For more details, refer to Reference Section 5.2: Language translation or page summary.

Does not directly provide links to similar terms or pages. However, you can use its document summarizer to extract keywords, either at the time of search analysis or later for an individual finding. These keywords become part of the Copernic-created metadata about a document file, and can serve as a basis for further searches.

Google

Provides various links for finding related pages or terms:

- In a Web or Directory search, click on the "Similar Pages" link on Google's findings page, provided for each individual result.

> **Whatever** ~ By Eliot Lucas
> ... Today's Episode: #99 "He had it coming",
> Make with the clicky! Vote for **Whatever!**
> Chartruesse ...www.geocities.com/red_today/
> - 15k - Cached - Similar pages

Here is a finding from a Web search on the term whatever.

In the words of Google Help: When you click on the "Similar Pages" link for a search result, Google automatically scouts the web for pages that are related to this result.

The Similar Pages feature can be used for many purposes. If you like a particular site's content, but wish it had more to say, Similar Pages can find sites with similar content with which you may be unfamiliar. If you are looking for product information, Similar Pages can find competitive information so you can make direct comparisons. If you are interested in researching a particular field, Similar Pages can help you find a large number of resources very quickly.

The more specialized a page is, the fewer results Google will be able to find for you. For example, Similar Pages may not be able to find related pages for your personal home page if it does not have enough information to authoritatively associate other pages with yours. Also, if companies use multiple URLs for their pages (such as company.com and www.company. com), Similar Pages may have little information on one URL, but lots on the other.

Reference Manual Section 5.2:
Findings Display &
Handling Interfaces

366

Links from
Findings Display

- In a Groups search, Google shows related groups at the top of the results.

   For a search on cat, you get the related discussion group rec. music.artists.springsteen.

- For a local search, Google shows "References" beneath each listing. These are inverse links pointing *toward* the website of the commercial establishment.

MSN Search

These search aids do not appear on its results pages.

General	AlltheWeb	AltaVista	Copernic	Google	MSN

Related entries from other catalogs

⇨ For more explanation, refer to Chapter 5: Links from findings display.

Links may be provided to other catalogs for each finding or for all the findings on the page as a group. It all depends on which catalog your search first addresses.

Most of our featured search engines have this ability, with the exception of Copernic.

General	AlltheWeb	AltaVista	Copernic	Google	MSN

AlltheWeb

Its ability to display findings from other catalogs exists only if you do a Web search. In this case, the following appear:

- Paid listings ("Sponsored Search Listings"): occur before the Web ones.
- News catalog items: "flashed in" between the paid listings and the Web ones.

Reference Manual Section 5.2:
Findings Display &
Handling Interfaces
367
Links from
Findings Display

AltaVista

Links to paid listings ("Sponsored Matches") are listed above the other findings for Web and multi-media (audio/video/image) searches.

Copernic

Related entries from other catalogs are unavailable.

Google

- If you do a Web search, the following may appear:
    - › Paid listings ("Sponsored Search Listings"): occur in a column in the right margin of the page.
    - › News catalog items: "flashed in" above the Web listings.
    - › Other items, such as stock quotes if you enter the symbol of a stock.
- Related entries from Google's Directory may be obtained using a link from the Google toolbar (➪ Reference Section 6.4: Software integration).
- For local search, Google displays a link to driving directions (from MapQuest) for each finding of a commercial establishment.

MSN Search

For a Web search, the following may appear:

- Paid listings ("Sponsored Search Listings"): occur before the Web ones, as well as down the right margin.
- Items "flashed in" between the paid listings at the top and the Web results:
    - › News catalog items: if your terms relate to a current news item.
    - › Local search findings: if your terms include a city or state name.
    - › Other items: e.g., stock quotes: if your terms include the symbol of a stock.

For local search, MSN displays a link to driving directions for each finding.

General	AlltheWeb	AltaVista	Copernic	Google	MSN

Language translation links

⇨ For more explanation, consult Chapter 5: Links from findings display.

These are links to translate your finding to and from different languages.

Of the search engines featured in this book, only AltaVista and Google provide such links.

🔨 However, all featured search engines have parameters to select documents according to language.

| General | AlltheWeb | AltaVista | Copernic | Google | MSN |

AlltheWeb

Language translation is unavailable.

AltaVista

With findings not in your chosen language(s), if the page is in a language supported by Babel Fish, AltaVista displays a language translation link. This allows you to translate the finding to any language of your choice, provided that the target language is supported by Babel Fish.

À Mon **Chat** clinique vétérinaire
Nous sommes la seule clinique vétérinaire à offrir des soins exclusivement aux chats sur la Rive Sud de Montréal. Vous considérez votre **chat** comme un membre de la famille? Nous aussi!
www.amonchat.qc.ca • Translate

Reference Manual Section 5.2:
Findings Display &
Handling Interfaces

369

Links from
Findings Display

Click "Translate" on the findings page to branch to AltaVista's language translation screen.

⇨ For an image of the translation screen, refer to Reference Section 5.2: Language translation or page summary.

Copernic

Language translation is unavailable.

Google

Google only provides a language translation link when the language of the finding is different from that of the user site controls, e.g., different from English, if that is your setting. For English users: this feature is currently available for pages published in Italian, French, Spanish, German, and Portuguese. [Google Help]

Click "Translate this page" on the findings page, if this link appears next to a finding, to go directly to the translated version.

⚲ To arrive at the same interface, click "Language tools" in the simple search interface.

⇨ For an image of the translation screen, see Reference Section 5.2: Language translation or page summary.

MSN Search

Language translation is unavailable.

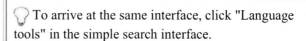

General   AlltheWeb   AltaVista   Copernic   Google   MSN

Additional links

⇨ For more explanation, refer to Chapter 5: Links from findings display.

These include dictionary definitions, cached versions of webpages, page format translation utilities, commercial links, and so on.

Except for AlltheWeb, all our featured search engines have one or more additional kinds of links from their findings displays.

General	AlltheWeb	AltaVista	Copernic	Google	MSN

AlltheWeb

In the bar at the top of the findings, search terms for which dictionary definitions can be found are linked to these definitions.

🔊 Enter lobotomy as a search term, and this term will be underlined as a hyperlink as seen in the accompanying.

1 - 2 of 2 Results for lobotomy

AltaVista

Additional links are not available.

Copernic

⇨ For an image of the Summarizer dialog box, see Reference Section 5.2: Language translation or page summary.

You can
choose Copernic's Summarizer from the File menu, to extract document keywords and produce a document summary.

Google

⇨ More details: Reference Section 3: Intelligent avoidance of formal parameter entry.

Has links to:

- **Dictionary definitions:** In Web, Directory, and Group searches, next to each term in the statistics bar, click the "Definition" link to go to Google Answers.

- **Cached pages, i.e., original versions of webpages as they were at the time they were indexed:** This applies to Web and Directory searches.

 As explained in Google Help:

- Google takes a snapshot of each page examined as it crawls the web and caches these as a back-up in case the original page is unavailable. If you click on the "Cached" link, you will see the web page as it looked when we indexed it. The cached content is the content Google uses to judge whether this page is a relevant match for your query.
- When the cached page is displayed, it will have a header at the top which serves as a reminder that this is not necessarily the most recent version of the page. Terms that match your query are highlighted on the cached version to make it easier for you to see why your page is relevant.
- The "Cached" link will be missing for sites that have not been indexed, as well as for sites whose owners have requested we not cache their content.

- **Translate non-HTML files into corresponding HTML versions:** Google searches document files in many formats other than just HTML including:

  PDF documents, ... Microsoft Office, PostScript, Corel WordPerfect, Lotus 1-2-3, and others. The new file types will simply appear in Google search results whenever they are relevant to the user query [Google Help].

  When documents found are in these other, non-HTML formats, Google:

  ... offers the user the ability to "View as HTML", allowing users to examine the contents of these file formats even if the corresponding application is not installed. The "View as HTML" option also allows users to avoid viruses which are sometimes carried in certain file formats [Google Help].

  Click on "View as HTML" in the finding below to display the page in HTML format, that is, without invoking the Word program on your computer to view the document. To see the actual HTML source code, simply use the same browser commands as for any page coded in HTML.

Reference Manual Section 5.2:
Findings Display &
Handling Interfaces

372

Links from
Findings Display

- If you have the Google toolbar:
  - › **Page rankings:** Information about the relative ranking of a page you are viewing, based on Google's algorithm for this.
  - › **Page hierarchy navigation:** For moving up and down the hierarchy of pages in a website organized hierarchically.

For more information: ⇨ Reference Section 6.4: Software integration.

MSN Search

For Web search, it provides a link to the cached version of each finding, i.e., original versions of webpages as they were at the time they were indexed.

General	AlltheWeb	AltaVista	Copernic	Google	MSN

Post-Processing of Findings

Search within findings

Searching within findings generally means searching within the set of catalog entries corresponding to the previous set of findings. It can also

⇨ For more explanation, refer to:

- Chapter 5: Post-processing of findings.
- Reference Section 6.3: Search within findings.

mean search of the referenced files themselves, if they can be downloaded to your computer.

Reference Manual Section 5.2:
Findings Display &
Handling Interfaces
373
Post-Processing
of Findings

Copernic is the only one of our featured search engines that has a sophisticated search within findings ability.

| General | AlltheWeb | AltaVista | Copernic | Google | MSN |

AlltheWeb

After the list of findings, and before any repeat of an advanced search entry form, you will find a link labeled "search within your results." This allows you to further restrict the scope of the search.

⚠ Non-additive changes to the search requirements require a change to the search string from the previous round of searching, before selecting "search within your results." You can only further restrict what you find by adding more terms.

AltaVista

A search within findings feature is unavailable.

Copernic

You can use any combination of search based on:

- Term-based filters.
- Metadata-based filters.
- Finding processing status, as in the drop-down menu you see here.

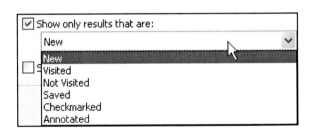

There are many dialog boxes and drop-down menus not discussed here. For more details on where these screens lead and how to interpret them in Copernic, ⇨:

- Reference Section 6.1: Term-Based Search Filters.
- Reference Section 6.2: Metadata-Based Search Filters.
- Reference Section 6.3: Search within findings.

Google

By choosing "Search within results" under the search string

⚠ Non-additive changes to the search requirements require a change to the search string from the previous round of searching, before selecting "Search within results." Otherwise, you can simply narrow your findings by adding more search terms.

generated by the previous round of searching, you can add new search requirements into an empty text box.

The Google toolbar, if you installed it, also allows you to search within a single page using term highlighting and find tools. For more on these, ⇨ Reference Section 6.4: Software integration.

You can also search within your search history, if you have an account with Google and have activated this feature. For more on this, see ⇨ Appendix 5.2: Search follow-up.

MSN Search

A search within findings feature is unavailable. However, the MSN toolbar, if you installed it, allows you to search within a single page using a term highlighting tool. For more on this, ⇨ Reference Section 6.4: Software integration.

General   AlltheWeb   AltaVista   Copernic   Google   MSN

Grouping and sorting

⇨ For more explanation, consult:

- Chapter 5: Post-processing of findings.
- Reference Section 6.3: Overall ordering.

Any number of criteria can be used to group and sort findings including domain, page status, page last modification date, and so on. Post-processing of findings permits even more exhaustive and powerful methods of doing this. Grouping of results may also involve complex techniques such as dynamic topic clustering.

Of our featured search engines:

- AlltheWeb, AltaVista, and Google all have the ability to sort news findings by date or by relevance.
- Google Groups search can sort by date.

- Google Directory search results can be sorted by title or by relevance.
- Copernic has a sophisticated set of options for sorting findings.
- None have dynamic topic clustering abilities.

General	AlltheWeb	AltaVista	Copernic	Google	MSN

AlltheWeb

Its News search findings page has a control to sort the findings by date or by relevance: ⇨ Reference Section 6.3: Overall ordering.

AltaVista

Using controls at the top of the results listing, its News search findings can be sorted by date or relevance: ⇨ Reference Section 6.3: Overall ordering.

Copernic

Many options are provided for both grouping and sorting findings. If grouping is applied, sorting is still possible, but is applied within each group as a secondary sort criterion: ⇨ Reference Section 6.3: Overall ordering.

Google

Has links for alternative sorting of findings from its News, Groups, and Directory searches: ⇨ Reference Section 6.3: Overall ordering.

MSN Search

Various MSN specialty searches available via the MSN subject directory can sort findings on a post-processing basis. MSN Search has a search entry parameter that can pre-determine the order in which findings are displayed. For more on the latter, see ⇨ Reference Section 6.3: Overall ordering.

General	AlltheWeb	AltaVista	Copernic	Google	MSN

Reference Manual Section 5.2:
Findings Display &
Handling Interfaces

376

Post-Processing
of Findings

Language translation or page summary

⇨ For more explanation, see:

- Chapter 5: Post-processing of findings.
- Reference Section 6.3: Language translation or page summary.

Special interfaces are needed to translate documents from one language to another or to summarize documents and extract keywords.

Of our featured search engines:

- AltaVista and Google have interfaces for translating document files.
- Copernic has an interface for document summarization.

General	AlltheWeb	AltaVista	Copernic	Google	MSN

AlltheWeb

Features for language translation or page summary are unavailable.

AltaVista

Has a language translation tool to translate text or entire websites. The interface is seen here.

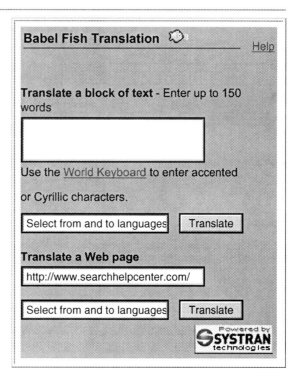

Reference Manual Section 5.2:
Findings Display &
Handling Interfaces

377

Post-Processing
of Findings

📷 Choose to and from languages using the drop-down menu in the form on the previous page. Then click "Translate" to translate your webpage accordingly.

⚠ Its block translation cannot handle more than 150 words at a time.

Clicking above (previous page) on the "World Keyboard" link brings you to the screen seen below. The virtual keyboard provides an easy way of entering characters from several foreign languages. Simply use the drop-down menu in the lower left corner of the keyboard to select one of the available languages — English, French, German, Italian, Portuguese, Russian, Spanish.

Image of "World Keyboard" for Entering Other Language Characters
Reproduced by permission of AltaVista Company. All rights reserved.

Reference Manual Section 5.2:
Findings Display &
Handling Interfaces

378

Post-Processing
of Findings

Copernic

Its summarizer technology has the ability to extract keywords and to produce document summaries in English. You can activate it through the context or file menus. The "Summarize" choice will be available (not grayed out) if a particular finding has been highlighted before doing this.

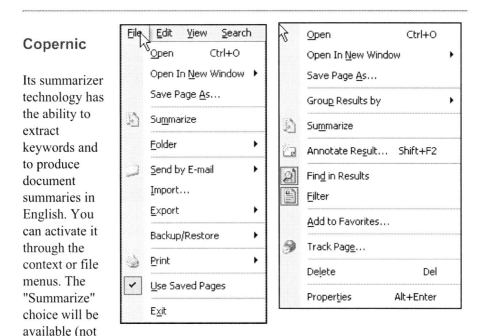

In the page summary in the screenshot below, a summary of 100 words is given.

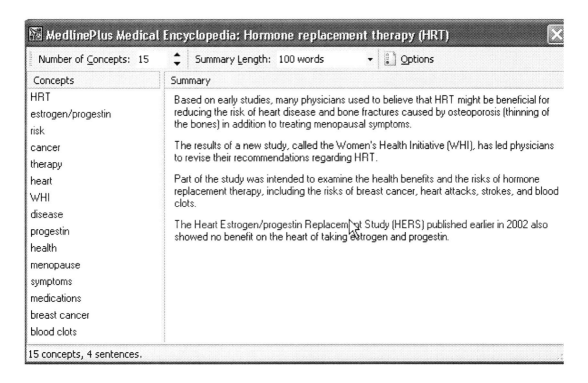

MedlinePlus Medical Encyclopedia: Hormone replacement therapy (HRT)

Number of Concepts: 15   Summary Length: 100 words   Options

Concepts

HRT
estrogen/progestin
risk
cancer
therapy
heart
WHI
disease
progestin
health
menopause
symptoms
medications
breast cancer
blood clots

15 concepts, 4 sentences.

Summary

Based on early studies, many physicians used to believe that HRT might be beneficial for reducing the risk of heart disease and bone fractures caused by osteoporosis (thinning of the bones) in addition to treating menopausal symptoms.

The results of a new study, called the Women's Health Initiative (WHI), has led physicians to revise their recommendations regarding HRT.

Part of the study was intended to examine the health benefits and the risks of hormone replacement therapy, including the risks of breast cancer, heart attacks, strokes, and blood clots.

The Heart Estrogen/progestin Replacement Study (HERS) published earlier in 2002 also showed no benefit on the heart of taking estrogen and progestin.

Reference Manual Section 5.2:
Findings Display &
Handling Interfaces

379

Post-Processing
of Findings

⇨ For more about the different summary length and other options, refer to:

- Reference Section 6.3: Language translation or page summary.
- Default settings for Summarizer in Reference Section 6.4: Handling of findings.

Google

Has a language translation tool to translate text or entire websites.

You can enter either the text to be translated in the "Translate text" box or the URL of a webpage to be translated in the "Translate a web page" box.

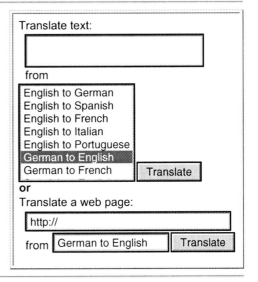

Translate text:

from

English to German
English to Spanish
English to French
English to Italian
English to Portuguese
German to English
German to French   Translate

or
Translate a web page:

http://

from German to English   Translate

MSN Search

Features for language translation or page summary are unavailable.

General   AlltheWeb   AltaVista   Copernic   Google   MSN

Search follow-up

⇨ For more explanation, refer to:

- Chapter 5: Post-processing of findings.
- Reference Section 6.3: Search follow-up.

This involves keeping records of searches and their findings, sharing searches and search results, and setting up user alerts for tracking pages or updating searches.

Of our featured search engines, Copernic has the best functionality in this area, followed by Google.

| General | AlltheWeb | AltaVista | Copernic | Google | MSN |

AlltheWeb

A search follow-up feature is unavailable.

AltaVista

A search follow-up feature is unavailable.

Copernic

Has many search follow-up capabilities, namely:

1. **Keep records of searches and their findings:**

    a. **Organize search history:**
    Step one is to organize automatically-kept searches into hierarchical search history folders. The first

    ⇨ For details on search parameters, see Reference Section 6.3: Search follow-up.

    screenshot below (next page) is the application search history panel with search history folders on the right. Their individual contents are on the left. The second screenshot is the search history seen after clicking the appropriate link near the top in the browser view of Copernic findings.

Reference Manual Section 5.2:
Findings Display &
Handling Interfaces

381

Post-Processing
of Findings

(🔨 To see the first screenshot below in full resolution, go to ⇨ www.SearchHelpCenter.com/effective-internet-search-copernic-screenshots.html, "History view in application panes."

For the second one, use www.SearchHelpCenter.com/effective-internet-search-copernic-screenshots.html, "History view in browser.")

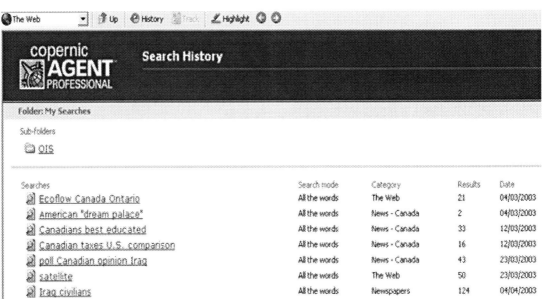

Reference Manual Section 5.2:
Findings Display &
Handling Interfaces

382

Post-Processing
of Findings

b. **Manage search history details:** History of individual findings can also be managed such as deleting and annotating them, etc.

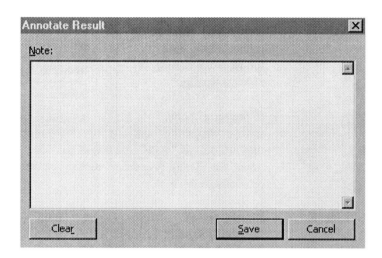 You can annotate either a search or any individual result (finding) from that search, using the following kinds of dialog boxes. Any annotation/note you enter in either of the text boxes below automatically appears in the other.

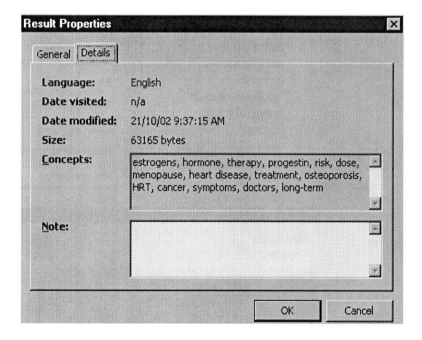

Reference Manual Section 5.2:
Findings Display &
Handling Interfaces

383

Post-Processing
of Findings

To delete individual findings kept for a search, annotate them, and so on, use the following menu selections:

- Choose one of "Annotate Result ...", "Delete," or "Copy" from the context menu (see accompanying screenshot), obtained by right-clicking your mouse when floating it above a finding.

- In the same menu, choose "Properties" and then fill out the "Note" text box in the "Details" tab of the "Result Properties" dialog box (see previous page).

- Choose one of "Annotate Result ...", "Delete," "Cut," "Copy," or "Paste" from the Edit pull-down menu on the menu bar (see accompanying screenshot). Note: "Annotate Result" is grayed out here because no finding has been selected in the results pane.

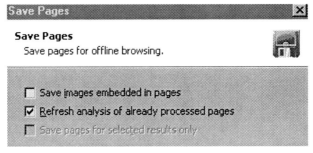

c. **Save individual files referenced from findings metadata to user's local computer:** Copernic can access the file corresponding to a finding on the Internet and then save that file on your own computer.

To save all findings for a specific search already in your search history, float your mouse over it and right-click to obtain the context menu seen here. Then select "Save Pages ..." and the "Save Pages" dialog box (see screenshot at bottom of previous page) will appear.

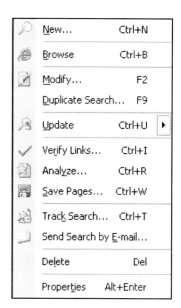

The Results pull-down menu will also bring up the dialog box, shown here.

Files corresponding to your findings can also be saved as an option when you select "optimal analysis" for your search (see the "Analyze..." choice in the above pull-down menu). Notice that "Save pages to disk for offline viewing" is checked in the screenshot below (top and bottom parts of dialog box not visible).

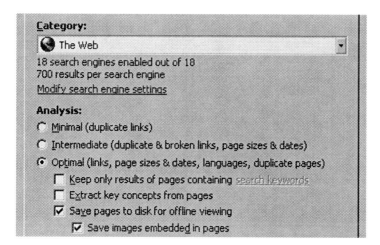

2. **Update, modify, and delete searches kept in the search history:** Whole searches can be deleted from the search history with all their findings. They can also be updated, causing them to rerun from the start using the same set of filters and other parameters set for that search. Or, search parameters can be modified and the search rerun, thereby replacing the earlier search. Alternatively, the search can simply be duplicated. All these choices are shown in the menu on the previous page.

3. **Share search findings:** You can export or import searches, including the search specifications and all the search findings. As well, you can send e-mail.

To export the findings of a search or to send e-mail, choose "Export" or "Send by E-mail," respectively, from the pull-down menu (shown here for the second time in this section). These selections lead to a further level of choices: whether to export all of the results of a search or only those selected in the results pane. Then:

- For e-mail: selected contents of the results pane are attached to an e-mail message ready for you to address. The attachment is in HTML format. When ready, use your e-mail program, e.g., Outlook Express, to send it.
- For "Export": the following dialog box appears for specifying the name of the file and other options.

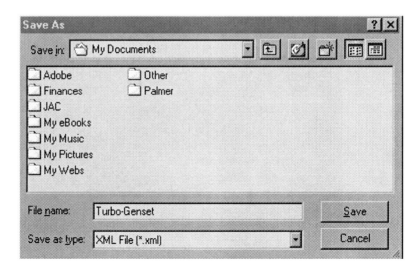

Reference Manual Section 5.2:
Findings Display &
Handling Interfaces

386

Post-Processing
of Findings

For "Import...": in the above File pull-down menu, a dialog box similar to the one below appears:

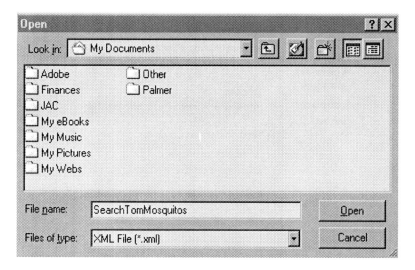

4. **Set up user alerts (search tracking):** User alerts are standing orders to the search engine to continue to track searches or particular search results on your behalf.

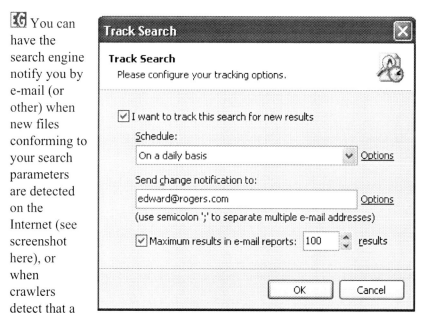

You can have the search engine notify you by e-mail (or other) when new files conforming to your search parameters are detected on the Internet (see screenshot here), or when crawlers detect that a designated file has been modified since your search or since your last alert (see screenshot below).

Reference Manual Section 5.2:
Findings Display &
Handling Interfaces

387

Post-Processing
of Findings

Copernic also has a tracking manager interface, a screenshot of which is shown below.

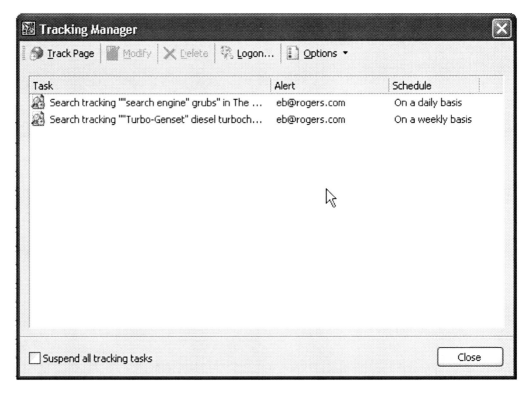

To obtain access to the above dialog boxes:

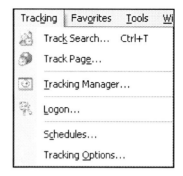

- Use the Tracking pull-down menu or button on the toolbar below the menu bar at the top of the screen. Menu choices can be seen here.
- Select "Track Search ..." on the context menu from right-clicking your mouse when it is over a particular search in the search history pane. See item '1c' (four pages above) for the screenshot of this menu.

⇨ For details on search tracking options, refer to:

- Reference Section 6.3: Search follow-up for tracking parameters.
- Reference Section 6.4: Handling of findings for setting up preferences for tracking parameter values.

Google

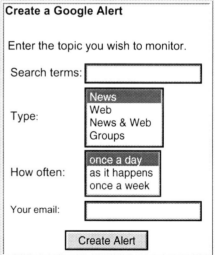

- Has alerts for changes to each of its News, Web, News & Web, and Groups catalogs. You receive an e-mail to alert you of new content in Google's catalogs conforming to your search keywords. It will run a daily, as it happens, or once a week search for you, as seen in the accompanying screen representation.
- Google has a simple search history feature that allows you to keep searches and their individual results on a Google server in chronological order. You can delete entire searches or individual results within any search, and access the searches based on a calendar. Also, you can search within your previous searches. To use this feature, you need to open a Google account.

- If you have installed the Google toolbar, it also has features to "blog" information from a page you are viewing, and to "vote" on that page (thereby expressing your opinion of it to Google). For more on these, ⇨ Reference Section 6.4: Software integration.

MSN Search

Provides alerts for certain specialty searches, such as news. For more on this, see ⇨ alerts.msn.com/Alerts/Default.aspx.

General	AlltheWeb	AltaVista	Copernic	Google	MSN

> ⇨ This section cross-links with Chapter 5: Search Support: User Tool Interfaces.

Search Support: User Tool Interfaces

Preference settings

With these, you can customize/ personalize the search engine as you like. You can set preferences for the default value for filter parameters, the display of findings, features of interface screens, and others.

Our featured search engines all have special interfaces for setting end user preferences. However, the degree of sophistication varies widely. AlltheWeb and Copernic have the most sophisticated sets of options.

> ⇨ For more explanation, see:
>
> - Chapter 5: Setting user preferences.
> - Reference Section 6.4:
>
>   ⌐ Filter Default Value Preferences.
>
>   ⌐ Findings Display & Handling Preferences.
>
>   ⌐ Interface Screen Features Preferences.
>
>   ⌐ Software Integration & Efficiency Preferences.

General	AlltheWeb	AltaVista	Copernic	Google	MSN

AlltheWeb

Provides a sophisticated set of user preference setting interface screens. These are broken down into ones for "Basic Settings," "Advanced Settings," "Languages," and "Look and Feel." Organizing them as we have in the book, their settings include:

1. **Filter default value preferences:**

- **Language of search results:** See "Language" settings screen (⇨ Reference Section 6.4: Document language).

- **Offensive content reduction:** See "Basic Settings" screen (⇨ Reference Section 6.4: Potentially offensive content).

2. **Findings display preferences:** Most of these cannot be dynamically changed from search entry interfaces for individual searches (⇨ Reference Section 6.4: Findings page organization).

- **Basic Settings screen:** Provides options to set maximum number of search results shown per page, open results screen in a new window, and highlight search terms.
- **Advanced Settings screen:** Has options for:
    › **Site collapse:** Suppress the display of more than one result per website.
    › **Number of news items to flash in:** Show news catalog findings above Web results in Web search.

3. **Interface screen feature preferences** (⇨ Reference Section 6.4: Interface options made available)**:**

- **Basic Settings screen:** Set text size to use on the search entry form and display certain options for boxes used to enter Boolean logic on the simple Web and News search interfaces.
- **Advanced Settings screen:** Can customize:
    › **Default search catalog interface:** Choose AlltheWeb's start-up search interface; provides choices of Web, Pictures, Videos, Audio, or News.
    › **Autocompletion in browser:** Select automatic completion of a text string based on the first few characters entered.
- **Look and Feel interface:** Show certain colors or artistic themes on search pages (⇨ Reference Section 6.4: Interface language or style).

4. **Software integration and efficiency preferences:**

- **Integrate access to AlltheWeb into your browser:** ⇨ Reference Section 6.4: Software integration.

AltaVista

Provides a single "Settings" interface (www.altavista.com/web/res?ref=Lw) for various parameters, some of which you may also set dynamically (in connection with each search). The parameters control the following areas:

1. **Filter default value preferences:**

- **Language preferences:** Search documents in particular languages, meaning language of findings. To apply a set of languages as a default for all your searches, use the settings interface (⇨ Reference Section 6.4: Document language).

- **Country:** Specify the country to which you can choose to limit your findings. To apply as a default for all your searches, use the settings interface (⇨ Reference Section 6.4: Other filter setting preferences).

- **Family filter interface:** To guard against potentially offensive material; can be reached from most of search or preference settings interfaces (⇨ Reference Section 6.4: Potentially offensive content).

> 💡 AltaVista also has a tool for reporting offensive websites (⇨ Reference Section 5.3: Additional end user-specific tools).

2. **Findings display preferences:** Most must be set as preferences, meaning they cannot be dynamically changed for individual searches. Choices include:

- **Fields of information to display for each finding.**
- **Number of findings to display per page.**

3. **Interface screen feature preferences:**

- **Language of site controls:** (⇨ Reference Section 6.4: Interface language or style).

4. **Software integration and efficiency preferences:**

- **Integrate access to AltaVista in your browser:** ⇨ Reference Section 6.4: Software integration.

Copernic

Provides a sophisticated set of use preference setting interface screens:

1. **Filter default value preferences:**

- **Analysis options:** Check for broken links to files on the Internet, eliminate duplicate files from different URL's, and filter using Boolean logic.

- **Spellchecking on search terms:** Specify dictionary to be used, whether to check as you type, internal word letter formations to be ignored, rules to be used in suggesting word replacements, and degree of accuracy to be required.
- **Performance options:** Indicate maximum file size for analysis by the Copernic Analyzer, length of timeouts for Internet communication, and number of simultaneous transfers.
- **Proxy options:** Related to use of proxy servers; specify whether to apply the proxy option to all users of the computer.
- **Search category options:**
    - ○ **Organizing search categories:** Based on existing category set-up; activate or deactivate search engines assigned to each category, and set the maximum number of findings per search engine in a category.
    - ○ **Creating new, custom search categories or category groups:** Choose search engines available from existing categories for assignment to the new category or category group.
    - ○ **Installing additional search engine categories and category groups:** Options and search sets available, but not automatically activated when you install Copernic's software.

2. **Findings display preferences:**

- **View saved findings:** Display the saved page when that finding is accessed rather than re-access it from the Internet.
- **View detail level:** Control level of detail for viewing historical searches in search history pane or search metadata in results listing panes.
- **Search term highlighting:** Use of colors to highlight search terms in finding lists and when reviewing finding file itself.

3. **Findings handling preferences:**

- **Summarizer settings:** Applicable to Copernic Summarizer; indicate how to summarize document files and extract terms representing the document concepts.
- **Analyzer preferences:** Specify whether to extract keyword concepts, save the files referenced in the results list to your computer, or extract modification dates and file sizes from the referenced files.
- **E-mail settings:** Select whether to send tracking results, e-mail protocol to be used, or send shared findings or receive tracking reports as file attachments.
- **Tracking schedules:** Specify default frequency and times of day for results tracking.
- **Spellchecking on annotation results or searches:** Select dictionary to be used, whether to check as you type, internal word letter formations to be

ignored, rules to be used in suggesting word replacements, and degree of accuracy to be required in these rules. These same settings also apply to spellchecking of words in search terms (see #1 above in this list).

4. **Interface screen feature preferences:**

- **Visual settings:** Specify whether to show ToolTips when passing cursor over searches, or individual findings, or show advertising banners.
- **Toolbar customization:** Choose buttons and icons to show on any given toolbar, whether to show the toolbar or not, and options for creating new toolbars.
- **Menu commands customization:** Indicate commands to include on each menu, at each level of menu choices.
- **Options for toolbars or menu commands:** Specify whether to show most recently used menu commands first or show shortcut keys in ToolTips.
- **Confirmation or warning messages:** Indicate if these messages should be used when deleting searches from the search history or when certain fields are left out of certain forms.
- **Default browser:** Choose Internet Explorer or Netscape, and options for using that browser, e.g., whether to use saved results or open findings in a new window.

5. **Software integration and efficiency preferences:**

- **Integration of Copernic into other software, especially Microsoft Internet Explorer:** Integrate with your e-mail application and with proxy servers you may use to access the Internet (⇨ Reference Section 6.4: Software integration).
- **Improvement of software efficiency:** Choose disk clean-up and setting performance level of computer (⇨ Reference Section 6.4: Software efficiency).
- **Obtaining updates to your Copernic software:** Determine the frequency with which you automatically check for changes may occur in the search engines accessed from the various Copernic categories or in the Copernic software itself (⇨ Reference Section 6.4: Software efficiency).

Google

Provides a single "Preferences" interface (www.google.ca/preferences?hl=en) for customizing the search engine on your behalf. You can also set some features here dynamically for each search. The parameters control the following areas:

1. **Filter default value preferences:**

- **Language preferences:** Search documents in particular languages (⇨ Reference Section 6.4: Document language).
- **Safe search filter setting:** Dynamically specify whether or not to use this filter in various search interfaces, including the advanced Web search and the Image search (⇨ Reference Section 6.4: Potentially offensive content).

2. **Findings display preferences** (⇨ Reference Section 6.4: Findings page organization)**:**

- **Number of results per page.**
- **Display search results in a new window.**

3. **Interface screen feature preferences:**

- **Language of the site controls:** (⇨ Reference Section 6.4: Interface language or style).

4. **Software integration and efficiency preferences:**

- **Integrate access to Google in your browser:** applies especially Internet Explorer (⇨ Reference Section 6.4: Software integration).

MSN Search

Provides a single "Preferences" interface for customizing the search engine on your behalf. The parameters control the following areas:

1. **Filter default value preferences:**

   > 🔍 MSN Search has no customization options for metadata-based filters. To prevent offensive material, options are available in Microsoft's Internet Explorer web browser (⇨ Reference Section 6.4: Potentially offensive content).

- **Language preferences:** Search documents in particular languages (⇨ Reference Section 6.4: Document language).
- **Safe search filter setting:** Dynamically specify whether or not to use this filter in various search interfaces, including the advanced Web search and the Image search (⇨ Reference Section 6.4: Potentially offensive content).
- **Default location:** This is used in local search, and can be applied to sorting web results according to the location of the host server (⇨ Appendix 6.2: Geographical region of server).

2. **Findings display preferences:**

- **Number of results per page:** ⇨ Reference Section 6.4: Findings page organization.

3. **Interface screen feature preferences:**

- **Language of the site controls:** ⇨ Reference Section 6.4: Interface language or style.

4. **Software integration and efficiency preferences:**

- **Software integration:** Integrate access to MSN Search in your browser, Windows, and certain other Microsoft applications (⇨ Reference Section 6.4: Software integration).

| General | AlltheWeb | AltaVista | Copernic | Google | MSN |

Additional end user-specific tools

⇨ For more explanation, refer to Chapter 5: Other user tools.

Other tools specifically designed for end users include those for setting up accounts, reporting offensive websites, setting text-only search mode, and so on.

A varied set of end user tools is available, depending on the search engine.

| General | AlltheWeb | AltaVista | Copernic | Google | MSN |

AlltheWeb

The following end user tools are described elsewhere in this book:

- **Converter** and **Spellchecker:** ⇨ Reference Section 3: Intelligent avoidance of formal parameter entry.

AltaVista

Has the following additional end user tools:

- **Reporting offensive websites:** "Report Search Spam" ⇨ add.yahoo.com/ fast/help/us/ysearch/cgi_reportsearchspam.
- **Text-only search:** Search the Web with a faster, graphics-free version of AltaVista's Web search (⇨ www.altavista.com/web/text).

Some are also described elsewhere in this book:

- **Shortcuts (conversion calculator, exchange rates, time zones), and Spellchecker:** ⇨ Reference Section 3: Intelligent avoidance of formal parameter entry.
- **Language translation:** ⇨ Reference Section 5.2: Language translation or page summary.
- **Toolbar:** ⇨ Reference Section 6.4: Software integration.

Copernic

Has some end user tools for contacting them. As seen in this menu screenshot, these include forms to send feedback and to submit reports of software bugs.

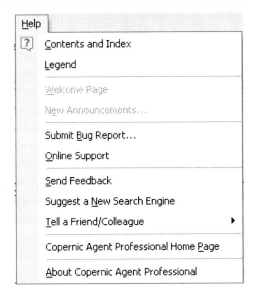

When completing the latter form, if you check "Add system information to report," details of your computer's configuration will be sent along with the e-mail to Copernic. You can also save the information on a problem sent in a file on your computer, using the appropriate links shown in the screen image on the next page.

Some other end user tools are also described elsewhere in this book:

- **Page summarizer:** ⇨ Reference Section 5.2: Language translation or page summary.

Google

Has the following additional end user tools:

- **Wireless** (www.google.com/options/wireless.html): Google search from wireless, mobile devices.

Some are also described elsewhere in this book:

- **Language assistance (spelling, definitions), Search by number or code (flights, airports, registration numbers for various kinds of equipment, patents, product codes, stock quotes), Built-in calculator:** ⇨ Reference Section 3: Intelligent avoidance of formal parameter entry.
- **Language Translation:** ⇨ Reference Section 5.2: Language translation or page summary.
- **Toolbar** and **Browser buttons**: ⇨ Reference Section 6.4: Software integration.

MSN Search

Has the following additional end user tools:

- **Reporting offensive websites:** "Report Search Spam" ➪ search.msn.com/docs/help.aspx?t=SEARCH_CONC_ContactUs.htm&FORM=CCDD2#B.

Some are also described elsewhere in this book:

- **Shortcuts:** ➪ Reference Section 3: Intelligent avoidance of formal parameter entry.
- **Toolbar:** ➪ Reference Section 6.4: Software integration.

Other user tools

➪ For more explanation, see Chapter 5: Other user tools.

Other user tools are those
applicable to webmasters, search engine clients, and perhaps to some end users.
Examples include Help, submitting a website for indexing, and adding the search
engine search interface to a website.

Of our featured search engines featured:

- All, except meta search engine Copernic, provide some sort of interface to submit a website for indexing by the search engine or by the company that supplies data to the search engine. This includes using the search engine to advertise your site with sponsored listings.
- All have Help and "Contact Us" interfaces.

General   AlltheWeb   AltaVista   Copernic   Google   MSN

AlltheWeb

Has user tools to:

⇨ For more details on these various options, go to www.alltheweb.com/help/webmaster/faq

- **Submit websites for indexing:** Instructions are provided to webmasters for submitting websites for indexing. Webmasters can submit paid inclusions in the Yahoo catalogs.

- **Investigate particular URL's:** Described in AlltheWeb Help as follows:

  If you've ever entered a URL as a keyword in the search box on AlltheWeb, you've discovered the URL Investigator. Below are some general questions and answers about this feature.

  Type a URL into the search box on AlltheWeb, and click the search button.

  For example:

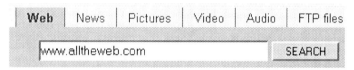

  The URL Investigator will return a page full of information about a specific URL including the following:

  - › Who owns the domain
  - › What language the site is written in
  - › The size of the page
  - › The date it was last updated
  - › A list of subdomains
  - › How many pages link to that URL
  - › How many pages are indexed from the given domain
  - › A link to see how the site looked in the past

- **Integrate AlltheWeb into a website:** Provides the following form (www.alltheweb.com/help/webmaster/add_to_site):

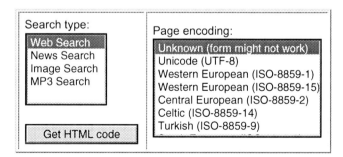

AltaVista

Has user tools to:

- **Submit websites for indexing:** This is now done through Yahoo. For details, see the relevant links at www.altavista.com/addurl/default.

- **Do Webmaster search:** This helps webmasters determine:

  ⇨ See the screenshot in Chapter 5: Other user tools, or see the actual screen at www.altavista. com/web/webmaster.

  - ◦ Other websites linked to theirs.
  - ◦ Other sites considered to be similar to theirs.

- **Integrate AltaVista into a website:** A web creator can download an AltaVista Web search or translation box (⇨ www.altavista.com/help/free/ free_searchbox).

Copernic

Provides the usual Help and Contact Us screens. All Copernic tools are for the end user (see preceding item, "Other end user tools").

Google

Has tools described at www.google.com/options, including:

- **Blogger** (www.blogger.com)**:** Create a web blog to post your thoughts to the web, and have it indexed by Google.
- **Google in your language** (https://services.google.com/tc/Welcome.html)**:** Have the Google interface in a language you request, in case your language is not currently available.
- **Submit websites for indexing** (www.google.ca/addurl.html)**:** Use Google's simple "Add URL" page to submit websites for indexing.
- **Web API's** (www.google.ca/apis)**:** Integrate Google into a website using its Web API's; of particular interest to website creators.

In addition, the Google toolbar (⇨ Reference Section 6.4: Software integration), if installed, has links to tools for:

- **Learning about popular searches:** Google Zeitgeist reports on trends in user searches across the globe.
- **Filling out Web forms.**
- **Blocking pop-ups.**

MSN Search

Has user tools to:

- **Submit websites for indexing:** ⇨ search.msn.com/docs/submit.aspx? FORM=WSDD2.
- **Integrate MSN Search into a website:** ⇨ search.msn.com/docs/siteowner. aspx?t=SEARCH_WEBMASTER_REF_AddMSNSearchToYourSite.htm&FORM =WADD.
- **Play around with experimental MSN Search features:** See "MSN Sandbox: ⇨ sandbox.msn.com.
- **Access the MSN Search Blog:** ⇨ blogs.msdn.com/msnsearch.

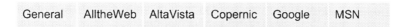

| General | AlltheWeb | AltaVista | Copernic | Google | MSN |

Reference Manual Section 6.1: Term-Based Search Filters

⇨ This section cross-links with Chapter 6: Term-Based Search Filters.

Term Variation

Wildcards, substrings, stemming

⇨ For more explanation, see Chapter 6: Term variation filters.

Wildcards: Are operators that act as placeholders for yet-to-be-determined characters or groups of characters in a word. Of our featured search engines:

- Google has wildcards for whole words. It also has automatic stemming, which produces the same effect as wildcards at the end of a word stub.
- None have wildcards that can act as stand-ins for individual characters or replace characters at the start of a word.

Substrings: Widen a search from just matching words to other words also containing that sequence of letters, e.g., searching on the substring technol as opposed to the word technology, will pick up more matches. Of our featured search engines, Copernic has substring recognition in its "Find in Results" function.

Stemming: Allows finding other kinds of variations on a same word, due to such things as differences in tense or mood or one word being the verb equivalent of a particular noun. Of our featured search engines, Google, and possibly MSN Search, give the user the possibility of turning word stemming on and off. In this case, stemming may simply refer to a wildcard of variable length at the end of a word, rather than the richer definition of stemming defined in Chapter 6.

None of our featured search engines provide examples of the kind of sophistication in word variations you can obtain through masks based on regular expressions. The now discontinued AlltheWeb FTP search provided an example of this, and is used here for illustrative purposes. Among current search engines, Exalead, discussed in Chapter 6, has regular expressions.

General	AlltheWeb	AltaVista	Copernic	Google	MSN

AlltheWeb

Does not have wildcards or automatic stemming.

FTP searches: On an academic note, it *used* to be able to do sophisticated FTP searches using wildcards. The drop-down menu box seen here was available in both simple and advanced FTP search interfaces.

The old AlltheWeb Help explained its use of wildcards and other types of searching as follows:

AlltheWeb supports 13 different search types:

Search type:
- substring search
- substring search, case sensitive
- substring match
- substring match, case sensitive
- multiple substrings search
- wildcard search
- wildcard search, case sensitive
- wildcard match
- wildcard match, case sensitive
- regular expression search
- regular expression match
- exact search
- browse directory

Substring search: Searches for parts of a filename. Treats uppercase and lowercase letters equally.

Substring search, case sensitive: Searches for parts of a filename. Treats uppercase and lowercase letters differently.

Multiple substrings search: Will match all search terms (separated by space) with same order in the filename. The search "ssh rpm" will e.g. match the file openssh-2.2.0p1-0.ppc.rpm. Case is significant.

Wildcard search: Similar to wildcards in e.g. UNIX shells, DOS, etc. The character '?' will match any single character while '*' will match zero or more of any character.

Wildcard search, case sensitive: Similar to above but case is significant.

Browse directory: Lets you browse an FTP server's filesystem without actually logging on to it. Set "Search type" to "Browse directory" and search for "ftp. server.host/" or "ftp.server.host/directory". ... If this field does not contain any slashes, wildcard matching for ftp server hostnames are performed.

Regular expression search: Searches for parts of a filename with a regular expression. Regular expressions are a powerful way of matching text strings.

Exact search: Searches for the exact filename. Case is significant.

Substring match;, Substring match, case sensitive; Wildcard match; Wildcard match, case sensitive; Regular expression match: Like their "search" counterparts, but you will only get the unique file names matching your query, without any information like size, path etc. You can then click on each file name to do an exact search.

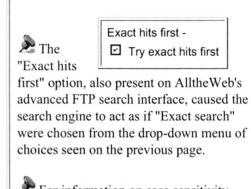

 The "Exact hits first" option, also present on AlltheWeb's advanced FTP search interface, caused the search engine to act as if "Exact search" were chosen from the drop-down menu of choices seen on the previous page.

For information on case sensitivity, refer to Reference Section 6.1: Formatting masks.

AltaVista

Before being taken over by Yahoo, AltaVista allowed the use of a wildcard character, the asterisk (*). However, this feature is no longer supported. Nevertheless, it does seem that the asterisk acts as a single word wildcard, similar to what you see in Google (see below). AltaVista does not have word stemming.

Copernic

Its "Advanced Find" dialog allows you to select a string within a word or to "Find whole words only" (see checkboxes here). Finding partial words, when the box is unchecked, acts as a kind of wildcarding ability.

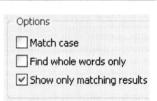

You can also access the above choices using a drop-down menu box on the control panel above the results list, seen here.

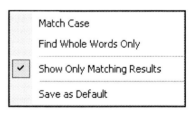

If Copernic takes you to the search interface of a particular search engine, as it does in some cases (e.g., when searching for image files), you can also use any wildcarding abilities supported there.

Google

Wildcarding is unavailable within or at the end of words. But in the latter case it is not needed because Google has automatic stemming for individual words (not for phrases). This can be disabled, however, by placing a plus sign in front of a word, or by placing a word inside a phrase.

You can use the asterisk (*) as a wildcard for a whole word.

> 🔎 Searching for **six * pencils** would find **six big pencils** and **six blue pencils**.

Such whole word wildcards can also be used within certain fielded search strings, where the field content syntax involves separation by periods, such as:

- inurl: or site: ⇨ Chapter 6: URL (resource) or site Internet address.

  > 🔎 If you want to find all sites that have **baylin** in the second position of their host name address, you could enter **site:*.baylin. ***. (Of course, this assumes that the last asterisk stands for any domain suffix and the host name ends there; also that only one qualifying name precedes **baylin**.)

- group: ⇨ Chapter 6: Additional document file content characteristics.

  > 🔎 If you want to find all sites that have **comp** in the first position of their group name, **os** in the second position, and any further qualifying group sub-division, you could enter **comp.os.***.

Note: You can use single word wildcards either within or outside a phrase. These are often used to get around Google's ten-word query limit (also counting otherwise ignored words within phrases).

MSN Search

Does not have wildcards or word stemming in the usual form, but it has an option that allows you specify the degree of match between your search terms and what is found. If you use "Search Builder," you can specify the degree of match using the slider you see on the next page. Or, you can type in an operator parameter directly to represent the state of the slider, using {mtch=999} in front of your search term(s) to specify the degree of match, where 999 represents an integer percentage from 0, for "Exact match," to 100, for "Exact match."

📖 Enter cat dog as terms, and slide the slider upwards until it reaches 89%. The search string then shows in the text entry box as cat dog {mtch=89}.

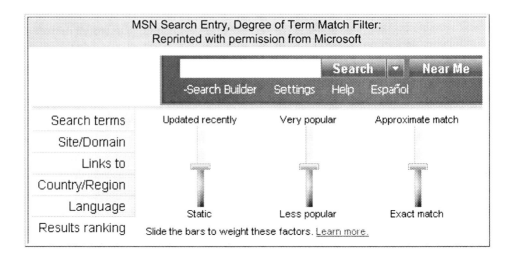

MSN Search Entry, Degree of Term Match Filter:
Reprinted with permission from Microsoft

General   AlltheWeb   AltaVista   Copernic   Google   MSN

Different spellings or phonetic matching

⇨ For more explanation, see:

- Chapter 6: Term variation filters.
- Reference Section 3: Intelligent avoidance of formal parameter entry.

Alternative spellings: The ability to automatically suggest and/or include different spellings of the same word sometimes helps to increase the number of relevant findings. All our featured search engines can do spellchecking, although none have filters that allow you to vary whether or how spellchecking is done in a given search.

Phonetic matching: Is based on the sound of the word rather than on the spelling. None of our featured search engines have this option. However, it is possible that some phonetic matching is done to check for spelling variations. **Note:** Exalead is a good example of a search engine with a phonetic match option.

Customization of spellchecking: ⇨ Reference Section 6.4: Other filter setting preferences.

Formatting masks

⇨ For more explanation, consult Chapter 6: Term variation filters.

Are often used in programs to cause data to be displayed to the user in a way that enhances readability. Formatting masks refer to the "superficial" appearance characteristics of terms. Of our featured search engines, only Copernic has any formatting mask abilities, specifically case sensitive searching within results.

However, if English-looking characters with diacritical marks are considered to be "formatting," Google and other search engines can use them to make distinctions. Diacritical mark are symbols (signs, accents, cedillas, etc.) placed above or below individual letters in certain alphabets to indicate different sounds or values of a letter, or to add a particular vowel before or after a consonant.

Note: AlltheWeb's now discontinued FTP search had a sophisticated ability to match formatting patterns, and is discussed below for illustration purposes.

| General | AlltheWeb | AltaVista | Copernic | Google | MSN |

AlltheWeb

⇨ For more on regular expression handling, refer to Reference Section 6.1: Wildcards, substrings, stemming.

Format mask search is presently unavailable. However, it used to be available in AlltheWeb's now discontinued FTP search, which had the ability to handle regular expressions. This meant that it could not only support the use of wildcards, but also handle recognition of different formats.

AltaVista

AltaVista Help's "Basic Web Search Tips" states: Uppercase and lowercase are treated the same. To maintain a certain capitalization, put the word in quotes. However, our own testing failed to determine whether or not capitalization made any difference in the findings when a phrase was used.

AltaVista treats English-like characters with diacritical marks added from non-English alphabets as being distinct from the apparently identical characters in English.

Copernic

Its "Advanced Find" dialog allows you to select according to case (see "Match case" checkbox shown here).

Options

- ☑ Match case
- ☐ Find whole words only
- ☑ Show only matching results

This same choice is also available from a drop-down menu in the control panel above the results list, as seen in the accompanying screen image.

| Options ▾ | Advanced Find | Clear |

- ✔ Match Case
-    Find Whole Words Only
- ✔ Show Only Matching Results
-    Save as Default

Google

Format mask search is unavailable. However, Google treats English-like characters with diacritical marks added from non-English alphabets as being distinct from the apparently identical characters in English.

MSN Search

Based on our testing, it does not appear to support case sensitivity, even within phrases.

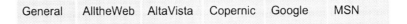

| General | AlltheWeb | AltaVista | Copernic | Google | MSN |

Ignored words or characters

⇨ For more explanation, refer to Chapter 6: Term variation filters.

Words ignored when matching terms (words and/or phrases) to documents are often called **stop words**. These usually include articles (such as a, the), prepositions (such as at, to, in), various forms of the verb "to be" (been, is), and other so-called "parts of speech." Also ignored are most punctuation characters, such as periods, commas, and colons.

AltaVista, Copernic, Google, and MSN Search, allow the user to actively control which characters are ignored in search terms.

AlltheWeb

Control over ignored words or characters is unavailable.

AltaVista

AltaVista automatically ignores special characters and common numeric digits (such as '1'), unless the search term is placed in quotes, forming a phrase. In phrases, all alphabetical characters are respected, but special characters (such as punctuation marks) are still ignored.

Copernic

It relies on the features of the search engines it invokes. Therefore, in general, it automatically ignores special characters and common numeric digits (such as '1'), unless the search term is a phrase (placed in quotes). Regardless, even in phrases, while all alphabetical characters may be respected, special characters (such as punctuation marks) are still ignored.

Google

 Google will also indicate if your query exceeds the 32-word limit (including dropped stop words).

At the top of the findings page, Google rewrites your query and notes any words that have been dropped. As explained in Google Help:

Google ignores common words and characters such as "where" and "how", as well as certain single digits and single letters... Google will indicate if a common word has been excluded by displaying details on the results page below the search box.

If a common word is essential to getting the results you want, you can include it by putting a "+" sign in front of it. (Be sure to include a space before the "+" sign.)

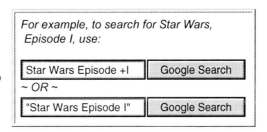

For example, to search for Star Wars, Episode I, use:

Star Wars Episode +I   Google Search

~ OR ~

"Star Wars Episode I"   Google Search

Another method for doing this is conducting a phrase search, which simply means putting quotation marks around two or more words. Common words in a phrase search (e.g., "where are you") are included in the search.

Specifically, Google ignores the following punctuation and special characters: , . ; ? [ ] ( ) @ / # .

On the other hand, Google does *not* ignore a term with an apostrophe. Thus we're as a search term produces different results than the term were.

Note: Diacritical marks are not ignored. These are signs, accents, cedillas, etc., used to indicate different sounds or values of a letter. Thus, a character in a term with an accent doesn't match a similar English character without an accent.

MSN Search

Control over ignored words is available by surrounding them by quotation marks, i.e., including them inside a phrase. You can also force an ignored word to be included by placing a plus sign (+) in front of it.

General	AlltheWeb	AltaVista	Copernic	Google	MSN

Term Relationship

Phrases

⇨ For more explanation, see Chapter 6: Term relationship filters.

Consist of multiple words separated by a space treated as a single term. In a phrase, the individual words must be in the specified order.

All our featured search engines can handle phrases.

General	AlltheWeb	AltaVista	Copernic	Google	MSN

AlltheWeb

To indicate a series of words is a phrase:

- Surround it with quotation marks. Type the phrase including quotes into the search string entry text box, e.g., "Breast cancer".

- Use the text boxes under "Word filters" in advanced Web search, simply typing in your phrase. Anything entered into one of these text boxes is assumed to be a phrase if you surround it with quotes.

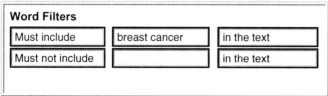

- Choose "the exact phrase" from the appropriate drop-down menu box in the advanced news, simple Web, or advanced Web search interfaces.

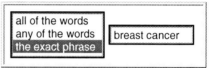

  Then enter your phrase in the accompanying text box. Quotation marks are unnecessary.

AltaVista

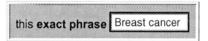

To indicate a series of words is a phrase:

- Surround it with quotation marks. Type the phrase including quotes into any search string entry text box, e.g., **"Breast cancer in Canada"**.

> ⚠ If you put two words not surrounded by quotes and with nothing but a space in between them in "this Boolean expression" text box, AltaVista assumes that the two words form part of a phrase. (⇨ Reference Section 6.1: AND, OR, and NOT.)

- Type the exact desired phrase in "This exact phrase" text box. Quotes are then not needed.

Copernic

To indicate a series of words is a phrase:

> ⚠ Do not enter quotation marks in a text box accompanied by some other indicator (e.g., using a checkbox or a radio button) telling Copernic the text box contains a phrase. In such cases, it will signal a syntax error.

- Surround it with quotation marks. Type the phrase including quotes into any search string entry text box, as in "Breast cancer".
- Use the appropriate text box to indicate an exact phrase in Copernic's advanced search interfaces, which look as follows.

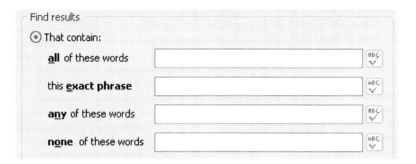

- Check the "exact phrase" checkbox associated with the search string entry text box in simple search interfaces.

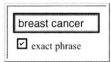 Type **breast cancer** into the text box. No quotes are needed if some other indicator connected with that box indicates a phrase is in the box.

Google

To indicate a series of words is a phrase:

- Surround it with quotation marks. Type the exact phrase including quotes in an appropriate text box.

- Type the desired phrase in the "with the exact phrase" text box. Quotes are then not needed.

MSN Search

To indicate a series of words is a phrase:

- Enter the term surrounded with quotation marks.

- Use the "Search Builder" drop-down menu box seen below, choosing "This exact phrase." This will place your terms in the search entry box surrounded by quotation marks. You can generate phrases and other constructs all in the same search by using this feature of "Search Builder" several times in succession.

 To generate the search string "Uncle Joe" (dog OR cat), use "Search Builder" once to generate "This exact phrase" Uncle Joe, and then use it again to generate (dog OR cat) by selecting "Any of these terms."

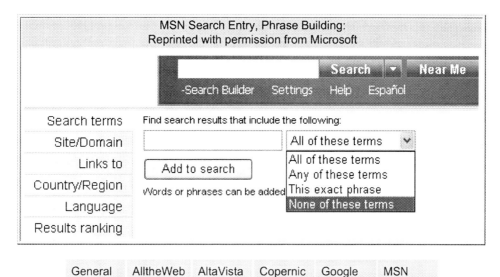

MSN Search Entry, Phrase Building:
Reprinted with permission from Microsoft

Search terms	Find search results that include the following:
Site/Domain	
Links to	Add to search
Country/Region	Words or phrases can be added
Language	
Results ranking	

All of these terms
- All of these terms
- Any of these terms
- This exact phrase
- None of these terms

General   AlltheWeb   AltaVista   Copernic   Google   MSN

AND, OR, and NOT

⇨ For more explanation, see Chapter 6: Term relationships using Boolean logic.

Boolean logic may be expressed by inserting connectives (operator parameters) between or before terms to express the ideas of conjunction (AND), inclusion (OR), and negation (NOT).

Although the mechanics may vary quite a bit, the abilities of the various search engines are fairly similar when it comes to this kind of feature. However, each search engine has a fairly unique set of problems and quirks. For example see ⇨ Chapter 4: Case #3: Health-Related Search.

Boolean logic can be expressed in a number of ways: (a) by using operator parameters, (b) by filling in boxes that do not involve use of operator parameters, or (c) by a combination of these two methods. To further complicate matters:

- Search engines do not always use the same syntax for Boolean operators. Fortunately, there is more uniformity now than ever before.

> ⇨ See also "Important information on using Boolean logic" in Chapter 6: Term relationships using Boolean logic.

- The way the ideas are expressed can vary depending upon which boxes and which search entry interfaces are employed, even when all operator parameters are used.

- Expressing the same ideas, whether with or without the use of operator parameters, does not necessarily produce identical results, even in the same search engine.

🕮 This can happen when the **OR** condition is used as an operator parameter between terms versus entering terms into a box for "any of the words" or its equivalent. Also, using plus and minus signs (see below) instead of **AND** and **OR** can sometimes produce slightly different numbers of findings.

All our featured search engines require explicit syntax when Boolean logic is entered using operator parameters into text boxes explicitly designated for such use. Most have such boxes on their advanced Web search. Here are more details:

1. **Text entry box specifically and explicitly designated for Boolean search strings with all kinds of Boolean relationships allowed:**

> 🔨 MSN Search requires that you designate whether the single search term entry box is to contain Boolean operators by using a choice in an accompanying drop-down menu. AlltheWeb has a similar feature in one of its interfaces, provided you use certain boxes.

   AlltheWeb, AltaVista, and Copernic have such a box in their advanced search entry interfaces.

🕮 AltaVista uses the text box seen here.

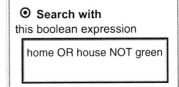

In these specially designated text boxes, you must place an explicit Boolean operator (e.g., AND, OR) between terms. If not, the terms taken together will not be properly understood, and may be taken to form a phrase or to have an **OR** between them.

UPPERCASE letters are required for Boolean operators by all our featured search engines, except for Copernic. The required Boolean operators accepted by the different search engines in such advanced Boolean search string entry text boxes are:

- **For conjunction:** Use **AND** or the **plus sign** (+ with a space before but not after) between terms, and a plus sign if it is in front of the first term, for most of our featured search engines. Examples: dog AND cat, dog +cat, +dog +cat, +dog AND cat.

- **For negation:** Use **NOT, AND NOT,** or **minus sign** (- with space before but not after) between terms, and a minus sign if it is in front of the very first term, for most of our featured search engines. **AND NOT** or **EXCEPT** is used by Copernic between terms, and the minus sign or **NOT** alone is used in front of the first term. **AND NOT** may be required between terms, or may produce slightly different results from **NOT** in some search engines. Examples: dog AND NOT cat, dog -cat, -dog AND cat, NOT dog AND cat, pets EXCEPT cat, pets -dog -cat.

- **For inclusion:** Use **OR** for all featured search engines. Example: dog OR cat.

> ⚠ In all our featured search engines, if you put nothing between terms, **AND** is the default, if defaults are accepted in a given search term entry box. Therefore, OR has to be explicit.

- **For inclusion combined with negation:** Use **OR** followed by the term preceded by a **minus sign**. Example: friend OR NOT pet, friend OR -pet. In Copernic, you can also use **OR NOT**.

2. **Text entry boxes not specifically designated for multi-purpose Boolean search strings:** The following rules apply provided that:

> For a discussion of the possibilities of entering Boolean operator parameters using simple search text boxes, see ⇨ Reference Section 3: Support for operator parameters.

- The box has not already been designated by some other selection (e.g., using radio button, checkbox, or dropdown menu choice) for a particular type of Boolean relation between terms *other than* "All these terms" or "All these words".

- Operator parameters, including Boolean ones, are recognized in that text entry box (not the case in AlltheWeb and AltaVista unless you use the one specially designated box).

In such cases, the default is **AND** for our featured search engines. Otherwise, the Boolean operator, if accepted in that box as a Boolean operator, must be explicitly entered.

🔲 dog cat means that *both* dog *and* cat are mandatory terms, and is equivalent to entering dog AND cat in text boxes that require the formal Boolean syntax.

General	AlltheWeb	AltaVista	Copernic	Google	MSN

AlltheWeb

Using operator parameters:

The use of Boolean operators with operator parameters is explained for all the search engines at the top of this section. The box on AlltheWeb's advanced Web search form designated for entering Boolean operators appears here below.

> 🔨 For more subtleties using Boolean logic in AlltheWeb, consult our health-related search case example: ⇨ Chapter 4: AlltheWeb.

Without using operator parameters:

Use the following method to specify Boolean logic without using operator parameters:

> ⦿ Boolean - Create a boolean query using the operators **AND**, **OR** and **NOT**. [cat NOT dog]

- Use the text box selected by a radio button at the top of the advanced Web search form. Then, from the

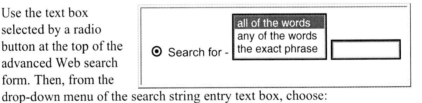

> ⦿ Search for - [all of the words / any of the words / the exact phrase] [   ]

drop-down menu of the search string entry text box, choose:

> ○ "all of the words" — to have the effect of **AND**.
> ○ "any of the words" — to have the effect of **OR**.
> ○ "the exact phrase.

> 💡 AlltheWeb gives you the choice whether to activate the above drop-down menu on its simple Web search (⇨ Reference Section 6.4: Interface options made available). It is automatically made available on its advanced Web and news (advanced or simple) search entry forms.

- Use the text boxes under "Word filters" in the drop-down menu to the left of the box for entering your phrase or word. Choices include:

> "Must include" — to have the effect of **AND**.
> "Must not include" — to have the effect of **NOT**.

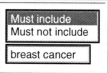

Unfortunately, the "Should include" option, to indicate **OR**, is no longer available in these drop-down menus since AlltheWeb was taken over by Yahoo.

> 💡 For Boolean logic choices with "domain" filtering, use the "Only Include" and "Exclude" text entry boxes to specify the ideas of **AND** and **NOT** for these metadata-based filters. ⇨ Reference Section 6.2: URL (resource) or site Internet address.

AltaVista

> 🔨 For more subtleties using Boolean logic in AltaVista, consult our health-related search case example: ⇨ Chapter 4: AltaVista.

The use of Boolean operators with operator parameters is explained for all the search engines at the top of this section. Therefore, the description here focuses on how to specify Boolean logic when you do not use operator parameters.

Here's a search string placed in the box on the advanced Web search form designated for entering Boolean operators.

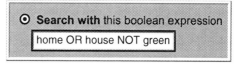

The method to specify Boolean logic without using operator parameters on the advanced Web search entry form is as follows:

- **OR:** Type the search terms into the "any of these words" text box; e.g., type home house in the "any of these words" text box.
- **NOT:** Type the unwanted search terms into the "none of these words" text box. At the same time, type the wanted term in another appropriate text box.

🔲 Enter house in a text box for terms that are wanted and green in the "none of these words" text box.

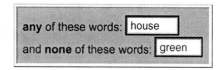

- **AND:** Type the search terms into the "all of these words" text box.

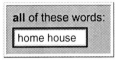

Typing house home into this box is the same as specifying home AND house in the "Boolean expression" text box.

Copernic

The use of Boolean operators with operator parameters is explained for all the search engines at the top of this section. However, a little more explanation is needed for Copernic, because of the complexity of its dialog boxes for Boolean search string entry.

To obtain an interface in which to enter a complex Boolean search string in Copernic, either use the dialog boxes provided when you do an "Analysis" or use the "Advanced Find in Results" dialog box.

1. First select the "Optimal Analysis," as seen using a radio button in the screenshot below. Also, check the "Keep only results of pages matching" checkbox. Then click on the link next to that label to arrive at the dialog box that then appears (seen on next page).

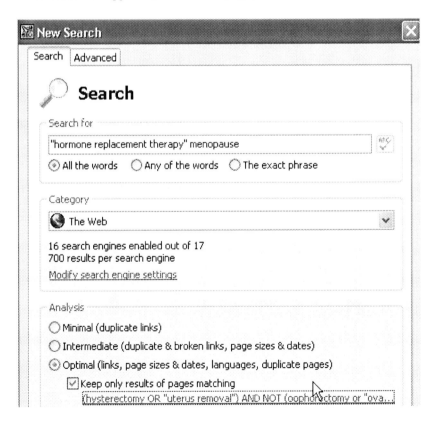

In this box, select the second radio button and then enter the Boolean string into the text box under it, as you see here. Then choose "OK" to return to the previous dialog box, from which you can execute your search.

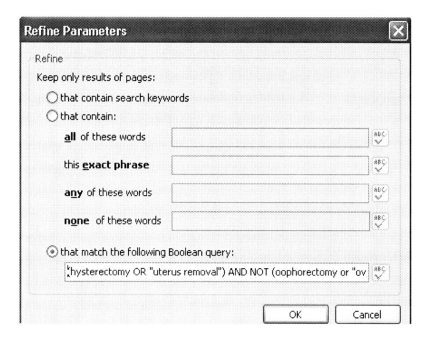

2. Use the "Advanced Find in Results" dialog box, either to enter your Boolean search string using operator parameters, or to enter it using various boxes designated for terms subject to particular Boolean relationships. Whichever method you choose, the other one is also shown. (For more about this dialog box, see ⇨ Reference Section 6.3: Search within findings.)

3. Copernic's "simple" search interface, seen here, provides you with a dialog boxes seen at the bottom of the next page to indicate Boolean relationships between terms, except that you cannot represent OR relationships or prioritize Boolean operator application.

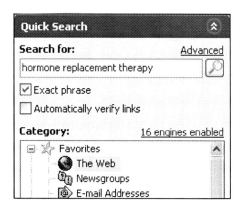

In this interface, if you choose the "Exact phrase" option, you must not surround your term with quotation marks. If you choose the other two options, you can use both individual words and phrases indicated by quotation marks as terms (despite the fact that the label simply says "words"). You cannot use Boolean operators in these dialog boxes or these will be themselves interpreted as search terms.

Google

> For more subtleties using Boolean logic in Google, consult our health-related search case example: ⇨ Chapter 4: Google.

The use of Boolean operators with operator parameters is explained for all the search engines at the top of this section. However, here is some clarification.

Google restricts the entry of Boolean operators to text boxes found on its simple search entry interfaces and ones on a few of its advanced search entry forms labeled "with all of these words." These boxes accept phrases, indicated by surrounding quotation marks, in addition to just "words" (despite their label). In these boxes (and only in these boxes), you can enter complex Boolean search string with operator parameters.

Here are the various methods for indicating Boolean relationships between terms in Google:

> ⚠ Boolean operators **must** be in uppercase in Google. Fortunately, Google will inform you when a word is not interpreted as a Boolean operator, in this case, the word "or" — as follows.

1. **Using operator parameters:**

   > The word **"or"** was ignored in your query — for search results including one term or another, use capitalized "OR" between words. [details]

   - Prefix terms with plus (+) or minus (-).
   - Separate them with the OR in uppercase letters or by the pipe (|) character (the equivalent of OR).

   - Enter these in any order and combination, e.g., "Star Wars" +I +bass -music OR vacation +(London | Paris).

   In this example, the required terms are the phrase Star Wars, the I, the bass, one or both of music and vacation, and one or both of London or Paris.

2. **Without using operator parameters:**

- **OR:** Type the search terms into the "with at least one of the words" text box, without specifying OR. To have the effect of hot OR cold, just type the type search terms into this text box.

> with **at least one** of the words | hot cold |

- **Minus (-):** Type the unwanted search terms into the "without the words" text box. At the same time, type the required term in an appropriate text box.

> with **at least one** of the words | hot |
> **without** the words | cold |

- **Plus (+):** Type the words into the "with all the words" text box.

  Type "Star Wars" "episode I" (in this case two phrases) into the "with all the words" text box.

> with **all** of the words
> | "Star Wars" "episode I" |

Guidelines when using Boolean Logic with Google

Typing nothing between words is equivalent to + when the terms are typed into the single search string text entry box in simple search.

If you type **AND** between terms in a text box that understands Boolean operators, the AND is ignored and Google informs you of this. In other words, the same idea is represented by a blank space between terms.

For Boolean logic with the "File Format" filter, use the "only" and "don't" drop-down menu options to specify the ideas of **AND** and **NOT** for these metadata-based filters. ⇨ Reference Section 6.2: File format.

For Boolean logic with the "Domain" filter, use the "only" and "don't" drop-down menu options to specify the ideas of **AND** and **NOT** for these filters. ⇨ Reference Section 6.2: URL (resource) or site Internet address.

For further discussion of the use of Boolean logic in Google, consult our health-related search case example: ⇨ Chapter 4: Google and Reference Section 6.3: Search within findings.

MSN Search

🔨 For more subtleties using Boolean logic in MSN Search, consult our health-related search case example: ⇨ Chapter 4: MSN Search.

The plus (or the &) and minus signs work in place of AND and NOT between terms. Also, the pipe (|) character is equivalent to OR.

🔢 Typing Monica AND Bellucci AND photos NOT nude will produce the same result as entering Monica +Bellucci +photos -nude. Thus, you can simply leave nothing between terms to achieve the same result as placing an AND between them.

Also, you can generate AND and NOT logic between terms through the "Search Builder" choices seen below:

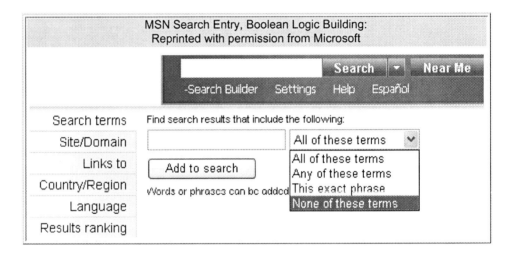

MSN Search Entry, Boolean Logic Building:
Reprinted with permission from Microsoft

General   AlltheWeb   AltaVista   Copernic   Google   MSN

Proximity

⇨ For more explanation, see Chapter 6: Term relationships using Boolean logic.

The AND operator can have sub-types (specialized kinds), generally called **proximity** or **adjacency** operators, such as NEAR to find terms before or after a term within a specified number of words.

Of our featured search engines, only Copernic has this feature, although Google has a partial means of doing proximity search.

AlltheWeb

There is no option for proximity Boolean operators.

AltaVista

There is no option for proximity Boolean operators.

Copernic

In any text box that accepts Boolean operators, use the NEAR operator in front of a term. This finds documents where the term occurs within a pre-determined number of words of another designated term.

Google

Although it sorts webpages, placing ones with your search terms near one another earlier in your results, Google has no explicit option for proximity Boolean operators. You can, however, use its single word replacement wildcard character (the asterisk) to achieve controlled nearness.

> 🔍 To find the words oil and slick within 2 words of one another, with oil before slick, enter the search string: "oil slick" OR "oil * slick" OR "oil * * slick".

If you want to search for two terms separated by no more than two words, where either word could come first, you may need multiple queries if you exceed Google 32-word limit. This is because inverting the word order and adding more OR clauses generates many more words in the search string. For searches of that kind, you might want to try out GAPS, a third-party Google-based search tool available at www.staggernation.com/cgi-bin/gaps.cgi, which gives you the following choices (among others not shown here):

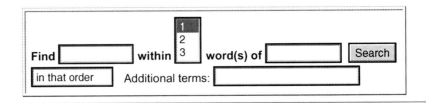

MSN Search

There is no explicit option for proximity Boolean operators.

General   AlltheWeb   AltaVista   Copernic   Google   MSN

Prioritizing term relationship operators

> ⇨ For further discussion of the quirky nature of this feature with all our featured search engines, see Chapter 6: Term relationships using Boolean logic and Chapter 4: Case #3: Health-Related Search.

Complex Boolean expressions usually involve the use of precedence operators, which are tertiary parameters, usually in the form of brackets nested to one or more levels. **The expressions within brackets are evaluated first, from innermost to outermost bracket levels**.

In theory, our featured search engines handle the prioritization of term relationship operators in a fairly similar way, although the implementation varies. The one exception is that the use of brackets may make no difference with Boolean searches in Google, indicating that Google cannot handle term relationship operator prioritization.

Note: Prioritizing term relationship operators does not appear to be covered in the Help documentation of any of our featured search engines, except perhaps for MSN Search in some unclear way.

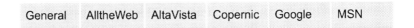

General   AlltheWeb   AltaVista   Copernic   Google   MSN

AlltheWeb

You need to use the advanced Web search Boolean search text box to enter searches where term relationships can be prioritized. If you use any of the text boxes on simple search entry forms, you can use a single level of brackets, but these will be used to signify OR relationships between terms (⇨ Reference Section 6.1: AND, OR, and NOT) rather than to prioritize term relationships.

⚠ You may find that using brackets and Boolean operators in conjunction with field operators will not work quite as consistently as you might like.

🔣 If you enter kangaroo AND (site:au OR site:mx), you will probably obtain a different number of findings as compared to entering kangaroo AND site:(au OR mx).

For further discussion of this feature in AlltheWeb, consult our health-related search case example: ⇨ Chapter 4: AlltheWeb.

AltaVista

In its "Search with this Boolean expression" text box, type the search terms with AND, OR, or NOT, using brackets to set up the priority of each term for your search. The expression can also be written into the single text box provided by AltaVista's simple search interfaces.

🔣 (salt AND pepper OR music) NOT spices

🔣 (salt AND pepper) OR (music AND NOT spices) NOT cinnamon NOT (peppermint OR garlic). Notice how the brackets are used to apply the second NOT operator to either peppermint or garlic.

🔨 Using brackets and Boolean operators in conjunction with field operators does not work consistently in AltaVista.

🔣 If you enter kangaroo AND (domain:au OR domain:mx), you will obtain many more findings as compared to entering kangaroo AND domain:(au OR mx).

For further discussion of this feature in AltaVista, refer to our health-related search case example: ⇨ Chapter 4: AltaVista.

Copernic

It is possible to use brackets to several levels when you enter a Boolean search string into a text box using Copernic. This complexity will not be passed to any sourced search engine, but will be applied in the sense of "Find in Results."

Google

Google Help does not mention the use of brackets, and our tests seem to indicate that brackets and prioritization of term operators does not seem to work.

MSN Search

Parentheses in Boolean queries give higher priority.

> 🔣 Enter Microsoft AND games NOT ("Urban Mess" OR "Fast Action"). This should return findings containing the words Microsoft and games, but not the phrases Urban Mess or Fast Action.

General	AlltheWeb	AltaVista	Copernic	Google	MSN

Other kinds of term relationships

> ⇨ For more explanation, see Chapter 6: Term relationship filters.

These include:

- **Fuzzy AND's, OR's, and NOT's:** For instance, when a term is optional but preferred, we have what in fuzzy logic is known as a **fuzzy AND** (or **fuzzy conjunction**). Of our featured search engines, only MSN Search uses fuzzy logic. Also, the Exalead supplementary search engine was mentioned in Chapter 6.

- **Range comparisons:** These involves testing for whether one term is greater than (>), less than (<), or equal to (=) another term. Sometimes, you can achieve this by including many **OR**'s, if not dealing with a continuous range, involving sets with infinite numbers of members. None of our featured search engines support comparison filters.

MSN Search

Has the prefer: fielded search operator, to indicate that a term is preferred, even if not strictly required. All other things being equal, webpages having the preferred term will sort higher in the results list than those without that term.

Enter Microsoft prefer:Seattle. This should return findings containing the words Microsoft and, preferably, also the word Seattle.

General	AlltheWeb	AltaVista	Copernic	Google	MSN

Reference Manual Section 6.2: Metadata-Based Search Filters

⇨ This section cross-links with Chapter 6: Metadata-Based Search Filters.

File Structure Characteristics

File format

⇨ For more explanation, refer to Chapter 6: File structure characteristics.

File formats (or **file types**) are usually identified by extensions to the file name.

All our featured search engines can search by file format, but not all have the same set of predefined formats (selectable from a list). With respect to predefined file formats:

- **Document file formats:** Google provides the greatest assortment of choices, followed by AlltheWeb and then AltaVista.
- **Multi-media file formats:** AltaVista has the largest assortment of choices, followed by AlltheWeb and then Google.
- **Other file formats:** AlltheWeb's former FTP search was able to distinguish file formats in a way useful for that kind of application. Although this search is no longer supported by AlltheWeb, it is shown below for illustrative and instructive purposes.

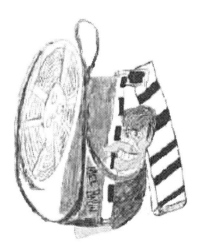

General	AlltheWeb	AltaVista	Copernic	Google	MSN

Reference Manual Section 6.2:
Metadata-Based
Search Filters

430

File Structure
Characteristics

AlltheWeb

Any format
Adobe PDF (.pdf)
Microsoft Word (.doc)
Microsoft Excel (.xls)
Microsoft Power Point (.ppt)
HTML
Text (.txt)

1. **Document files:**

Use the drop-down menu box in AlltheWeb's advanced Web search to choose either "Any format" (which includes HTML files), or any of the other file formats shown.

2. **Multi-media files:**

- In its Pictures search interface, you have the set of choices for file format seen here.

  File Format: ☑ All formats ☐ JPEG ☐ GIF ☐ BMP

- In its Video search interface, you have the set of choices for file format, seen here.

  ☑ All ☐ AVI ☐ AVI/DivX ☐ MPEG ☐ Real ☐ QuickTime

3. **FTP File Formats**

In AlltheWeb's former advanced FTP search interface, you were able to choose to hide certain file formats, because they are related

Hide - ☐ Packages ☐ Distfiles ?
☐ FreeBSD ☐ OpenBSD
☐ NetBSD ☐ Linux

to the server operating system, and therefore, not of interest.

As was explained in AlltheWeb Help of old, the above choices were:

- **Hide -** Hide most of the files in one of the following categories:
- **Packages** - FreeBSD/OpenBSD/NetBSD packages and ports.
- **Distfiles** - Distribution files used by FreeBSD/OpenBSD/ NetBSD port system.
- **FreeBSD** - FreeBSD related files.
- **NetBSD** - NetBSD related files.
- **OpenBSD** - OpenBSD related files.
- **Linux** - Linux related files.

AltaVista

1. **Document files:**

   In its advanced Web search interface, AltaVista allows the choices you see here.

2. **Multi-media files:**

- Click on the checkboxes for the type of format of the audio file sought (e. g., WAV, MP3, etc.).

   If searching for MP3's from the group Less Than Jake, select only the MP3 checkbox and type "Less than Jake" in the text box. Leave the play duration filter at "All Durations." (Also see ⇨ Reference Section 6.2: Additional multi-media file content characteristics).

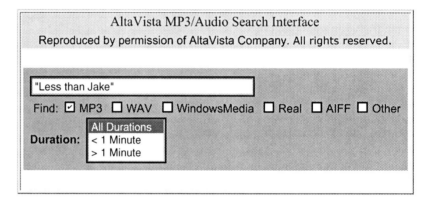

   Choose all video file formats for videos with the names indicated in the text box below.

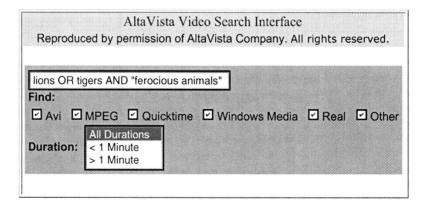

Reference Manual Section 6.2:
Metadata-Based
Search Filters
432
File Structure
Characteristics

The Image search does not provide an explicit

Find: ☑ Photos ☑ Graphics ☐ Buttons/Banners

choice by file format on the assumption that all web image file formats (GIF and JPEG, in particular) are selected. However, "Photos" basically translates to the JPEG (JPG) file format, while Graphics and Buttons/Banners are likely GIF or PNG types.

Copernic

Allows the choices of file formats you see here.

Since the file name is part of the metadata Copernic amasses in constructing its results, you can

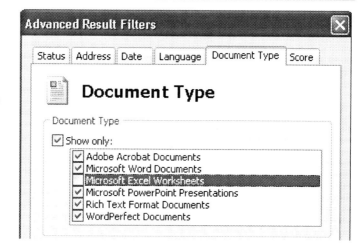

also do a "Find in Results" procedure to search on particular file formats, based on file name extensions.

> ℹ️ Find all results that are contained in Adobe Acrobat files by searching on pdf.

Copernic also has access to specialized types of searches based on file format, some of which provide interfaces you can use to select particular ones.

> ℹ️ One category of search allows you to search image files, from which you can access AlltheWeb's image file search interface.

Google

Search not using operator parameters:

> 🔨 For more on the indexing of different file formats by Google, ⇨ www.searchenginewatch.com/sereport/01/11-google.html.

1. **Document files:**

   Type your search term in an appropriate text box. Select "Only" or "Don't" from the drop-down menu to specify whether to include or

Reference Manual Section 6.2:
Metadata-Based
Search Filters

433

File Structure
Characteristics

exclude a given choice of file formats. Then select the file format(s) from the associated drop-down menu.

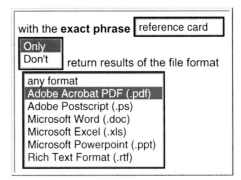 Type reference card as a phrase in an appropriate text box. Then select "Only" return results of the file format along with "Adobe Acrobat PDF (. pdf)" file format from the drop-down menu.

2. **Multi-media files:**

Using the advanced image search interface, the user can choose any image file format or zero in on GIF and JPG (JPEG) files using a drop-down menu.

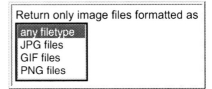

Fielded search using operator parameters:

No matter the file type, you can use the filetype: keyword followed by the file extension.

△ The field name filetype: must be in lowercase.

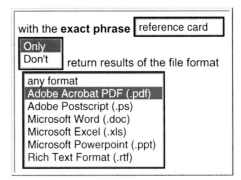 Enter **"trailing indicators" filetype:ppt** to find PowerPoint files with the phrase trailing indicators.

MSN Search

△ The field name filetype: must be in lowercase, and there must be no space after the colon.

No matter the file type, you can use the filetype: keyword followed by the file extension.

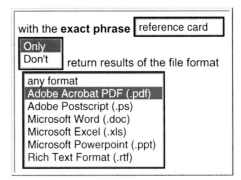 Enter **"trailing indicators" filetype:ppt** to find PowerPoint files with the phrase trailing indicators.

General   AlltheWeb   AltaVista   Copernic   Google   MSN

Embedded content

⇨ For more explanation, see Chapter 6: File structure characteristics.

Occurs when a document file contains a link to a multi-media file to be displayed on the webpage along with the text. Embedded content also includes programs inside the document file, including those in VBScript, JavaScript, or ActiveX, as well as Java applets and the like.

Except for MSN Search, none of our featured search engines has the ability to make distinctions by embedded content.

MSN Search

⚠ The field name **contains**: must be in lowercase, and there must be no space after the colon.

You can select files linked to from within a webpage (document) based on the extension used for file format.

🔲 Enter **music contains:wma** to find webpages having the term music as well as embedded links to Windows Media Audio (wma) files.

General	AlltheWeb	AltaVista	Copernic	Google	MSN

Document file section or location

⇨ For more explanation, consult Chapter 6: File structure characteristics.

HTML documents have two major sections, the header and the body, with a title sub-section found in the header. In addition to file section, you can often choose particular locations within the document file where these are demarcated using HTML tags. Such tags identify, for example, tables, scripts, frames, anchors (places for hyperlinks), and so on.

Most of our featured search engines can distinguish the title, and often the body (text) document sections.

- AltaVista cannot restrict search to the text section.
- Copernic does not have a precisely equivalent ability, but provides its own variation on this general idea.
- AlltheWeb, Google, and MSN Search can choose either the title or the body section of the HTML document.

- Google and MSN Search have the ability to find text inside page hyperlinks (ANCHOR HTML tags).

Other than the above, none of our featured search engines have the ability to locate text in other kinds of places, e.g., HTML tables, frames, and scripts.

General   AlltheWeb   AltaVista   Copernic   Google   MSN

AlltheWeb

To restrict terms to either the title or the text (body) sections of a web document (webpage):

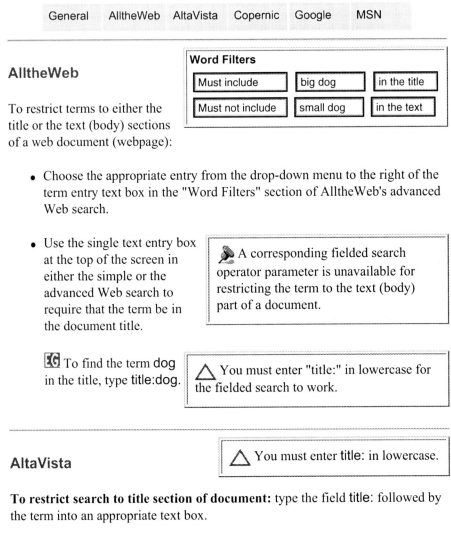

Word Filters

| Must include | big dog | in the title |
| Must not include | small dog | in the text |

- Choose the appropriate entry from the drop-down menu to the right of the term entry text box in the "Word Filters" section of AlltheWeb's advanced Web search.

- Use the single text entry box at the top of the screen in either the simple or the advanced Web search to require that the term be in the document title.

  A corresponding fielded search operator parameter is unavailable for restricting the term to the text (body) part of a document.

  To find the term dog in the title, type title:dog.

  ⚠ You must enter "title:" in lowercase for the fielded search to work.

AltaVista

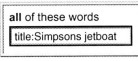

⚠ You must enter title: in lowercase.

To restrict search to title section of document: type the field title: followed by the term into an appropriate text box.

title:Simpsons means the word Simpsons must be in the title section.

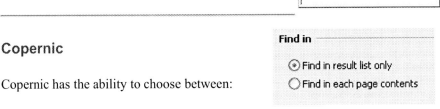

all of these words

title:Simpsons jetboat

Copernic

Copernic has the ability to choose between:

Find in

◉ Find in result list only
○ Find in each page contents

Reference Manual Section 6.2:
Metadata-Based
Search Filters

436

File Structure
Characteristics

- Finding in the "results list" (the file's metadata, in effect). This idea is somewhat similar to searching within the document title, since the title is the most important metadata item.

- Doing a search within "each page contents." In this case, Copernic accesses the actual file out on the Internet when it does a "Find in results" procedure, rather than looking in the already downloaded text in the detailed results list.

| Result list |
| Each page contents |

Google

| with the **exact phrase** | Boogey Wugie |

Return results where my terms occur

| anywhere in the page |
| in the title of the page |
| **in the text of the page** |
| in the url of the page |
| in links to the page |

1. **To restrict search to body section of document:**

   a. Type the search query in an appropriate text box. Then select "in the text of the page" in the "Return results where my terms occur" drop-down menu.

   b. Use a fielded search string with one of:

   - **intext:** searches only body text.

     ⚏ Enter intext:"Bill Clinton" to find the phrase in the body of the document.

   - **allintext:** searches for all the text in the search string following the colon, as opposed to just the first term following the field identifier (similar to the idea of the **allintitle** field in #2 next).

     ⚏ This search finds both the phrase search up and the word hello in the text body of the document.

   ⚠ **intext:** not only ignores titles, but also displays URL's and hyperlinks inside the body of the document.

   ⚠ If you use **allintext:**, everything in your search string that follows this field identifier must be in the body part of the document.

   ⚠ You must enter **intext:** and **allintext:** in lowercase for the fielded search to work.

| with **at least one** of the words |
| allintext: "search up" hello |

2. **To restrict the search to title section of document**: use one of the following options:

Reference Manual Section 6.2:
Metadata-Based
Search Filters

437

File Structure
Characteristics

a. Type the search query in an appropriate text box, select "in the title of the page" from the "Return results where my terms occur" drop-down menu.

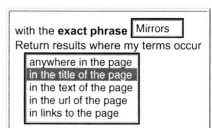

with the **exact phrase** | Mirrors |
Return results where my terms occur

| anywhere in the page |
| in the title of the page |
| in the text of the page |
| in the url of the page |
| in links to the page |

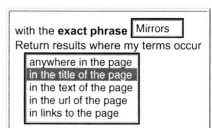 Type Mirrors in an appropriate text box, select "in the title of the page" from the "Return results where my terms occur" drop-down menu.

b. Use a fielded search with one of the following [explained in Google Help]:

⚠ You must enter intitle: and allintitle: in lowercase.

• **intitle:** If you include "intitle:" in your query, Google will restrict the results to documents containing that word in the title. Note there can be no space between the "intitle:" and the following word. **Note:** Putting "intitle:" in front of every word in your query is equivalent to putting "allintitle:" at the front of your query. For example, "intitle: google search" will return documents that mention the word "google" in their title, and mention the word "search" anywhere in the document (title or not). For instance, "intitle:google intitle: search" is the same as "allintitle: google search".

🔨 For further discussion of this feature in Google, consult our health-related search case example: ⇨ Chapter 4: Google.

• **allintitle:** If you start a query with "allintitle:", Google will restrict the resultsto those with all of the query words in the title. For example, "allintitle: google search" will return only documents that have both "google" and "search" in the title.

with **at least one** of the words

| allintitle: google search |

c. In Google's advanced groups search, enter the discussion subject in the following box (or use the title fielded search syntax above).

Subject Return only messages where the

subject contains [   ]

3. **To restrict search to displayed text of a document hyperlink:** use the field name inanchor: or allinanchor: in front of your search term.

⚇ Enter inanchor:Gamespot to find documents where the user can select hyperlinks having the wordGamespot in them.

⚠ You must enter inanchor: in lowercase for the fielded search to work.

MSN Search

Returns pages that contain the specified term in the anchor, body, or title of the site, respectively.

⚇ To find pages that contain jones in an anchor (hyperlink), and the terms hyper and agitating in the title and body text, respectively, type: inanchor:jones intitle:spaces inbody: agitating.

General	AlltheWeb	AltaVista	Copernic	Google	MSN

File Content Characteristics

File age

⇨ For more explanation, see Chapter 6: File content characteristics.

On the Internet, date and time of creation or last modification of a file is usually coincident with the date a webcrawler detected a new file or a file change.

All our featured search engines, except for MSN Search, can select by file age, although the mechanisms for doing so vary. MSN Search can, however, filter based on the frequency with which a file is updated (as opposed to its contents remaining static).

General	AlltheWeb	AltaVista	Copernic	Google	MSN

AlltheWeb

Only find results updated	☐ after	1	January	1980
	☐ before	29	March	2003

- Select document files according to how old these are in AlltheWeb's advanced Web search.

Reference Manual Section 6.2:
Metadata-Based
Search Filters

439

File Content
Characteristics

Make the appropriate selections of day, month, and year of each start and end dates from the drop-down menus.

- In AlltheWeb's advanced news search, you have the choices you see here.

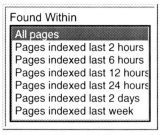

AltaVista

- In AltaVista's advanced Web search, type the term(s) sought in an appropriate text box. Then, use either the "by time frame" drop-down menu or specify the date range as shown here.
- In News search, choose the age of the news item from the drop-down menu.

 Type car sale in an appropriate text box and select "Anytime" from the "by timeframe" drop-down menu:

Copernic

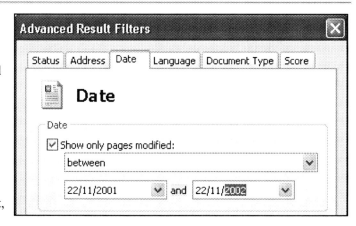

In its "Advanced Filters" dialog box, check the checkbox to enable date selection. Then enter a start and end date in dd/mm/yyyy format, as shown here.

Reference Manual Section 6.2:
Metadata-Based
Search Filters

440

File Content
Characteristics

Google

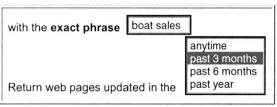

- In its advanced Web search interface, type the search term in an appropriate text box. Then using the "Return web pages updated in the" drop-down menu, select the appropriate time since that page has been created or last modified.

    🔟 Type boat sales in the "with exact phrase" text box. Then use the "Return web pages updated in the" drop-down menu to "Date" to select "past 3 months."

- Select dates of discussion group messages via Google's advanced group search Interface.

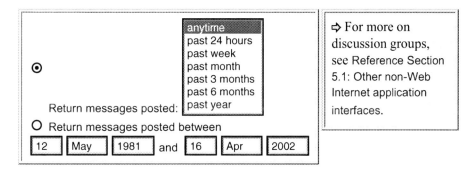

The following third-party Google-based search tools provide other ways of obtaining results by file age:

- **Fagan Finder** (⇨ www. faganfinder.com/ engines/google.shtml) lets you choose specific ranges of dates, as shown here.

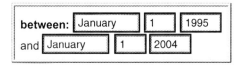

- In virtually any Google search entry interface, use the daterange: fielded search to find files by age — using Julian, as opposed to Gregorian dates. (The Julian date is the number of days since noon, January 1, 4713 BC.)

    🔟 Enter "George Samuels" daterange:2452389-2522450. The dash (-) between the start and end dates is part of the syntax. To convert the date to Julian in the first place, go to wwwmacho. mcmaster.ca/JAVA/JD.html.

⚠ Daterange field warnings:

- You must enter **daterange:** in lowercase for the fielded search to work.
- Fractions of days represent time, but with Google, you should use the closest integer to obtain the best results.

MSN Search

While it cannot filter based on date of first or last change detection, it can filter based on the degree to which the file contents change frequently. The slider shown in the screenshot below covers the spectrum between "Updated frequently" and "Static." The degree to which a file is static is expressed as a percent, ranging from 0, for "Static," to 100, for "Updated recently."

If you drag the slider to near the "Static" end in a search for cat cow dog, the "Search Builder" generates a string.

> 🔲 Enter **cat cow dog** as your search terms. Then drag the slider toward the bottom, until you see {frsh=15} after the search terms in the text entry box. 15 indicates that the file is only 15% dynamic. Rather than generating it by the slider, you can also type this operator parameter yourself directly into the search string, as in cat cow dog {frsh=15}.

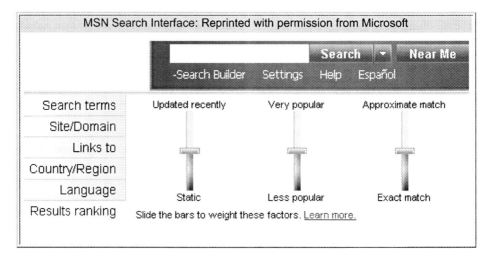

Document language

⇨ For more explanation, see Chapter 6: File content characteristics.

Search engines will often
default to searching for documents in all languages, unless otherwise specified.

All of our featured search engines handle document languages in a fairly similar way. However, each one includes a somewhat different set of languages, and there are considerable differences in the number of languages detected.

In addition to selecting the language of the documents found, some search engines have options to translate the findings, to select the language of the interface (site controls), and to set defaults for the language of documents found.

⇨ For more details on those related features, consult:

- Reference Section 5.2: Language translation or page summary.
- Reference Section 6.4: Interface Screen Features Preferences: Interface language or style.
- Reference Section 6.4: Filter Default Value Preferences: Document language.

General	AlltheWeb	AltaVista	Copernic	Google	MSN

AlltheWeb

In advanced News search, choose document language along with your browser's encoding scheme, using the drop-down menu seen here.

Preferred	Unicode (UTF-8)
Any language	Western European (ISO-8859-1)
Afrikaans	Western European (ISO-8859-15)
Albanian	Central European (ISO-8859-2)
Arabic	Celtic (ISO-8859-14)
Basque	Turkish (ISO-8859-9)
Bulgarian	South European (ISO-8859-3)
Byelorussian	Baltic (ISO-8859-4)
Catalan	Baltic (ISO-8859-13)
Chinese (simp)	Cyrillic (ISO-8859-5)

The choices are the same for
advanced Web search, except the encoding scheme menu does not appear.

The "Preferred" choice shown above depends on your filter setting preferences (⇨ Reference Section 6.4: Document language).

Reference Manual Section 6.2:
Metadata-Based
Search Filters

443

File Content
Characteristics

AltaVista

Language can either be chosen dynamically (for a particular

> ⚠ For language search to work, the "family filter" feature of AltaVista must be in the "off" state.

search), or based on user preference settings. To set dynamically, click on the hyperlink labeled with the language set (see screenshot below). Then choose one or more languages from the set of checkboxes provided for document language choices: ⇨ Reference Section 6.4: Document language.

Language and country are closely related in AltaVista.

> ⇨ For more details on specifying a country, either dynamically or through user preferences, see Reference Section 6.2: Geographical region of server.

⛬ If you access AltaVista Canada in the English interface, radio buttons appear giving you the option of restricting the web server location to Canada (the default being "Worldwide"), and the language defaults to to English (which you can change). On the other hand, for the United States (AltaVista.com) the default is "All languages." You might want to restrict the search to the United Stated, and set English and Spanish as your languages, as in the following:

SEARCH: ○ Worldwide ◉ U.S. RESULTS IN: ○ All languages ◉ English, Spanish

Copernic

Several languages can be detected. To do this, you must use the set of checkboxes from the "Language" section of the "Advanced Filters" dialog box.

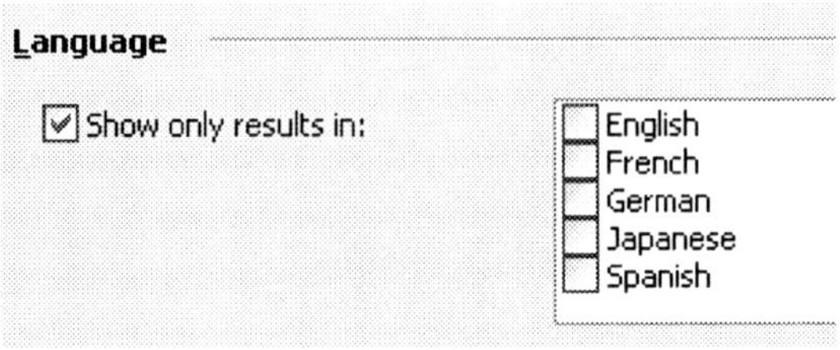

Language

☑ Show only results in:

☐ English
☐ French
☐ German
☐ Japanese
☐ Spanish

> ⚠ Language is only detected when you do a search using the "optimal analysis" setting. You can set Copernic preferences to default to optimal analysis mode (⇨ Reference Section 6.4: Other filter setting preferences).

Google

You can set multiple languages to search in as preferences: ⇨ Reference Section 6.4: Document language. To select a single or all languages dynamically, for a particular search, select a language in the "Return Pages written in" drop-down list.

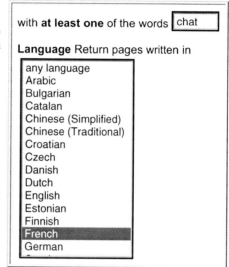

🔎 Type chat in an appropriate text box. On the "Language" list, select "French" in the drop down list in the "Return Pages written in." Click "Search" at the top of the page.

For a more sophisticated language interface, including translation of search terms *to* a language and of documents found *from* a language, go to the simple search interface, and click on "Language tools." Choose a language in the "Search pages written in:" drop-down menu under the heading "Search Specific languages or Countries." Type the search terms in an appropriate text box. For details, ⇨ Reference Section 5.2: Language translation or page summary.

Third-party Google Ultimate Interface (⇨ www.faganfinder.com/google.html) also provides filtering by language (and by country) in the directory search entry interface.

MSN Search

You can use the "Search Builder" option to access the drop-down menu seen below (next page) to specify document language. This generates a search string with the appropriate operator parameter incorporated. Or you can simply type the language operator parameter yourself directly into the search string.

🔎 Type chien chat (language:it OR language:fr) as your search string to search for chien and chat in either Italian or French. Alternatively:

1. Type chien chat into the search string.

Reference Manual Section 6.2:
Metadata-Based
Search Filters

445

File Content
Characteristics

2. Choose "Italian" and then "French," using the "Search Builder," making two selections in a row from the drop-down menu provided.

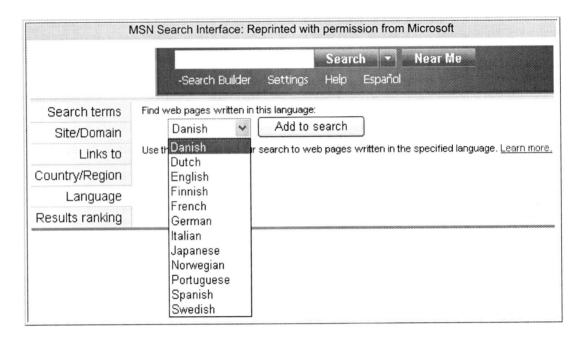

General   AlltheWeb   AltaVista   Copernic   Google   MSN

Potentially offensive content

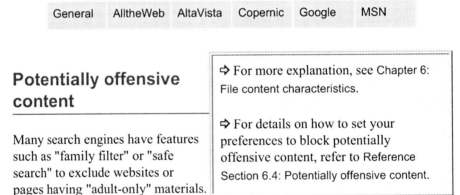

⇨ For more explanation, see Chapter 6: File content characteristics.

⇨ For details on how to set your preferences to block potentially offensive content, refer to Reference Section 6.4: Potentially offensive content.

Many search engines have features such as "family filter" or "safe search" to exclude websites or pages having "adult-only" materials.

With respect to our featured search engines:

- AlltheWeb, AltaVista, Google, and MSN Search all provide filters in this area. However, only AlltheWeb and Google allow the filter to be set *dynamically*, that is, for an individual search without changing your preference settings for blocking offensive content.
- Copernic has no offensive content filter.

General   AlltheWeb   AltaVista   Copernic   Google   MSN

Reference Manual Section 6.2:
Metadata-Based
Search Filters

446

File Content
Characteristics

AlltheWeb

Offensive content reduction is On

Set the parameter dynamically (without affecting the preference setting). You can do this on its advanced Pictures and Video search interfaces, using the drop-down menu.

On how to set your offensive content preferences, consult ➪ Reference Section 6.4: Potentially offensive content.

AltaVista

You cannot change your offensive content filter for each search (dynamically) without also altering your preference settings: ➪ Reference Section 6.4: Potentially offensive content. All multi-media search interfaces have special links to this preference setting feature.

Attention: The Family Filter has detected adult content
- See adult content by changing your settings.
- See results without adult content

If you do an image search on hot sex and your filter is set to block offensive content on multi-media searches, you will receive the message seen here.

Copernic

An offensive content control feature is unavailable.

Google

➪ On how to set the SafeSearch filter as a preference, also see Reference Section 6.4: Potentially offensive content.

Set the parameter dynamically (without affecting the preference setting) on its advanced Web and advanced Group search interfaces using the radio buttons you see here.

In its advanced image search entry interface, you get the following, more fine-grained set of choices:

SafeSearch ○ No filtering ◉ Use moderate filtering ○ Use strict filtering

Moderate filtering applies only to images, while strict filtering also excludes offensive text.

MSN Search

You cannot change your offensive content filter for each search (dynamically) without also altering your preference settings: ⇨ Reference Section 6.4: Potentially offensive content.

General	AlltheWeb	AltaVista	Copernic	Google	MSN

Additional document file content characteristics

⇨ For more explanation, see Chapter 6: File content characteristics.

Examples of this include the publication, publisher, author, the company or its stock symbol, and message identifier.

The abilities of our featured search engines to handle miscellaneous parameters varies greatly. AltaVista does not provide examples in this category, while MSN Search provides by far the widest variety of all our featured search engines.

General	AlltheWeb	AltaVista	Copernic	Google	MSN

AlltheWeb

News sources:

Its advanced News search allows selection of news articles according to the sources you see here.

File size: AlltheWeb used to have filters for this, but no longer does.

☑ All

☐ International   ☐ US News

☐ Various Local News ☐ Business

☐ Finance   ☐ Technology

☐ Sports   ☐ Traffic

☐ Weather   ☐ Entertainment

AltaVista

Filters based on other document characteristics were not detected.

Copernic

When doing a "Find in Results" procedure with Copernic, you can select findings within your overall results as follows:

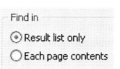

- According to whether what you are looking for is in the metadata ("results list") or in the file itself.

- According to whether the link to the file was detected as being broken during Copernic's analysis 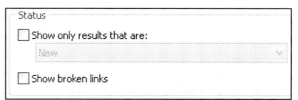 phase (where an attempt is made to access the actual file as it now exists on the Internet).

Google

Phonebook: You can do fielded searches as follows:

> Google can automatically detect when you are looking for a phone number: ⇨ Reference Section 3: Intelligent avoidance of formal parameter entry.
>
> Reverse phone book look-ups are available (e.g., phonebook:(708) 482-6659), although they don't always work.

- Use the bphonebook: field for U.S. business listings.

Enter bphonebook: mexican food dallas for Mexican food places in Dallas. You receive the following:

Reference Manual Section 6.2:
Metadata-Based
Search Filters

449

File Content
Characteristics

Business Phonebook Results **1 - 18** of **18** for **mexican food dallas**. (**0.10** seconds)

Reyes **Mexican Food** - (214) 398-6145 - 1310 N Jim Miller Rd, **Dallas**, TX 75217 - Yahoo! Maps - >
MapQuest
Pepitos **Mexican Food** - (214) 428-6755 - 1835 S Harwood St, **Dallas**, TX 75215 - Yahoo! Maps -
MapQuest

> ⚠ Warnings [based on research from Google Hacks: 100 Industrial-
> Strength Tips & Tools: www.amazon.com/exec/obidos/ASIN/0596004478/ref%
> 3Dnosim/researchbuz03-20/102-1651225-2500151]:
>
> - Do not combine the above fielded search syntaxes with other ones or
>   the results may be unexpected.
> - For the feature to work, you must use lowercase for the field name; e.
>   g., use phonebook: instead of Phonebook:.
> - Wildcards don't work in phonebook search.
> - Negations don't work. Suppose you want to exclude Baylins in NY
>   from your search, the minus sign in front of NY will not work in the
>   following: phonebook:baylin -NY.
> - OR only works properly where you specify something other than a
>   state code and in the middle of your search string, e.g., phonebook:
>   fruit (lemons | oranges) CA. On the other hand, phonebook:fruit
>   (CA | NY) will not work, since Google will look for a state whose
>   code is the whole string (CA | NY).

- Similarly, use the rphonebook: field identifier for U.S. residential listings.

  🔍 Type rphonebook: smith dallas for someone having the name
  Smith in Dallas.

- Instead of the above, simply use phonebook: for either business or
  residential listings.

Company stock symbol: Google Help explains:

If you begin a query with the "stocks:" parameter, Google will treat the rest of the
query terms as stock ticker symbols, and will link to a page showing stock
information for those symbols. (Note you must type the ticker symbols, not the
company name.) This functionality is also available if you search just on the
stock symbols (e.g. "intc yhoo") and then click on the "Show stock quotes" link
on the results page.

🔍 stocks:intc yhoo will show
information about Intel and Yahoo.

with **at least one** of the words
stocks:intc yhoo

⚠ **Warnings:**

- You have to enter the field name **stocks:** in lowercase.
- A stock query may not function as expected if the **stocks:** field is used along with other field names in the search string. This should be a stand-alone field name in the context of the search string.

Website information: From Google Help:

The query "info:" will present some information that Google has about that web page. Note there can be no space between the "info:" and the web page url. This functionality is also

with **at least one** of the words
info:www.google.com

accessible by typing the web page url directly into a Google search box. For instance, "info:www.google.com" will show information about the Google homepage.

Advanced group search: Google provides a number of different methods to locate particular groups:

- Specify a particular group:

Group	Return only messages from the **group**	_(blank field)_ (Example: rec.games.misc, comp.os.*, *linux*)

You can also specify the above as a fielded search, as in **group: comp.os.***. The asterisk at the end, which is a wildcard, means find all further divisions into groups below that level.

- Specify a particular author or author e-mail address.

Return only messages where
the **author** is Chauncey Gardner

You can also specify author as a fielded search, as in **author:"Chauncey Gardner"**.

The author can be a full or partial name, and can be an e-mail address: e.g., **nilyab@yahoo.com**.

- Specify a particular message identifier:

> Find the message with **message**
> **ID** mod-ng-faq-1-98@swc.com

> Specifying other fields on the advanced group search entry form is dealt with elsewhere, as follows:
>
> - Specify a particular subject of discussion: ➪ Reference Section 6.2: Document file section or location.
> - Specify the message language: ➪ Reference Section 6.2: Document language.
> - Specify a range of dates: ➪ Reference Section 6.2: File age.
> - Set the offensive content filter: ➪ Reference Section 6.2: Potentially offensive content.
>
> ⚠ Other than group: and author:, the only field operator that works in group search is intitle: ➪ Reference Section 6.2: URL (resource) or site Internet address.

Advanced catalog search: In this specialized search interface, the user is able to choose:

> **Category**
> Return results from the category
> Any category
> Apparel & Accessories
> Arts & Crafts
> Automotive
> Books, Music & Film

- Category of the catalog through a drop-down menu.

- Catalog age, by distinguishing between "current" and "past" catalogs, using a radio button to select it.

> **Date**
> ⦿ Search only current catalogs
> ○ Search all catalogs, including past catalogs

Cache: When document links do not work, another potential way to get your desired content is using the cache: fielded search, which accesses files at the time they were indexed by Google.

> ➪ For an explanation of this feature, consult Reference Section 5.2: Additional links.

The query [cache:] will show the version of the web page that Google has in its cache. Note there can be no space between the "cache:" and the web page url [Google Help].

> with **at least one** of the words
> cache:www.google.com

Reference Manual Section 6.2:
Metadata-Based
Search Filters
452
File Content
Characteristics

> ⚠ You must enter all the field names in the above fielded searches in lowercase for the fielded search to work.

Local search: Location as a filter is discussed in Appendix 6.2: Geographical region of the server. However, where the server is versus where the business or residence is located are not necessarily related, so part of the discussion of that filter probably belongs here. Nevertheless, to avoid duplication, we discuss the subject in that section.

MSN Search

Specialty searches associated with the MSN subject directory provide a large variety of further metadata-based filters based on other document characteristics. The following tables will give you an idea of some of these field filters in relation to each of the top-level (or sometimes lower) subject directory branches.

> 🔍 **Local search:** Location as a filter is discussed in Appendix 6.2: Geographical region of the server. However, where the server is versus where the business or residence is located are not necessarily related, so part of the discussion of that filter probably belongs here. Nevertheless, to avoid duplication, we discuss the subject in that section.

To see the various fields in each case, you will need to expand the drop-down menu boxes, either by visiting the MSN subject directory website. See ➪ special. msn.com/insidemsn.armx, for one version, or special.msn.com/directory.armx, for another, somewhat different, arrangement of this directory.

General	AlltheWeb	AltaVista	Copernic	Google	MSN

Going Places	
City Guides	Enter the city name [ ] or search by zip code: [ ]
Traffic Updates	Enter [ZIP Code]
Maps & Directions, & Local Traffic	Country/Region [United States] Street Address [ ] City [ ] State [ ] ZIP Code [ ] [Get Map] [Get Directions]

Reference Manual Section 6.2:
Metadata-Based
Search Filters
453
File Content
Characteristics

Currency Converter	Number of units: [ ]
	Currency to convert from: [US dollars]
	Currency to convert to: [US dollars]

Travel (Air Tickets at expedia .com)	⦿ Flight only ⦿ Hotel only ⦿ Car only ⦿ Cruise
	⦿ Flight + Hotel ⦿ Flight + Hotel + Car ⦿ Hotel + Car
	Departing from: [ ] Depart: [mm/dd/yy] [Anytime]
	Going to: [ ] Return: [mm/dd/yy] [Anytime]
	Adults: (age 19-64) [1] Seniors: (65+) [0] Children: (0-18) [0]

Car Rentals (at expedia .com)	**Where do you want to pick up your car?**
	⦿ At an airport ⦿ Near a Place ⦿ Near a US address
	Pick-up airport or city name (e.g. DEN, or Denver): [ ]
	Place name (e.g. New York or Times Square): [ ]
	Street: [ ] City: [ ] State: [ ] Zip code: [ ]
	Pick-up date: (MM/DD/YY) [mm/dd/yy] [11:00 AM]
	Drop-off date: (MM/DD/YY) [mm/dd/yy] [11:00 AM]
	☐ My drop-off location is different from pick-up location.
	Drop-off location: [ ] Search how far from this place? [10 mile(s)]
	Do you have a car class preference? ⦿ [No Preference]
	⦿ Minivan ⦿ SUV ⦿ Sports Car ⦿ Convertible
	Do you have a discount code?
	⦿ None ⦿ Corporate or Contracted Rate (Code required)
	⦿ Special or Advertised Rate (Code required)
	Do you have a car company preference?
	Rental car company: [Preferred Vendors]

Look it up		

| White Pages | First or Initial [   ] Last [   ] (required) |
| | City [   ] State [All States] |

Yellow Pages	Category (browse): [ ]
	or Business Name: [ ]
	City: [ ] State: [choose a state...]

Financial	
Money	Search MSN Money [_____] Symbol(s): [_____] [Get Quote]

Entertainment	
Celebrities	Select search type [music artist] Enter your search query [_____]
Entertainment News	Select search type [movie] Enter your search query [_____]
Music Radio Plus	Select search type [artist] Enter your search query [_____] Also see ⇨ Reference Section 6.2: Additional multi-media file content characteristics.
TV Listings	Select search type [show] Enter your search query [_____] Type your ZIP or postal code: ZIP: [_____]
Tickets (Ticket Master)	[Choose Event] [This Weekend] [Enter Zip Code or City] Enter City or Zip Code [_____] [Select Category] [Select Date]

People	
MSN Member Directory (Options from form for advanced search, if you follow the link from that page)	Sympatico / MSN Nickname [_____] First Name [_____] Last Name [_____] Gender [No Preference] Age Range [No Preference] Marital Status [No Preference] Country/Region [No Preference] [_____] City [_____] ☐ View only profiles with pictures ☐ Include adult profiles in search results

Reference Manual Section 6.2:
Metadata-Based
Search Filters

455

File Content
Characteristics

Buy	
Cars	No specialized search terms entry box. You can only find your information from options (such as you see below) or from links, or from a general Web search. However, search entry boxes may appear at levels below this node in the subject directory hierarchy. ⊙ New ⊙ Used Make: [ ] Model: [ ] Find by Category: [Category:]

Living	
Find a Job (URL given here for advanced search option, if you follow the link from that page)	Enter Keywords(s): [ ] Using: [All of These Words] Select Job Category (Up to 3): [- Select Job Category 1 -] [- Select Job Category 2 -] [- Select Job Category 3 -] Select up to 3 locations: Enter City 1: [ ] Select State 1: [- ALL -] Enter City 2: [ ] Select State 2: [- ALL -] Enter City 3: [ ] Select State 3: [- ALL -] Include Jobs Within: [30 miles] of these locations [ ] ☐ Exclude national and regional jobs Jobs Posted Within: [Last 30 Days] Your Degree: [Graduate Degree] ☑ Include all lower degrees Employment Type: ☑ Full-time ☑ Contractor ☐ Part-Time ☑ Intern Salary Range: [$0] [> $120,000] ☐ Exclude jobs that don't include salary information
Get a Date	I am [M] seeking [W] between [18] and [35] Located [25] miles of zip/postal code: [city or 7⊞] ☑ Photos only
Buy a House	City: [ ] State: [Select a State] Zip: [ ] **Or** Price Range: [$0] [No Maximum]

Additional multi-media file content characteristics

⇨ For more explanation, see Chapter 6: File content characteristics.

Examples of this include the artist, song name, and duration of play of audio or video files.

AlltheWeb, AltaVista, Copernic, and Google have a number of these features.

General	AlltheWeb	AltaVista	Copernic	Google	MSN

AlltheWeb

- Its advanced Pictures search has options for image type and background:

> **Image Type:** ☑ All types ☐ Color ☐ Grayscale ☐ Line Art
> **Background:** ⦿ Both types ⦿ Transparent ⦿ Non-Transparent

- Its advanced Video search has options for video delivery method:

> **Streams or Downloads:** ⦿ Both ⦿ Downloads Only ⦿ Streams Only

- Its former (now discontinued) advanced FTP search had filters applicable to files of any type. Details of this are given elsewhere (⇨ Reference Section 6.2: Additional document file content characteristics).

AltaVista

Has special searches for video, image, and audio. All of these work in essentially the same way.

- The video and audio searches have "duration of play" options. Using the appropriate interface for audio or video file formats, choose the play duration as less than or greater than one minute.

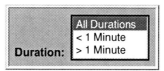

- Its image search has options for image resolution, for black and white versus color images, and to distinguish photos from graphics from buttons/banners.

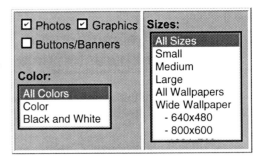

In addition, it has options for including "sources" for obtaining findings. Source can mean anything from a type of Internet application, to a particular subject matter area, to a partner site. These can be selected using a drop-down menu options box, as shown here.

Copernic

Features in this area are the same as for document files (➪ Reference Section 6.2: Additional document file content characteristics).

Google

Use its advanced image search to specify image size or coloration.

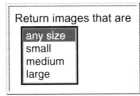
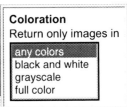

MSN Search

The Music and TV searches from the MSN subject directory allow you to filter sound files by genre and TV shows by show, keyword, or person, as you see in the drop-down menus here.

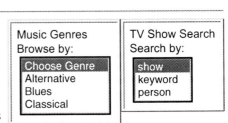

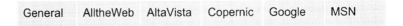

General   AlltheWeb   AltaVista   Copernic   Google   MSN

Hosting Site Characteristics

Geographical region of server

⇨ For more explanation, refer to Chapter 6: Hosting site characteristics.

This restricts the findings to files located on servers in particular continents, countries, states, provinces, or cities, etc.

A general problem for many search engines is that geographical region is determined from the domain suffix, that is, the highest level of the domain name. Unfortunately, servers in many countries often use suffixes such as net, com, gov, org, and so on, rather than the country domain suffix, thus making it more difficult to identify geographical region.

All our featured search engines can restrict files by geography, although the specific breakdown into regions varies significantly. Google does not handle geographical distinctions except in its ability to filter by domain suffix code.

⇨ For information on specifying the domain so the domain suffix can be used to identify geographical region, see Reference Section 6.2: URL (resource) or site Internet address.

| General | AlltheWeb | AltaVista | Copernic | Google | MSN |

AlltheWeb

Determines geographical regions from the domain suffix. They can be specified in AlltheWeb's advanced Web search using the drop-down menu seen here.

AltaVista

Geographical location is done by country. This can be specified dynamically (in connection with each search) or by default (based on user preference settings).

- To dynamically choose the country, click on the default country name (e. g., AltaVista U.S.A.) in the upper right-hand corner of one of the simple search interface screens. Then make your one choice from the following radio buttons (see next page):

Choose your country

O Australia - Australia	O France - France	O Portugal - Portugal
O Austria - Österreich	O Germany - Deutschland	O Spain - España
O Belgium (French) - Belgique	O India - India	O Sweden - Sverige
O Belgium (Dutch) - België	O Ireland - Ireland	O Switzerland (German) - Schweiz
O Brazil - Brasil	O Italy - Italia	O Switzerland (French) - Suisse
O Canada (English) - Canada	O Korea - 한국	O Switzerland (Italian) - Svizzera
O Canada (French) - Canada	O Netherlands - Nederland	O U.K. - United Kingdom
O Denmark - Danmark	O New Zealand - New Zealand	⦿ U.S. - United States
O Finland - Suomi	O Norway - Norge	

- You can also reach the above set of choices from the "Settings" interface to establish a default country setting, which then appears as a radio button on all search interfaces. This allows you to choose between searching websites within that country or searching worldwide (the default).

SEARCH: ⦿ Worldwide O U.S. RESULTS IN: O All languages ⦿ English, Spanish

Note: Your country setting is related to the way AltaVista makes document language choices available to you and the default interface language.

⇨ For more details, see:

- Reference Section 6.2: Document language.
- Reference Section 6.4: Document language.

Copernic

Copernic provides a drop-down menu for choosing region when doing a "Find in Results" procedure. You can see the regions available in the accompanying screenshot seen here.

> Any
> Africa
> Asia
> Australasia
> Central America
> Europe
> Middle East
> North America
> South America

Google

Google does not have filters on most of its search entry pages for selecting by geographical region. So, you have to use the domain suffix filters (which really are what most of the other featured search engines use anyways for geographical region): ⇨ Appendix 6.2: URL (resource) or site Internet address. Notwithstanding:

- In its simple search interface, click on "Language Tools." One of the boxes there enables selection of a particular country. In that interface, enter a search term in the appropriate box and then select the country from the appropriate drop-down menu, which you see here.

- Third-party Google Ultimate Interface (⇨ www.faganfinder.com/google. html) also provides filtering by country in Web, directory, groups, and images searches.
- Geographical region of the server is also a filter in Local search. However, this is presumably only one factor in determining the location of an organization or business. Locality filters are also based partially on file content characteristics, and are therefore also mentioned in Appendix 6.2: Additional document file content characteristics.

MSN Search

To specify geographical region, type the search term in the text box, and then use the "Country/Region" drop-down menu of the "Search Builder" (see next page) one or more times to select the appropriate country(ies). This automatically inserts the loc: operator parameter followed by a 2-character country country code into the search string. If you select more than one country, an OR is placed between the alternatives.

You can also type this operator parameter and country code directly into the search string.

> 🔟 Enter cat dog (loc:BE OR loc:AT) to search on the terms cat and dog on websites hosted in Belgium or Austria.

Geographical region of the server is also a filter in Local search. However, this is presumably only one factor in determining the location of an organization or business. Locality filters are also based partially on file content characteristics, and are therefore also mentioned in Appendix 6.2: Additional document file content characteristics.

To restrict the search to files hosted on servers local to your area, use the "Near Me" button on the search entry interface. This button is, however, currently available only if your settings indicate that you are using the United States search entry interface. In the case of other countries, you will get a checkbox at the bottom of the search entry screen, allowing you to restrict searches to that country albeit not particular locations within that country.

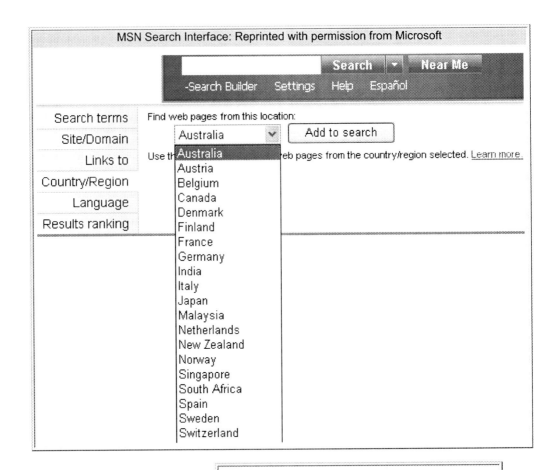
MSN Search Interface: Reprinted with permission from Microsoft

A "Near Me" search is, in effect, a Local search, and the default location depends on your country and locality preference setting values. But, you can change that dynamically, for an individual search, regardless of your preference settings, by including a different city name in the text box for location in Local search.

> Initially, MSN Search automatically sets your search entry interface country default (based on your IP address), but you can change that using preference settings, as explained in ⇨ Section 6.4: Interface language or style. MSN will also default your city/state location if you are within the U.S. based on its automatic determination of the location of your Internet server. Again, you can, reset this by preference settings, as explained in ⇨ Reference Section 6.4: Other filter setting preferences.

Also, if you do a Web search and include a valid American city name, but do not press the "Near Me" button to start your search, a number of local search findings with be flashed in above the Web results. Clicking on one of those will bring you to the results page for the corresponding Local search.

General   AlltheWeb   AltaVista   Copernic   Google   MSN

Reference Manual Section 6.2:
Metadata-Based
Search Filters
462
Hosting Site
Characteristics

URL (resource) or site Internet address

> ⇨ For more explanation, see Chapter 6: Hosting site characteristics.

A URL (uniform resource locator or Internet address) consists of:

- **Protocol identifier:** indicates the type of Internet application — http:// (Hypertext Transfer Protocol) for the Web, FTP:// (File Transfer Protocol), Mailto: (for e-mail), and so on.
- **Site or host identification** (server address, full domain name): includes the domain suffix at the end. The host identifier is usually a name, although it can also be an IP (Internet Protocol) number such as 28.1.1.128.

All our featured search engines can limit or exclude particular findings using domain names, although the way they achieve this varies. Currently, only MSN Search can filter using the numeric IP address.

General	AlltheWeb	AltaVista	Copernic	Google	MSN

AlltheWeb

Domain filters: In its advanced Web or advanced news document searches, particular domain names can be limited or excluded from the findings, using the text entry boxes shown here.

> Filter results from specific domains (com, gov, dell.com, etc.)
> **Domain Filters -** Include results from [   ]
> Exclude results from [   ]

As explained in AlltheWeb Help:

Multiple entries in either box are allowed, and should be separated by spaces. The user may also "only include" some domains, while "excluding" others. An important note here is that these filters operate at the domain level only, (i.e. dell. com) and not at the host level (www.dell.com), so the former is a valid entry, the latter is not.

Specification of Internet address using operator parameters: You can also specify Internet address using the site: and url: fielded searches, that is, with operator parameters. AlltheWeb Help [www.alltheweb.com/help/faqs/ query_language] describes it as follows:

Reference Manual Section 6.2:
Metadata-Based
Search Filters
463
Hosting Site
Characteristics

- **site:** Enter auctions site:shopping.com. Finds pages for auctions within shopping.com. This can be helpful in obtaining highly relevant results from a specific site. By default, the site: keyword anchors the value of the keyword to match the *end* of the hostname, in this case, shopping.com. This query will find pages for auctions within shopping.com, but not in shopping.com.sg.
- **url:** Enter URL:football. Finds pages with the specific word or phrase in the URL. This example will find all pages that have the term football anywhere in the URL (e.g. http://www.domain.com/football.html would be in the results).

Interesting features of the former AlltheWeb: We cover these here for instructional purposes, as they provide examples of other ways in which sites or file paths may be obtained. FTP search no longer exists in today's AlltheWeb, and searching by IP number is no longer supported.

1. **IP-style specification of Internet address:** In AlltheWeb's former version of advanced

   > Only find results from the following IP-address(es) and/or range(s) 66.77.74.20/24

   Web search, the IP (Internet Protocol) number was used for the host part of the URL. However, it is first important that you gain a technical understanding of how the IP protocol numbers worked, or at least what they signified. You were able to use ranges of IP numbers, e.g., to choose by class of IP address.

   As explained in a former version of AlltheWeb Help:

   The IP Address Filter enables you to restrict search to, or exclude results from, web servers with specified IP-addresses or within specified IP-address ranges.

   An IP-address is specified using the common "dotted" syntax, e.g. 66.77.74.20 (IP-address for AlltheWeb.com). An IP-address range can be specified using a number of common syntax:

   - Address/Network bits, e.g. 66.77.74.20/24
   - Address/Netmask, e.g. 66.77.74.20/255.255.255.0
   - Start address:End address, e.g. 66.77.74.0:66.77.74.255

   No prefix in front of an IP-address (or range) will restrict all results to this specification while a minus (-) will exclude that IP-address (or range) from the results.

   If there is an error parsing one of the IP-addresses (or ranges), the text "ERROR:" will occur in front of the problematic term. Remove this text and correct the error before you resubmit your query. If you don't, the problematic term will be removed.

Reference Manual Section 6.2:
Metadata-Based
Search Filters

464

Hosting Site
Characteristics

For example: Restricting a result to web servers only with IP-addresses in AlltheWeb.com's class C net while excluding AlltheWeb.com itself would give the IP-address restriction: "66.77.74.20/24 -66.77.74.20" (do not include quotes). Image below shows what happens when using the invalid IP-address 666.77.74.20 for AlltheWeb.com.

2. **FTP search specification of Internet address:** In

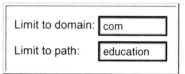

its former version of advanced FTP search, you were allowed to specify a particular domain name and a path to the file.

To find files in the private company sector that have the word education in the path to the file name, you could have entered what you see here.

| Limit to domain: | com |
| Limit to path: | education |

AlltheWeb Help explained it as follows:

- **Limit to Domain:** Only get hits where the hosts have the given parameter at the end of their domain name. Having **edu** here would exclude hits from everywhere but *.edu.

The "Limit to path" string actually allowed term variation logic:

- **Limit to Path:** Limit results to files with this term in its path (directory name). Multiple terms are separated by colons, negation is done by prefixing each term with an exclamation mark. **For example:**

  › RedHat - Include only files with "RPMS" in the directory name
  › !mac - Exclude files with "mac" in the directory name
  › netbsd:openbsd - Include only files with "netbsd" or "openbsd" in the directory name.

AltaVista

1. In its advanced Web search, you can choose:

- The domain part of the URL, or any part of it.
- The URL as a whole, or any part of it, including just the host (server identification) part.

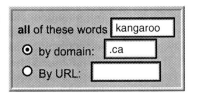 Choose the domain ca, for Canada in conjunction with the word kangaroo to find that word on servers whose host name ends with a Canadian identifier.

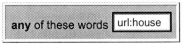

2. Type the field url: followed by the search term in one of the appropriate text boxes, e.g., url:house will find the string house somewhere in the URL.

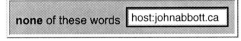

3. To zero in on just the host identifier part of the URL string (in this instance meaning the full domain name, rather than the IP number), use the host: field, as in host:johnabbott.ca.

4. To zero in on any part of the host name, including just the domain suffix, type the search term along with the field domain: followed by the domain suffix in any text box.

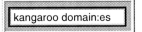 To find the term kangaroo on a website located in Spain, enter kangaroo domain:es.

Copernic

Here you can apply domain filters during a "Find in Results" procedure. Use the following checkboxes and accompanying text entry boxes in the "Advanced Filters" dialog box. Some guidelines:

- More than one domain string can be entered in each box.
- A comma followed by a blank is needed to separate entries.
- An exact domain name can be entered in full or an exact domain suffix preceded by a period.

Reference Manual Section 6.2:
Metadata-Based
Search Filters
466
Hosting Site
Characteristics

Google

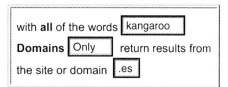

Occurrences: Return results where my terms occur
- anywhere in the page
- in the title of the page
- in the text of the page
- **in the url of the page**
- in links to the page

- In the "Occurrences" section of the advanced Web search entry form, choose "in the url of the page."
- Type the search term in one of the appropriate text boxes. Then, in the "Domains" text box, type the domain suffix, making sure that the "Only" (as opposed to "Don't" to exclude a domain) is selected in the drop-down menu.

🦘 Type kangaroo in the appropriate text box, and in the domains text box type es, for Spain.

with **all** of the words [kangaroo]
Domains [Only] return results from
the site or domain [.es]

- To specify just the domain suffix part of the host identifier or any part of it in Google's advanced image search entry interface, enter the necessary string into the text box provided for this purpose.

Domain: Return images from the site or domain [.com]

Specification using operator parameters:

- allinurl: To quote [Google Help]: If you start a query with [allinurl:], Google will restrict the results to those with all of the query words in the url.

  Note that [allinurl:] works on words, not url components. In particular, it ignores punctuation. Thus, [allinurl: foo/bar] will restrict the results to page with the words "foo" and "bar" in the url, but won't require that they be separated by a slash within that url, that they be adjacent, or that they be in that particular word order. There is currently no way to enforce these constraints.

  For instance, type [allinurl: google search] will return only documents that have both "google" and "search" in the url.

  with **all** of the words
  [allinurl: google search]

- inurl: To quote [Google Help]: If you include [inurl:] in your query, Google will restrict the results to documents containing that word in the url. Note there can be no space between the "inurl:" and the following word.

  ... [inurl:] works on words, not url components. In particular, it ignores punctuation. Thus, in the query [google inurl:foo/bar], the "inurl:" parameter will affect only the word "foo", which is the single word following the inurl: parameter, and will not affect the word bar.

The query [google inurl:foo inurl:bar] can be used to require both "foo" and "bar" to be in the url.

Putting "inurl:" in front of every word in your query is equivalent to putting "allinurl:" at the front of your query: [inurl:google inurl:search] is the same as [allinurl: google search].

For instance, [inurl:google search] will return documents that mention the word "google" in their url, and mention the word "search" anywhere in the document (url or no).

> with **at least one** of the words
>
> inurl:google inurl:search

- site: Just the host (website/server) part of the URL can be specified as a fielded search with site. To quote [Google Help]:

  > with **at least one** of the words
  >
  > site:www.google.com

  If you include [site:] in your query, Google will restrict the results to those websites in the given domain. Note there can be no space between the "site:" and the domain .... For instance, [help site:www.google.com] will find pages about help within www.google.com. [help site:com] will find pages about help within .com url's.

⚠ **Warnings for allinurl:, inurl:, and site: fields:**

- You must enter the field name in lowercase for the search to work.
- You should not enter the protocol prefix, such as HTTP://, in a URL or site address. In the case of the site: field, it will be ignored; in the case of allinurl: and inurl:, you are likely to obtain no results from your search.

MSN Search

To specify domain, enter the search term in the text box, and then use the "Site/Domain" drop-down menu of the "Search Builder" (see next page) to select the appropriate domain(s). You can enter several domains separated by spaces in the text box, along with just one of the two radio buttons to include or exclude the listed domain(s). This automatically inserts the site: operator parameter followed by the domain details you typed into the search string. Note that you can specify just the domain suffix, such as edu, or a larger part of the name, or the entire name, such as berk.edu.

You can also type this operator parameter and the domain list(s) directly into the search string.

⬚ Type cat dog site:gov edu -site:berk.edu to to restrict findings to the gov and edu domains, unless the domain is berk. edu.

In addition to the fielded search filtering with the site: operator parameter, you can also use the following fielded search identifiers:

- For a full URL, including the site, the path to the file, and the file, use url:, as in url:search.msn.com/docs/toolbar.aspx?FORM=TBDD2.
- For a string of characters embedded in a URL, use inurl:, as in inurl:docs/toolbar.aspx.
- For the domain suffix part of a site, you might want to try loc:com, as an example.
- To find one or more domains (sites) hosted at a given server IP address, use the ip: operator parameter, as in ip:207.46.249.252.

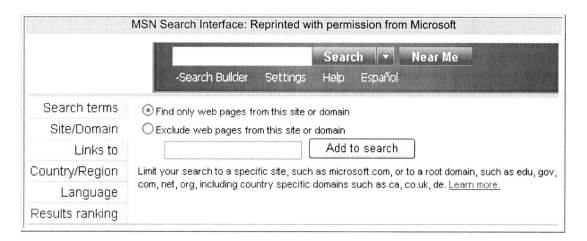

MSN Search Interface: Reprinted with permission from Microsoft

General   AlltheWeb   AltaVista   Copernic   Google   MSN

Findings shown per site

⇨ For more explanation, refer to Chapter 6:
Hosting site characteristics.

Many websites have hundreds, if not thousands of different pages, interlinked in an assortment of ways. There are numerous methods to restrict the number of findings.

Various parameters exist in our featured search engines, which allow you to control the number of findings shown per website.

AlltheWeb

You can control the number of findings shown in several ways:

To display all the findings for a website:

- Limit the search to that website ("domain").
- Change the "site collapse" preference setting to allow all findings for a site to display (⇨ Reference Section 6.4: Findings page organization).

⇨ For directions to specify a single domain, refer to:

- Reference Section 5.2: More same-site findings.
- Reference Section 6.2: URL (resource) or site Internet address.

For illustrative purposes, we include a description of how the former AlltheWeb FTP search used to handle the problem of same-site findings. You could do the following:

Max hits: 15
Hits: Max matches:
Max hits/match:

- Control the number of times the same file is found (is "hit") on different FTP sites, or even within the same FTP site.
- Control how many files are "matched" (found) per site and the number of hits per match (per file).

AltaVista

To display more than two findings per website and to allow all of them to be displayed, use the "site collapse" parameter. This is an option on AltaVista's advanced search interface.

When site collapse is on (check box is checked), AltaVista shows a maximum of two results per site. When site collapse is off, AltaVista shows all results, listed in order of relevance, with results from the same site indented below the first result from the site [AltaVista Help].

It may appear AltaVista is ignoring this parameter setting, showing only two findings per website. This may occur because the different findings from the same site do not appear one after the other due to differences in how AltaVista ranks their relevance.

As a result of site collapse, the second finding below from URL
www.med.jhu.edu/hg/faculty.html is indented:

Display: ☑ site collapse (on/off)

Human Genetics
... Acad Sci USA 91: 974-978, 1994. STEPHEN **BAYLIN**, M.D., Professor of Oncology Molecular
Determinants of ... L, Zink MC, Mankowski JL, Donovan DM and **Baylin** SB. Mice Deficient in the
Candidate Tumor
...www.med.jhu.edu/hg/facultyhome.html •
 Translate More pages from www.med.jhu.edu

   Welcome to Adobe GoLive 5
   ... Acad Sci USA 91: 974-978, 1994. STEPHEN **BAYLIN**

Copernic

Findings shown per site cannot be controlled by a filter here. Depending on the
source search engine defaults, only the default number of results per site are
displayed. You can select all the findings from a given site by doing a "Find in
Results" procedure. However, this does not control the number of findings per
site sourced from each search engine.

Google

To display all the findings
for a website, you need to
limit the search to that
website ("domain").
Otherwise, only up to two
findings per site are
displayed.

⇨ For directions to specify a single domain,
refer to:

- Reference Section 5.2: More same-site
  findings.
- Reference Section 6.2: URL (resource) or
  site Internet address.

MSN Search

To display all the findings for a website, you need to limit the search to that
website ("domain"). Otherwise, only one, two (the default), or three findings per
site are displayed, based on a preference setting: ⇨ Reference Section 6.4: Findings
page organization.

> ⇨ For directions to specify a single domain, refer to:
>
> - Reference Section 5.2: More same-site findings.
> - Reference Section 6.2: URL (resource) or site Internet address.

General   AlltheWeb   AltaVista   Copernic   Google   MSN

Related Documents or Sites

Similarity of meaning

> ⇨ For more explanation, consult Chapter 6: Related documents or sites.

Phrases such as "Similar Pages" or "concept search" are used to refer to various relationships between files. On the basis of these, you may want to look at certain other suggested files or websites to satisfy a search.

Of our featured search engines, only Google can find related pages or sites based on parameters entered in their search entry interfaces, and on a "Similar Pages" link from its listing of each finding.

General   AlltheWeb   AltaVista   Copernic   Google   MSN

AlltheWeb

Has no search filters for this feature, although it does provide certain links on its findings pages by suggesting terms to narrow the search (⇨ Reference Section 5.2: Links for refining searches).

AltaVista

Has no search filters for this feature.

Copernic

Filters based on similarity of meaning are unavailable, although it does provide certain links on its findings pages by extracting search keywords (⇨ Reference Section 5.2: Related pages or terms).

Google

> Google also has links to similar pages on its findings pages:
> ⇨ Reference Section 5.2: Related pages or terms.

- To search to any site that has the similar or related subject: Type in the field related: followed by a URL.

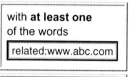

  related:www.google.com will list webpages that are similar to the Google homepage.

> with **at least one** of the words
> related:www.abc.com

- To find similar pages: Use "Page Specific Search" on the advanced web search interface. Just type the URL into the "Find pages similar to the page" text box.

> Find pages similar to the page
> www.abc.com/hlp.htm

MSN Search

Has no search filters for similarity of meaning.

General	AlltheWeb	AltaVista	Copernic	Google	MSN

Inverse page links

> ⇨ For more explanation, consult Chapter 6: Related documents or sites.

This involves finding documents that link *to* a particular URL, rather than *from* it.

Our featured search engines are quite similar in their ability to handle inverse relationships, except Copernic, which cannot do it. MSN Search has the extra ability to find links to *any* page in a domain.

General	AlltheWeb	AltaVista	Copernic	Google	MSN

AlltheWeb

Can limit results to files that link to a given URL. To do this, use the "link:" field identifier as an operator parameter. link: must be in lowercase.

Reference Manual Section 6.2:
Metadata-Based
Search Filters

473

Related Documents
or Sites

KG Enter link:www.alltheweb.com to find all webpages that link to www.alltheweb.com.

You can also use AlltheWeb's URL Investigator: ⇨ Reference Section 5.3: Other user tools.

AltaVista

This feature is achieved by typing the field "link:" followed by the exact link in an appropriate text box, as in link:www.gamespot.com. link: must be in lowercase.

AltaVista also has a special webmaster search interface for finding inverse page links (⇨ Reference Section 5.3: Other user tools).

Copernic

Inverse page links feature is unavailable.

Google

It can limit results to files that link to a given URL in the following ways:

- Type the field link: following by the exact link in an appropriate text box, as in link:www. baylin.com.

- Use the "Page Specific Search > Links" section of the form.

△

Warnings:

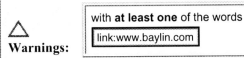

- The field name link: must be in lowercase.
- Link: is a stand-alone kind of field operator. Thus, the link: syntax cannot be used along with any other kind of fielded search such as domain: or inurl:.
- Inverse links go to a specific page. Google has no direct way of finding the links to all the pages in a domain (on a site).

Reference Manual Section 6.2:
Metadata-Based
Search Filters

474

Related Documents
or Sites

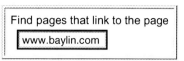
Find pages that link to the page

www.baylin.com

Type www.gamespot.com into the "Find pages that link to the page" text box.

Note: If you enter a site's URL as your search keyword, Google not only displays a link to it, along with a brief description and the normal links to cached and similar pages for the site, but also links to pages that:

- Link to the site entered.
- Contain the site's URL.

MSN Search

To limit results to pages that link to a given URL, use the "Links to" option of the "Search Builder" (see below) to select the appropriate domain(s) (using the full domain name) or specific resources (URL's) within those domains. You must enter one, and not more than one, full domain name or URL at a time.

You can add many successive domains/URL's in succession, in which case OR is automatically inserted in the generated search string between the different ones. Each one is specified in the search string with the link: operator parameter followed by the domain/URL details you typed.

You can also type this operator parameter and the domain(s)/URL(s) directly into the search string.

Type link:www.microsoft.com OR link:www. searchhelpcenter.com/index.html to find pages that link either to the full Microsoft domain name or to the index.html page's URL at www.searchhelpcenter.com.

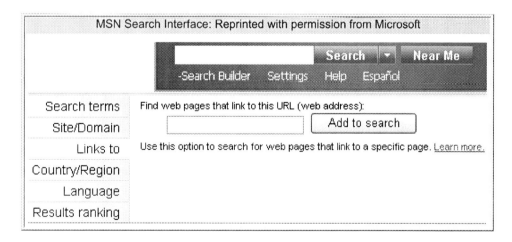

In addition to the link: fielded search, which simply identify which domains link to a given domain, MSN Search also has a linkdomain: operator parameter. With this, you can find links from other sites to any page (not just the single one specified) in a given site.

> Type linkdomain:www.searchhelpcenter.com to find pages that link to *any* pages hosted at www.searchhelpcenter.com. By doing this, you can find sites that link, say, to pages below the home page, in addition to ones that link specifically to the home page.

General	AlltheWeb	AltaVista	Copernic	Google	MSN

Reference Manual Section 6.2:
Metadata-Based
Search Filters

476

Related Documents
or Sites

Reference Manual Section 6.3: Findings Display & Handling Parameters

⇨ This section cross-links with Chapter 6: Findings Display & Handling Parameters.

Organization of Findings Display

Overall ordering

While the usual way of ordering findings is according to relevance or importance, the user sometimes has other choices.

⇨ For more explanation, see:

- Chapter 6: Organization of findings display.
- Reference Section 5.2: Overall ordering.

Our featured search engines vary in their ability to handle ordering of display of findings on a results page. The default for ordering is always by relevance. However:

- You can often re-sequence the findings *on a post-processing basis*. This is especially true for Copernic, which has all kinds of regrouping and sorting abilities. With AltaVista, AlltheWeb, and Google, you can also sequence results of News searches by date. Google has additional options to sequence directory and groups searches using findings display choices.

- You can sometimes instruct the search engine to sequence the findings in a particular way *in advance of* producing its findings:

  › **MSN Search:** you can specify that equally relevant findings be sorted by degree of finding update frequency, exactness of match, site popularity, or some combination thereof.

  › **AlltheWeb:** you can tell the News document search in advance to present findings in order of date rather than by relevance.

  › **Google:** using certain third-party search tools, you can cause sequencing to tend to be in a certain order, or explicitly achieve a different order.

General	AlltheWeb	AltaVista	Copernic	Google	MSN

Reference Manual Section 6.3:
Findings Display &
Handling Parameters

477

Organization of
Findings Display

AlltheWeb

Sort results - ⊙ Relevance ○ Date

To choose whether findings are to be displayed in order of relevance or of date: check the appropriate radio button on the advanced News search *entry* interface.

The News search *findings* page also has a control to sort the findings by date or by relevance, seen here.

Sort by: Relevance ▸ Date

AltaVista

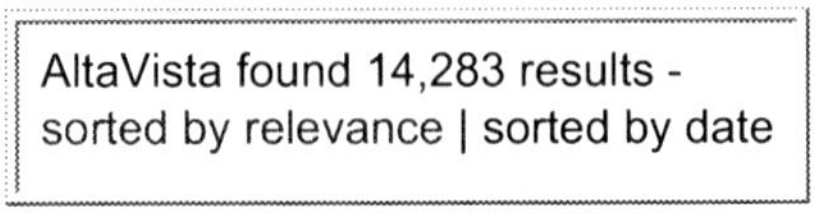

AltaVista found 14,283 results - sorted by relevance | sorted by date

Using controls at the top of the results listing, News search findings can be sorted by date or by relevance.

Copernic

Here you can control the overall ordering of the findings display on a post-processing basis, after you have downloaded the metadata (the results list). Otherwise, Copernic uses the relevance orderings of the various search engines it sources. It uses its own algorithms, however, to decide which search engine's findings to display first when more than one search engine is sourced.

The ordering parameters used for a given search are stored along with it in the search history folder.

Using the drop-down menu controls, you can group and/or sort the results list. If you both group and sort, the sorting occurs within the group, thus in effect providing a two-level sort.

You can group by:

- **Score:** relevancy ranking.
- **Domain:** host part of URL of a finding.
- **Status:**
    - ○ **New:** finding is from the latest search run and has not yet been accessed.

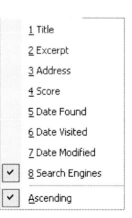

- › **Visited:** finding has been accessed.
- › **Saved:** finding has been saved on the searcher's computer.
- › **Annotated:** finding has been annotated during review of the findings list.
- › **Checkmarked:** user has checked the finding using the checkbox provided on the results list for each finding.

- **Date:**

  - › **Found:** date the search was run.
  - › **Visited:** date the searcher accessed the finding by linking from results list to the Internet.

  - › **Modified:** date of finding; in effect, date the crawler found the file.

    ⇨ For a screenshot showing grouping of findings by date modified, refer to Chapter 4: Case #1: Stock Investment Search.

- **Annotation Contents:** what the search entered as an annotation for the finding.
- **Languages:** finding language, as detected during Optimal analysis, if optimal analysis was set for the search.
- **Same Contents:** whether two files are the same, despite differences in their URL's, as detected during Optimal analysis.

You can sort by:

- **Title:** title of finding, if it is a document.
- **Excerpt:** text produced due to certain choices connected with Optimal analysis.
- **Address:** URL of finding.
- **Score:** relevancy ranking of finding.
- **Date:**

  - › **Found:** date the search was run.
  - › **Visited:** date the searcher accessed the finding by linking to it from results list.

The grouping menu options shown:

1 No Group
2 Score
3 Domain
4 Status: New
5 Status: Visited
6 Status: Saved
7 Status: Annotated
8 Status: Checkmarked
9 Date Found
A Date Visited
B Date Modified
C Annotation Contents
D Languages
E Same Contents

The sorting menu options shown:

1 Title
2 Excerpt
3 Address
4 Score
5 Date Found
6 Date Visited
7 Date Modified
8 Search Engines
Ascending

- **Modified:** date of finding; in effect, date the crawler found the file.
- **Search Engines:** search engine used to source the result.

Note that "Ascending" is checked in the above menu (previous page). If it is unchecked, the sort is in descending order.

The above grouping and sorting options only apply when the results are displayed in the Copernic application pane. When you view the findings in your browser window, you cannot group them. You can sort them, however, based on title, score, and address, as you can in the Copernic application pane, shown here.

● Sort by Score
Sort by Title
Sort by Address
Sort Ascending
✔ Display Address
✔ Use Saved Pages
Open Copernic Agent
Close Toolbar

Google

You cannot pre-specify how Google must sort its findings, but the sequence in which you place your search terms affects the ordering of the results you get. Thus, you should enter search terms in the sequence in which you would expect to find them on the pages for which you are searching.

A search for fat nose gives priority to pages about fatty tissue found in noses, while the query nose fat gives priority to pages about noses with a fat appearance.

As well, Google lists pages where your search terms are found nearer to one another before those where they are farther apart.

For certain types of search, you can sort certain findings lists on a *post-processing* basis, as follows:

- News and Groups search results can be sorted by date or by relevance using controls on the findings pages.

  Sorted by relevance   Sort by date

- Directory searches have a link to sort the findings alphabetically by title.

Finally, among the several third-party products built around Google:

- **Anacubis** (⇨ www.anacubis.com/Products/ViewManager) allows users to select different visual arrangements of Google results and to post-process findings.

- **GAPS** (➪ www.staggernation.com/cgi-bin/gaps.cgi),
which specializes in proximity search (➪ Reference
Section 6.1: Proximity), allows you to pre-specify the
results sort order by title, URL, normal Google
ranking, or proximity.

MSN Search

For Web search, you can specify that equally relevant findings be sorted by
degree of finding update frequency, exactness of match, site popularity, or any
three of these in different combinations of degrees for each. You can modify the
emphasis placed on each of these secondary factors using the following sliders
(shown below):

- **Update frequency:** the frequency of change of a URL, as detected on the
Internet by the Microsoft crawler: ➪ Reference Section 6.2: File age.
- **Site popularity:** the number and importance of links from other websites.
- **Exactness of match:** the degree of precision with which your terms match
the finding: ➪ Reference Section 6.1: Wildcards, substrings, stemming.

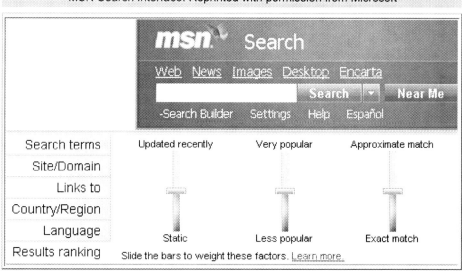

MSN Search Interface: Reprinted with permission from Microsoft

As you manipulate the sliders in the "Results ranking" part of the "Search Builder," various operator parameters and their values are generated inside the search string. You can also type these yourself, directly into the search string.

🔲 Enter cat dog as terms, and slide the:

- "Frequency of update" slider upwards to 83%.
- "Site popularity" slider downwards to 20%.
- "Exactness of match" slider downwards until it reaches 9%.

The search string that then shows in the text entry box becomes cat dog {frsh=83} {popl=20} {mtch=9}.

| General | AlltheWeb | AltaVista | Copernic | Google | MSN |

Page organization

⇨ For more explanation, refer to:

- Chapter 6: Organization of findings display.
- Reference Section 5.2: Page organization.

Another aspect of the overall organization of findings is how the findings are organized into pages and within pages.

Many of the page organization features can only be controlled through setting preferences (⇨ Reference Section 6.4: Findings page organization). The following search engine-specific write-up is restricted to page organization parameters that you can set dynamically, that is, apply to the single search you are doing.

All our featured search engines can limit the number of findings reported per page. This feature can also be set as a preference. As well:

- AltaVista's site collapse feature can be used to control whether to show all findings from a single website.
- Copernic provides two basic formats for results page organization, one using a browser window and the other not.

| General | AlltheWeb | AltaVista | Copernic | Google | MSN |

AlltheWeb

To control the number of findings shown per page in its advanced Web and News search, use the following drop-down menu choices:

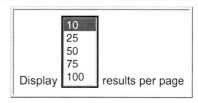

Display [100] results per page

> ⇨ For other AlltheWeb page organization parameters, refer to Reference Section 6.4: Findings page organization.

AltaVista

In its advanced Web search:

- To quote [AltaVista Help]: When Site Collapse is on (check box is checked), AltaVista displays a maximum of two results per site. This lets you see many different sites in your results. When Site Collapse is off, AltaVista displays all results from each site, indenting pages from the same site below the first result listed in order of relevance. This makes it easy to see results from deep within sites.

Display: ☑ site collapse (on/off)

- To control the number of results displayed per page for a particular search, select the number of findings per page from the drop-down menu shown here:

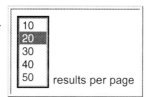

results per page

Copernic

> ⇨ For an example, see the Copernic screenshot in Chapter 3: Local application interfaces.

It has two basic page organizations for browsing findings:

1. The primary organization provides a large pane on the right and bottom two-thirds of the screen to display the results listing.

2. When the results are displayed in the preceding pane, you can select "Browse Results" in the "Common Tasks" pane on the lower left. This takes you to a browser interface that has the results listed in very short form on a scrollable frame to the left of the browser window. The results themselves are seen in the much larger scrollable frame on the right of that same window.

If you select one of the findings from the left pane, or from the hyperlink for that finding in the right frame, the finding itself opens in the right frame. You can also display the findings one by one by choosing "Previous" or "Next" options in the toolbar at the top of the frame on the left (see screenshot below).

- Sort by Score
- Sort by Title
- Sort by Address

- Sort Ascending

✓ Display Address

✓ Use Saved Pages

Open Copernic Agent

Close Toolbar

To return to the findings list in the right frame after viewing an individual finding, click on the leftmost icon on the toolbar at the top of the left frame (⇨ see screenshot below, or, for a larger one, see ⇨ Chapter 5: Organization of findings display).

To close the left frame, either choose the "X" in the upper right-hand corner of that frame, or select the "Close Toolbar" option in the Options menu, shown here, accessible in the toolbar at the top of the left frame.

If you use Internet Explorer as your browser, you can control the number of findings displayed per browser window page using a preference setting.

⇨ For details, see the screenshot in Reference Section 6.4: Software integration.

(To see the screenshot in full resolution, go to ⇨ www.SearchHelpCenter.com/effective-internet-search-copernic-screenshots.html, "Browser view controls.")

Reference Manual Section 6.3:
Findings Display &
Handling Parameters
484
Organization of
Findings Display

Google

To select the number of results to display per page, go to the advanced Web search page Use a drop-down menu with options of 10, 20, 30, 50, and 100 findings per page (default value is 10).

MSN Search

Page organization can only be controlled by preference settings (⇨ Reference Section 6.4: Findings page organization); no options are available for each individual search.

General   AlltheWeb   AltaVista   Copernic   Google   MSN

Presentation of Individual Findings

Finding fields to display

The metadata displayed for each finding are divided into fields for document title, description, or extract (usually containing the keywords), URL, and various links (to similar websites, for translation, and so on). Parameters can sometimes be used to control the fields to be displayed, even the contents of each field, and how to format the display of this content for that finding.

⇨ For more explanation, see:

- Chapter 6: Presentation of individual findings.
- Reference Section 5.2: Presentation of individual findings.

Most of our featured search engines cannot dynamically control fields to display for each finding. Copernic can, however, and Google has a feature to control file format field display. Otherwise, most of the findings field display features can only be controlled by setting preferences (⇨ Reference Section 6.4: Individual findings detail).

General   AlltheWeb   AltaVista   Copernic   Google   MSN

AlltheWeb

Findings field display cannot be controlled for each individual search.

AltaVista

Findings field display cannot be controlled for each individual search. However, AltaVista provides preference settings that give you quite a bit of control over which fields to display (⇨ Reference Section 6.4: Individual findings detail).

Copernic

The choices available for the details of each findings depend on whether you view the results in the Copernic application pane or in your browser.

> ⚠ The description here assumes familiarity with the fields and icons Copernic can display for each finding. For an explanation,
> ⇨ Reference Section 5.2: Presentation of individual findings.

You have more choices for the level of finding detail shown if you use the Copernic application pane. However, search term highlighting and "use saved pages" options are the same with both methods of viewing, each of which is described below.

Copernic application pane method options:

> 🔨 The following description could also have been included with setting user preferences (⇨ Reference Section 6.4: Individual findings detail).

When you change the following findings detail parameter values for an individual search, the latest values become your defaults from that point on.

The options are as follows:

1. **Result detail level:** Choose "Result layout" from the toolbar or use the View>Result Layout menu (see screenshot on next page) choice from the menu bar at the top of the screen. This will provide you with choices of compact, standard, and detailed display of findings seen here, as well as with result highlighting options (see #2 below).

In Reference Manual section 5.2 (⇨ Reference Section 5.2: Presentation of individual findings), you will notice screenshots corresponding to each of the following view detail levels:

- **Compact:** displays one line of the title. If the title is unavailable, the URL will show in the case of a document file or the file name in the case of a multi-media file. A checkbox is also shown, possibly along with a marker (⇨ Reference Section 5.2: Presentation of individual findings), the first line of any title, and on the far right, the relevancy score is displayed graphically.

- **Standard:** in addition to the contents of the compact view, two or more lines of an extract are shown under the full title, the relevancy score displayed numerically, the URL, and the search engines from which this finding was obtained.

- **Detailed:** in addition to the contents of the standard view, fields are displayed that may be extracted with the ⚠ The Copernic Professional version is needed to obtain values for these fields.

right optimal search choices. These are: concepts, language, and date modified. The date found (date the search reported the finding) and any notes added to the finding through user annotation are also shown.

2. **Search term highlighting:** These options allow you to switch between:

- **No highlight:** search terms are not highlighted in the title or in the excerpt fields of the findings detail.
- **Singe-color highlight:** search terms are highlighted in a single color, e.g., yellow.
- **Multi-color highlight:** each search term is highlighted in a different color.

3. **Use saved results:** If you saved the file corresponding to the finding, you have the option of displaying results based on that file as it was when you saved it, rather than the file as it may now be cataloged or is now on the Internet (see menu choice on next page).

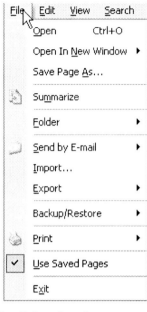

⇨ For saving results, consult Reference Section 6.3: Search follow-up.

Browser frame method options:

The options are the same as those for the Copernic pane view, except for the following:

- The findings are always displayed in standard detail, but the relevancy score is not given graphically (just numerically).

- In the left frame, if you uncheck the "Display Address" option, shown here, the URL will not show under the first several words of the document title in the left frame.

- The "Use Saved Pages" option (⇨ preceding screenshot) is chosen from the drop-down menu at the top of the left frame on the browser window, rather than from the File menu in the Copernic application window.

- The options for highlighting are only available by a drop-down menu in the Copernic toolbar near the top of your browser window.

💡 The toolbar option is also available at the top of the Copernic panes.

Google

Has one parameter to control findings field display for individual searches. To quote [Google Help]: If you prefer to see a particular set of results without file types (for example, PDF links), simply type **filetype:[extension]** (for example, **filetype:pdf**) within the search box along with your search term(s).

form 1040 filetype:pdf

MSN Search

Cannot control findings field display for each individual search.

General	AlltheWeb	AltaVista	Copernic	Google	MSN

Finding language translation

Language translation here refers to translating the results of the search back into the language of the interface employed by the user, or sometimes into another selected target language.

> ⇨ For more explanation, see:
>
> - Chapter 6: Presentation of individual findings.
> - Reference Section 5.2: Language translation links.

None of our featured search engines have parameters that control whether the finding is automatically translated (without requiring you to make selections using links on the findings display). However, AltaVista and Google provide you with the option of branching to a language translation utility.

Other Post-Processing of Findings

Search within findings

Search within findings is generally used to further filter what has already been found. Ideally, you should be able to use any of the filters available for your original search to search within findings.

> ⇨ For more explanation, see:
>
> - Chapter 6: Post-processing of findings.
> - Reference Section 5.2: Search within findings.

Of our featured search engines, only Copernic has a sophisticated search within findings ability. AlltheWeb and Google can also search within findings, but in a much more limited way.

General	AlltheWeb	AltaVista	Copernic	Google	MSN

Reference Manual Section 6.3:
Findings Display &
Handling Parameters

489

Other Post-
Processing of Findings

AlltheWeb

Allows you to add further search terms to limit the scope of the result.

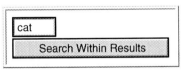 Enter cat as a search term, and AlltheWeb produces 6,780,276 matches. The accompanying message shows near the bottom of the findings page.

You select "search within your results" from the above and another text entry box presents. In that, you enter donkey sheep and then press the "Search Within Results" button to re-execute your search.

AlltheWeb now renders just 13,719 matches. That is, the donkey sheep was interpreted as having been conjuncted (with a logical AND) to the previous search string, thereby narrowing the scope of the findings. Donkey and sheep are themselves connected by conjunction, i.e., using AND logic.

Now do the same but type donkey OR sheep into the "Search Within Results" box. This time you receive 1,925,384 results. It is equivalent to entering your original search as cat AND donkey OR sheep.

> ⚒ For more on entering Boolean operators with AlltheWeb, ⇨ Reference Section 6.1: AND, OR, and NOT.

Based on the above example, it is difficult to see how AlltheWeb really searches within results, because you should never have more results than in your original search, even when OR is used as in this example.

AltaVista

Does not have a search within findings feature.

Copernic

You can use any combination of the following techniques:

Reference Manual Section 6.3:
Findings Display &
Handling Parameters

490

Other Post-
Processing of Findings

1. **Search based on term-based filters:** You have a choice to either:

   a. Enter your Boolean logic directly into the "Look for:" text entry box on the control panel. If you do this, choose either "Result list" or "Each page contents" from the drop-down menu labeled as "In:"

   Finding in the results list looks only in the file metadata already in your computer, while finding in each page's contents involves accessing the referenced document file on the Internet to apply the Boolean logic.

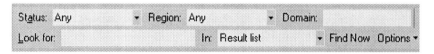

You also have various choices from an options drop-down menu (downward arrowhead on the bottom right of the above command bar), equivalent to those seen at the bottom of the "Advanced Find in Results" dialog box on the next page.

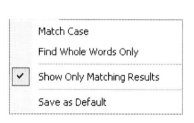

After making your various entries to start the procedure of finding within results, select the "Find Now" button.

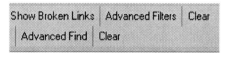

   b. Enter the logic in the "Advanced Find in Results" dialog box (see next page). If you do this, use the radio buttons shown and the checkboxes at the bottom to make the same choices as in option "a" above.

2. **Search based on metadata-based filters:** Again you have two choices, one more advanced than the other:

- Simpler alternative: use any combination of the drop-down menu choices for region, the text entry box for domains, and the "Show Broken Links" button to show findings whose links to Internet sites do not work.
- More complex alternative: use the set of dialog boxes, obtainable by selecting the various tabs, shown on the page after the next page.

Reference Manual Section 6.3:
Findings Display &
Handling Parameters
491
Other Post-
Processing of Findings

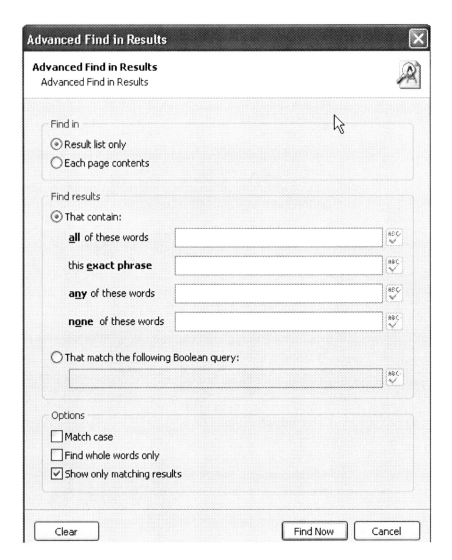

3. **Search based on finding processing status:** The "Advanced Result Filters" dialog box (see next page) has a drop-down menu choice for "status." You can also make the same choices from the "Status" drop-down menu box on the control panel. **Status** refers to what has already been done with the result during the process of reviewing findings. Status has the following values that you can select from the drop-down menu seen here:

- **Any:** Any status.
- **New:** The finding has not yet been accessed on the Internet for inspection during your review of findings. Also, the search results have just been updated (or obtained for the first time), and the file in question was not present in the last set of results for this search.

- **Visited:** The finding has already been accessed for inspection.
- **Not Visited:** The finding is not "new" and has also not yet been accessed.
- **Saved:** The finding has been saved on your local storage; you may or may not have accessed the file yet.
- **Checkmarked:** You placed a checkmark next to the finding in the results listing.
- **Annotated:** You made some notes about that result.

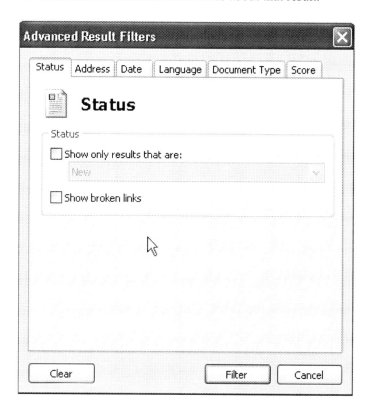

The above simply gives you a glimpse of the interface screens. From these, there are many additional dialog boxes and drop-down menus. For more details on where these screens lead and how to interpret them in Copernic, ⇨:

- Reference Section 5.2: Search within findings.
- Reference Section 6.1: Term-Based Search Filters.
- Reference Section 6.2: Metadata-Based Search Filters.

Reference Manual Section 6.3:
Findings Display &
Handling Parameters

493

Other Post-
Processing of Findings

Google

Allows you to add further search terms to limit the scope of the result.

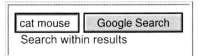 Enter cat mouse as a search term and Google produces about 4,500,000 matches. Near the bottom of your findings page, you see a "Search Within Results" choice. Select this, and a new text entry box appears. Enter OR sheep into that box; then press the "Search Within Results" button to re-execute your search. This time, Google finds about 5,860,000 matches. The new search string is equivalent to cat mouse OR sheep. But, when you do a completely new search with cat mouse OR sheep, that's exactly the number of results you receive.

Based on this example, it appears that Google doesn't really search *within* results, since it would be logically impossible to receive more than the original number of findings by doing so. What the "Search within results" is, it appears, is just another way of editing your original search string.

> For more on entering Boolean operators with AlltheWeb, ➪ Reference Section 6.1: AND, OR, and NOT.

MSN Search

Does not have a search within findings feature.

General	AlltheWeb	AltaVista	Copernic	Google	MSN

Language translation or page summary

These allow the text of the findings to be changed for your convenience in reviewing the finding.

> ➪ For more explanation, consult:
>
> • Chapter 6: Post-processing of findings.
> • Reference Section 5.2: Language translation or page summary.

Reference Manual Section 6.3:
Findings Display &
Handling Parameters

494

Other Post-
Processing of Findings

While AltaVista and Google provide links to language translators, these programs do not have secondary parameters that allow you to control how these tasks are completed.

Only Copernic provides a document summarizer function that may be parameterized in a few different ways.

AlltheWeb

Does not have language translation of page summary abilities.

AltaVista

Has language translation abilities. You parameterize the translation interface by choosing source and target languages, as well as language keyboard to be used (⇨ Reference Section 5.2: Language translation or page summary).

Copernic

> ⇨ For details of this interface, see Reference Section 5.2: Language translation or page summary.

Its summarizer technology has the ability to extract keywords and to produce document summaries in English. You can change the workings of the summarizer for each finding, using the "Number of Concepts" spin box, and the "Summary Length" drop-down menu shown below. See ⇨ Reference Section 5.2 screenshot for a full screenshot of the Summarizer.

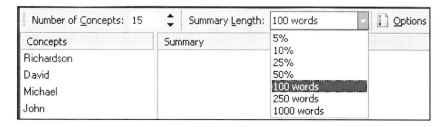

Note: Click on "Options" in the above to go to set the length and other Summarizer options as user preferences. For more on these, consult ⇨ Reference Section 6.4: Handling of findings.

Reference Manual Section 6.3:
Findings Display &
Handling Parameters
495
Other Post-
Processing of Findings

Google

Has language translation abilities. You can parameterize the translation interface only by choosing source and destination language ($\Rightarrow$ Reference Section 5.2: Language translation or page summary).

MSN Search

Does not have language translation of page summary abilities.

General	AlltheWeb	AltaVista	Copernic	Google	MSN

Search follow-up

This involves keeping records of searches and their findings, sharing searches and search results, and setting up user alerts for tracking pages or updating searches.

> $\Rightarrow$ For more explanation, see:
>
> - Chapter 6: Post-processing of findings.
> - Reference Section 5.2: Search follow-up.

Of our featured search engines:

- Copernic has sophisticated search follow-up abilities.
- Google and MSN Search have alerts of updates to Web and news searches.

General	AlltheWeb	AltaVista	Copernic	Google	MSN

AlltheWeb

Search follow-up features are unavailable.

AltaVista

Search follow-up features are unavailable.

Reference Manual Section 6.3:
Findings Display &
Handling Parameters
496
Other Post-
Processing of Findings

Copernic

Copernic has the ability to:

> ⚠️ If you are not already familiar with the various Copernic interfaces for search follow-up, begin by reviewing ⇨ Reference Section 5.2: Search follow-up. The following discussion builds upon that knowledge by describing the various options available in each of the following areas.

1. **Keep records of searches and their findings:**

a. **Organize search history:** Use the context menu shown here (which you obtain by right-clicking your mouse over the search history folders pane) to make or remove folders, rename them, move records of searches from one folder to another, and so on.

b. **Manage search history details:** There are no parameters other than the choices described in Reference Manual section 5.2 for this item.

c. **Save individual files referenced from findings metadata to user's local computer:** When you use the dialog box shown here

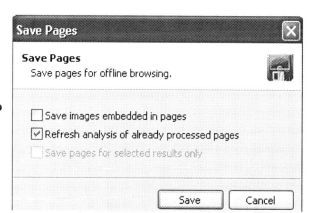

to save your results, you can choose any combination of the following:

- **Save images embedded in pages:** This saves image files linked to and from a webpage and displayed along with its textual contents.
- **Save pages for selected results only:** It applies if you have selected some results in the Copernic results pane. Note that it is grayed out in the below screenshot.

Reference Manual Section 6.3:
Findings Display &
Handling Parameters

497

Other Post-
Processing of Findings

- **Refresh analysis of already processed pages:**
  If the file has already been saved, re-access it on the Internet to see if there is a later version of the file; if so, save the later version.

If you save your files using the checkboxes connected with optimal analysis (⇨ Reference Section 5.2: Search follow-up), it is assumed you will refresh any already processed files with later versions. You also have the choice of saving the image files linked to and from (embedded in) webpages (see first checkbox in screenshot on previous page).

To arrive at the above "Save Pages" screen, user either the "Results" pull-down menu (shown here), or the context menu obtained by floating your mouse over an individual search in the search history pane and then right-clicking that search.

Results	Tracking	Favorites
Browse		Ctrl+B
Verify Links...		Ctrl+I
Analyze...		Ctrl+R
Save Pages...		Ctrl+W
Filter		
Find in Results		

d. **Update, modify, duplicate, and delete searches kept in search history:** If you have filters set during the analysis phase, either for a new search or when redoing the analysis, Copernic permanently drops the filtered findings from results for that search. If you want otherwise, do not set these filters before doing analysis, but only set them when performing a "Find in Results" procedure.

2. **Share search findings:** First choose the specific file from the specific folder to send or receive. Then select the file format for exporting results, using the "File of type" drop-down menu at the bottom of the dialog box. You can choose between comma separated values (CSV), ordinary text (TXT), Microsoft Word (DOC), regular webpage (HTML), and XML file formats for exporting (saving) a search.

Although the "File of type" dialog box is available to search import, only the XML file format was available as a choice at the time of writing this book. If you wish to send the search results as an e-mail attachment, the HTML format is automatic and the only available choice.

Reference Manual Section 6.3:
Findings Display &
Handling Parameters

498

Other Post-
Processing of Findings

3. **Set up user alerts (search tracking):**

a. The options available to track a
whole search for new findings that
might appear on the Internet
include:

	Tracking	Favorites	Tools	Wi
📇	Track Search...		Ctrl+T	
🌐	Track Page...			
📅	Tracking Manager...			
👤	Logon...			
	Schedules...			
	Tracking Options...			

- **Schedule:** multiple times
per day, daily, weekly,
monthly frequencies of
looking for and reporting changes.
- **E-mail address:** to which to send tracking
results.

If you select the "Options"
link in search tracking (⇨
Reference Section 5.2: Search
follow-up for screenshot), you
will be taken to the screen
setting preferences for tracking multiple times per day.

> ⇨ To set tracking preferences,
> see Reference Section 6.4:
> Handling of findings.

b. Further to the options available in "a," when tracking an
individual result (⇨ Reference Section 5.2: Search follow-up
for screenshot), you need the URL and the minimum
required change in the number of words in the finding to
trigger Copernic's reporting as you have altered it.

c. You can also set up tracking for an advanced search at time
of doing the search, using the "Advanced" tab in the dialog
box shown on the next page.

Google

Has search follow-up abilities: ⇨ Reference Section 5.2: Search follow-up for
screenshots. In addition to the search string and the e-mail address to which you
would like the search tracking results delivered, you have various options. These
are:

- **The catalog involved:** Web, News, Web and News, or Groups search.
- **The frequency of monitoring for changes:** once a day, once a week, as it
happens.

MSN Search

Has search follow-up abilities (⇨ Reference Section 5.2: Search follow-up),
although we do not describe associated parameters here.

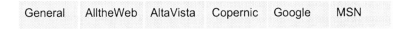

Reference Manual Section 6.4: User Preference Setting Parameters

> ⇨ This section cross-links with Chapter 6: User Preference Setting Parameters.

Filter Default Value Preferences

Document language

> ⇨ For more explanation, consult Chapter 6: Filter default value preferences.

One of the most frequently used metadata-based filters is the languages of documents from various document file catalogs. Its default values can be set as a preference.

In helping you set your preferred document languages, some search engines initially assume certain language defaults based on your site control language: ⇨ Reference Section 6.4: Interface language or style. But you can still change the document language for individual searches: ⇨ Reference Section 6.2: Document language.

Except for Copernic, all our featured search engines can set document language preferences. In the cases of AlltheWeb and AltaVista, a relationship is also made between geographical location of your server and the default document language settings.

| General | AlltheWeb | AltaVista | Copernic | Google | MSN |

AlltheWeb

> Results in:- ⦿ Any Language
> ⦿ Preferred Language(s) - define below

You can set AlltheWeb to filter pages based on preferences for one or more of its supported languages. Preferred language is at first set to values that correspond to your geographical location, which AlltheWeb automatically detects.

Reference Manual Section 6.4:
User Preference
Setting Parameters

501

Filter Default
Value Preferences

You also need to select a character encoding scheme that matches your language(s), For instance, the Unicode (UTF-8) code supports all languages. You can select up to 8 languages from the 36 ones available.

```
Unicode (UTF-8)
Western European (ISO-8859-1)
Western European (ISO-8859-15)
Central European (ISO-8859-2)
Celtic (ISO-8859-14)
```

To quote [AlltheWeb Help]: AlltheWeb automatically detects your local language, and by default, searches for results written in that language as well as English.

🔨 To set language on an individual search basis,
⇨ Reference Section 6.2: Document language.

You can select any language using the checkboxes shown below.

☐ Albanian / Shqip	☐ Finnish / Suomi	☐ Norwegian / Norsk
☐ Arabic / العربية	☐ French / Français	☐ Persian / فارسى
☐ Bulgarian / български	☐ German / Deutsch	☐ Polish / Polski
☐ Catalan / Català	☐ Greek / Ελληνικά	☐ Portuguese / Português
☐ Chinese (simp) / 汉语	☐ Hebrew / עברית	☐ Romanian / Româna
☐ Chinese (trad) / 漢語	☐ Hungarian / Magyar	☐ Russian / Русский
☐ Croatian / Hrvatski	☐ Icelandic / Íslenska	☐ Slovak / Slovenčina
☐ Czech / Česky	☐ Italian / Italiano	☐ Slovenian / Slovenščina
☐ Danish / Dansk	☐ Japanese / 日本語	☐ Spanish / Español
☐ Dutch / Nederlands	☐ Korean / 한국어	☐ Swedish / Svenska
☐ English / English	☐ Latvian / Latviski	☐ Thai / ภาษาไทย
☐ Estonian / Eesti	☐ Lithuanian / Lietuviškai	☐ Turkish / Türkçe

AltaVista

⚠ For language search to work, AltaVista's "family filter" feature must be in the "off" state (⇨ Reference Section 6.4: Potentially offensive content).

Whether you set document language dynamically (⇨ Reference Section 6.2: Document language) or select it based on user preference settings, you arrive at the checkboxes seen below (next page). From these, you can choose one or more languages for documents found.

Language and country are closely related in AltaVista, as are document language and language of the site controls (⇨ Reference Section 6.4: Interface language or style).

⇨ To specify a country, see Reference Section 6.4: Other filter setting preferences.

Reference Manual Section 6.4:
User Preference
Setting Parameters

502

Filter Default
Value Preferences

If you access
AltaVista Canada,

SEARCH: ⊙ Worldwide ⊙ U.S.
RESULTS IN: ⊙ All languages ⊙ English, Spanish

radio buttons appear giving you the option of restricting the web
server location to Canada and the language to English or French.
On the other hand, for the United States the languages choices are
English and Spanish, as seen here.

Search Languages: Search only for pages written in these language(s):

☐ Albanian - Shqip   ☐ German - Deutsch   ☐ Polish - Polski
☐ Arabic - العربية   ☐ Greek - Ελληνικά   ☐ Portuguese - Português
☐ Bulgarian - български   ☐ Hebrew - עברית   ☐ Romanian - Română
☐ Catalan - Català   ☐ Hungarian - Magyar   ☐ Russian - Русский
☐ Croatian - Hrvatski   ☐ Icelandic - Íslensk   ☐ Simplified Chinese (China) - 汉语
☐ Czech - Český   ☐ Italian - Italiano   ☐ Slovak - Slovenčina
☐ Danish - Dansk   ☐ Japanese - 日本語   ☐ Slovenian - Slovenščina
☐ Dutch - Nederlands   ☐ Korean - 한국어   ☐ Spanish - Español
☑ English - English   ☐ Latvian - Latviešu   ☐ Swedish - Svenska
☐ Estonian - Eesti   ☐ Lithuanian - Lietuvių   ☐ Thai - ภาษาไทย
☐ Finnish - Suomi   ☐ Norwegian - Norsk   ☐ Traditional Chinese (Taiwan) - 漢語
☐ French - Français   ☐ Persian - فارسی   ☐ Turkish - Türkçe

Copernic

Cannot set document
language preferences.

However, you can choose document language
dynamically at the time of each search (⇨ Reference
Section 6.2: Document language).

Google

It allows you to specify
document language
preferences

⇨ Also see: Reference Section 6.2: Document
language to set language for an individual search;
and Reference Section 6.4: Interface language or style,
concerning site controls for language.

dynamically or by setting user preferences. Use the selections on the following
form to set document language through preferences:

MSN Search

⇨ Also see: Reference Section 6.2: Document language to set language for an individual search; and Reference Section 6.4: Interface language or style, concerning site controls for language.

It allows you to specify document language preferences dynamically or by setting user preferences. Use the selections on the below form to set document language through preferences.

⊙ Search pages written in any language
○ Limit my searches to pages written in the following languages:
☐ Danish ☐ Dutch ☑ English ☐ Finnish ☐ French ☐ German
☐ Italian ☐ Japanese ☐ Norwegian ☐ Portuguese ☐ Spanish ☐ Swedish

General	AlltheWeb	AltaVista	Copernic	Google	MSN

Potentially offensive content

⇨ For more explanation, see Chapter 6: Filter default value preferences.

Potentially offensive content filtering is sometimes called "Safe Search" or "Family Filtering." Of our featured search engines:

- All, except for Copernic, have the ability to set potentially offensive content filtering preferences.
- AlltheWeb and Google can set this parameter both dynamically (for each search) or as a preference. AltaVista and MSN Search can only do so through the latter.

Reference Manual Section 6.4:
User Preference
Setting Parameters

504

Filter Default
Value Preferences

General	AlltheWeb	AltaVista	Copernic	Google	MSN

AlltheWeb

Offensive content filter --	⊙ On ⊙ Off

To quote [AlltheWeb Help]: The Offensive Content Reduction filter reduces the amount of offensive material displayed in the search results. Please note that the filter is not 100% accurate, and offensive material will in some cases slip through the filter and be displayed in the search results. Some pages that are not offensive may also be incorrectly filtered out. The filter only supports English documents.

You can override the offensive content reduction default setting from the advanced Picture and Video search interfaces.

➪ For further information, consult Reference Section 6.2: Potentially offensive content.

AltaVista

In addition to using the "Settings" link on most search entry screens, you can access AltaVista's "Family Filter" using a link from the findings pages for the various multi-media file searches. This takes you to the preference setting screen seen below.

Choose your Family Filter preference.

- ○ **Multimedia Only** - filters image, video and audio search only.
- ○ **All** - filters all searches: web pages, images, audio and video.
  Note: With the Family Filter set to "All", you can perform Web searches in only English, French, German and Spanish.
- ⊙ **None** - will not filter any search

Password Protection (Optional):
Makes it necessary to enter a password to change your Family Filter preferences.

Enter Optional Password: [ ]

Re-enter Optional Password: [ ]

> ⇨ Also see:
>
> - AltaVista's tool for reporting offensive websites: Reference Section 5.3: Additional end user-specific tools.
> - Reference Section 6.2: Potentially offensive content.

Copernic

A potentially offensive content control feature is unavailable.

Google

> ⇨ To set this filter dynamically, consult Reference Section 6.2: Potentially offensive content.

Use the "Preferences" interface to choose one of three levels of potentially offensive content control, as seen next.

> **SafeSearch Filtering** Google's SafeSearch blocks web pages containing explicit sexual content from appearing in search results.
>
> ○ Use strict filtering (Filter both explicit text and explicit images)
> ◉ Use moderate filtering (Filter explicit images only - default behavior)
> ○ Do not filter my search results.

MSN Search

> **Safe Search** Choose how you want to filter results.
>
> ◉ Strict - Filter sexually explicit text and image results
> ◉ Moderate - Filter sexually explicit images only
> ◉ Off - Do not filter search results

Use the "Settings" interface to choose one of three levels of potentially offensive content control, as seen here.

| General | AlltheWeb | AltaVista | Copernic | Google | MSN |

Reference Manual Section 6.4:
User Preference
Setting Parameters

506

Filter Default
Value Preferences

Other filter setting preferences

> ⇨ For more explanation, refer to Chapter 6: Filter default value preferences.

Other common default filter preferences include the spelling dictionary or settings to be used to help filter search terms, geographical region of the server, default location for local search, categories of news results to display, etc. Such settings vary widely across our featured search engines.

General	AlltheWeb	AltaVista	Copernic	Google	MSN

AlltheWeb

Has no other kinds of filter preference settings.

AltaVista

> Country - **Canada**
> Select a country to focus your search

Geographical region of the server
(country): This parameter can be entered either dynamically or from the settings interface. In the latter, click "country." This will take you to the same set of choices as you see when setting the country dynamically (⇨ Reference Section 6.2: Geographical region of server).

Country and language are related (⇨ Reference Section 6.4: Document language and Reference Section 6.4: Interface language or style). When you choose a particular country, AltaVista automatically establishes a default setting for one or more languages.

English and Spanish are the American defaults for the language of results, while English is the United States default for the interface language.

> ⇨ Reference Section 6.2: Document language, for another example.

Reference Manual Section 6.4:
User Preference
Setting Parameters

507

Filter Default
Value Preferences

Copernic

Is able to set default values for filters in the following areas:

1. **Whether to use saved versions of pages instead of re-accessing the page on the Internet when displaying the results of an updated search:** Set this option using:

   - "File" pull-down menu in the Copernic application, shown here.
   - Browser default preference settings (⇨ Reference Section 6.4: Interface options made available), where you can set the "Use saved pages when opening results" checkbox shown below.

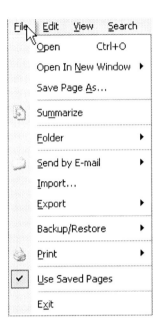

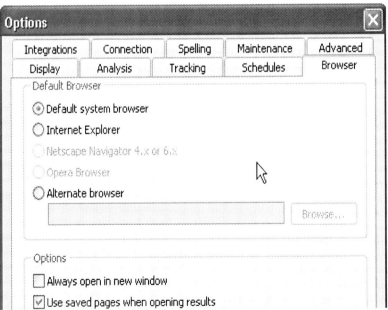

Reference Manual Section 6.4:
User Preference
Setting Parameters

508

Filter Default
Value Preferences

- "Options" pull-down menu in the browser results listing, shown here.

2. **General and dictionary options for spellchecking search terms:** These options (see screenshot below) also apply to spellchecking annotations made during post-processing of findings (⇨ Reference Section 6.4: Handling of findings).

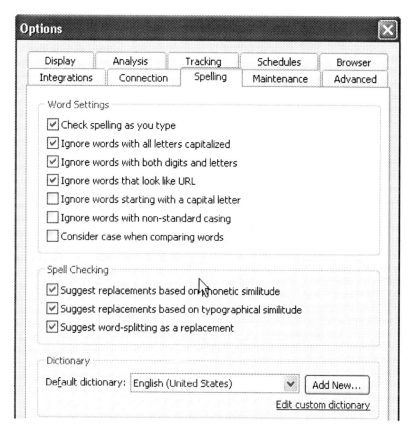

3. **Analysis options:** including ones for the Copernic Summarizer, as seen in the screenshot on the next page.

Except for the "Use default language when detection fails" option on the "Analysis" preference setting dialog box, you can override all these settings dynamically. More specifically:

Reference Manual Section 6.4:
User Preference
Setting Parameters

509

Filter Default
Value Preferences

- You can change any of the "Default Level" group of options each time you do an advanced search or run an analysis, where the same set of choices is made available. See ⇨ Reference Section: Advanced web search interfaces.

- You can dynamically change the "Summaries" options using the options on the summarizer display. See ⇨ Reference Section: Language translation or page summary.

- You can save all the results of a search at any time. See ⇨ Reference Section 6.3: Search follow-up.

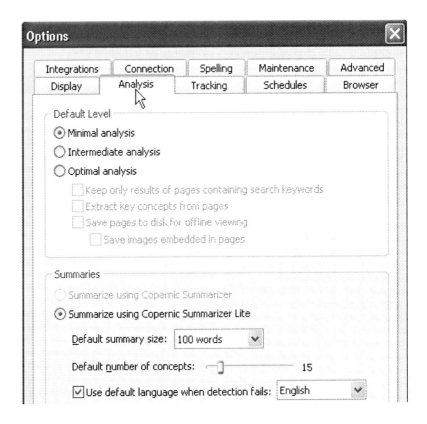

Google

- It allows you to customize your news search news topic categories, to:
    - ɔ Add or delete main news categories, such as business and sports.
    - ɔ Add sections from any of the country-specific versions of Google News.
    - ɔ Create your own section on any topic that interests you. Define the section using keywords for a topic of interest.

Reference Manual Section 6.4:
User Preference
Setting Parameters

510

Filter Default
Value Preferences

- In Local search, Google has a checkbox that allows you to set your default location. Initially, Google sets that automatically, based on the IP address of your server.

MSN Search

You can set preferences for the country whose location you want to assume. Initially, MSN Search determines your default automatically, based on your server's IP address. To change that, go to MSN Search Help, and select the "Worldwide" link. You will receive the following list of countries:

MSN Search Worldwide
- Australia · Austria · Belgium · Belgium (French) · Brazil · Canada
- Canada (French) · Denmark · Finland · France · Germany · Hong Kong S.A.R.
- India (English) · Italy · Japan · Korea · Latin America · Malaysia (English)
- Mexico · Netherlands · New Zealand · Norway · Singapore (English)
- South Africa (English) · Spain · Sweden · Switzerland · Switzerland (French)
- Taiwan · United Kingdom · United States · United States (Spanish)

Initially, MSN Search automatically sets your preferred locality, based on the knowledge it has of the location of

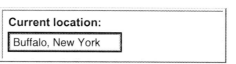

Current location:

Buffalo, New York

your Internet server, which is associated with your computer's Internet Protocol (IP) address. However, using preference setting, you can change your default location for local search. Simply type your city and state/province into the text box provided, as you see here.

General   AlltheWeb   AltaVista   Copernic   Google   MSN

Reference Manual Section 6.4:
User Preference
Setting Parameters
511
Filter Default
Value Preferences

Findings Display & Handling Preferences

Findings page organization

These parameters allow you to control things such as the maximum number of findings to show per website, and the overall ordering of findings across different pages of findings display and within each such page.

> ⇨ For more explanation, see:
>
> - Chapter 6: Findings display and handling preferences.
> - Reference Section 5.2: Overall ordering.
> - Reference Section 5.2: Page organization.
> - Reference Section 6.3: Organization of Findings Display.

All our featured search engines can control the number of findings displayed per page. AlltheWeb, Copernic, and Google have more options than others.

General   AlltheWeb   AltaVista   Copernic   Google   MSN

AlltheWeb

Unless otherwise indicated, none of the following preference settings can be dynamically changed, that is, revised from the search entry interfaces for individual searches. For Web search, options include:

- **Number of findings shown per domain:** This involves the site collapsing option. To quote [AlltheWeb Help]: By default, AlltheWeb shows one page per domain. Disabling this feature may return more results. Some matches may be redundant.

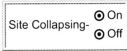

- **Search results per page:** This setting can be overridden for individual searches in the advanced Web, News, and Pictures search interfaces (⇨ Reference Section 6.3: Page organization).

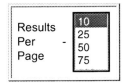

Reference Manual Section 6.4:
User Preference
Setting Parameters

512

Findings Display &
Handling Preferences

- **Open results in new window:** To quote [AlltheWeb Help]: When this feature is enabled AlltheWeb will open the search results in a new window. Note that you can choose to open your results in a shared window or open each result in its own window.

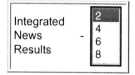

- **Number of integrated news results:** To quote [AlltheWeb Help]: This option controls the number of integrated news results displayed above your ordinary results.

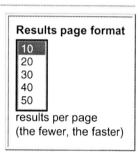

AltaVista

For Web search, can set the preferred number of results to show per page.

This setting can be overridden for individual searches in the advanced Web search interface (⇨ Reference Section 6.3: Page organization).

Copernic

Copernic has a couple of different ways of setting preferences for finding page organization. These are as follows:

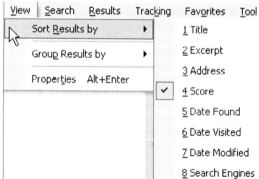

- **View menu:** You can use the following sub-menus of the View pull-down menu:
  - ○ **Sort Results By:** establishes the default sort order for findings. The choices are shown here.
  - ○ **Group Results By:** establishes the default scheme for grouping findings. The choices are shown on the next page.

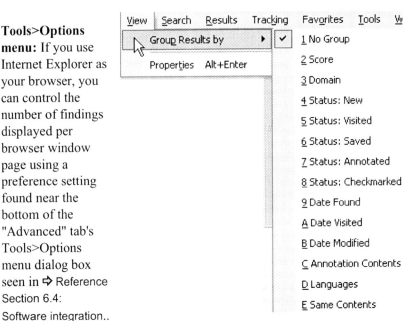

- **Tools>Options menu:** If you use Internet Explorer as your browser, you can control the number of findings displayed per browser window page using a preference setting found near the bottom of the "Advanced" tab's Tools>Options menu dialog box seen in ⇨ Reference Section 6.4: Software integration..

Google

For Web search, can set preferences to control:

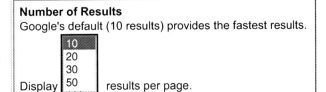

Number of Results
Google's default (10 results) provides the fastest results.

Display [10 / 20 / 30 / 50] results per page.

- Number of results
  to show per page. This setting can be overridden for individual searches in the advanced Web search interface (⇨ Reference Section 6.3: Page organization).

- Display of results in a new window.

Results Window
☐ Open search results in a new browser window.

For news search, Google allows you to change the search entry form layout. This can be done in two different ways, by:

- Using the controls found in a light blue box in the upper right corner of the screen.
- With a Javascript "widget" that permits you drag and drop sections into new locations.

Options are also provided allowing you to:

Reference Manual Section 6.4:
User Preference
Setting Parameters

514

Findings Display &
Handling Preferences

- Restore the default Google news page.
- View the text-only version of the standard page.
- Share your customization choices with others. This can be achieved by sending the unique URL Google creates for your particular customization choices to others.

MSN Search

For Web search, can set preferences for:

- Number of results to show per page.

- Display of results in a new window.

☐ Open links in a new browser window

- Whether to group the findings from the same site (the default), and, if so, whether to show up to one, two, or three of them in a group. Selecting one result is, presumably, equivalent to un-checking the box shown here.

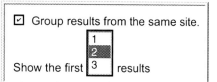

General   AlltheWeb   AltaVista   Copernic   Google   MSN

Individual findings detail

These parameters control factors such as the level of detail and the fields of information to display for each finding, and options for highlighting of search terms in the results.

Of our featured search engines:

- AlltheWeb, AltaVista, and Copernic have options to emphasize (bold or highlight) keywords (search terms) in the findings list. **Note:** You can also do this with all of our featured search engines' (Google and MSN Search included) toolbars for integration into your browser (see ⇨ Reference Section 6.4: Software integration).

⇨ For more explanation, see:

- Chapter 6: Findings display and handling preferences.
- Reference Section 5.2: Presentation of individual findings.
- Reference Section 6.3: Presentation of Individual Findings.

- AltaVista and, in particular, Copernic have different kinds of options to control the level of detail shown in each finding.

General	AlltheWeb	AltaVista	Copernic	Google	MSN

AlltheWeb

Has the following preference setting option:

- **Highlight search terms:** To quote [AlltheWeb Help]: Search terms can be highlighted in the search result, if the document summary contains the terms used in the search. You will see cases where your search terms are not found within the document summary but are found in the document. AlltheWeb searches the full HTML document, not only the document summary presented in the search result.

> Highlight Search Terms- ⦿ On ⦿ Off

The above appears on the "Basic Settings" preferences customization screen.

AltaVista

From almost any AltaVista search interface, link to "Settings," where you will see a number of options that control the fields shown for each finding.

The options are specified using checkboxes, shown here.

> **Web Page information:**
> ☑ Description ☑ URL ☐ Page size ☐ Page language
> **Useful Links:** ☑ Translate
> **Results page format:** ☑ Bold the search term in the results

- **Description:** description of the finding, usually consisting of a few lines.
- **URL:** web address of the finding.
- **Page size:** size of the finding, in terms of number of bytes or characters.
- **Page language:** language in which the found document is written.
- **Translation link:** translates the found document into the language of the interface.
- **Results page format:** whether to bold (in heavier font) search term occurrences in the description and the number of findings to display on each findings page.

Reference Manual Section 6.4:
User Preference
Setting Parameters

516

Findings Display &
Handling Preferences

Copernic

Has the following Display preference setting options (see "Display" tab screenshot below):

- **Extraction of keywords during analysis for detailed viewing of results:** In connection with doing an optimal analysis, you can set other preferences for the detail level to show *if* you also choose to extract keywords at the time of doing that analysis. To set this related

> You can set optimal analysis as a preference on the "Analysis" tab in the screenshot below: see ⇨ Reference Section 6.4: Other filter setting preferences for details of that dialog box.

preference, check the "Switch to detailed layout when extracting key concepts" box in the screenshot below.

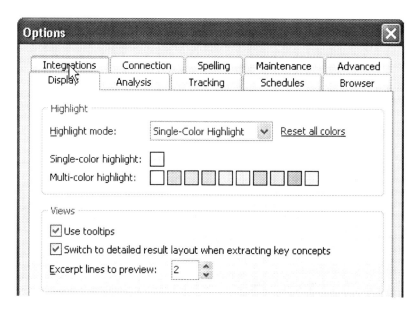

- **Search term (keyword) highlighting:**

  - › **No highlight:** Keywords are not highlighted in the findings list and in the findings themselves when displayed in the browser.
  - › **Single-color highlight:** Keywords are highlighted in one color only.
  - › **Multi-color highlight:** Each search term is highlighted in a different color when more than one keyword is used.
- **Whether to show search and result tooltips when not viewing in detailed mode:** These allow all details for the search or finding to appear

Reference Manual Section 6.4:
User Preference
Setting Parameters

517

Findings Display &
Handling Preferences

on your screen when you pass you mouse over the item, even though the item details are not otherwise displayed.

- **Number of excerpt lines from text of a document finding to display:** In standard or detailed viewing of results.

As well, certain "View" pull-down menu options become defaults, and may therefore be seen as "preference settings." The "Results Layout" options on the View menu also controls individual results detail, based on the choices shown here.

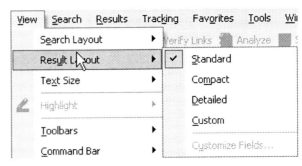

Google

Has no preference settings for displaying individual findings.

MSN Search

Has no preference settings for displaying individual findings.

| General | AlltheWeb | AltaVista | Copernic | Google | MSN |

Handling of findings

This involves using various links from the findings display and post-processing of findings by searching within findings, grouping and sorting, language translation, page summarization, and search follow-up.

Of our featured search engines, only Copernic has preference setting options of this kind.

⇨ For more explanation, consult:

- Chapter 5: Post-Processing of Findings.
- Chapter 6: Findings display and handling preferences.
- Reference Section 5.2: Post-Processing of Findings.
- Reference Section 6.3: Other Post-Processing of Findings.

| General | AlltheWeb | AltaVista | Copernic | Google | MSN |

Reference Manual Section 6.4:
User Preference
Setting Parameters

518

Findings Display &
Handling Preferences

AlltheWeb

Has no preference setting options for handling of findings.

AltaVista

Has no preference setting options for handling of findings.

Copernic

Has preference settings for:

1. **Findings page summarization options:** These occur on the "Analysis" tab of the screenshot on the next page. The options are:

    - Use of a default language when automatic language detection fails, and the default language to use in such a case.
    - Choice of using the "Lite" or more thorough version of the Copernic Summarizer.

    - Default summary size in words or percent of webpage size.
    - Number of concept terms to extract, up to 15.

2. **Search tracking options:** These occur on the "Tracking" and "Schedules" tabs of the two screenshots you see at the bottom of the next page and the top of the page after that. Options include:

    - **E-mail setup:** whether and how to send e-mail messages for tracked searches or webpages.
    - **E-mail address:** for sending tracking results.
    - **Default minimum number of words:** that have to change in a tracked webpage before it will be reported as having changed.
    - **Method to send the tracking results (URL's):** as an e-mail attachment or as part of the message body.
    - **Schedule for performing tracking of changes:** to searches or to individual webpages.

Reference Manual Section 6.4:
User Preference
Setting Parameters

519

Findings Display &
Handling Preferences

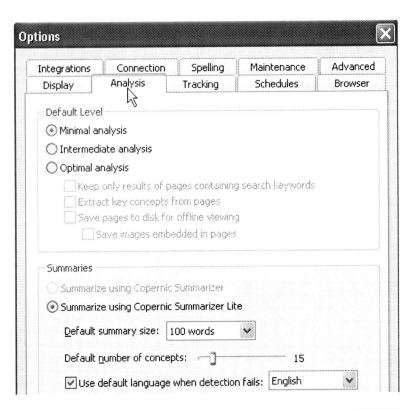

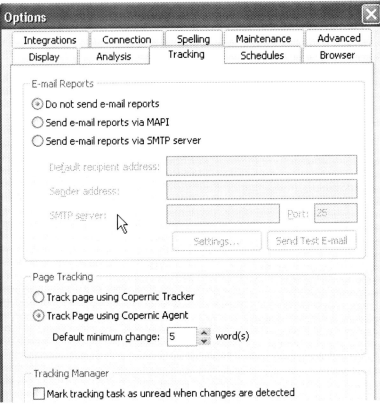

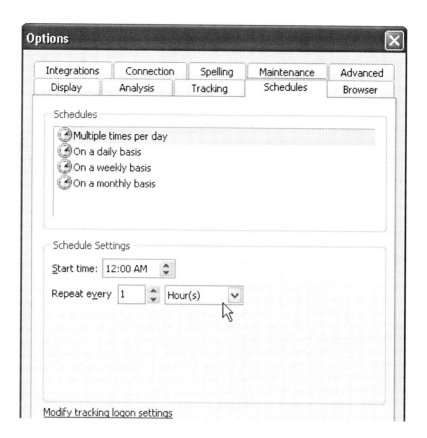

Google

Has no preference setting options for handling of findings.

MSN Search

Has no preference setting options for handling of findings.

Reference Manual Section 6.4:
User Preference
Setting Parameters

521

Findings Display &
Handling Preferences

Interface Screen Features Preferences

Interface options made available

⇨ For more explanation, refer to Chapter 6: Interface screen features preferences.

These parameters control the boxes, menu choices, and toolbars to be displayed on particular interfaces; also the choices made available in certain selection boxes or box sets.

Of our featured search engines, only AlltheWeb and Copernic provide options in this area. Copernic has particularly sophisticated ones, partially because it is an application that runs on your computer rather than on the server.

General	AlltheWeb	AltaVista	Copernic	Google	MSN

AlltheWeb

Has preference setting options for:

- **Simple search form option for search type display:** To quote [AlltheWeb Help]: By default the search type menu (any, all, phrase, or boolean), and Exact Phrase are not shown on the search form.

  Display-
  - ⊙ Menu (any, all, phrase, or boolean)
  - ⊙ Exact Phrase
  - ⊙ Neither

  The "Menu" selection applies to the Web and News searches only, while the "Exact Phrase" choice applies to all the simple search entry interfaces.

The remaining two options are accessed from AlltheWeb's Advanced Settings preferences customization screen.

- **Query autocompletion in browser:** This controls a browser feature, which is described in your browser's help. To quote [AlltheWeb Help]: By default, Internet Explorer and Mozilla will autocomplete your search phrases. If you want to disable this, click "off."

  Autocomplete-
  - ⊙ On
  - ⊙ Off

Reference Manual Section 6.4:
User Preference
Setting Parameters

522

Interface Screen
Features Preferences

- **Default search catalog:** The
default catalog determines which
catalog's tab is highlighted when
you start the search engine. To
quote [AlltheWeb Help]: AlltheWeb can perform five different search types,
and does by default a basic web search. By changing this default setting,
AlltheWeb will automatically perform your chosen type of search the next
time you enter AlltheWeb.

Default catalog - ⊙ Web ⊙ Video
⊙ News ⊙ Audio
⊙ Pictures

AltaVista

Does not have preferences for interface screen options.

Copernic

Has options for:

Search engine categories configuration

Install Additional Categories...
Create Custom Category...
Organize Categories...

These give you control over the
categories of search engines.

Using the interface on the next page, you can organize already installed
categories of search engines. You can:

- Using the checkboxes, choose which of these search engines to activate
  for use in searching within a category.
- Set the maximum number of results per search engine in your category (or
  for all categories) up to a ceiling of 700 results.
- Suggest new search engines for a category, using the link at the bottom
  left of the screen.
- Visit a given search engine from the install screen, using the appropriate
  choice obtainable from the context menu when your mouse is over a
  particular search engine in the list.
- Add a link to a particular search engine to your browser favorites by
  checking it in the provided list and then selecting "Add to Favorites."
- Sort alphabetically the list of search engines in a category, using the
  "Reset Order" button.

- Delete a highlighted search engine from a category (which is different from simply unchecking it), using the delete icon in the toolbar at the top of the dialog box.
- Delete an entire group of categories when the group is selected in the left pane, rather than the individual category.
- Expand or contract any category group by clicking on the plus and minus signs.
- Expand or contract any individual category to show or hide its search engines by clicking on the plus and minus signs.
- Select a group of categories to see the group description displayed or click on a category to see the category description displayed.
- Choose either "Install Additional Categories" or "Create Custom Category" to branch to dialog boxes for those purposes (next page).

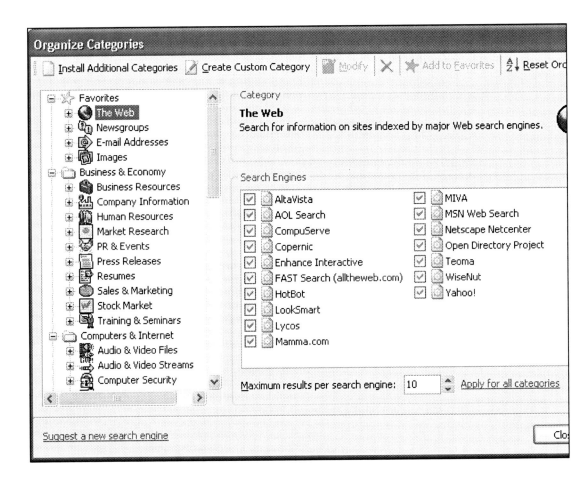

Reference Manual Section 6.4:
User Preference
Setting Parameters

524

Interface Screen
Features Preferences

(To see the screenshot on the previous page in full resolution, go to ⇨ www. SearchHelpCenter.com/effective-internet-search-copernic-screenshots.html, "Search engine customization #3.")

Copernic permits you to add some additional categories over and above those already present when you first install the software. Use the provided checkboxes in the screen seen below either to install a group of categories or to install individual categories within that group. The individual categories and their checkboxes will be visible once you click the plus signs for the category groups. After selecting all the checkboxes you want at different levels, click the "Install" button to add them to the set you can access when you do your next search.

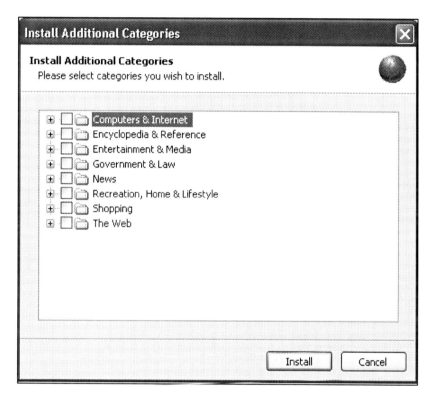

You can move whole categories as well as individual search engines within categories. As well, you can create custom categories of your own from the set that has already been defined. To do this:

- Enter your new category name at the top of the appropriate dialog box (shown on next page).
- In the left pane of that dialog box, click on the plus signs until you see the search engines you want located below a given category.

Reference Manual Section 6.4:
User Preference
Setting Parameters

525

Interface Screen
Features Preferences

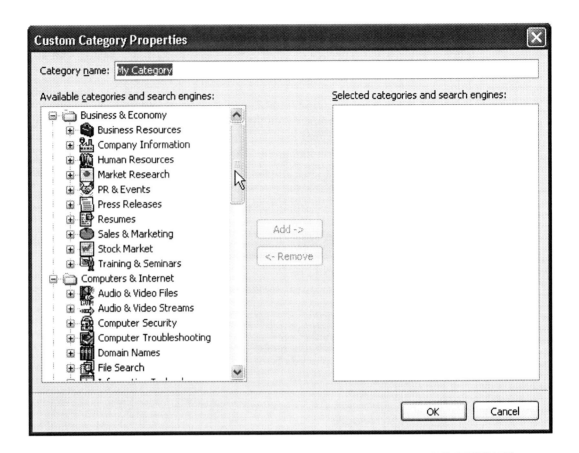

- Choose the "Add" button to move desired search engines from the left pane to the search engines listed in your selected category on the right. You can also choose the "Remove" button to undo that move.

⇨ For a review of the layout of the Copernic application screen, see Chapter 3: Local application interfaces.

- When finished adding search engines to your category, choose the "OK" button.

Whether to show various control items and panes on the screen

These options can be selected using the View menu, as sub-choices of the "Toolbars," "Command Bar," and "History Pane" options (shown here).

- **Toolbars:** provides choices to show various toolbars or search within results control panel items. These items are:

Reference Manual Section 6.4:
User Preference
Setting Parameters

526

Interface Screen
Features Preferences

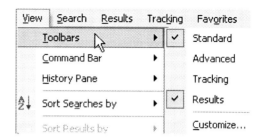

> **Standard toolbar:** Contains the most frequently used controls, including new search, modify search, update search, verify links, analyze results, save pages, browse results, and delete results. Two buttons on this toolbar, the "Find in Results" and "Filter" buttons, are used to activate/ deactivate the toolbars above the results pane for searching within findings.

> **Advanced toolbar:** Adds some extra controls for sending searches by email, annotating results, highlighting results, organizing categories, and getting help with the Copernic application.

> **Tracking toolbar:** Adds choices for tracking searches, tracking pages, and managing tracking.

> **Results toolbar:** Has controls for grouping, sorting, and laying out results.

> **Customize:** Branches to a sub-application for customizing existing toolbars and making new ones.

- **Command Bar:** This controls the appearance or disappearance of the the series of panes running down the left of the Copernic application screen,

consisting from top to bottom of the Search, Common Tasks, and View panes. Options include selectively displaying or not the following items:

> **Show command bar:** Shows/hides the rest of the panes in this list, as a whole.

> **Search bar pane:** Shows/hides the "Quick Search" and "Categories" areas for entering simple searches.

> **Common tasks pane:** Shows/hides the pane for context-sensitive choices, such as viewing results in browser window, analyzing results, organizing categories, etc.

> **View pane:** Shows/hides the pane that gives a thumbnail view of each finding.

Reference Manual Section 6.4:
User Preference
Setting Parameters

527

Interface Screen
Features Preferences

- **History Pane:** This
  has options to show or
  hide the panes for
  search history and
  search history folders.

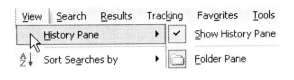

Customization choices available from the menu bar and the toolbars

One of the Toolbar menu options, discussed above, is called "Customize." As
mentioned, this is used to customize the toolbars, including making new ones. It
is also used to customize the pull-down menu bar choices, and to set options on
how all these bars are to react in given situations.

The three dialog boxes on the "Toolbars" tab of this customization interface are
shown below. If you are familiar with today's popular operating systems, such as
Windows XP, you will recognize that these follow the fairly standard patterns of
all applications in these environments.

- **Toolbars
  tab dialog
  box:** used
  to create
  new tool
  or menu
  bars, or
  rename,
  delete or
  reset (to
  defaults)
  the
  existing
  ones.

- **Commands
  tab dialog
  box:** used
  to
  reconfigure
  the choices on each toolbar or menu.

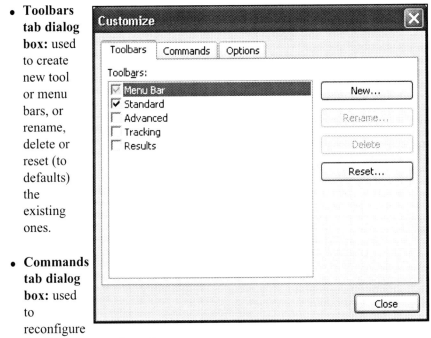

Reference Manual Section 6.4:
User Preference
Setting Parameters

528

Interface Screen
Features Preferences

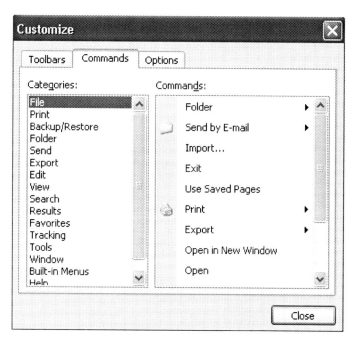

- **Options tab dialog box:** used to control various features of how toolbar and menu choices are to behave.

Display of various confirmations and warnings

Various preference settings for these are shown in the upper half of the screenshot below.

Reference Manual Section 6.4:
User Preference
Setting Parameters

529

Interface Screen
Features Preferences

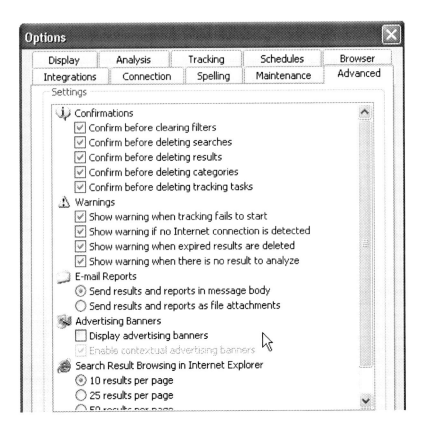

Browser options

These options concern which Internet browser to use to display results in the browser window, as well as some choices determining how it will behave in conjunction with Copernic. Settings are shown on the screenshot below.

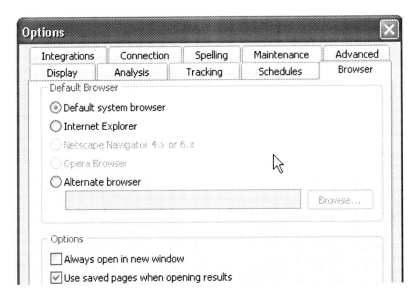

Reference Manual Section 6.4:
User Preference
Setting Parameters

530

Interface Screen
Features Preferences

Visual settings

Among these are provisions for showing advertising banners. See the screenshot for the "Advanced" options tab on the previous page.

View of search history pane

These settings can be made from two sub-menus on the "View" pull-down menu. They concern:

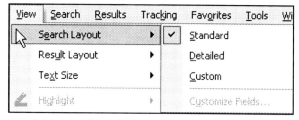

- **Search layout:** concerns the level of detail for showing search history. The choices are shown here.

- **Search sort order:** concerns the sequencing of the searches listed in the search history pane. The choices are shown here.

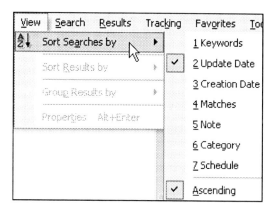

Google

Does not have preferences for interface screen options.

MSN Search

Does not have preferences for interface screen options.

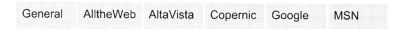

General   AlltheWeb   AltaVista   Copernic   Google   MSN

Interface
language or style

⇨ For more explanation, see Chapter 6: Interface screen features preferences.

Interface style has to do with the cosmetics of the search engine website, including screen text size on the search entry form, and colors or themes.

Interface (site control) language choices allow you to choose your own language for interfacing with the search engine. Some search engines will default it to one related to where you are located.

Of our featured search engines:

- AltaVista, Google, and MSN Search provide alternatives for language of site controls. As for Copernic, you can buy the software in different languages, particularly French.
- AlltheWeb, in particular, and Copernic provide options related to style.

General	AlltheWeb	AltaVista	Copernic	Google	MSN

AlltheWeb

Has preference setting options for:

Select a
text size

small
normal
large
larger

- **Default Text Size:** To quote AlltheWeb Help: allows you to customize how large or small the default text for AlltheWeb is. In some cases our font may be too small to read easily, so you can select from the following to increase or decrease the default setting.
- **Look and feel:** These items appear on the Look and Feel preferences customization screen. For more details, ⇨ see AlltheWeb "skins gallery" at www.alltheweb.com/help/alchemist/gallery.

AltaVista

Country - **USA**
Select a country to focus your search.

Setting the language of your site controls is based on your choice of country. Select the "Country" link shown here (set to your current country choice or default).

In response, you will receive the following set of radio buttons for making your single choice of the interface (site control) language:

Reference Manual Section 6.4:
User Preference
Setting Parameters
532
Interface Screen
Features Preferences

Country

○ Australia - Australia	○ France - France	○ Portugal - Portugal
○ Austria - Österreich	○ Germany - Deutschland	○ Spain - España
○ Belgium (French) - Belgique	○ India - India	○ Sweden - Sverige
○ Belgium (Dutch) - België	○ Ireland - Ireland	○ Switzerland (German) - Schweiz
○ Brazil - Brasil	○ Italy - Italia	○ Switzerland (French) - Suisse
○ Canada (English)	○ Korea - 한국	○ Switzerland (Italian) - Svizzera
○ Canada (French)	○ Netherlands - Nederland	○ U.K. - United Kingdom
○ Denmark - Danmark	○ New Zealand - New Zealand	○ U.S. - United States
○ Finland - Suomi	○ Norway - Norge	

⇨ For more details on specifying a country, consult Reference Section 6.4: Other filter setting preferences.

Copernic

Provides an option related to text size for the application screen, as shown here.

You can also buy Copernic in a few different interface languages, in particular, French as well as English.

Google

Allows a large selection of site control interface language choices. Simply select your single language choice from the drop-down menu you see here.

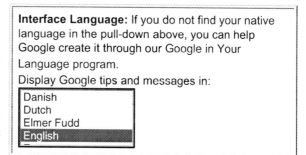

MSN Search

It supports interfaces in several different countries. The language of the interface is determined by which country you are in (automatically detected), or by which country you actively choose as your preference.

In countries having more than one widespread language, links are provided on the search entry interface to enable you to switch between your country's languages, e.g., between English and Spanish in the United States, or between English and French in Canada.

General   AlltheWeb   AltaVista   Copernic   Google   MSN

Software Integration & Efficiency Preferences

Software integration

> ⇨ For more explanation, refer to Chapter 6: Software integration and efficiency preferences.

The most common parameters are those that make the search engine part of the Internet browser. The search engine may also be integrated with other kinds of applications, such as word processors and e-mail, and with the operating system, such as Windows.

All our featured search engines have methods of integrating links to the search engine from within other software, especially browsers (and in particular Internet Explorer).

General   AlltheWeb   AltaVista   Copernic   Google   MSN

AlltheWeb

Provides tools to add AlltheWeb search to a user's browser. For more details on the following kinds of tools, see ⇨ www.alltheweb.com/help/tools/index, and then link to the information for your browser:

- Make AlltheWeb your browser homepage.
- Make AlltheWeb your default search engine.
- Create a search button for AlltheWeb in your browser. You can use this in conjunction with highlighting the text on a webpage and then choosing the AlltheWeb" button in your toolbar. Highlighted text will be automatically be searched for in AlltheWeb.
- Enable keyword search in your browser. In Internet Explorer, for instance, this will allow you to type atw followed by a space and then your query terms in the location bar, whereupon AlltheWeb will perform a search on these terms.
- Create a URL investigator button.

Reference Manual Section 6.4:
User Preference
Setting Parameters

534

Software Integration &
Efficiency Preferences

Your choice of browser determines which of the above are available.

AltaVista

Has a toolbar, described at ➪ www.altavista.com/toolbar/hlp/features. Its various options can be seen on the next page.

Copernic

Has preference setting options to:

Integrate Copernic quick searching and software activation into Microsoft software, especially Internet Explorer and Windows. As shown in the below screenshot, you can choose to:

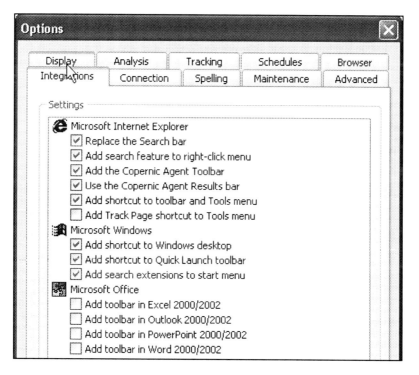

- Have the Copernic interface open in the left pane of Internet Explorer when the search icon is chosen. With this, you replace the MSN Search in the search bar on the left (activated by selecting the Search icon in the IE toolbar) with the same Copernic search bar you see on the left of the Copernic browser results window.

- Create a Copernic toolbar in Internet Explorer.
- Add shortcuts and extensions to Windows.
- Add Copernic toolbars to MS Office applications.

Integrate Copernic with your e-mail sending application, so that you can contact Copernic for help with problems, to request new search engines to add to search engine categories, etc. You do this using the SMTP (outgoing mail server) setup, the screen for which is shown on the next page.

AltaVista Toolbar Menu

Toolbar Menu, accessed through clicking on the AV logo or the drop-down arrow next to the logo, provides the following links to Toolbar settings and AltaVista webpages:

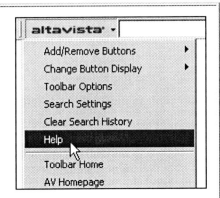

Add/Remove Buttons	Opens a list of all buttons you can display or hide on the Toolbar.
Change Button Display	Lets you determine how you want to see the Toolbar buttons: with icons and text or icons-only.
Toolbar Options	Takes you to the Toolbar configuration page.
Search Settings	Takes you to the AltaVista Search Settings Page.
Clear Search History	Clears the Toolbar search history.
Help	Takes you to the Toolbar Help page.
Toolbar Home	Takes you to the Toolbar Homepage.
AV Homepage	Takes you to the AltaVista Homepage.
AV Images	Takes you to the AltaVista Image Search Page.
AV Audio	Takes you to the AltaVista Audio Search Page.
AV Video	Takes you to the AltaVista Video Search Page.
AV News	Takes you to the AltaVista News Search Page
AV Advanced Search	Takes you to the AltaVista Advanced Search Page.
Hide Toolbar	Hides the Toolbar
Uninstall	Uninstalls the Toolbar
Privacy Information	Takes you to the Toolbars Privacy Information Page
About	Displays Toolbar Version information

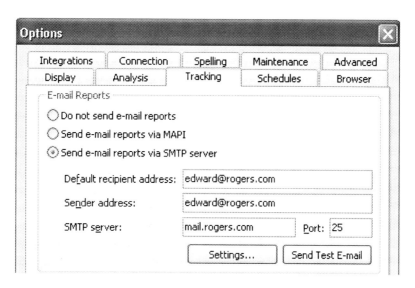

Take into account programs and methods you use to connect to the Internet, since the software is integrated with Internet access. Thus, it needs to know if you are directly connected or connected behind a firewall involving a proxy server (often used in business). Copernic has to know if it is dealing with a proxy server and how to contact it. Several advanced technical options in this area can be called upon if you choose the "Advanced" button seen grayed out in the screen image below.

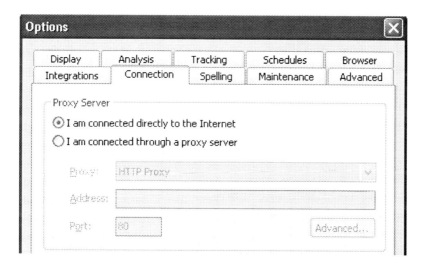

Google

Allows you to add their access
buttons to your browser. If you are
using Internet Explorer and the
Windows operating system, there is
a special utility to install a Google
search toolbar. To quote [Google
Help]: Adding Google Browser
Buttons to your personal toolbar

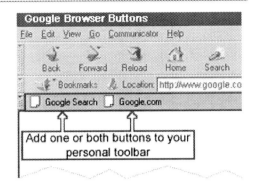

gives you access to Google's search technology, without taking up extra screen
space. ... Browser buttons let you search the Internet simply by highlighting a
word (or phrase) on any web page and clicking the **Google Search** button. ...
The **Google.com** button instantly takes you to Google's homepage.

For more Google power, you can install the Google toolbar below:

The Google toolbar, available in a number of languages, has a complex and
sophisticated set of features, including blocking of pop-ups, spellchecking,
immediately translation of foreign language words into English, filling out forms,
setting options for the preceding, and, of course, various kinds of search. For
more on these various options, play the Google Toolbar Tour at ⇨ toolbar.google.
com/T3/tour/toolbar.html.

For more details, go to the Toolbar Help page at ⇨ www.google.com/support/
toolbar/bin/static.py?page=features.html. There, you will receive more detailed
explanations of each of the toolbar options. Here are a few more from among
those not mentioned in the previous paragraph:

- **Autolink:** As described by Google: The online review of a great new
  restaurant has the place's address but no map. You could type the
  restaurant's street, city, and ZIP code into the search box, but why bother,
  when clicking the Toolbar's AutoLink button will automatically create a link
  to an online map (US addresses only)? AutoLink can also link package
  tracking numbers to delivery status, VIN numbers (US) to vehicle history,
  and publication ISBN numbers to Amazon.com listings.

Reference Manual Section 6.4:
User Preference
Setting Parameters

538

Software Integration &
Efficiency Preferences

- **PageRank Display:** As described by Google: Wondering whether a new website is worth your time? Use the Toolbar's PageRank™ display to tell you how Google's algorithms assess the importance of the page you're viewing.

- **Highlight Search Terms:** As described by Google: Once you've used the Google Toolbar to find a web page, there's no need to scroll around looking for your search terms. The Highlight button instantly lights them up on the page, making it easier to find relevant information.

- **Word Find Buttons:** As described by Google: Finding a particular word on a web page can be frustrating. With the Google Toolbar however you easily jump to the first instance of a word by typing it into the Toolbar search box, then clicking on the Toolbar's Word Find button to find each additional occurrence of the word.

MSN Search

It provides a suite of toolbars, which you can download and install on your computer. These can be integrated with a number of Microsoft programs, as well as with different browsers. Many preferences can be set, depending on the toolbar. While the toolbar provides the same kind of functions as the Google one (see above), there are also significant differences in what each of these toolbars can do.

Because of the complexity of MSN's toolbar suite, we simply refer you to MSN Search Help on the matter: ⇨ search.msn.com/docs/toolbar.aspx?FORM=TBDD2.

AlltheWeb	AltaVista	Copernic	Google	MSN

Software efficiency

⇨ For more explanation, refer to Chapter 6: Software integration and efficiency preferences.

This applies especially to client-side search software, and includes functions such as getting rid of files no longer needed, setting options related to tradeoffs between search speed and other factors, and updating client-side software with newer versions or with the latest settings.

Of our featured search engines, only Copernic has options like this. The reason is only Copernic is a client-side application, installed on the user's own computer.

General	AlltheWeb	AltaVista	Copernic	Google	MSN

Reference Manual Section 6.4:
User Preference
Setting Parameters
539
Software Integration &
Efficiency Preferences

AlltheWeb

Has no preference settings governing software efficiency.

AltaVista

Has no preference settings governing software efficiency.

Copernic

Has preference setting options for:

Maintenance: As seen on the below screenshot, these include options for:

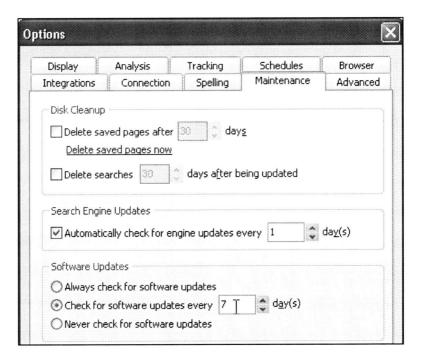

- **Disk cleanup:** To get rid of saved pages or search history items after specified periods of time.
- **Updates of search engines and of Copernic software itself:** These can be obtained from the Tools menu at any time. However, updates can also be scheduled at regular intervals through preference settings.

Reference Manual Section 6.4:
User Preference
Setting Parameters

540

Software Integration &
Efficiency Preferences

Note that the default frequency to check for search engine updates is "every 1 days." This is because search engines available for use by Copernic to support its various search engine categories can change frequently. This can happen for a number of reasons, including the possibility that a search engine may decide to deny access to Copernic.

System performance tuning: As seen in the bottom half of the below screenshot, these include options for:

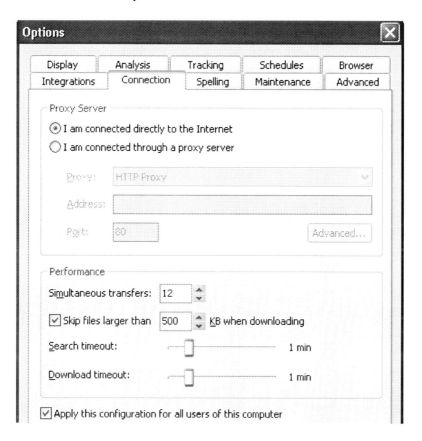

- **Speed:** Number of simultaneous transfers from search engines. This is related to how many search engines your categories search in parallel, since more search engines mean you may need more simultaneous transfers.
- **Maximum download file size:** Limits to file sizes whose findings are accessed during optimal analysis. PDF files, for example, may be important for your search and for your search to analyze, although they often have a very large file size and so are skipped during the Copernic analysis phase of the search.
- **Timeouts:** For each of search and file download. The latter has to do with tolerances for how long your computer will wait for a download from the Internet during the analysis phase of a search.

The network version of Copernic has even more options, although these are not shown on the above screenshot.

Google

Has no preference settings governing software efficiency.

MSN Search

Has no preference settings governing software efficiency.

General	AlltheWeb	AltaVista	Copernic	Google	MSN

Lightning Source UK Ltd.
Milton Keynes UK
29 July 2010

157510UK00001B/11/A